Datsun
Owners
Workshop
Manual

by J H Haynes
Member of the Guild of Motoring Writers
and Peter Strasman

Models covered

UK: Datsun 120Y Saloon (2 & 4 door). 1171 cc
         Datsun 120Y Hatchback Coupe. 1171 cc
         Datsun 120Y Estate. 1171 cc

USA: Datsun B-210 Sedan (2 & 4 door) 78.6 & 85.2 cu.in.
         Datsun B-210 Hatchback Coupe 78.6 & 85.2 cu.in.

ISBN 0 85696 228 7

Printed in England   *(228 - 11J3)*

ABCD

THE
BOOK

MEMBER

HAYNES PUBLISHING GROUP
SPARKFORD YEOVIL SOMERSET BA22 7JJ ENGLAND
distributed in the USA by
HAYNES PUBLICATIONS INC
861 LAWRENCE DRIVE
NEWBURY PARK
CALIFORNIA 91320
USA

Acknowledgements

Thanks are due to Nissan Motor Company Limited of Japan for the supply of technical information and certain illustrations. Castrol Limited provided lubrication details.

Champion Sparking Plug Company Limited for the provision of spark plug photographs. The bodywork repair photographs used in this manual were provided by Lloyds Industries Limited who supply 'Turtle Wax', Holts 'Dupli Color' and a range of other Holts products.

Tor View Garage, Edgarley, Glastonbury, Somerset, were very helpful and provided the Datsun 120Y used in our workshops for original research. We particularly thank Peter Knowles of that establishment.

Lastly, special thanks are due to all of those people at Sparkford who helped in the production of this manual. Particularly, Martin Penny and Les Brazier who carried out the mechanical work and took the photographs respectively; Rod Grainger who edited the text and Stanley Randolph who planned the layout of each page.

About this manual

Its aims

The aim of this book is to help you get the best value from your car. It can do so in two ways. First it can help you decide what work must be done, even should you choose to get it done by a garage, the routine maintenance and the diagnosis and course of action when random faults occur. But it is hoped that you will also use the second and fuller purpose by tackling the work yourself. This can give you the satisfaction of doing the job yourself. On the simpler jobs it may even be quicker than booking the car into a garage and going there twice, to leave and collect it. Perhaps most important, much money can be saved by avoiding the costs a garage must charge to cover their labour and overheads.

The book has drawings and descriptions to show the function of the various components so that their layout can be understood. Then the tasks are described and photographed in a step-by-step sequence so that even a novice can cope with complicated work. Such a person is the very one to buy a car needing repair yet be unable to afford garage costs.

The jobs are described assuming only normal spanners are available, and not special tools. But a reasonable outfit of tools will be a worthwhile investment. Many special workshop tools produced by the makers merely speed the work, and in these cases guidance is given as to how to do the job without them, the oft quoted example being the use of a large hose clip to compress the piston rings for insertion in the cylinder. But on a very few occasions the special tool is essential to prevent damage to components, then their use is described. Though it might be possible to borrow the tool, such work may have to be entrusted to the official agent.

To avoid labour costs a garage will often give a cheaper repair by fitting a reconditioned assembly. The home mechanic can be helped by this book to diagnose the fault and make a repair using only a minor spare part.

The manufacturer's official workshop manuals are written for their trained staff, and so assume special knowledge; detail is left out. This book is written for the owner, and so goes into detail.

Using the manual

The book is divided into thirteen Chapters. Each Chapter is divided into numbered Sections which are headed in **bold type** between horizontal lines. Each Section consists of serially numbered paragraphs.

There are two types of illustration: (1) Figures which are numbered according to Chapter and sequence of occurrence in that Chapter. (2) Photographs which have a reference number on their caption. All photographs apply to the Chapter in which they occur so that the reference figure pinpoints the pertinent Section and paragraph number.

Procedures, once described in the text, are not normally repeated. If it is necessary to refer to another Chapter the reference will be given in Chapter number and Section number thus: Chapter 1/16.

If it is considered necessary to refer to a particular paragraph in another Chapter the reference is given in this form: 1/5:5. Cross-references given without use of the word 'Chapter' apply to Sections and/or paragraphs in the same Chapter (eg; 'see Section 8') means also 'in this Chapter'.

When the left or right side of the car is mentioned it is as if looking forward from the rear of the car.

Great effort has been made to ensure that this book is complete and up-to-date. The manufacturers continually modify their cars, even in retrospect.

Whilst every care is taken to ensure that the information in this manual is correct no liability can be accepted by the authors or publishers for loss, damage or injury caused by any errors in, or omissions from, the information given.

Contents

Introduction to the Datsun B-210 and 120Y

The Datsun B-210 (North America) or the 120Y (other territories) are very similar in construction and general appearance. The vehicles marketed in North America have engines of slightly larger capacity, different front and rear end styling, impact absorbent bumpers and full emission control equipment. A starter interlock system is installed in conjunction with the two front seat belts.

Other than for North America, the range includes an Estate Wagon and supersedes the previous 'Sunny' 1200 range. The design is extremely conventional and incorporates a solid rear axle with leaf type road springs and a recirculatory ball type steering gear. However, the model is reliable and easy to service and maintain, and is very fully equipped. Automatic transmission is available on the Saloon/Sedan versions.

Datsun 120Y 2-door Saloon - UK Specification

Datsun 120Y Estate - UK Specification

Datsun 120Y 4-door Saloon - UK Specification

Datsun 120Y Hatchback Coupe - UK Specification

Buying
spare parts and vehicle identification numbers

Buying spare parts

Spare parts are available from many sources, for example: Datsun garages, other garages and accessory shops, and motor factors. Our advice regarding spare parts is as follows:

Officially appointed Datsun garages - This is the best source of parts which are peculiar to your car and otherwise not generally available (eg; complete cylinder heads, internal gearbox components, badges, interior trim etc). It is also the only place at which you should buy parts if your car is still under warranty; non-Datsun components may invalidate the warranty. To be sure of obtaining the correct parts it will always be necessary to give the storeman your car's engine and chassis number, and if possible, to take the old part along for positive identification. Remember that many parts are available on a factory exchange scheme - any parts returned should always be clean! It obviously makes good sense to the specialists on your car for this type of part for their are best equipped to supply you.

Other garages and accessory shops - These are often very good places to buy material and components needed for the maintenance of your car (eg; oil filters, spark plugs, bulbs, fan belts, oils and grease, touch-up paint, filler paste etc). They also sell general accessories, usually have convenient opening hours, charge lower prices and can often be found not far from home.

Motor factors - Good factors will stock all of the more important components which wear out relatively quickly (eg; clutch components, pistons, valves, exhaust systems, brake cylinders/pipes/hoses/seals/shoes and pads etc). Motor factors will often provide new or reconditioned components on a part exchange basis - this can save a considerable amount of money.

Vehicle identification numbers

Modifications are a continuing and unpublicised process in vehicle manufacture quite apart from major model changes. Spare parts manuals and lists are compiled upon a numerical basis, the individual vehicle number being essential to correct identification of the component required.

The vehicle identification number is located on the top surface of the instrument panel cowl and it is visible through the windscreen on vehicles manufactured for and operating in North America. Vehicles operating in other territories have the identification (chassis) number stamped on the engine compartment rear bulkhead. The key to the vehicle number is as follows:

Prefix	B	R.H. Drive
	L	L.H. Drive
	K	Coupe
	V	Estate car
	H	Equipped with A 13 type engine (B210 models only)

Suffix	U	For North America
	R	Two door model
	T	Manual gearbox
	A	Automatic transmission

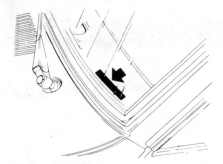

Vehicle identification number (N. America)

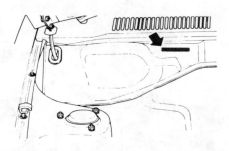

Vehicle identification number (UK and other territories)

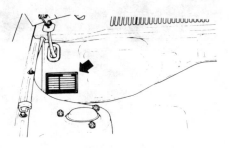

Model identification plate

The model identification plate is fixed to the engine compartment rear bulkhead. It indicates the type of vehicle, engine capacity, maximum bhp, the wheelbase engine number and vehicle serial number.

The body colour coding is shown on a plate attached to the top surface of the radiator support crossmember.

The engine number is duplicated on rear, right-hand side of the engine block.

The M.V.S.S. certificate label is affixed to the centre pillar on the driver's side.

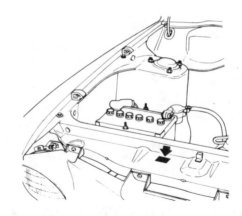

Body colour code plate

Details of vehicle identification number within engine compartment

Details of engine number

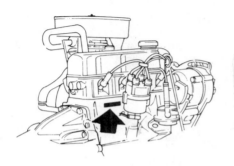

Location of engine number

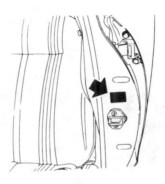

Location of MVSS certificate

Routine maintenance

Maintenance is essential for ensuring safety and desirable for the purpose of getting the best in terms of performance and economy from the car. Over the years the need for periodic lubrication - oiling, greasing and so on - has been drastically reduced if not totally eliminated. This has unfortunately tended to lead some owners to think that because no such action is required the items either no longer exist or will last for ever. This is a serious delusion. It follows therefore that the largest initial element of maintenance is visual examination. This may lead to repairs or renewals.

In the summary given here the essential for safety' items are shown in **bold type**. These **must** be attended to at the regular frequencies shown in order to avoid the possibility of accidents and loss of life. Other neglect results in unreliability, increased running costs, more rapid wear and more rapid depreciation of the vehicle in general.

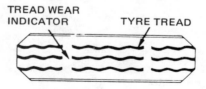

Tyre tread wear indicator

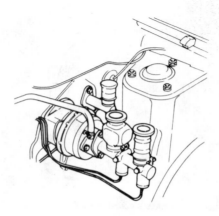

Brake and clutch fluid reservoir

Every 250 miles (400 km) travelled or weekly - whichever comes first

Steering
    Check the tyre pressures.
    Examine tyres for wear or damage.
    Is steering smooth and accurate?

Brakes
    Check reservoir fluid level.
    Is there any fall off in braking efficiency?
    Try an emergency stop. Is adjustment necessary?

Lights, wipers and horns
    Do all bulbs work at the front and rear?
    Are the headlamp beams aligned properly?
    Do the wipers and horns work?
    Check windscreen washer fluid level.

Engine
    Check the sump oil level and top up if required. (photo)
    Check the radiator coolant level and top up if required.
    Check the battery electrolyte level and top up to the level of the plates with distilled water as needed.

Windscreen washer reservoir

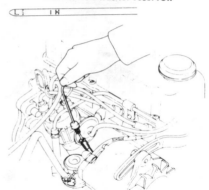

Checking engine oil level

Topping-up brake master cylinder
reservoir (non-servo type)

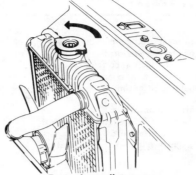

REMOVE SLOWLY

Removing radiator cap

3,000 miles (4800 km)

Every 3,000 miles or 4 monthly, whichever comes first, or earlier if indications suggest that safety items in particular are not performing correctly.

Steering
Examine all steering linkage rods, joints and bushes for signs of wear or damage.
Check front wheel hub bearings and adjust if necessary.
Check tightness of steering box mounting bolts.
Check the steering box oil level.

Brakes
Examine disc pads and drum shoes to determine the amount of friction material left. Renew if necessary.
Examine all hydraulic pipes, cylinders and unions for signs of chafing, corrosion, dents or any other form of deterioration or leaks.
Adjust drum type brakes.

Suspension
Examine all nuts, bolts and shackles securing the suspension units, front and rear. Tighten if necessary.
Examine the rubber bushes for signs of wear and play.

Engine
Change oil.
Check distributor points gap.
Check and clean spark plugs.

Gearbox (manual and automatic)
Check oil level and top up if necessary.

Clutch
Check fluid reservoir level and top up if necessary.

Body
Lubricate all locks and hinges (photo).
Check that water drain holes at bottom of doors are clear.

Inspecting battery electrolyte level

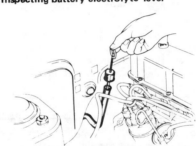

Checking automatic transmission fluid level

Topping-up the engine oil

6,000 miles (9600 km)

Engine
Check fan belt tension and adjust if necessary.
Check cylinder head bolt torque setting.
Check valve clearances and adjust if necessary.
Renew oil filter.
Lubricate distributor.
Clean air cleaner element.
Clean fuel pump.

Steering
Rotate roadwheels and rebalance if necessary.

Brakes
Check pedal free movement and for oil leakage at cylinders.

Clutch
Check pedal free movement and for oil leakage at cylinders.

Transmission
Check oil level in rear axle and top up if necessary.

12,000 miles (19000 km)

Engine
Renew crankcase fume emission valve.
Check fuel storage evaporative emission control system.
Check exhaust emission control system.
Clean carburettor float chamber and jets.
Renew fuel line filter unit.

Fit new distributor points.
Clean carburettor float chamber and jets.
Renew fuel line filter unit.
Check HT ignition leads for deterioration.

Steering
Check wheel alignment.

Suspension
Check shock absorber operation.

Transmission
Check security of propeller shaft bolts.

24,000 miles (38000 km)

Engine
Flush cooling system and refill with anti-freeze mixture.
Renew air cleaner element.

Brakes
Lubricate handbrake linkage.
Check pressure regulator valve.
Renew brake fluid by draining system.
Renew wheel bearing grease in front hubs.

30,000 miles (48000 km)

Transmission
Drain manual gearbox and refill with fresh oil.
Drain rear axle and refill with fresh oil.
Check propeller shaft universal joints for wear and re-condition if necessary.

Steering
Grease balljoints by removing plug and screwing in a nipple. (photo)

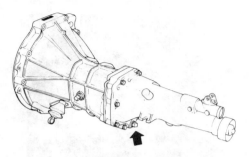

Location of gearbox drain plug

Headlights
Check beams and adjust if required.

8,000 miles (77000 km)

Brakes
Drain hydraulic system, renew all cylinder seals and refill with fresh fluid. Bleed system.

Clutch
Drain hydraulic system, renew master and slave cylinder seals, refill with fresh fluid. Bleed system.

Additionally the following items should be attended to as time can be spared:

Cleaning
Examination of components requires that they be cleaned. The same applies to the body of the car, inside and out, in order that deterioration due to rust or unknown damage may be detected. Certain parts of the body frame, if rusted badly, can result in the vehicle being declared unsafe and it will not pass the annual test for roadworthiness.

Exhaust system
An exhaust system must be leakproof, and the noise level below a certain minimum. Excessive leaks may cause carbon monoxide fumes to enter the passenger compartment. Excessive noise constitutes a public nuisance. Both these faults may cause the vehicle to be kept off the road. Repair or replace defective sections when symptoms are apparent.

Lubricating the hinges

Removing a balljoint grease plug

Jacking and Towing

Towing points

If the vehicle has to be towed, any rope or cable should be connected to the hook attached to the front sidemember. On vehicles equipped with automatic transmission, the towing speed should not exceed 20 mph (30 km/h) nor the towing distance 6 miles (10 km) otherwise the transmission may be damaged due to lack of lubrication. If towing distances are excessive, disconnect the propeller shaft from the rear axle pinion flange and tie the shaft up out of the way.

Where another vehicle is being towed, always attach the rope or cable to the rear road spring shackle.

Jacking points

The pentograph type jack supplied with the vehicle must only be used at the positions below the body sills. Other types of jack should be located below the front crossmember or rear axle differential casing. If axle stands are to be used, then they must be positioned under the bodyframe sidemembers or rear axle casing. No other positions should be used for jacking or support purposes.

Front towing hooks

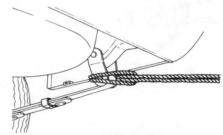

Rear tow line attachment point

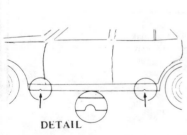

Car jack (pantograph) lifting points

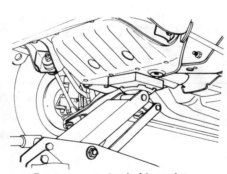

Front crossmember jacking point

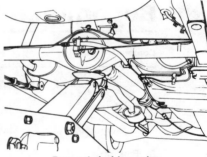

Rear axle jacking point

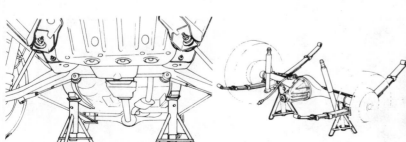

Front axle support positions

Rear axle support positions

Storage position for lifting jack

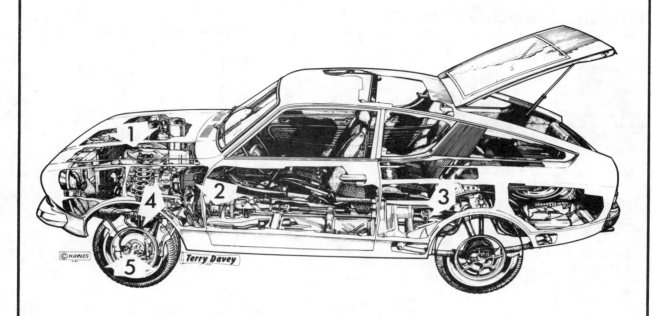

Recommended lubricants

Component									Castrol Product
1 Engine	...	...	...	...	...	...	...	...	**Castrol GTX**
2 Gearbox:									
Manual	...	...	...	...	...	...	...	...	**Castrol Hypoy**
Automatic		...	...	...	...	...	...	...	**Castrol TQ Dexron ®**
3 Final drive (differential)		...	...	...	...	...	...	...	**Castrol Hypoy B**
4 Steering gearbox	...	...	...	...	...	...	...	...	**Castrol Hypoy**
5 Wheel bearings (front) and chassis					...	...	...	...	**Castrol LM Grease**

Note: The above recommendations are general: lubrication requirements vary from territory-to-territory. Consult the operators handbook supplied with your car.

Refill capacities

	US	Imperial	Metric
Fuel tank:			
Saloon	12 3/8 gal.	10 3/8 gal.	47 litres
Coupe	11 3/8 gal.	9½ gal.	43 litres
Estate wagon	10 5/8 gal.	8¾ gal.	40 litres
Cooling system (includes heater)	5 3/8 qt	4½ qt	5.1 litres
Engine oil	3 3/8 qt	2 7/8 qt	3.2 litres
Transmission:			
Manual	2½ pt	2 1/8 pt	1.2 litre
Automatic	11¾ pt	9¾ pt	5.5 litres
Differential (rear axle)	1 7/8 pt	1 5/8 pt	0.9 litre
Steering box	5/8 pt	½ pt	0.27 litre

Overall dimensions

Length
- 2 and 4 door Sedan (N. America) ... ...   160.6 in. (407.9 cm)
- Hatchback ... ...   160.0 in. (406.4 cm)
- 2 and 4 door Saloon (UK and other territories) ... ...   155.5 in. (395.0 cm)
- Coupe (UK and other territories) ... ...   155.5 in. (395.0 cm)
- Estate Wagon (UK and other territories) ... ...   157.0 in. (398.5 cm)

Width
- All models ... ...   61.0 in. (154.5 cm)

Height
- Hatchback (N. America) ... ...   53.1 in. (134.9 cm)
- All other models ... ...   54.0 in. (137.2 cm)

Track
- Front ... ...   50.2 in. (127.5 cm)
- Rear ... ...   49.8 in. (126.5 cm)

Ground clearance
- All models ... ...   6.7 in. (17.0 cm)

Kerb weight

	Manual	Automatic
2 door Sedan (N. America)	1915 lb (868 kg)	1960 lb (889 kg)
4 door Sedan (N. America)	1960 lb (889 kg)	2005 lb (909 kg)
Hatchback (N. America)	1960 lb (889 kg)	2005 lb (909 kg)
2 door Saloon (UK and other territories)	1675 lb (760 kg)	1720 lb (780 kg)
4 door Saloon (UK and other territories)	1709 lb (775 kg)	1754 lb (796 kg)
Coupe (UK and other territories)	1675 lb (760 kg)	1720 lb (780 kg)
Estate Wagon (UK and other territories)	1764 lb (800 kg)	—

Use of English

As this book has been written in England, it uses the appropriate English component names, phrases, and spelling. Some of these differ from those used in America. Normally, these cause no difficulty, but to make sure, a glossary is printed below. In ordering spare parts remember the parts list will probably use these words:

Glossary

English	American	English	American
Accelerator	Gas pedal	Leading shoe (of brake)	Primary shoe
Alternator	Generator (AC)	Locks	Latches
Anti-roll bar	Stabiliser or sway bar	Motorway	Freeway, turnpike etc.
Battery	Energizer	Number plate	Licence plate
Bonnet (engine cover)	Hood	Paraffin	Kerosene
Boot lid	Trunk lid	Petrol	Gasoline
Boot (luggage compartment)	Trunk	Petrol tank	Gas tank
Bottom gear	1st gear	'Pinking'	'Pinging'
Bulkhead	Firewall	Propellor shaft	Driveshaft
Camfollower or tappet	Valve lifter or tappet	Quarter light	Quarter window
Carburettor	Carburetor	Retread	Recap
Catch	Latch	Reverse	Back-up
Choke/venturi	Barrel	Rocker cover	Valve cover
Circlip	Snap ring	Roof rack	Car-top carrier
Clearance	Lash	Saloon	Sedan
Crownwheel	Ring gear (of differential)	Seized	Frozen
Disc (brake)	Rotor/disk	Side indicator lights	Side marker lights
Drop arm	Pitman arm	Side light	Parking light
Drop head coupe	Convertible	Silencer	Muffler
Dynamo	Generator (DC)	Spanner	Wrench
Earth (electrical)	Ground	Sill panel (beneath doors)	Rocker panel
Engineer's blue	Prussion blue	Split cotter (for valve spring cap)	Lock (for valve spring retainer)
Estate car	Station wagon	Split pin	Cotter pin
Exhaust manifold	Header	Steering arm	Spindle arm
Fast back (Coupe)	Hard top	Sump	Oil pan
Fault finding/diagnosis	Trouble shooting	Tab washer	Tang; lock
Float chamber	Float bowl	Tailgate	Liftgate
Free-play	Lash	Tappet	Valve lifter
Freewheel	Coast	Thrust bearing	Throw-out bearing
Gudgeon pin	Piston pin or wrist pin	Top gear	High
Gearchange	Shift	Trackrod (of steering)	Tie-rod (or connecting rod)
Gearbox	Transmission	Trailing shoe (of brake)	Secondary shoe
Halfshaft	Axle-shaft	Transmission	Whole drive line
Handbrake	Parking brake	Tyre	Tire
Hood	Soft top	Van	Panel wagon/van
Hot spot	Heat riser	Vice	Vise
Indicator	Turn signal	Wheel nut	Lug nut
Interior light	Dome lamp	Windscreen	Windshield
Layshaft (of gearbox)	Counter shaft	Wing/mudguard	Fender

Miscellaneous points

An "Oil seal" is fitted to components lubricated by grease!

A "Damper" is a "Shock absorber" it damps out bouncing, and absorbs shocks of bump impact. Both names are correct, and both are used haphazardly.

Note that British drum brakes are different from the Bendix type that is common in America, so different descriptive names result. The shoe end furthest from the hydraulic wheel cylinder is on a pivot; interconnection between the shoes as on Bendix brakes is most uncommon. Therefore the phrase "Primary" or "Secondary" shoe does not apply. A shoe is said to be Leading or Trailing. A "Leading" shoe is one on which a point on the drum, as it rotates forward, reaches the shoe at the end worked by the hydraulic cylinder before the anchor end. The opposite is a trailing shoe, and this one has no self servo from the wrapping effect of the rotating drum.

Chapter 1 Engine

Contents

Specifications

Engine (general)		A 12	A 13
Engine design		Four cylinders, in-line, overhead valve	
Displacement		71.5 cu. in. (1171 cc)	78.59 cu. in. (1288 cc)
Bore		2.87 in. (73.0 mm)	
Stroke		2.760 in. (70.0 mm)	3.030 in. (77.0 mm)
Compression ratio		9.0 : 1	8.5 : 1
Maximum power		69 BHP @ 6000 rev/min	67 BHP @ 6000 rev/min
Maximum torque		70 lb/ft @ 4000 rev/min	71 lb/ft @ 3600 rev/min
Oil pressure (hot) @ 2000 rev/min		43 to 50 lb/in^2 (3 to 3.5 kg/cm^2)	

Cylinder block

Material		Cast iron	

Crankshaft

Number of main bearings		Five	
Journal diameter		1.9666 to 1.9671 in. (49.951 to 49.964 mm)	
Maximum journal taper and out of round		0.0004 in. (0.01 mm)	
Crankshaft endfloat		0.0020 to 0.0059 in. (0.05 to 0.15 mm)	
Crankpin diameter		1.7701 to 1.7706 in. (44.961 to 44.974 mm)	

Maximum crankpin taper and out of round ... ... less th 0.0012 in. (0.03 mm)
Main bearing thickness ... ... 0.0719 to 0.0722 in (1.827 to 1.835 mm)
Main bearing clearance ... ... 0.0008 to 0.0024 in (0.020 to 0.062 mm)
Main bearing clearance (wear limit) .. .. 0.0059 in (0.15 mm)

Connecting rods

Bearing thickness ... ... 0.0591 to 0.0594 in (1.500 to 1.508 mm)
Big-end endfloat ... ... 0.008 to 0.012 in (0.2 to 0.3 mm)
Big-end endfloat (wear limit) ... ... less than 0.016 in (0.4 mm)
Big-end bearing clearance ... ... 0.0008 to 0.0020 in (0.020 to 0.050 mm)

Pistons

Type ... ... Aluminium
Diameter:
   Standard ... ... 2.8727 to 2.8747 in. (72.967 to 73.017 mm)
   Oversize 50 ... ... 2.8924 to 2.8944 in. (73.467 to 73.517 mm)
   Oversize 100 ... ... 2.9121 to 2.9140 in. (73.967 to 74.017 mm)
   Oversize 150 ... ... 2.9318 to 2.9337 in (74.467 to 74.517 mm)
Bore clearance ... ... 0.0009 to 0.0017 in (0.023 to 0.043 mm)

Piston rings

Number ... ... Two compression (top), one oil control
Ring groove width:
   Compression ... ... 0.0796 to 0.0804 in. / 0.0787 in.
   (2.022 to 2.042 mm) / (1.9815 mm)
   Oil control ... ... 0.1578 to 0.1588 in. / 0.1575 in.
   (4.008 to 4.034 mm) / (3.993 mm)
Ring side clearance:
   Compression ... ... 0.0016 to 0.0028 in. (0.04 to 0.07 mm)
Ring end gap:
   Compression ... ... 0.0079 to 0.0138 in. (0.20 to 0.35 mm)
   Oil control ... ... 0.0118 to 0.0354 in. (0.30 to 0.90 mm)

Gudgeon pins

Diameter ... ... 0.6869 to 0.6871 in. (17.447 to 17.452 mm)
Length ... ... 2.5681 to 2.5779 in.(65.23 to 65.48 mm)
Clearance in piston ... ... 0.0002 to 0.0003 in. (0.006 to 0.008 mm) @ 68° F (20° C)
Interference fit in small end bush ... ... 0.0007 to 0.0013 in. (0.017 to 0.034 mm)

Camshaft

Number of bearings ... ... Five, bored in-line
Drive ... ... Double roller chain
Endfloat ... ... 0.0008 to 0.0031 in. (0.02 to 0.08 mm) / 0.0004 to 0.0020 in (0.01 to 0.05 mm)

Lobe lift:
   Inlet ... ... 0.2224 in. (5.65 mm) / 0.2224 in. (5.65 mm)
   Exhaust ... ... 0.2224 in. (5.65 mm) / 0.2331 in. (5.92 mm)
Journal diameter:
   1st ... ... 1.7237 to 1.7242 in. (43.783 to 43.796 mm)
   2nd ... ... 1.7041 to 1.7046 in (43.283 to 43.296 mm)
   3rd ... ... 1.6844 to 1.6849 in. (42.783 to 42.796 mm)
   4th ... ... 1.6647 to 1.6652 in. (42.283 to 42.296 mm)
   5th ... ... 1.6224 to 1.6229 in. (41.208 to 41.221 mm)
Bearing inner diameter:
   1st ... ... 1.7257 to 1.7261 in. (43.833 to 43.843 mm)
   2nd ... ... 1.7056 to 1.7060 in. (43.323 to 43.333 mm)
   3rd ... ... 1.6865 to 1.6868 in. (42.836 to 42.846 mm)
   4th ... ... 1.6663 to 1.6667 in. (42.323 to 42.333 mm)
   5th ... ... 1.6243 to 1.6247 in. (41.258 to 41.268 mm)
Journal to bearing clearance:
   1st ... ... 0.0015 to 0.0024 in. (0.037 to 0.060 mm)
   2nd ... ... 0.0011 to 0.0020 in. (0.027 to 0.050 mm)
   3rd ... ... 0.0016 to 0.0025 in. (0.040 to 0.063 mm)
   4th ... ... 0.0011 to 0.0020 in. (0.029 to 0.050 mm)
   5th ... ... 0.0015 to 0.0024 in. (0.037 to 0.060 mm)

Cylinder head

Material ... ... Aluminium

Valves

Clearance:
   HOT (inlet and exhaust) ... ... 0.0138 in. (0.35 mm)
   COLD (inlet and exhaust) ... ... 0.0098 in. (0.25 mm)
Valve head diameter:
   Inlet ... ... 1.378 in. (35.0 mm) / 1.46 in. (37.0 mm)
   Exhaust ... ... 1.142 in. (29.0 mm) / 1.18 in. (30.0 mm)
Valve stem diameter:

Inlet	0.3128 to 0.3134 in. (7.945 to 7.960 mm)	
Exhaust	0.3128 to 0.3134 in. (7.945 to 7.960 mm)	
Valve length (inlet and exhaust)	0.1588 to 0.1591 in. (4.034 to 4.041 mm)	0.1606 to 0.1611 in. (4.0807 to 4.0925 mm)
Valve lift:		
Inlet	0.3346 in. (8.51 mm)	0.3114 in. (7.91 mm)
Exhaust	0.3346 in. (8.51 mm)	0.3236 in. (8.22 mm)
Valve spring free-length	1.831 in. (46.5 mm)	
Valve guide length	2.087 in. (53.0 mm)	1.929 in. (49.0 mm)
Valve guide height from cylinder head surface	0.709 in. (18.0 mm)	0.728 in. (18.5 mm)
Valve guide inner diameter	0.3150 to 0.3156 in. (8.000 to 8.015 mm)	
Valve guide outer diameter	0.4737 to 0.4742 in (12.033 to 12.044 mm)	
Valve guide to stem clearance:		
Inlet	0.0006 to 0.0018 in. (0.015 to 0.045 mm)	
Exhaust	0.0016 to 0.0028 in. (0.040 to 0.070 mm)	
Valve seat width:		
Inlet	0.0512 in. (1.3 mm)	
Exhaust	0.0709 in. (1.8 mm)	
Valve seat angle (inlet and exhaust)	45°	
Valve seat interference fit	0.0025 to 0.0038 in. (0.064 to 0.096 mm)	
Valve guide interference fit	0.0009 to 0.0017 in. (0.022 to 0.044 mm)	

Oil pump and lubrication

Type (pump)	Rotor, camshaft gear driven
Type (system)	Pressure feed
Filter	Canister, disposable, full-flow type
Pressure relief valve	Ball and spring, non adjustable

Oil Capacity ... ...
2 7/8 qt. (Imp) 3 7/8 qt (U.S.) 3.2 litres

Torque wrench settings

	lb f ft	kg f m
Cylinder head bolts (Cold)	54	7.5
Rocker shaft pillar bolts	18	2.5
Big-end nuts	27	3.8
Flywheel to crankshaft bolts	60	8.3
Camshaft sprocket bolts	35	4.8
Camshaft locking plate bolts	5	0.7
Main bearing cap bolts	45	6.2
Sump drain plug	22	3.0
Crankshaft pulley bolt	145	20.0
Clutch bellhousing to engine	16	2.2
Torque converter housing to engine	36	5.0

1 General description

The B-210 models are fitted with the longer stroke 1288 cc engine and the 120Y models have the smaller 1171 cc engine. Both engines are similar but reference should be made to Specifications Section for detail differences.

The engine is front mounted four cylinder, in-line overhead valve and water-cooled. The cylinder block embodies five main bearings for the crankshaft, the latter being of forged steel construction and incorporates oil drillings for lubrication of the main bearings.

The pistons are of aluminium construction, the connecting rods are of forged steel with gudgeon pins which are interference fit in the connecting rod small ends but fully floating in the pistons.

The cylinder head is of light alloy with pressed in valve seats.

A cast iron camshaft is fitted, which is supported by five bearings and driven by a double roller chain from the crankshaft. The overhead valve mechanism comprises conventional camshaft operated tappets, pushrods and rocker shaft and arms. The valves are fitted with single coil springs and split cotters are employed to retain the valve spring caps.

The inlet manifold is aluminium and the exhaust manifold is cast iron.

The power unit is mounted at three points, one each side of the engine crankcase and one below the gearbox housing. The mountings are of the bonded rubber/metal type acting under compression of steel brackets.

Throughout this Chapter, the figures show the 1288 cc type engine with full emission control while the photographs illustrate the 1171 cc engine without emission control. All the operations described apply equally to both power units unless specifically indicated as being applicable to only one model.

2 Major operations possible with the engine in position in the vehicle

The following operations can be carried out with the engine still in position in the bodyframe:

1 *Removal and installation of the cylinder head assembly.*
2 *Removal and installation of the timing gear and chain.*
3 *Removal and installation of the oil pump.*
4 *Removal and installation of the engine mountings.*

With the front crossmember removed (see Chapter 11) the following operations can also be undertaken although it is preferable to remove the complete power unit the time saved is marginal.

5 *Removal and installation of the sump.*
6 *Renewal of the main bearings.*
7 *Renewal of the big-end bearings.*
8 *Removal and installation of the piston/connecting rod assemblies.*

3 Major operations only possible with the engine removed

1 *Removal and installation of the crankshaft.*
2 *Removal and installation of the flywheel.*

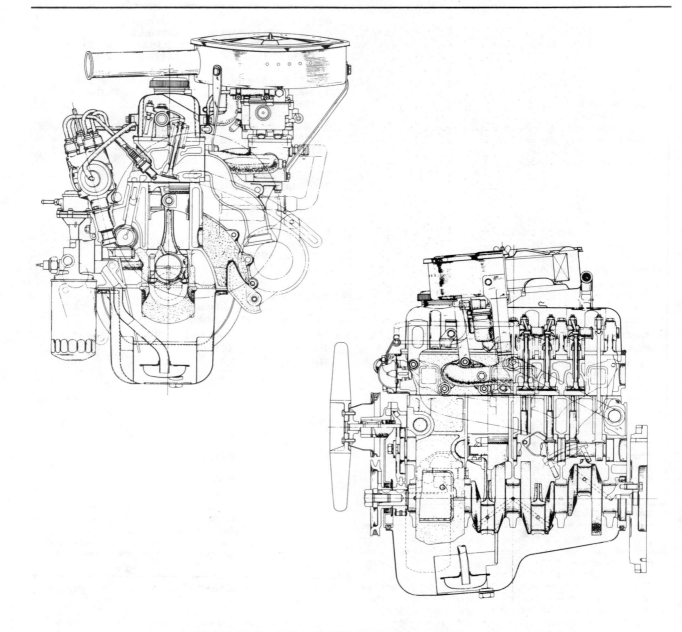

Fig. 1.1. Sectional views of 1171cc engine fitted to 120Y model

3   Renewal of the crankshaft rear bearing oil seal.
4   Removal and installation of the camshaft.

---

4   Engine - method of removal

The engine complete with gearbox or automatic transmission unit can be lifted upward and out of the engine compartment. Removal of the engine only is very difficult due to lack of forward clearance required to clear the gearbox primary shaft or driveplate.

---

5   Engine/transmission - removal

1   Disconnect the lead from the battery negative (—) terminal and the fusible link at its connector. (photo)

2   Mark the position of the hinge plates on the bonnet lid brackets (to facilitate installation) and then with the help of an assistant, remove the hinge bolts and lift the bonnet away. (photo)
3   Remove the splash shield from beneath the engine.
4   Drain and retain the engine coolant, drain and discard the engine oil.
5   Remove the air cleaner from the carburettor.
6   Disconnect the radiator upper and lower hoses and then remove the radiator (four bolts) from the engine compartment. (photo)
7   Disconnect the earth cable at the engine end.
8   Disconnect the HT cable (coil to distributor).
9   Disconnect the LT cable from the distributor.
10 Disconnect the leads from the water temperature transmitter unit and the oil pressure switch. (photo)
11 Disconnect the leads from the starter motor solenoid. (photo)

5.1 Battery location

5.2 Removing a bonnet hinge bolt

5.6A Radiator upper hose

5.6B Radiator lower hose and heater hose

5.6C Removing radiator

5.10 Location of oil pressure switch

5.11 Starter motor solenoid and leads

Fig. 1.2. Bonnet hinge

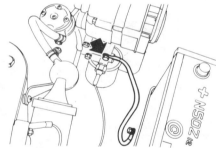

Fig. 1.3. Location of engine earth cable

12 Identify and then disconnect the leads from the alternator.

13 Disconnect the accelerator cable from the carburettor, and the choke cable (1207 models). (photo)

14 Disconnect the lead to the automatic choke (B210 models).

15 Disconnect the fuel inlet hose from the fuel pump.

16 Disconnect the heater water hoses.

17 Disconnect the brake vacuum servo hose from the inlet manifold.

18 *On vehicles equipped with emission control systems disconnect:*

   The lead from the thermal transmitter.

   The lead from the fuel cut-off solenoid.

   The lead from the throttle opener solenoid.

   The lead from the exhaust gas recirculation (EGR) solenoid.

   The lead from the vacuum cut-off solenoid.

19 Disconnect the hose which connects the air cleaner to the flow guide valve (see Chapter 3).

20 Disconnect the leads from the reversing lamp, neutral and top gear switches. (photo)

21 *On cars equipped with automatic transmission,* disconnect the leads from the inhibitor switch and downshift solenoid by disconnecting the multi-pin plug.

22 *On B-210 models and LHD 120Y models* unbolt the clutch

hydraulic operating cylinder from the clutch bellhousing and tie it up out of the way, there is no need to disconnect the hydraulic hose.

23 *On RHD 120Y models,* disconnect the clutch operating cable from the release fork.

24 Disconnect the speedometer cable from the gearbox rear extension housing. (photo)

25 *On vehicles equipped with manual transmission,* remove the centre console and then unscrew the retaining ring from the gearlever rubber boot up the lever and then disconnect the lever by removing the circlip and pivot pin (see Chapter 6). (photos)

26 *On cars equipped with automatic transmission,* disconnect the selector range lever.

27 *On all cars:* Disconnect the exhaust downpipe at the manifold flange. (photo)

28 Mark the edges of the propeller shaft rear flange and the pinion driving flange (for exact replacement) and then unscrew the four flange securing bolts. Push the propeller shaft slightly forward, lower it and then withdraw it from the transmission rear extension. It is a good plan to slip a plastic bag over the end of the extension housing and secure with a strong rubber band in order to prevent loss of oil when the unit is inclined at a steep angle during removal.

29 Bend down the tabs of the locking plates located below the fan securing bolts. Unscrew and remove the bolts, the fan and the spacer and pulley. (photos)

30 Support the transmission on a jack and remove the engine rear mounting both from the bodyframe and the transmission housing. (photo)

31 Attach suitable hoisting tackle to the engine lifting eyes and take the weight of the engine. Remove the front engine mounting bracket to insulator bolts.

32 Lift the combined engine/transmission from the engine compartment. (photo)

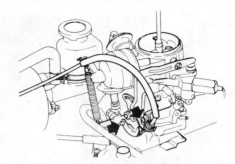

Fig. 1.4. Accelerator control linkage

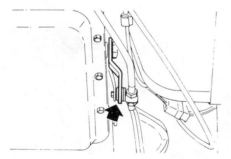

Fig. 1.5. Fuel inlet hose at fuel pump

Fig. 1.6. Connector plug for inhibitor switch and downshift solenoid leads (automatic transmission)

Fig. 1.7. Clutch operating cylinder (B210 models and LHD 120Y models)

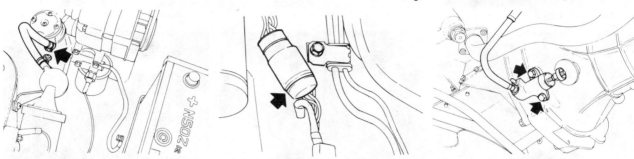

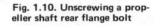

Fig. 1.8. Speed selector range lever (automatic transmission)

Fig. 1.10. Unscrewing a propeller shaft rear flange bolt

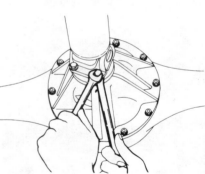

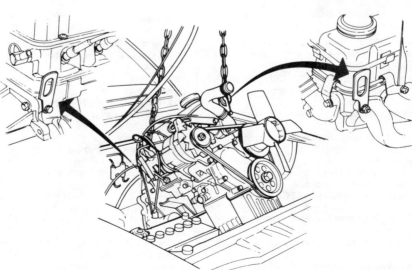

Fig. 1.11. Hoisting engine/transmission from engine compartment

5.13 Choke cable and throttle control connections at carburettor

5.20 Location of reversing lamp switch on transmission casing

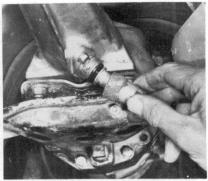
5.24 Disconnecting speedometer cable

5.25A Removing centre console

5.25B Gearshift lever boot and retainer

5.25C Gearshift lever pivot pin

5.25D Withdrawing gearshift lever

5.27 Exhaust downpipe connection

5.29A Fan lockplates and bolts

5.29B Removing fan, spacer and pulley

5.30 Engine rear mounting

5.32 Removing engine/transmission unit

6 Engine - separation from manual gearbox

1 With the engine and gearbox now removed from the vehicle, unscrew and remove the bolts which connect the clutch bell-housing to the engine block. Remove the starter motor. (photo)
2 Pull the gearbox from the engine in a straight line and support the gearbox so that its weight does not hang upon the gearbox primary shaft, even momentarily, whilst it is still engaged with the clutch mechanism.

6.1 Removing starter motor

7 Engine - separation from automatic transmission

1 Remove the converter housing lower cover and unscrew and remove the torque converter to drive plate securing bolts. The drive plate will have to be rotated to reach each of the bolts in turn. Mark the relative position of the drive plate to the converter housing using a spirit pen or dab of quick drying paint so that they can be fitted in their original relative positions, (see Chapter 6).
2 Unscrew and remove the bolts which secure the automatic transmission to the engine and remove the starter motor. Pull the automatic transmission unit from its connection with the engine, keeping it in a straight line and supporting its weight during the operation.

8 Engine dismantling - general

1 It is best to mount the engine on a dismantling stand but if one is not available, then stand the engine on a strong bench so as to be at a comfortable working height. Failing this, the engine can be stripped down on the floor.
2 During the dismantling process the greatest care should be taken to keep the exposed parts free from dirt. As an aid to achieving this, it is a sound scheme to thoroughly clean down the outside of the engine, removing all traces of oil and congealed dirt.
3 Use paraffin or a good water soluble solvent. The latter compound will make the job much easier, as, after the solvent has been applied and allowed to stand for a time, a vigorous jet of water will wash off the solvent and all the grease and filth. If the dirt is thick and deeply embedded, work the solvent into it with a wire brush.
4 Finally wipe down the exterior of the engine with a rag and only then, when it is quite clean should the dismantling process begin. As the engine is stripped, clean each part in a bath of paraffin or petrol.

5 Never immerse parts with oilways in paraffin, i.e. the crankshaft, but to clean, wipe down carefully with a petrol dampened rag. Oilways can be cleaned out with wire. If an air line is present all parts can be blown dry and the oilways blown through as an added precaution.
6 Re-use of old engine gaskets is false economy and can give rise to oil and water leaks, if nothing worse. To avoid the possibility or trouble after the engine has been reassembled ALWAYS use new gaskets throughout.
7 Do not throw the old gaskets away as it sometimes happens that an immediate replacement cannot be found and the old gasket is then very useful as a template. Hang up the old gaskets as they are removed on a suitable hook or nail.
8 To strip the engine it is best to work from the top down. The sump provides a firm base on which the engine can be supported in an upright position. When this stage where the sump must be removed is reached, the engine can be turned on its side and all other work carried out with it in this position.
9 Wherever possible, replace nuts, bolts and washers fingertight from wherever they were removed. This helps avoid later loss and muddle. If they cannot be replaced then lay them out in such a fashion that it is clear where they belong.

9 Removing engine ancillary components

1 Unbolt the clutch assembly from the flywheel (see Chapter 5). (photo)
2 Loosen the alternator mounting bolts and the adjustment strap bolt. Push the alternator in towards the engine and remove the driving belt. Remove the alternator mounting bolts and adjustment strap bolt and lift the unit away. Some mountings incorporate shims to eliminate endfloat. Return them to their original positions. (photo)
3 Remove the oil dipstick.
4 Remove the distributor cap complete with HT leads.
5 Disconnect the vacuum pipe from the distributor and then unbolt and withdraw the distributor.
6 Disconnect the fuel inlet hose from the carburettor.
7 Remove the fuel pump, gaskets and insulating spacer. (photo)
8 Unbolt the thermostat housing and extract the thermostat. (photos)
9 Remove the engine mounting brackets. (photos)
10 Remove the oil pump/filter assembly. If the filter is being renewed, it will be easier to unscrew the filter before unbolting and withdrawing the oil pump. (photos)
11 Remove the crankcase ventilation valve (PCV valve).
12 Unbolt and remove as an assembly, the inlet and exhaust manifolds complete with carburettor. (photo)
13 Unbolt and remove the water pump assembly.

10 Cylinder head - removal

1 Unscrew and remove the five rocker shaft pillar securing bolts. Lift the rocker shaft assembly from the cylinder head. (photo)
2 Withdraw each of the pushrods and keep them in sequence so that they can be returned to their original positions. A piece of wood with two rows of holes drilled in it and numbered will provide a very useful rack for both pushrods and valves. (photo)
3 Unscrew each of the cylinder head bolts a turn or two each at a time in the sequence shown.
4 Lift off the cylinder head. Should it be stuck, do not attempt to prise it from the engine block but tap it all round using a hardwood block or plastic faced mallet. Remove the cylinder head gasket.

11 Valves - removal

1 The valves can be removed from the cylinder head by the following method. Compress each spring in turn with a valve

Fig. 1.13. Removing manifolds complete with carburettor

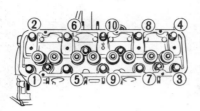

Fig. 1.15. Cylinder head bolt removal sequence diagram

Fig. 1.16. Removing the cylinder head

9.1 Removing clutch mechanism from flywheel

9.2 Removing alternator from mounting

9.7 Removing fuel pump

9.8A Thermostat housing

9.8B Thermostat

9.9A Left-hand engine mounting bracket

9.9B Right-hand engine mounting bracket

9.10A Oil filter

9.10B Withdrawing oil pump

9.12 Removing manifold assembly complete with carburettor

10.1 Removing rocker shaft assembly

10.2 Withdrawing pushrods

spring compressor until the two halves of the collets can be removed. Release the compressor and remove the spring and spring retainer.

2 If, when the valve spring compressor is screwed down, the valve spring retaining cap refuses to free to expose the split collet, do not continue to screw down on the compressor as there is a likelihood of damaging it.

3 Gently tap the top of the tool directly over the cap with a light hammer. This will free the cap. To avoid the compressor jumping off the valve spring retaining cap when it is tapped, hold the compressor firmly in position with one hand.

4 Slide the rubber oil control seal off the top of each valve stem and then drop out each valve through the combustion chamber.

5 It is essential that the valves are kept in their correct sequence unless they are so badly worn that they are to be renewed.

12 Rocker assembly - dismantling

1 The components of the rocker assembly are removed simply by sliding the pillars, arms and springs from the shaft.

2 If the original parts are to be refitted, mark their position with a numbered piece of masking tape before dismantling begins.

13 Sump - removal

1 Unscrew each of the sump securing bolts a turn at a time in order to prevent distortion. Remove the sump.

2 The gauze strainer and oil intake pipe will now be exposed and they should be detached after removal of the two flange securing bolts.

14 Timing cover, gear and chain - removal

1 Unscrew the crankshaft pulley securing bolt. This is achieved by using a 'slogger' type ring spanner. One or two hefty clouts with a club hammer on the shaft of the spanner should loosen the nut. It is useless to attempt to unscrew the pulley bolt using hand pressure alone as the crankshaft will simply rotate. Alternatively, the starter ring gear can be jammed while the bolt is being released.

2 Unbolt and remove the timing cover.

3 Remove the oil thrower disc from the crankshaft.

4 Unbolt and remove the chain tensioner.

5 Unscrew and remove the camshaft sprocket bolt.

6 Remove the camshaft and crankshaft gearwheels simultaneously complete with doublt roller chain. Use tyre levers behind each gear and lever them equally and a little at a time. If they are stuck on their shafts, the use of a puller may be required.

7 When the gearwheels and chain are removed, extract the Woodruff key from the crankshaft and retain it safely.

15 Piston, connecting rod and big-end bearing - removal

1 With the cylinder head and sump removed undo the big-end retaining bolts.

2 The connecting rods and pistons are lifted out from the top of the cylinder block, after the carbon or 'wear' ring at the top of the bore has been scraped away.

3 Remove the big-end caps one at a time, taking care to keep them in the right order and the correct way round. Also ensure that the shell bearings are kept with their correct connecting rods and caps unless they are to be renewed. Normally, the numbers 1 to 4 are stamped on adjacent sides of the big-end caps and connecting rods, indicating which cap fits on which rod and which way round the cap fits. If no numbers or lines can be found then, with a sharp screwdriver or file, scratch mating marks across the joint from the rod to the cap. One line for connecting rod No. 1, two for connecting rod No. 2 and so on. This will ensure there is no confusion later as it is most important that the caps go back in the correct position on the connecting rods from which they were removed.

4 If the big-end caps are difficult to remove they may be gently tapped with a soft hammer.

5 To remove the shell bearings, press the bearings opposite the groove in both the connecting rod, and the connecting rod caps and the bearings will slide out easily.

6 Withdraw the pistons and connecting rods upwards and ensure they are kept in the correct order for replacement in the same bore. Refit the connecting rod, caps and bearings to the rods if the bearings do not require renewal, to minimise the risk of getting the caps and rods muddled.

16 Flywheel - removal

1 Mark the relationship of the flywheel to the crankshaft mounting flange.

2 Unscrew and remove the securing bolts. To hold the flywheel still during this operation, wedge the crankshaft with a block of wood between the web and the crankcase.

17 Main bearings and crankshaft - removal

1 Unscrew and remove the securing bolts from the main bearing caps. The caps are numbered 1 to 5 starting from the timing cover end of the engine and arrows are marked on the caps and these point towards the timing cover to ensure correct orientation of the caps when refitting. If arrows are not visible, dot punch the caps on the side nearer the camshaft.

2 Withdraw the bearing caps complete with the lower halves of the shell bearings.

3 Remove the rear oil seal.

4 Lift the crankshaft from the crankcase and then remove each of the upper halves of the shell bearings.

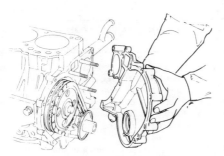

Fig. 1.17. Removing the timing cover

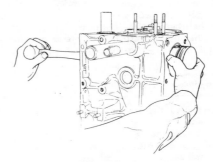

Fig. 1.18. Removing piston/connecting rod assembly from block

Fig. 1.19. Removing the crankshaft rear oil seal

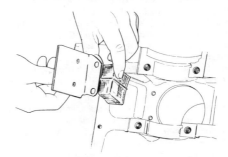

Fig. 1.20. Removing the baffle plate and mesh screen from the crankcase

5 Remove the baffle plate and the mesh screen from the crankcase.

18 Camshaft and cam followers - removal

1 With the engine block inverted, unscrew and remove the two bolts which secure the camshaft locating plate. Remove the plate and carefully withdraw the camshaft. Rotate the camshaft during the removal operation and take particular care not to damage the camshaft bearings as the lobes of the cams pass through them.
2 The tappet blocks may now be lifted from their original positions and retained in sequence so that they may be refitted in exactly the same order.
3 The engine is now completely dismantled and the individual components should be examined and serviced as described in later Sections of this Chapter.

19 Piston rings - removal

1 Each ring should be sprung open just sufficiently to permit it to ride over the lands of the piston body.
2 Once a ring is out of its groove, it is helpful to cut three ¼ in (6.35 mm) wide strips of tin and slip them under the ring at equidistant points.
3 Using a twisting motion this method of removal will prevent the ring dropping into a empty groove as it is being removed from the piston.

20 Gudgeon pin - removal

1 The gudgeon pins are an interference fit in the connecting rod small ends. It is recommended that removal of the gudgeon pin be left to a service station having a sufficiently powerful press to remove them.

2 Where a press is available to carry out the work yourself, the body of the piston must be supported on a suitably shaped distance piece into which the gudgeon pin may be ejected.

21 Lubrication system - description

The engine lubrication system is of the pressure feed type. An oil pump mounted on the right hand side of the cylinder block is driven by a meshing gear on the camshaft which also drives the distributor drive shaft. Oil is drawn from the sump through a filter screen and tube, pumped by the rotor type pump, through a full flow oil filter to the main crankcase oil gallery.

The main oil gallery supplies oil to the crankshaft main bearings and big-end bearings through drillings and a regulated quantity of oil ejected from small holes in the connecting rods lubricate the gudgeon pins and cylinder walls.

The timing chain is fed with oil from the main gallery and the

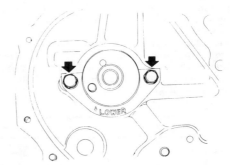

Fig. 1.21. Camshaft locating plate

chain tensioner is held against the timing chain partly by oil pressure and partly by a coil spring.

The camshaft bearings are lubricated with oil from the main gallery and the rocker shaft and valve gear obtain their lubrication through a drilling from the camshaft centre bearing.

22 Oil pump - inspection and servicing

1 Having removed the oil pump as previously described, unscrew and remove the two cover bolts, extract the inner end outer rotors and drive shaft.
2 Clean all components in paraffin and then check the following clearances using feeler gauges.

(i)   Side clearance 0.0020 to 0.0047 in (0.05 to 0.12 mm) with a wear limit of 0.0079 in (0.20 mm).
(ii) Rotor tip clearance, less than 0.0047 in (0.12 mm).
(iii) Outer rotor to body clearance 0.0059 to 0.0083 in (0.15 to 0.21 mm) with a wear limit of 0.0197 in (0.50 mm).
(iv) Rotor to body gap, 0.0020 in (0.05 mm) with a wear limit of 0.0079 in (0.20 mm).

Where measurements are outside the specified tolerances then the oil pump should be renewed as an assembly.
3 Apply a thin coating of gasket cement to the mating surfaces of the body and cover before reassembling and always use a new gasket when refitting the pump to the crankcase.

23 Oil pressure regulator valve - inspection and servicing

1 The oil pressure relief valve assembly is screwed into the rear face of the oil pump body. Unscrew the sealing plug and extract the shim, spring and valve.
2 No adjustment of the valve is provided for and the only check that can be carried out is to measure the length of the spring. This should be 1.71 in (43.43 mm). The best way to check this is to compare it with a new one.
3 Refit the relief valve components in their correct sequence, check the plug sealing washer and tighten the plug to between 29 and 36 lb/ft (4.0 and 5.0 kg/m)) torque.

24 Oil pressure relief valve - renewal

1 In the event of low oil pressure being indicated by the oil warning lamp lighting up, it must not be assumed that the fault lies with the pressure relief valve on the oil pump. Check for (i) blocked filter cartridge (ii) sump oil level correct (iii) oil pressure switch faulty and (iv) general excessive wear in main and big-end bearings. All these factors may be the cause of low oil pressure being indicated.
2 If all the foregoing prove satisfactory, check the operation of the relief valve by inserting a thin rod after the regulator valve has been removed.
3 The relief valve is sealed in position by a plug and this will first have to be drilled and extracted before a new relief valve ball and spring can be installed. The relief valve is very reliable in service and in the event of its malfunction, it will probably be better to renew the oil pump complete.

25 Oil filter cartridge - renewal

1 This should be unscrewed from the oil pump cover using a chain wrench or strap type oil filter removal tool.
2 When installing the new filter cartridge, apply grease to the rubber sealing ring and tighten it only with hand pressure. Remember a new filter element will absorb engine oil and the oil level should be topped-up after the engine has been operated for

a few minutes.

26 Crankcase ventilation control system - description and servicing

1 The system is designed to extract gas which has passed the pistons and entered the crankcase. These fumes are drawn through a closed circuit with valve to the inlet manifold.
2 During part-throttle openings the vacuum created in the inlet manifold draws fums through a valve screwed into the side of the inlet manifold and air to replace them is drawn into the clean side of the air cleaner through a hose which connects the air cleaner to the rocker cover and thence to the crankcase.
3 During full throttle operation, the inlet manifold vacuum is insufficient to draw the crankcase fumes through the valve and the flow is therefore in the reverse direction through the rocker cover to air cleaner hose.
4 The spring loaded valve which is essential to the accurate control of the system should be checked periodically in the following manner. With the engine idling, remove the hose from the valve. If the valve is operating correctly a hissing noise will be evident to prove that air is being admitted by the valve. A high vacuum should also be felt if a finger is placed over the valve inlet. Where these factors are not observed then the valve must be renewed.
5 Occasionally check the hoses for splits and security of connections. Pull a piece of rag through them to clean them.
6 A flame trap is interposed between the air cleaner and the rocker cover to prevent a blow-back from the carburettor reaching the engine interior. Check that this is securely fixed in the hose and regularly wash it free from oil contamination using paraffin, **not** petrol/gasoline.

27 Examination and renovation - general

With the engine stripped down and all parts thoroughly cleaned, it is now time to examine everything for wear. The items should be checked and where necessary renewed or renovated as described in the following Sections.

28 Crankshaft and main bearings - examination and renovation

1 Examine the crankpin and main journal surfaces for signs of scoring or scratches. Check the ovality of the crankpins at different positions with a micrometer. If more than specified out of round, the crankpin will have to be reground. It will also have to be reground if there are any scores or scratches present. Also check the journals in the same fashion.
2 If it is necessary to regrind the crankshaft and fit new bearings your local Datsun garage or engineering works will be able to decide how much metal to grind off and the size of new bearing shells.
3 Full details of crankshaft regrinding tolerances and bearing undersizes are given in Specifications.
4 The main bearing clearances may be established by using a strip of Plastigage between the crankshaft journals and the main bearing/shell caps. Tighten the bearing cap bolts to a torque of 45 lb/ft (6.3 kg/m). Remove the cap and compare the flattened Plastigage strip with the index provided. The clearance should be compared with the tolerances in Specifications.
5 Temporarily refit the crankshaft to the crankcase having refitted the upper halves of the shell main bearings in their locations. Fit the centre main bearing cap only, complete with shell bearing and tighten the securing bolts to 45 lb/ft (6.2 kg/m) torque. Using a feeler gauge, check the endfloat by pushing and pulling the crankshaft. Where the endfloat is outside the specified tolerance, the centre bearing shells will have to be renewed.
6 Finally check the pilot bush in the centre of the crankshaft rear flange. If it is worn or damaged, extract it by tapping a

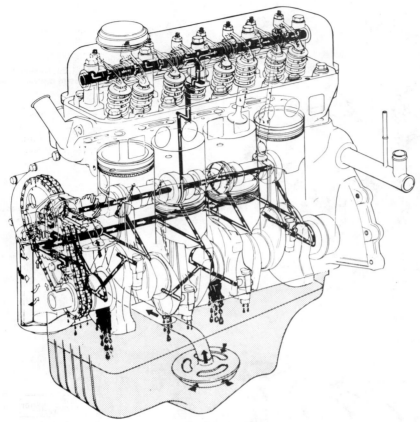

Fig. 1.22. Engine lubrication system

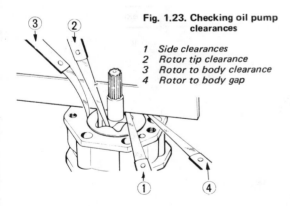

Fig. 1.23. Checking oil pump clearances

1 Side clearances
2 Rotor tip clearance
3 Rotor to body clearance
4 Rotor to body gap

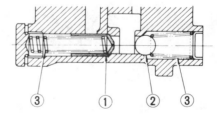

Fig. 1.24. Locations of oil pressure regulator valve (1) relief valve (2) and springs (3)

thread into it and then screwing in a bolt. Drive in the new bush which requires no lubrication.

29 Connecting rods and bearings - examination and renovation

1 Big-end bearing failure is indicated by a knocking from within the crankcase and a slight drop in oil pressure.
2 Examine the big-end bearing surfaces for pitting and scoring. Renew the shells in accordance with the sizes specifed in Specifications. Where the crankshaft has been reground, the correct undersize big-end shell bearings will be supplied by the repairer.
3 Should there be any suspicion that a connecting rod is bent or twisted or the small end bush no longer provides an interference fit for the gudgeon pin then the complete connecting rod assembly should be exchanged for a reconditioned one but ensure that the comparative weight of the two rods is within 0.18 oz (5g).
4 Measurement of the big-end bearing clearances may be carried out in a similar manner to that described for the main bearings in the previous Section but tighten the securing nuts on the cap bolts to 27 lb/ft (3.8 kg/m).

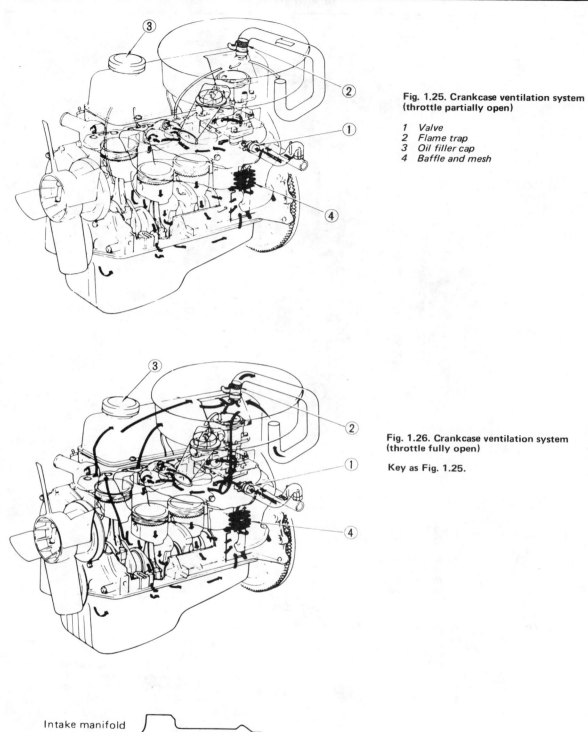

Fig. 1.25. Crankcase ventilation system
(throttle partially open)

1   Valve
2   Flame trap
3   Oil filler cap
4   Baffle and mesh

Fig. 1.26. Crankcase ventilation system
(throttle fully open)

Key as Fig. 1.25.

Intake manifold

Fig. 1.27. Sectional view of crankcase
emission control valve

30 Cylinder bores - examination and renovation

1 The cylinder bores must be examined for taper, ovality, scoring and scratches. Start by carefully examining the top of the cylinder bores. If they are at all worn a very slight ridge will be found on the thrust side. This marks the top of the piston ring travel. The owner will have a good indication of the bore wear prior to dismantling the engine, or removing the cylinder head. Excessive oil consumption accompanied by blue smoke from the exhaust is a sure sign of worn cylinder bores and piston rings.

2 Measure the bore diameter just under the ridge with a micrometer and compare it with the diameter at the bottom of the bore, which is not subject to wear. If the difference between the two measurements is more than 0.008 in (0.2032 mm) then it will be necessary to fit special pistons and rings or to have the cylinders rebored and fit oversize pistons. If no micrometer is available remove the rings from a piston and place the piston in each bore in turn about ¾ in below the top of the bore. If an 0.0012 in (0.0254 mm) feeler gauge slid between the piston and the cylinder wall requires less than a pull of between 1.1 and 3.3 lbs (0.5 and 1.5 kg) to withdraw it, using a spring balance then remedial action must be taken. Oversize pistons are available as listed in Specifications.

3 These are accurately machined to just below the indicated measurements so as to provide correct running clearances in bores bored out to the exact oversize dimensions.

4 If the bores are slightly worn but not so badly worn as to justify reboring them, then special oil control rings and pistons can be fitted which will restore compression and stop the engine burning oil. Several different types are available and the manufacturer's instructions concerning their fitting must be followed closely.

5 If new pistons are being fitted and the bores have not been reground, it is essential to slightly roughen the hard glaze on the sides of the bores with fine glass paper so the new piston rings will have a chance to bed in properly.

31 Pistons and piston rings - examination and renovation

1 If the original pistons are to be refitted, carefully remove the piston rings as described in Section 19.

2 Clean the grooves and rings free from carbon, taking care not to scratch the aluminium surfaces of the pistons.

3 If new rings are to be fitted, then order the top compression ring to be stepped to prevent it impinging on the 'wear ring' which will almost certainly have been formed at the top of the cylinder bore.

4 Before fitting the rings to the pistons, push each ring in turn down to the part of its respective cylinder bore (use an inverted piston to do this and to keep the ring square in the bore) and measure the ring end gap. The gaps should be as listed in Specifications Section.

5 Now test the side clearance of the compression rings which again should be as shown in Specifications Section.

6 Where necessary a piston ring which is slightly tight in its groove may be rubbed down holding it perfectly squarely on an oilstone or a sheet of fine emery cloth laid on a piece of plate glass. Excessive tightness can only be rectified by having the grooves machined out.

7 The gudgeon pin should be a push fit into the piston at room temperature. If it appears slack, then both the piston and gudgeon pin should be renewed.

32 Camshaft and camshaft bearings - examination and renovation

1 Carefully examine the camshaft bearings for wear. If the bearings are obviously worn or pitted then they must be renewed. This is an operation for your local Datsun dealer or local engineering works as it demands the use of specialized equipment. The bearings are removed with a special drift after which new bearings are pressed in, and in-line bored, care being taken to ensure the oil holes in the bearings line up with those in the block.

2 The camshaft itself should show no signs of wear, but, if very slight scoring on the cams is noticed, the score marks can be removed by very gentle rubbing down with a very fine emery cloth. The greatest care should be taken to keep the cam profiles smooth.

3 Examine the skew gear for wear, chipped teeth or other damage.

4 Carefully examine the camshaft thrust plate. Excessive end-float (more than 0.0039 in (0.10 mm) will be visually self evident and will require the fitting of a new plate.

33 Valves and valve seats - examination and renovation

1 Examine the heads of the valves for pitting and burning, especially the heads of the exhaust valves. The valve seatings should be examined at the same time. If the pitting on valve and seat is very slight the marks can be removed by grinding the seats and valves together with coarse, and then fine, valve grinding paste.

2 Where bad pitting has occurred to the valve seats it will be necessary to recut them and fit new valves. If the valve seats are so worn that they cannot be recut, then it will be necessary to fit new valve seat inserts. These latter two jobs should be entrusted to the local Datsun agent or engineering works. In practice it is very seldom that the seats are so badly worn that they require renewal. Normally, it is the valve that is too badly worn for replacement, and the owner can easily purchase a new set of valves and match them to the seats by valve grinding.

3 Valve grinding is carried out as follows:
   Smear a trace of coarse carborundum paste on the seat face and apply a suction grinder tool to the valve head. With a semi-rotory motion, grind the valve head to its seat, lifting the valve occasionally to redistribute the grinding paste. When a dull matt even surface finish is produced on both the valve seat and the valve, wipe off the paste and repeat the process with fine carborundum paste, lifting and turning the valve to redistribute the paste as before. A light spring placed under the valve head will greatly ease this operation. When a smooth unbroken ring of light grey matt finish is produced, on both valve and valve seat faces, the grrinding operation is completed.

4 Scrape away all carbon from the valve head and the valve stem. Carefully clean away every trace of grinding compound, taking great care to leave none in the ports or in the valve guides. Clean the valves and valve seats with a paraffin soaked rag then with a clean rag, and finally if an air line is available, blow the valves, valve guides and valve ports clean.

34 Valve guides - examination and renovation

1 Test each valve in its guide for wear. After a considerable mileage, the valve guide bore may wear oval. This can best be tested by inserting a new valve in the guide and moving it from side to side. If the tip of the valve stem deflects by about 0.0080 in (0.2032 mm) then it must be assumed that the tolerance between the stem and guide is greater than the permitted maximum as listed in Specification Section.

2 New valve guides are available in diameters of 0.0079 in (0.2 mm) oversize.

3 To remove and install valve guides, the cylinder head should be heated to between 302 and 392°F (150 to 200°C) in a domestic oven. Drive the old guides out towards the combustion chamber and then ream the valve guide holes in the cylinder head to 0.480 in (12.2 mm) diameter.

4 Press in the new guides from the combustion chamber end and then ream them to a diameter of 0.315 in (8.0 mm).

5 Unless the necessary reamers are available, it is preferable to leave valve guide renewal to your Datsun dealer.

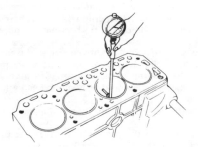

Fig. 1.28. Measuring a cylinder bore

Fig. 1.29. Measuring piston to cylinder bore clearance

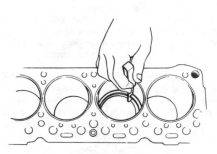

Fig. 1.30. Measuring piston ring end-gap

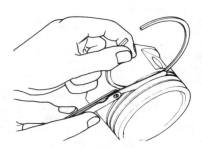

Fig. 1.31. Testing compression ring side clearance

Fig. 1.32. Testing the fit of a gudgeon pin in a piston

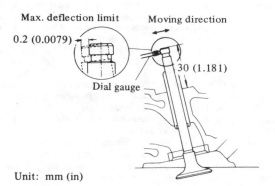

Max. deflection limit

0.2 (0.0079)

Moving direction

Dial gauge

30 (1.181)

Unit: mm (in)

Fig. 1.33. Valve guide wear test diagram

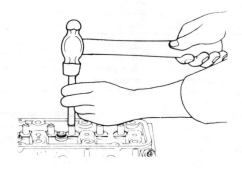

Fig. 1.34. Removing a valve guide

35 Timing gears and chain - examination and renovation

1 Examine the teeth on both the crankshaft gear wheel and the camshaft gear wheel for wear. Each tooth forms an inverted 'V' with the gearwheel periphery, and if worn the side of each tooth under tension will be slightly concave in shape when compared with the other side of the tooth (ie; one side of the inverted 'V' will be concave when compared with the other). If any sign of wear is present the gearwheels must be renewed.

2 Examine the links of the chain for side slackness and renew the chain if any slackness is noticeable when compared with a new chain. It is a sensible precaution to renew the chain at about 30,000 miles (48,000 km) and at a lesser mileage if the engine is stripped down for a major overhaul. The actual rollers on a very badly worn chain may be slightly grooved.

36 Rockers and rocker shaft - examination and renovation

1 Thoroughly clean the rocker shaft and then check the shaft for straightness by rolling it on plate glass. It is most unlikely that it will deviate from normal, but if it does, purchase a new shaft. The surface of the shaft should be free from any worn ridges caused by the rocker arms. If any wear is present, renew the shaft.

Check the rocker arms for wear of the rocker bushes, for wear at the rocker arm face which bears on the valve stem, and for wear of the adjusting ball ended screws. Wear in the rocker arm bush can be checked by gripping the rocker arm tip and holding the rocker arm in place on the shaft, noting if there is any lateral rocker arm shake. If shake is present, and the arm is very loose on the shaft, a new bush or rocker arm must be fitted.

Check the tip of the rocker arm where it bears on the valve

head for cracking or serious wear on the case hardening. If none is present reuse the rocker arm. Check the lower half of the ball on the end of the rocker arm adjusting screw. Check the push-rods for straightness by rolling them on the bench. Renew any that are bent.

37 Tappets - examination and renovation

Examine the bearing surface of the mushroom tappets which lie on the camshaft. Any indentation in this surface or any cracks indicate serious wear and the tappets should be renewed. Thoroughly clean them out, removing all traces of sludge. It is most unlikely that the sides of the tappets will prove worn, but, if they are a very loose fit in their bores and can readily be rocked, they should be exchanged for new units. It is very un-usual to find any wear in the tappets, and any wear is likely to occur only at very high mileages.

38 Flywheel starter ring gear - examination and renovation

1 If the teeth on the flywheel starter ring are badly worn, or if some are missing then it will be necessary to remove the ring and fit a new one, or preferably exchange the flywheel for a recon-ditioned unit.
2 Either split the ring with a cold chisel after making a cut with a hacksaw blade between two teeth, or use a soft headed hammer (not steel) to knock the ring off, striking it evenly and alternately at equally spaced points. Take great care not to damage the flywheel during this process.
3 Heat the new ring in either an electric oven to about 392°F (200°C) or immerse in a pan of boiling oil.
4 Hold the ring at this temperature for five minutes and then quickly fit it to the flywheel so the chamfered portion of the teeth faces the gearbox side of the flywheel.
5 The ring should be tapped gently down onto its register and left to cool naturally when the contraction of the metal on cooling will ensure that it is a secure and permanent fit. Great care must be taken not to overheat the ring, indicated by it turning light metallic blue, as if this happens the temper of the ring will be lost.

39 Cylinder head - decarbonising and examination

1 With the cylinder head removed, use a blunt scraper to remove all trace of carbon and deposits from the combustion spaces and ports. Remember that the cylinder head is aluminium alloy and can be damaged easily during the decarbonising opera-tions. Scrape the cylinder head free from scale or old pieces of gasket or jointing compound. Clean the cylinder head by washing it in paraffin and take particular care to pull a piece of rag through the ports and cylinder head bolt holes. Any dirt remaining in these recesses may well drop onto the gasket or cylinder block mating surface as the cylinder head is lowered into position and could lead to a gasket leak after reassembly is complete.
2 With the cylinder head clean, test for distortion if a history of coolant leakage has been apparent. Carry out this test using a straight edge and feeler gauges or a piece of plate glass. If the surface shows any warping in excess of 0.039 in (0.1015 mm) then the cylinder head will have to be resurfaced which is a job for a specialist engineering company.
3 Clean the pistons and top of the cylinder bores. If the pistons are still in the block then it is essential that great care is taken to ensure that no carbon gets into the cylinder bores as this could scratch the cylinder walls or cause damage to the piston and

rings. To ensure this does not happen, first turn the crankshaft so that two of the pistons are at the top of their bores. Stuff rag into the other two bores or seal them off with paper and masking tape to prevent particles of carbon entering the cooling system and damaging the water pump.
4 Rotate the crankshaft and repeat the carbon removal operations on the remaining two pistons and cylinder bores.
5 Thoroughly clean all particles of carbon from the bores and then inject a little light oil round the edges of the pistons to lubricate the piston rings.

40 Timing cover oil seal - renewal

1 Whenever a major engine overhaul is carried out, renew the timing cover oil seal as a matter of routine. Drive it out of its location using a piece of tubing as a drift.
2 Tap in the new seal squarely, making sure that the lips face the correct way. Refer to Section 42 for renewal of the crank-shaft rear oil seal.

41 Engine - preparation for reassembly

1 To ensure maximum life with reliability from a rebuilt engine, not only must everything be correctly assembled but all com-ponents must be spotlessly clean and the correct spring or plain washers used where originally located. Always lubricate bearing and working surfaces with clean engine oil during reassembly of engine parts.
2 Before reassembly commences, renew any bolts or studs the threads of which are damaged or corroded.
3 As well as your normal tool kit, gather together clean rags, oil can, a torque wrench and a complete (overhaul) set of gaskets and oil seals.

42 Engine - reassembly

1 Inspect the cylinder block for cracks and clean all the external surfaces. Probe the oil passages with a piece of wire.
2 Install the main bearing shells into their crankcase locations and into the main bearing caps. Note the centre bearing shell incorporates thrust washers. (photo)
3 Oil the bearing surfaces liberally with clean engine oil and carefully lower the cranksshaft into position in the crankcase. (photos)
4 Install the caps complete with shell bearings. Make sure that they are numbered 1 to 5 from the front of the engine and are fitted the correct way round. (photo) Apply sealant to the corners of the rear bearing cap.
5 Tighten the main bearing cap bolts to the specified torque. (photo)
6 Check that the crankshaft rotates smoothly and then test the endfloat (see Section 28).
7 Install a new crankshaft rear oil seal using a piece of tubing as a drift and making sure that the seal lips face the correct way.
8 The piston rings should be fitted to the pistons as described in Section 31 so that the markings on the rings are uppermost. The connecting rods will have been fitted with new bearings, pistons and gudgeon pins as necessary (see Sections 29 and 31).
9 Arrange the piston ring gaps at equidistant points of a circle so that they do not line up to cause gas blow-by; lubricate the rings and piston surfaces liberally and insert the connecting rod into the cylinder bore so that the number on the piston crown faces the timing cover end of the engine. If the original pistons are being refitted, ensure that they are returned to their original cylinders. On some piston crowns, an 'F' mark indicates the front.
10 Using a piston ring compressor, place the shaft of a hammer on the piston crown and strike the hammer head with the hand. This force should be quite sufficient to drive the piston/rod

assembly down the cylinder bore. Where this action does not have the desired effect, then the piston rings are either not sufficiently compressed or their end gaps are incorrect. (photo)

11 Connect each big-end to its appropriate crankshaft journal and install the big-end cap complete with shell. The caps and rods are numbered 1 to 4 and should be installed with the lowest number at the timing cover end of the engine. Make sure that the cap and rod numbers are adjacent and nearer the camshaft side of the engine. (photo)

12 Use plenty of oil when fitting the connecting rods to the crankshaft and engage the rod to the crankshaft when the crankshaft journal is at its lowest point.

13 Tighten the big-end bolt nuts to the specified torque. (photo)

14 Check the endfloat at each of the connecting rod big-ends after installation of the cap and bolts. The endfloat should be between 0.008 and 0.012 in (0.2 and 0.3 mm) when the crankshaft is aligned as shown.

15 With the engine still in the inverted position, install the cam followers in their original locations. A suction type valve grinding tool will be found useful during this operation. (photo)

16 Oil the camshaft bearings and gently slide the camshaft into position, taking care not to scratch or damage the bearing surfaces as the cam lobes pass through. (photo)

17 Install the camshaft locking plate so that the word 'lower' is to the bottom when the engine is the correct way up. Tighten the plate securing bolts to the specified torque. (photo)

18 Temporarily install the camshaft and crankshaft sprockets. Test their alignment with a straight edge and feeler blades. Any difference in alignment which exceeds 0.020 in (0.50 mm) must be corrected by installing a shim (available from your Datsun dealer) beneath the crankshaft sprocket.

19 Place the crankshaft and camshaft sprockets within the timing chain and install the complete assembly to the crankshaft and camshaft simultaneously. When correctly installed, a line drawn through the sprocket centres should also pass through the centre of the camshaft sprocket dowel hole and the crankshaft sprocket keyway. A double check can be made by making sure that the sprocket dot punch marks and the 'bright' chain plates are in alignment. The correct installation of the timing gear will call for rotation of the camshaft and crankshaft and repositioning of the sprockets within the loop of the chain on a trial and error basis until the alignment is correct. (photo)

20 When the timing is correct, tighten the camshaft sprocket bolt to the specified torque. (photo)

21 Install the timing chain tensioner and tighten the securing bolts. (photo)

22 Check the gap between the body of the tensioner and the rear face of the slipper. This must not exceed 0.591 in (15.0 mm). If the gap is greater than that specified, either the chain has stretched or the slipper has worn away and in either case, the component must be renewed.

23 Install the oil thrower disc to the front of the crankshaft, making sure that the projecting rim is towards the timing cover. (photo)

24 With a new oil seal installed in the timing cover, (see Section 40) clean the mating surfaces of the timing cover and cylinder block.

25 Apply a thin film of gasket cement to the mating surfaces of cover and block and position a new gasket on the block. Check that the gasket does not mask any of the bolt holes and then secure the cover by inserting and tightening the retaining bolts. (photo)

26 Install the oil pump pick-up tube using a new gasket at its mating flange with the crankcase. (photo)

27 Check that the crankcase breather tube baffle plate (and gauze filter on some models) are in position within the crankcase.

28 Apply a thin film of gasket cement to the lower face of the crankcase and stick a new sump gasket into position so that the holes in the crankcase are not masked by the gasket. (photo)

29 Insert the rubber sealing strips into the grooves of the front and rear main bearing caps and apply a little gasket cement to the corners. (photo)

30 Apply gasket cement to the mating flange of the sump and bolt it into position. Do not overtighten the bolts or the gasket will be damaged. (photo)

31 Oil the lips of the timing cover oil seal and install the crankshaft pulley. The pulley retaining bolt cannot be fully tightened at this stage but must wait until the flywheel (or driveplate) has been installed and the starter ring gear can be jammed to prevent the crankshaft rotating. (photo)

32 Install the water pump using a new gasket. On most models this gasket is combined with the timing cover gasket. (photo)

33 The cylinder head should now be reassembled ready for bolting to the engine cylinder block. Place the cylinder head on its side and having oiled the valve guides, insert the valves in their original locations or in the case of new valves into the seats into which they were previously ground. (photo)

34 To each valve in turn, fit a new oil seal, a new valve spring (if the engine has covered more than 20,000 miles/32,000 km) and a new valve spring cup and insert. Compress each spring in turn sufficiently to permit the split cotters to be inserted in the cut-out in the valve stem. Release the compressor gently and check that the split cotters have not been displaced. (photos)

35 When all the valve assemblies have been installed, place the cylinder head face downwards on the bench and using a hammer and a block of wood, strike the end of each valve stem squarely to settle the valve components.

36 Thoroughly clean the mating faces of cylinder block and head.

37 Place a new gasket on the cylinder block and carefully lower the cylinder head into position. (photo)

38 Screw in the cylinder head bolts finger-tight noting that the longer ones are located on the right-hand side and that one of them is of smaller diameter (waisted) than the rest. This particular bolt should be inserted in the middle hole on the right-hand side of the cylinder head. The bolt is marked 12T on its head. (photos)

39 Tighten the cylinder head bolts progressively, in stages and in the sequence shown until the specified torque is achieved. (photo)

40 Insert the pushrods into their original positions.

41 Slacken the rocker arm screws and locknuts right-off. Install the rocker shaft assembly and tighten the pillar bolts to the specified torque. Tighten the centre bolts first and then the front and rear ones.

42 The valve clearances should now be adjusted. Rotate the crankshaft during the adjustment procedure by applying a spanner or socket to the crankshaft pulley bolt.

43 The valve clearances obviously will have to be set with the engine cold to start with but when the unit is refitted to the vehicle and run up to normal operating temperature then they will have to be checked and readjusted when the engine is hot.

The importance of correct rocker arm/valve stem clearances cannot be overstressed as they vitally affect the performance of the engine. If the clearances are set too open, the efficiency of the engine is reduced as the valves open late and close earlier than was intended. If, on the other hand the clearances are set too close there is a danger that the stems will expand upon heating and not allow the valves to close properly which will cause burning of the valve head and seat and possible warping.

It is important that the valve clearance is set when the tappet of the valve being adjusted is on the heel of the cam (the lowest point) so that the valve is fully seated. One of two methods may be employed, first place a finger over No 1 spark plug hole, turn the engine and as soon as compression is felt, either observe the piston crown until it reaches its highest point (TDC). Alternatively, use as a guide a length of wire inserted through the spark plug hole. Rotate the engine until the guide wire reaches its highest point. Check the crankshaft pulley timing mark.

44 Set No. 1 cylinder inlet and exhaust valve clearances to 0.0098 in (0.25 mm) by adjusting the screw on the rocker arm while the appropriate feeler blade is inserted between the rocker arm and the end of the valve stem. (photo)

45 Rotate the crankshaft until No. 3 piston is at TDC and adjust

42.2 Main bearing shells installed in crankcase

42.3A Lubricating main shell bearings

42.3B Crankshaft in position in crankcase

42.4 Installing centre main bearing cap

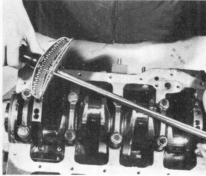
42.5 Tightening a main bearing cap bolt

42.7 Crankshaft rear oil seal

42.10 Piston ring compressor correctly fitted

42.11 Installing a big-end cap

42.13 Tightening a big-end cap bolt

42.15 Installing a cam follower

42.16 Installing camshaft

42.17 Camshaft locking plate

42,19 Timing gear correctly installed

42.20 Tightening camshaft sprocket bolt

42.21 Timing chain tensioner

42.23 Crankshaft oil thrower

42.25 Combined timing cover/water pump joint gasket

42.26 Installing oil pump pick-up tube

42.28 Installing sump gasket

42.29 Sealing main bearing cap strips

42.30 Fitting sump to crankcase

42.31 Crankshaft pulley and retaining bolt

42.32 Installing water pump

42.33 Inserting a valve into its guide

42.34A Valve stem oil seal

42.34B Valve spring and insert

42.34C Inserting valve spring split cotters

42.37 Installing cylinder head

42.38A Short and long cylinder head bolts

42.38B Location of waisted type 12T cylinder head bolt

42.39 Tightening a cylinder head bolt

42.44 Adjusting a valve clearance

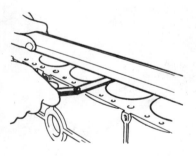
Fig. 1.35. Testing the cylinder head for distortion

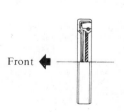
Front
Fig. 1.36. Correct installation of timing cover oil seal

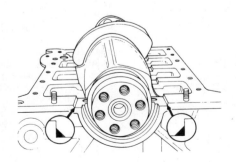
Fig. 1.37. Rear main bearing cap sealant application points

Fig. 1.38. Installing crankshaft rear oil seal

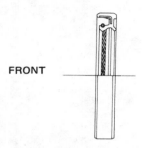

FRONT

Fig. 1.39. Correct installation
of crankshaft rear oil seal

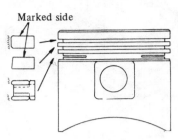

Marked side

Fig. 1.40. Piston ring installation diagram

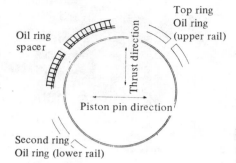

Top ring
Oil ring
(upper rail)

Oil ring
spacer

Thrust direction

Piston pin direction

Second ring
Oil ring (lower rail)

Fig. 1.41. Piston ring end gap
positioning diagram

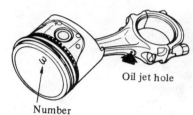

Oil jet hole

Number

Fig. 1.42. Correct piston to
connecting rod alignment

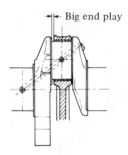

Big end play

Fig. 1.43. Crankshaft and connecting rod alignment prior to
checking end float

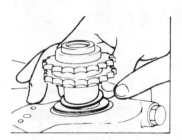

Fig. 1.44. Location of crankshaft sprocket alignment shim

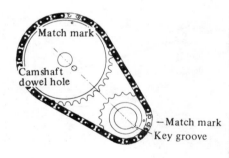

Match mark

Camshaft
dowel hole

Match mark
Key groove

Fig. 1.45. Timing sprocket and
chain alignment

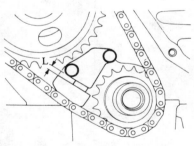

L

Fig. 1.46. Chain tensioner
clearance (L = 0.591 in
—15.0mm)

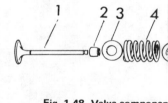

1   2 3   4   5 6

Fig. 1.48. Valve components

1 valve
2 oil seal
3 spring cup
4 valve spring
5 spring insert
6 split collets

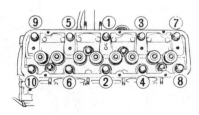

Fig. 1.49. Cylinder head bolt
tightening sequence diagram

No. 3 cylinder valve clearances.

46 Rotate the crankshaft until No. 4 piston is at TDC and adjust
No. 4 cylinder valves.

47 Finally, rotate the crankshaft until No. 2 piston is at TDC and
adjust No. 2 cylinder valves.

48 An alternative method of valve clearance adjustment, which
will probably be easier once the engine is installed in the vehicle,
is to turn the crankshaft until No. 1 piston is at TDC on its compression stroke (ignition timing marks in alignment).

49 Counting from the front of the engine, adjust valves:

1 exhaust
2 inlet
3 inlet
5 exhaust

50 By reference to the crankshaft pulley timing notch, rotate the
crankshaft one complete turn and adjust valves:

4 *exhaust*
6 *inlet*
7 *inlet*
8 *exhaust*

51 Adjustment of the clearance is made by conventional screw and locknut. Insert the feeler blade between the rocker arm face and the valve stem end face. Loosen the locknut, turn the screw until the blade cannot be withdrawn and then loosen the screw until the blade can be withdrawn just (stiffly), by a hard pull. Holding the slotted adjustment screw quite still, tighten the locknut with a ring spanner. When all the valve clearances have been adjusted, recheck them again before fitting the rocker box cover complete with a new sealing gasket.

52 Install the thermostat, a new gasket and the thermostat housing cover. Note that the right-hand securing bolt will carry the fuel pipe support clip.

53 Using a new gasket, fit the oil pump to the crankcase, check that the drive gear meshes correctly.

54 Screw a new oil filter cartridge into position. Lightly grease the rubber sealing ring before fitting it and tighten by using hand pressure only.

55 Install the fuel pump using a new gasket and making sure that the insulating spacer is in position.

56 Install the distributor by first setting No. 1 piston to TDC on the compression stroke. Hold the distributor over its hole in the crankcase and then turn the rotor arm in a clockwise direction 30° from the No. 1 firing position (indicated by a mark on the distributor cap). As the distributor is installed, and its drive gear meshes, the rotor will turn and align with the No. 1 mark.

57 Tighten the distributor clamp plate bolt to the crankcase.

58 Bolt the right-hand engine mounting to the crankcase. The mountings are not interchangeable and cannot be confused as the mounting holes are different.

59 Install the engine rear plate. (photo)

60 Install the flywheel (marks made before removal in alignment) and tighten the flywheel bolts to the specified torque. (photo)

61 Bolt the left-hand mounting to the crankcase.

62 Bolt the reinforcement bracket to the rear left-hand side of the crankcase but leave the bolts finger-tight at this stage. (photo)

63 Use a new gasket and install the manifold assembly complete with carburettor. Note the location of the engine lifting hook and air cleaner support strut under two of the manifold bolts. Install the fuel pipe between pump and carburettor. (photos)

64 Install the clutch assembly to the flywheel, centralising the driven plate as described in Chapter 5. Make sure that the longer projecting splined hub of the driven plate is towards the gearbox.

65 Couple the gearbox to the engine (see Chapter 6) and insert and tighten the clutch bellhousing to engine bolts to the specified torque.

66 In the case of cars fitted with automatic transmission, make sure that the alignment marks made on the driveplate and torque converter before removal, are correctly mated. Tighten the driveplate and torque converter housing to engine bolts to the specified torque.

67 Install the starter motor.

68 Install the alternator and adjustment strap. Fit the original mounting shims (if removed on dismantling). (photo)

69 Fit suitable slings to the engine/transmission unit and prepare to hoist the assembly into the engine compartment.

42.59 Engine rear plate

42.60 Install the flywheel

42.62 Installing crankcase reinforcement bracket

42.63A Details of engine lifting hook, air cleaner support and fuel pipe clips

42.63B Air cleaner main bracket and crankcase breather hose attachment

42.68 Alternator drivebelt adjustment strap and bolt

43 Engine/transmission installation - general

1 Although the engine can be replaced with one man using a
suitable winch, it is easier if two are present, one to lower the
engine into the engine compartment and the other to guide the
engine into position and to ensure it does not foul anything.
2 At this stage one or two tips may come in useful. Ensure all
the loose leads, cables, etc. are tucked out of the way. If not it is
easy to trap one and so cause much additional work after the
engine is replaced.
3 Two pair of hands are better than one when refitting the
bonnet. Do not tighten the bonnet securing bolts fully until it is
ascertained that the bonnet is on straight.

44 Engine/transmission - refitting to vehicle

1 Raise the engine/gearbox unit and either roll the vehicle
forward under it or if the hoist is mobile roll it forward so that
the unit is suspended above the engine compartment.
2 Lower the engine into the engine compartment at a steep
angle with the gearbox inclined downwards to the rear. Ensure
that nothing is fouled during the operation.
3 Fit the rear mounting bolts while the unit is still suspended
employing a jack if necessary to raise the gearbox sufficiently to
engage them.
4 Fit the engine front mounting pads, and lower the engine into
position. Remove the engine slings and hoist.
5 Refit the propeller shaft, ensuring that the rear flange marks
made before removal are aligned.
6 Remove the plug and reconnect the fuel line to the fuel
pump.
7 Refit the gearshift lever and the speedometer to drive cable to
the gearbox.
8 Connect the clutch cable or hydraulic slave cylinder

(according to type used) and connect the reversing lamp leads.
9 Fill the gearbox with the correct grade and quantity of oil.
10 Reconnect the throttle control.
11 Reconnect the choke control cable or automatic choke electrical lead (according to type used).
12 Connect the leads to the starter motor.
13 Connect the leads to the oil pressure gauge and the water
temperature transmitter.
14 Connect the exhaust downpipe to the manifold.
15 Check and adjust the ignition timing as described in Chapter
4.
16 Install the distributor cap and connect the HT and LT leads.
17 Connect the heater hoses to the inlet and outlet pipes on the
cylinder block.
18 Insert the engine oil dipstick.
19 Refit the air cleaner and connect the crankcase breather pipe.
(photo)
20 Reconnect the vacuum pipe between the distributor and the
carburettor. (photo)
21 Install the fan, spacer and pulley assembly, making sure to
include the lockplates and to bend them up after the bolts are
tightened.
22 Locate the fan belt over the crankshaft, water pump and
alternator pulleys and then with the alternator mountings and
adjustment strap slightly loosened, prise the alternator away
from the engine until the belt has a total deflection of ½in (12.4
mm) at the centre of its longest run. Tighten the mounting and
adjustment strap bolts without altering the belt tension. (photo)
23 Install the radiator.
24 Install the top and bottom radiator hoses.
25 Check for correct and positive connections of all emission
control system hoses and leads (see Chapter 3).
26 Refill the engine with oil.
27 Refill the cooling system (see Chapter 2).
28 Reconnect the negative lead to the battery.
29 Refit the bonnet lid.

44.19 Installing air cleaner

44.20 Routing of distributor vacuum
pipe and pump to carburettor fuel line

44.22 Checking fan belt tension

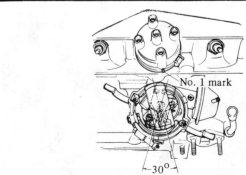

Fig. 1.51. Distributor installation diagram

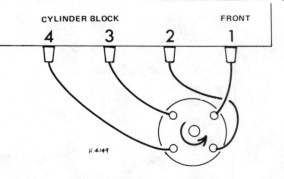

Fig. 1.52. HT lead connection diagram
(firing order 1-3-4-2)

45 Engine adjustment after major overhaul

1 With the engine refitted to the car and all controls leads and hoses properly connected, give a final visual check to make sure that no rags or tools have been left within the engine compartment.
2 Start the engine and check for any oil or water leaks, tightening any hose clips or bolts as may be necessary.

3 Run the car on the road until the engine reaches normal operating temperature. Switch off the engine and check the valve clearances, adjusting them to the **hot** clearances given in the Specifications Section.
4 Check all carburation and emission control settings as described in Chapter 3.
5 After 500 miles (800 km) running, check the torque of the cylinder head bolts (cold) and change the engine oil. Check the security of the engine mounting bolts.

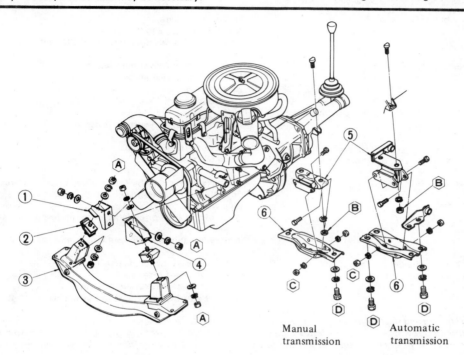

Manual transmission

Automatic transmission

Torque settings

	manual gearbox	auto. transmission
Ⓐ	9 lb/ft (1.2 kg/m)	9 lb/ft (1.2 kg/m)
Ⓑ	19 lb/ft (2.6 kg/m)	29 lb/ft (4.0 kg/m)
Ⓒ	6 lb/ft (0.8 kg/m)	6 lb/ft (0.8 kg/m)
Ⓓ	29 lb/ft (4.0 kg/m)	29 lb/ft (4.0 kg/m)

Fig. 1.54. Engine mounting components

1 Bracket
2 Insulator
3 Crossmember
4 Bracket
5 Insulator
6 Rear mounting cross-member

46 Fault diagnosis - engine

Symptom	Reason/s
Engine will not turn over when starter switch is operated	Flat battery. Bad battery connections. Bad connections at solenoid switch and/or starter motor. Defective starter motor.
Engine turns over normally but fails to start	No spark at plugs. No fuel reaching engine. Too much fuel reaching the engine (flooding).
Engine starts but runs unevenly and misfires	Ignition and/or fuel system faults. Incorrect valve clearances. Burnt out valves. Worn out piston rings.
Lack of power	Ignition and/or fuel system faults. Incorrect valve clearances. Burnt out valves. Worn out piston rings.
Excessive oil consumption	Oil leaks from crankshaft, rear oil seal, timing cover gasket and oil seal, rocker cover gasket, oil filter gasket, sump gasket, sump plug washer. Worn piston rings or cylinder bores resulting in oil being burnt by engine. Worn valve guides and/or defective valve stem seals.
Excessive mechanical noise from engine	Wrong valve ro rocker clearances. Worn crankshaft bearings. Worn cylinders (piston slap). Slack or worn timing chain and sprockets.

Note: When investigating starting and uneven running faults do not be tempted into snap diagnosis. Start from the beginning of the check procedure and follow it through. It will take less time in the long run. Poor performance from an engine in terms of power and economy is not normally diagnosed quickly. In any event the ignition and fuel systems must be checked first before assuming any further investigation needs to be made.

Chapter 2 Cooling system

Contents

Specifications

System type	Thermo syphon with pump assistance
Radiator type	Corrugated fin
Filler cap opening pressure	13 lb sq. in (0.9 kg sq. cm)
Thermostat type	Wax pellet
Thermostat starts to open	75 to 78°C (USA 80.5 to 83.5°C, Canada 86.5 to 89.5°C)
Coolant capacity (with heater)	9 pts. (5 3/8 US qts. 5.1 litres)

Torque wrench settings	lb f ft	kg f m
Water pump body securing nuts	10	1.4

1 General description

The cooling system comprises the radiator, top and bottom water hoses, water pump, cylinder head and block water jackets, radiator cap with pressure relief valve and flow and return heater hoses. The thermostat is located in a recess at the front of the cylinder head. The principle of the system is that cold water in the bottom of the radiator circulates upwards through the lower radiator hose to the water pump, where the pump impeller pushes the water round the cylinder block and head through the various cast-in passages to cool the cylinder bores, combustion surfaces and valve seats. When sufficient heat has been absorbed by the cooling water, and the engine has reached an efficient working temperature, the water moves from the cylinder head past the now open thermostat into the top radiator hose and into the radiator header tank.

The water then travels down the radiator tubes when it is rapidly cooled by the in-rush of air, when the vehicle is in forward motion. A four bladed fan, mounted on the water pump pulley, assists this cooling action. The water, now cooled, reaches the bottom of the radiator and the cycle is repeated.

When the engine is cold the thermostat remains closed until the coolant reaches a pre-determined temperature (see Specifications). This assists rapid warming-up.

Water temperature is measured by an electro-sensitive capsule located immediately below the thermostat housing. Connection between the transmitter capsule and the facia gauge is made by a single cable and Lucar type connector. The cooling system also provides the heat for the heater. The heater matrix is fed directly with water from the hottest part of the engine - the cylinder head - returning through a connection on the bottom radiator hose.

2 Cooling system - draining

1 Should the system have to be left empty for any reason both the cylinder block and radiator must be drained, otherwise with a partly drained system corrosion of the water pump impeller seal face may occur with subsequent early failure of the pump seal and bearing.

2 Place the car on a level surface and have ready a container having a capacity of two gallons which will slide beneath the radiator and sump.

3 Move the heater control on the facia to HOT and unscrew and

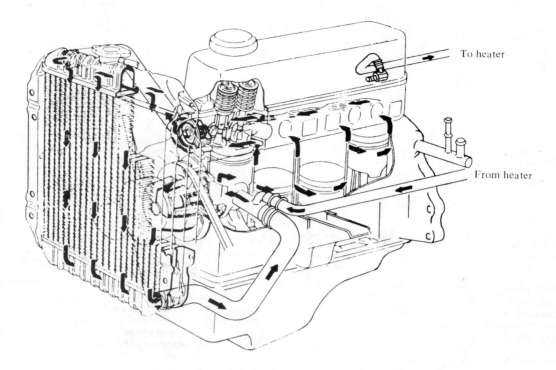

To heater

From heater

Fig. 2.1. Cooling system flow diagram (B210 models)

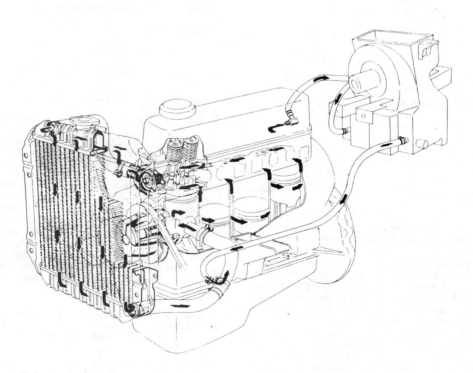

Fig. 2.1A Cooling system flow diagram (120Y models)

remove the radiator cap. If hot, unscrew the cap very slowly, first covering it with a cloth to remove the danger of scalding when the pressure in the system is released.

4 Unscrew the drain tap and/or remove the radiator bottom hose to allow the coolant to drain out. Retain the coolant for further use if it contains anti-freeze.

3 Cooling system - flushing

1 The radiator and waterways in the engine after some time may become restricted or even blocked with scale or sediment which reduce the efficiency of the cooling system. When this condition occurs or the coolant appears rusty or dark in colour the system should be flushed. In severe cases reverse flushing may be required as described later.

2 Place the heater controls to the 'HOT' position and unscrew fully the radiator and cylinder block drain taps.

3 Remove the radiator filler cap and place a hose in the filler neck. Allow water to run through the system until it emerges from both drain taps quite clear in colour. Do not flush a hot engine with cold water.

4 In severe cases of contamination of the coolant or in the system, reverse flush by first removing the radiator cap and disconnecting the lower radiator hose at the radiator outlet pipe.

5 Remove the top hose at the radiator connection end and remove the radiator as described in Section 7.

6 Invert the radiator and place a hose in the bottom outlet pipe. Continue flushing until clear water comes from the radiator top tank.

7 To flush the engine water jackets, remove the thermostat as described later in this Chapter and place a hose in the thermostat location until clear water runs from the water pump inlet. Cleaning by the use of chemical compounds is not recommended.

4 Cooling system - filling

1 Place the heater control to the 'HOT' position.

2 Screw in the radiator drain tap finger tight only and close the cylinder block drain tap.

3 Pour coolant slowly into the radiator so that air can be expelled through the thermostat pin hole without being trapped in a waterway.

4 Fill to the correct level which is 1 inch (25.4 mm) below the radiator filler neck and replace the filler cap.

5 Run the engine, check for leaks and recheck the coolant level.

5 Antifreeze mixture

1 The cooling system should be filled with Antifreeze solution in early Autumn. The heater matrix and radiator bottom tank are particularly prone to freeze if antifreeze is not used in air temperatures below freezing. Modern antifreeze soltuions of good quality will also prevent corrosion and rusting and they may be left in the system to advantage all year round, draining and refilling with fresh solution each year.

2 Before adding antifreeze to the system, check all hose connections and check the tightness of the cylinder head bolts as such solutions are searching. The cooling system should be drained and refilled with clean water as previously explained, before adding antifreeze.

3 The quantity of antifreeze which should be used for various levels of protection is given in the table below, expressed as a percentage of the system capacity.

Antifreeze volume	Protection to	Safe pump circulation
25%	$-26^{o}C$ $(-15^{o}F)$	$-12^{o}C$ $(10^{o}F)$
30%	$-33^{o}C$ $(-28^{o}F)$	$-16^{o}C$ $(3^{o}F)$
35%	$-39^{o}C$ $(-38^{o}F)$	$-20^{o}C$ $(-4^{o}F)$

4 Where the cooling system contains an antifreeze solution any topping-up should be done with a solution made up in similar proportions to the original in order to avoid dilution.

6 Radiator - removal, inspection, cleaning, refitting

1 Drain the cooling system as described in Section 2.

2 Disconnect the top hose from the radiator header tank.

3 Disconnect the bottom hose from the radiator outlet pipe.

4 Unscrew and remove the retaining bolts which secure the radiator to the front engine compartment mounting panel.

5 Lift out the radiator, taking care not to damage the cooling fins. Do not allow antifreeze solution to drop onto the bodywork during removal as damage may result.

6 Radiator repair is best left to a specialist but minor leaks may be tackled with a proprietary compound.

7 The radiator matrix may be cleared of flies by brushing with a soft brush or by hosing.

8 Flush the radiator as described in Section 3 according to its degree of contamination. Examine and renew any hoses or clips which have deteriorated.

9 Examine the plastic drain tap and its rubber washer, renewing if suspect.

10 Replacement of the radiator is a reversal of the removal procedure. Refill and check for leaks as described in Section 4.

7 Thermostat - removal, testing, refitting

1 A faulty thermostat can cause overheating or slow engine warm up. It will also affect the performance of the heater.

2 Drain off enough coolant through the radiator drain tap so that the coolant level is below the thermostat housing joint face. A good indication that the correct level has been reached is when the cooling tubes are exposed when viewed through the radiator filler cap.

3 Unscrew and remove the two retaining bolts and withdraw the thermostat cover sufficiently to permit the thermostat to be removed from its seat in the cylinder head.

4 To test whether the unit is serviceable, suspend the thermostat by a piece of string in a pan of water being heated. Using a thermometer, with reference to the opening and closing temperature in Specifications, its operation may be checked. The thermostat should be renewed if it is stuck open or closed or it fails to operate at the specified temperature. The operation of a thermostat is not instantaneous and sufficient time must be allowed for movement during testing. Never replace a faulty unit - leave it out if no replacement is available immediately.

5 Replacement of the thermostat is reversal of the removal procedure. Ensure the mating faces of the housing are clean. Use a new gasket with jointing compound. The word 'TOP' which appears on the thermostat face must be visible from above.

8 Water pump - description

The water pump is of conventional impeller type, driven by the fan belt. The impeller chamber is built into, and forms part of, the timing cover. The water pump detachable body is of die-cast aluminium in which runs the shaft. The shaft is fitted with bearings which are a shrink fit in the body and in the event of leakage or failure of the water pump, then it must be renewed as an assembly on an exchange basis.

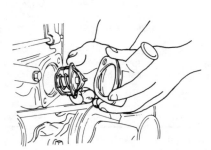

Fig. 2.2. Removing the thermostat

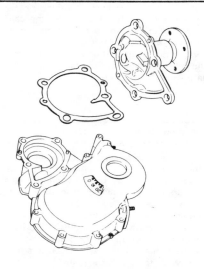

Fig. 2.3. Components of the water pump

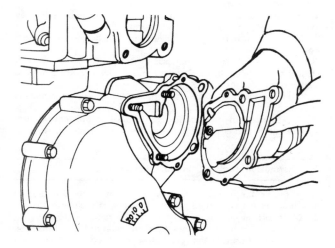

Fig. 2.4. Removing the water pump body

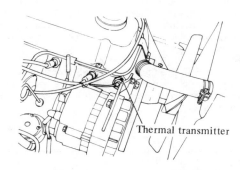

Thermal transmitter

Fig. 2.5. Location of water temperature transmitter

9 Water pump - removal and refitting

1 Drain the cooling system, retaining the coolant if required for further use.

2 Slacken the alternator mountings and adjustment strap bolt, push the alternator in towards the engine and slip the fan belt from the driving pulleys.

3 Unscrew and remove the four bolts which secure the fan and pulley to the water pump flange, remove the fan and pulley.

4 Unscrew and remove the securing nuts and bolts from the water pump housing flange and withdraw the water pump. Should the pump be stuck to the face of the timing cover, do not attempt to prise the mating flange apart as this will damage the soft aluminium and cause leaks after refitting. Grip the shaft extension housing firmly and lever from side to side to break the seal.

5 Refitting is a reversal of removal but ensure that the mating faces are clean and free from old pieces of gasket. Use a new gasket coated both sides with jointing compound and tighten the securing nuts to a torque of 10 lb/ft (1.4 kg/m).

6 Adjust the tension of the fan belt as described in Chapter 1, Section 42.

7 Refill the cooling system (Section 4).

10 Water temperature gauge - fault finding

1 Correct operation of the water temperature gauge is very important as the engine can otherwise overheat without it being observed.

2 The gauge is an electrically operated instrument comprising a transmitter unit screwed into the front of the cylinder head and transmitting through a spade type connector and cable to the dial mounted on the facia instrument panel. The instrument only operates when the ignition is switched on.

3 Where the water temperature gauge reads high-low inter-mittently, or not at all, then first check the security of the connecting cable between the transmitter unit and the gauge.

4 Disconnect the spade connector from the transmitter unit, switch on the ignition when the gauge should read 'COLD'. Now earth the cable to the engine block when the gauge needle should indicate 'HOT'. This test proves the gauge to be functional and the fault must therefore lie in the cable or transmitter unit. Renew as appropriate.

5 If the fuel gauge shows signs of malfunction at the same time as the water temperature gauge then a fault in the voltage stabilizer may be the cause.

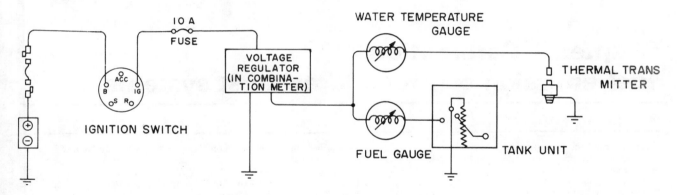

Fig. 2.6. Water temperature and fuel gauge circuits

11 Fault diagnosis - Cooling system

Symptom	Reason/s
Overheating	Low coolant level
	Slack fan belt
	Thermostat not operating
	Radiator pressure cap faulty or of wrong type
	Defective water pump
	Cylinder head gasket blowing
	Radiator core clogged with flies or dirt
	Radiator blocked
	Binding brakes
	Bottom hose or tank frozen
Engine running too cool	Defective thermostat
	Faulty water temperature gauge
Loss of coolant	Leaking radiator or hoses
	Cylinder head gasket leaking
	Leaking cylinder block core plugs
	Faulty radiator filler cap or wrong type fitted

Chapter 3 Carburation;
fuel, emission control and exhaust systems

Contents

Specifications

Fuel pump

Type	Mechanical, driven by camshaft
Pressure	3.4 lb/in^2 (0.24 kg/cm^2)

Fuel tank

Capacity:

Saloon	10 3/8 gal (Imp). 12 3/8 gal (U.S.) 47.0 litres.
Coupe	9½ gal. (Imp) 11 3/8 gal (U.S.) 43.0 litres.
Estate	8¾ gal. (Imp) 10 5/8 (U.S.) 40 litres.
Fuel octane rating	Above 90 (2 star)

Carburettors

Make	Hitachi

Application:

Model B210 (manual transmission)	DCH306 - 6
Model B210 (automatic transmission)	DCH306 - 7
Model 120Y	DCG 306

	Types DCH 306/4/5		Type DCG 306	
	Primary	Secondary	Primary	Secondary
Manifold port diameter ,..	1.024 in. (26.0 mm)	1.181 in. (30.0 mm)	1.024 in. (26.0 mm)	1.181 in. (30.0 mm)
Venturi diameter	0.787 in. (20.0 mm)	1.024 in. (26.0 mm)	0.787 in. (20.0 mm)	1.024 in. (26.0 mm)
Main jet	95	140	98	135
Main air bleed	80	80	80	80
Slow jet	43	50	43	50
Slow air bleed	215	100	220	100
Power jet	60		60	
Accelerator pump injector nozzle diameter	0.0197 in. (0.5 mm)		0.0197 in. (0.5 mm)	

Idling speed:

(B210) Manual transmission	800 rpm
(120Y) Manual transmission	600 rpm
Automatic transmission in 'D'	650 rpm
Exhaust CO analysis	1.5% $\pm$ 0.5%

Torque wrench settings

						lb f ft	kg f m
Carburettor to manifold nuts	...	...	...	...	...	18	2.5
Manifold to block nuts and bolts	...	...	...	...	...	18	2.5
Fuel pump nuts	...	...	...	...	...	20	2.8
Manifold to exhaust downpipe nuts		...	...	...	...	18	2.5

1 General description

The fuel system comprises a rear mounted tank from which fuel is drawn through a filter by means of a mechanically operated pump mounted on the right hand side of the crankcase. The fuel pump is operated by an eccentric on the camshaft and delivers fuel, under pressure, to a twin choke carburettor. The carburettor type varies according to the vehicle model and date or manufacture and reference should be made to Specifications for full details.

The carburettors fitted to all 120Y models have a manually-operated choke while the B210 models have a similar carburettor incorporating an electrically-heated automatic choke.

All vehicles are fitted with a crankcase fume emission control system (see Chapter 1) and B210 models are additionally equipped with exhaust emission control and fuel evaporative control systems also a temperature controlled air cleaner.

2 Air cleaner - servicing

1 The standard air cleaner comprises a body in which is housed a paper element type filter, a lid and the necessary connecting hoses and brackets.
2 Every 24,000 miles (38,000 km) the element should be renewed. Other than renewal, no servicing is required.
3 Unscrew and remove the wing nut which secures the air cleaner lid in position, remove the lid and extract the paper element. (photo)
4 Wipe the interior of the air cleaner body free from oil and dirt and install the new element.
5 Set the valve lever to 'SUMMER' to 'WINTER' position as required by climatic conditions. (photo)

3 Air cleaner - automatic temperature control type

1 This type of air cleaner is designed to keep air being drawn into the engine for combustion purposes at a consistent temperature of about 43°C (110°F). The system is installed to assist in reducing pollution emitted from the exhaust and consists, essentially of a temperature sensor and air control valves.
2 The temperature sensor will actuate the air control valve so that the correct mixture of hot air from the exhaust manifold and cold air entering the air cleaner inlet tube will be supplied to the carburettor at the specified temperature irrespective of the operating temperature of the engine itself.
3 Regular maintenance of this type of air cleaner is not required beyond renewal of the element as described for standard air cleaner in the preceding Section.

However, in the event of a fault developing and evidence of increased exhaust fumes being emitted, carry out the following operations.
4 Check the security, condition and correct location of all vacuum air supply hoses.
5 With the engine at normal operating temperature, switch off the ignition and holding a mirror to reflect the interior of the air cleaner intake pipe, check the position of the valve. The valve should be closed to exhaust manifold heated air. If this is not the case, check the valve linkage.
6 Disconnect the vacuum hose which connects the vacuum capsule to the inlet manifold. Suck the tube to actuate the vacuum capsule and check that the valve closes to cold air in-

take. If this is not the case then the air cleaner must be renewed as an assembly.
7 With the engine cold, check that the ambient temperature of the sensor is below 30°C (86°F).
8 Using a mirror as previously described, check that the valve is in the 'open to cold air' position.
9 Start the engine and run it at idling speed, the valve should close immediately to cold air and permit exhaust manifold heated air to be drawn into the cleaner.
10 As the engine warms up observe that the valve gradually opens to permit the entry of cold air into the air cleaner intake tube.
11 If the valve does not operate correctly at within the temperature range 38 to 55°C, 100°F to 131°F (checked by using a thermometer adjacent to its location) remove and renew the sensor unit by bending back the tabs of its retaining clips.

4 Idle compensator - checking and renewal

1 The idle compensator is a thermostatic valve located in the air cleaner to compensate for over-rich mixture when the under bonnet temperature is very high. The valve opens under temperature conditions of between 60° and 75°C (140° and 167°F).
2 A faulty idle compensator may be checked in-situ by making sure that the valve is shut (under bonnet temperature cool) and then disconnecting the hose and alternatively blowing and sucking with the mouth. If any air leakage is evident around the valve, renew it.
3 Operation of the valve can be checked by removing it (two screws after detaching air cleaner cover), and immersing it in water which is being heated to the valve operating temperature.

5 Fuel filter - servicing

1 The fuel filter is located in the tank to pump hose and is of the sealed paper element type.
2 Every 12,000 miles (19,000 km) renew the filter. It is preferable to carry out this operation when the fuel tank level is low otherwise when the fuel hoses are disconnected from the filter, the tank line will have to be plugged to prevent loss of fuel.
3 Check that the new filter is installed in the correct attitude.

6 Fuel pump - description

The fuel pump is actuated by the movement of its rocker arm on a camshaft eccentric. This movement is transferred to a flexible diaphragm which draws the fuel from the tank and pumps it under pressure to the carburettor float chamber. Inlet and outlet valves are incorporated to control the flow of fuel irrespective of engine speed.

7 Fuel pump - testing

Presuming that the fuel lines and unions are in good condition and that there are no leaks anywhere, check the performance of the fuel pump in the following manner: Disconnect the fuel pipe at the carburettor inlet union, and the high tension lead to the coil, and with a suitable container or a large rag in position to catch the ejected fuel, turn the engine over on the starter motor solenoid. A good spurt of petrol should emerge from the end of the pipe every second revolution.

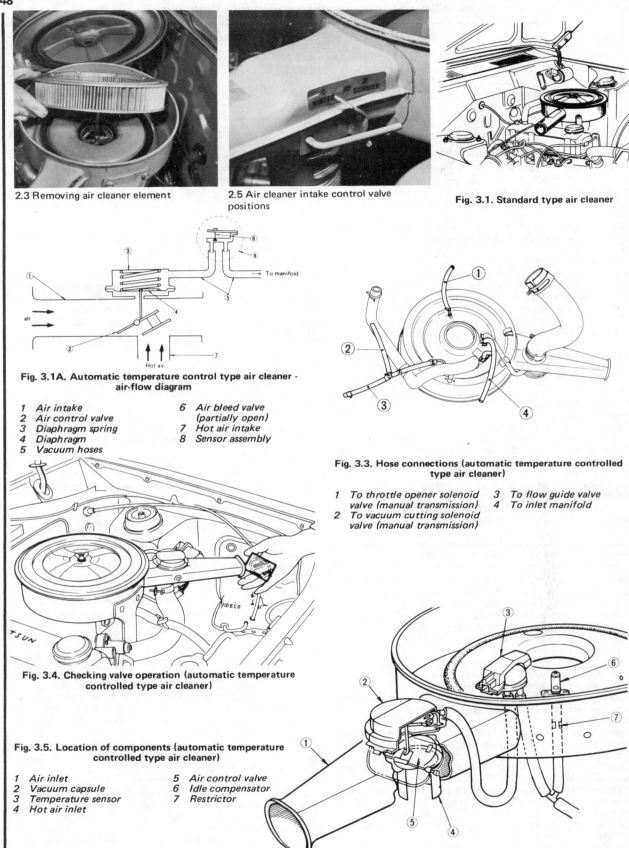

2.3 Removing air cleaner element

2.5 Air cleaner intake control valve positions

Fig. 3.1. Standard type air cleaner

Fig. 3.1A. Automatic temperature control type air cleaner -
air-flow diagram

1 Air intake
2 Air control valve
3 Diaphragm spring
4 Diaphragm
5 Vacuum hoses
6 Air bleed valve (partially open)
7 Hot air intake
8 Sensor assembly

Fig. 3.3. Hose connections (automatic temperature controlled
type air cleaner)

1 To throttle opener solenoid valve (manual transmission)
2 To vacuum cutting solenoid valve (manual transmission)
3 To flow guide valve
4 To inlet manifold

Fig. 3.4. Checking valve operation (automatic temperature
controlled type air cleaner)

Fig. 3.5. Location of components (automatic temperature
controlled type air cleaner)

1 Air inlet
2 Vacuum capsule
3 Temperature sensor
4 Hot air inlet
5 Air control valve
6 Idle compensator
7 Restrictor

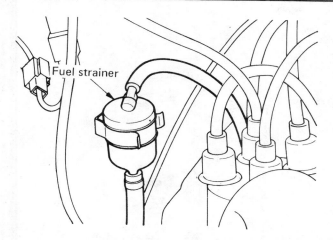

Fig. 3.6. Location of fuel filter

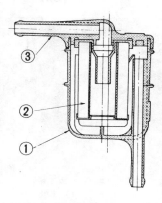

Fig. 3.7. Sectional view of fuel filter

1 *Body*   3 *Cover*
2 *Element*

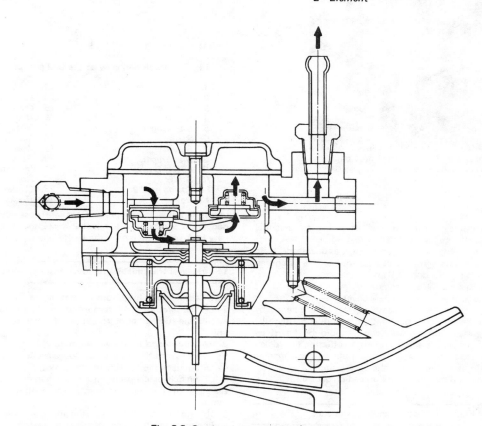

Fig. 3.8. Sectional view of the fuel pump

8 Fuel pump - removal and refitting

1 Disconnect the fuel pipes by unscrewing their two hose clips on the fuel pump which is located on the right hand side of the engine. Where the fuel tank contains more than a small amount of fuel it will probably be necessary to plug the inlet fuel line from the tank. (photo)

2 Remove the two nuts which secure the fuel pump to the crankcase. Lift away the pump noting carefully the number of gaskets used between the pump and crankcase mating faces.

3 Installation is a reversal of removal but note the routing of the fuel pipe to the carburettor. (photo)

9 Fuel pump - dismantling, inspection, reassembly

1 Scratch an alignment mark across the edges of the upper and lower body flanges to ensure correct reassembly.

2 Unscrew and remove the body securing screws.

3 Remove the cover screws and lift off the cover and gasket.

4 Remove the fuel pipe stubs.

5 Remove the retainer (two screws) and extract the two valves.

6 Press the diaphragm downwards and then grip the top of the pull rod and move the bottom end of the rod so that a sideways movement will disengage it from the rocker arm link. The diaphragm, diaphragm spring, lower body and washer may then

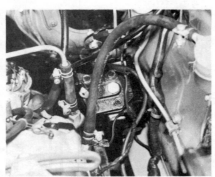

8.1 Fuel pump inlet (from filter) and outlet pipes

8.3 Fuel pump to carburettor pipe clip location on right hand side of engine

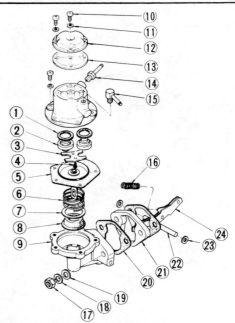

Fig. 3.9. Exploded view of the fuel pump

1	Seal	13	Gasket
2	Valve	14	Inlet nozzle
3	Retainer	15	Outlet nozzle
4	Screw	16	Rocker arm spring
5	Diaphragm	17	Nut
6	Spring	18	Spring washer
7	Retainer	19	Washer
8	Diaphragm	20	Gasket
9	Lower body	21	Insulator
10	Screw	22	Rocker arm pivot
11	Spring washer	23	Circlip
12	Cover	24	Rocker arm

be withdrawn.

7 The rocker arm pin is an interference fit and if it is essential to remove it, then it should be pressed or drifted out.

8 Check all components for wear and renew as necessary. Hold the diaphragm up to the light and inspect for splits or pin holes. Check the upper and lower body halves for cracks.

9 Reassembly is a reversal of dismantling. Apply grease to the rocker arm mechanism and install a new cover gasket.

10 When the pump has been reassembled, test its efficiency by either placing a finger over the inlet pipe and actuating the rocker arm when a good suction noise should be heard by connecting it to the tank fuel line and after actuating the rocker arm a few times, each successive stroke should be accompanied by a well defined spurt of fuel from the outlet pipe.

11 Refit the pump as described in the preceding Section.

10 Fuel tank and liner - description and maintenance

1 The fuel tank is mounted at the rear on all vehicles but varies in capacity and installation method according to the particular model.

2 The tank is fitted with a fuel level transmitter and a drain plug.

3 The coupe model is equipped with a reservoir tank and all vehicles destined for operation in North America and certain other territories have an evaporative emission control system.

4 Occasionally check the security of all hose clips and when the fuel level is low, remove the drain plug and release any accumulated water or sediment which may have collected in the bottom of the tank.

5 Should a leak develop in the fuel tank do not be tempted to solder over the hole. Fuel tank repair is a specialist job and

unless lengthy safety precautions are observed can be a very dangerous procedure. It is probably as cheap these days to buy a new tank rather than have the faulty one repaired.

11 Fuel level transmitter - removal, testing, refitting

1 Disconnect the lead from the battery negative terminal.

2 *On the saloon model,* remove the trim panel from the forward end of the luggage boot to expose the fuel tank and transmitter unit.

3 *On coupe and estate wagon models,* remove the small inspection cover from the floor of the luggage compartment.

4 Disconnect the leads from the tank transmitter unit and using a 'C' wrench or carefully applying a hammer and cold chisel to the tags of the locking ring, unscrew the unit and carefully remove it.

5 If a malfunction occurs in the fuel gauge, first check all leads and connections between the gauge and transmitter unit.

6 If the fuel gauge and the water temperature gauge become faulty at the same time, refer to Chapter 2, Section 10, as the instrument voltage stabiliser may be at fault.

7 Refitting is a reversal of removal but take care not to damage the float or arm of the transmitter unit when inserting it into the tank and always use a new rubber sealing ring.

12 Fuel tank (saloon) - removal and installation

1 Disconnect the lead from the battert negative terminal.

2 Remove the trim panel from the forward end of the luggage boot.

3 Remove the spare wheel from the luggage boot.

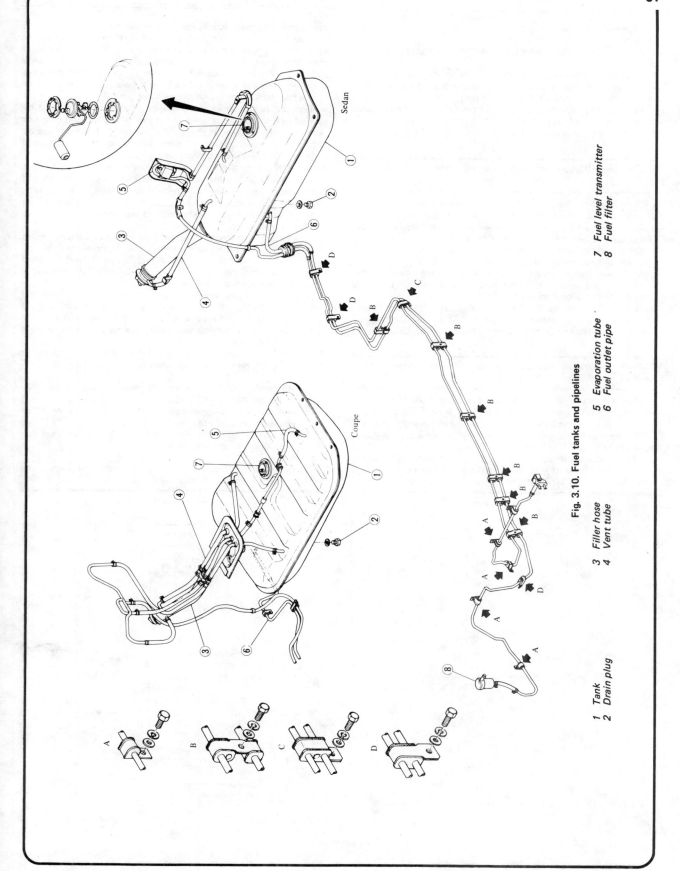

Fig. 3.10. Fuel tanks and pipelines

1 Tank
2 Drain plug

3 Filler hose
4 Vent tube

5 Evaporation tube
6 Fuel outlet pipe

7 Fuel level transmitter
8 Fuel filter

4 Remove the drain plug and drain the fuel into a suitable container.
5 Disconnect the fuel filler hose and all other pipes from the tank.
6 Disconnect the leads from the fuel level transmitter unit.
7 Remove the rear seat cushion and the seat back and then unscrew the two front tank mounting bolts.
8 Unscrew the tank mounting bolts from both sides and remove the tank from the luggage boot.
9 Installation is a reversal of removal.

13 Fuel tank (Coupe and Estate Wagon) - removal and installation

1 Disconnect the lead from the battery negative terminal.
2 Drain the fuel from the tank into a suitable container.
3 Remove the trim panel to gain access to the fuel filler hose. Disconnect all hoses and pipes from the tank.
4 *On coupe models,* disconnect the pipes from the reservoir tank and remove the spare wheel and reservoir tank.
   On estate wagon car models, remove the spare wheel carrier.
5 Remove the small inspection cover and disconnect the leads from the tank transmitter unit.
6 Release the tank flange mounting bolts and remove the tank.
7 Installation is a reversal of removal but use a new bead of mastic to seal the tank mounting flange to the floor pan.

14 Fuel evaporative emission control - description and maintenance

1 This system is designed to prevent vapour from the tank escaping to atmosphere and is fitted to vehicles operating in areas where stringent anti-pollution regulations are enforced.
2 The system comprises a tight sealing filler cap, a vapour-liquid separator, a vent line and a flow guide valve.
3 The principle of operation is such that with the engine switched off, the vent line, the separator and fuel tank are filled with fuel vapour. When the pressure of this vapour reaches a pre-determiend level it actuates a flow guide valve and passes to the crankcase. When the engine is started, the vapour which has accumulated in the crankcase, manifold and air cleaner is drawn into the inlet manifold for combustion within the engine cylinders. When the vapour pressure in the system becomes negative, then the flow guide valve will permit entry of fresh air to the fuel tank from the air cleaner.
4 Periodic preventative maintenance of the system should be carried out. Inspect all hoses and the fuel filler cap for damage or deterioration. Leakage at the fuel cap can only be determined by fitting a three-way connector, cock and manometer ('U' shaped glass tube will do) into the vent line as shown.
5 Blow through the cock until the level in the 'U' tube is approximately at the higher level illustrated. Close the cock and after a period of 2½ minutes check that the level in the 'U' tube has not dropped more than indicated in the illustrations. If the levels in the 'U' tube quickly become equalised, then the filler cap is not sealing correctly.
6 Assuming the previous test has proved satisfactory, again blow into the 'U' tube and shut the cock. Remove the filler cap quickly when the height of the liquid in the 'U' tube should immediately drop to zero, failure to do this will indicate a clogged or obstructed vent line.
7 The fuel filler cap imcorporates a vacuum release valve and this may be checked by gently sucking with the mouth. A slight resistance accompanied by a click shows the valve is in good condition. Further suction will cause the resistance to cease as soon as the valve clicks.
8 To check the operation of the flow guide valve, apply air pressure from a tyre pump in the following sequence:

   a) *Air applied to fuel tank nozzle should emerge freely from crankcase nozzle.*
   b) *Air applied to crankcase nozzle should not enter or emerge from any other nozzle.*
   c) *Air applied to air cleaner nozzle should emerge from one or both of the other two nozzles.*

Any deviations from the foregoing tests will necessitate renewal of the components as assemblies.

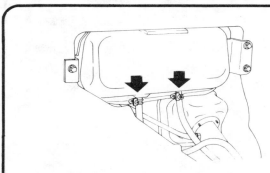

Fig. 3.11. Coupe reservoir tank connecting hoses

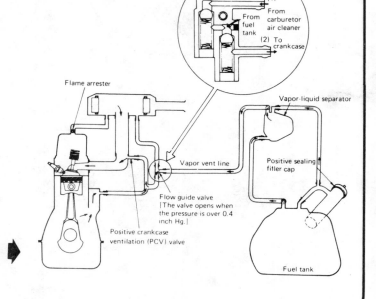

Fig. 3.12. Fuel evaporative emission control system

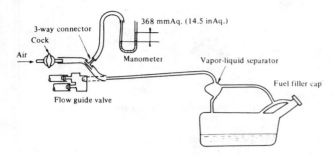

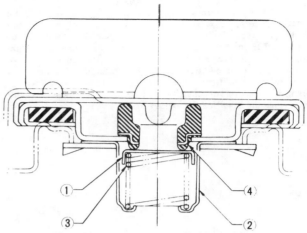

Fig. 3.13. Diagram for testing components of fuel evaporative emission control system

Fig. 3.14. Sectional view of fuel tank filler cap

1   Valve   3   Spring
2   Valve housing   4   Valve seat

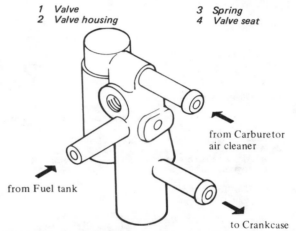

Fig. 3.15. Flow guide (fuel evaporative emission control system)

15 Accelerator linkage - adjustment

1 After a considerable mileage, the accelerator cable may stretch and the following adjustment may be carried out to remove the slack.

2 Check the security of the inner cable to the accelerator pedal and the threaded portion of the outer cable which is held by a nut to the engine bulkhead. Loosen clamp '1' and pull the outer cable in the direction 'P', until any further movement would cause the throttle arm on the carburettor to move. Now ease the outer cable in the opposite direction 'Q' no more than between 0.160 and 0.240 in (4.0 to 6.0 mm). Tighten the clamp.

3 The accelerator pedal should be adjusted by means of its stop bolt so that the pedal travel is as indicated and the carburettor butterfly valve is fully open when the pedal is fully depressed.

4 On vehicles having automatic transmission, adjust the 'kick-down' switch to operate when the accelerator pedal is fully depressed.

16 Carburettors - general description

All models are equipped with a Hitachi twin barrel carburettor of down draught type. An automatic, electrically heated choke is fitted to the carburettors on B210 vehicles while most 120Y models have carburettors equipped with a manually operated choke. (photo)

The carburettors vary in calibration details and those fitted on B120 models having manual transmission incorporate a throttle opener device. When these carburettors are fitted in conjunction with automatic transmission a dashpot is incorporated in the carburettor to prevent any tendency to stall the engine during deceleration. Refer to the Specifications Section for precise details and applications.

The carburettor is conventional in operation and incorporates a primary and main jet system and a mechanically operated accelerator pump.

Manually operated choke: This comprises a butterfly valve which closes one of the venturi choke tubes and is so synchronized with the throttle valve plate that the latter opens sufficiently to provide a rich mixture and an increased slow running speed for easy starting.

Automatic choke: This is essentially an electrically heated bi-metal strip. When the engine is switched on, the bi-metal strip which is linked to the now fully closed choke valve (cold engine) is heated electrically and over a pre-set period causes the choke valve to open until its fully open position coincides with the engine reaching normal operating temperature.

For idling and slow running, the fuel passes through the slow running jet, the primary slow air bleed and the secondary slow air bleed. The fuel is finally ejected from the by-pass and idle holes.

The accelerator pump is synchronized with the throttle valve.

During periods of heavy acceleration, the pump which is of simple piston and valve construction, provides an additional metered quantity of fuel to enrich the normal mixture. The quantity of fuel metered can be varied according to operating climatic conditions by adjusting the stroke of the pump linkage.

The secondary system provides a mixture for normal motoring conditions by means of a main jet and air bleed. The float chamber is fed with fuel pumped by the mechanically operated pump on the crankcase. The level in the chamber is critical and must at all times be maintained as specified.

17 Slow running - adjustment

1 Run the engine to normal operating temperature and then set the throttle adjusting screw (1) (Fig. 3.21) to provide the correct idling speed as given in the Specifications, according to the particular model. The gear selector lever in neutral (manual transmission) or in 'D' (automatic transmission). If the vehicle is fitted with a tachometer then the setting of engine speed will be no problem. Where an instrument is not available then a useful guide may be obtained from the state of the ignition warning lamp. This should just be going out at the correct idling speed.

2 Setting of the mixture screw (2) may be carried out using 'Colortune' or a vacuum gauge attached to the inlet manifold. In either case follow the equipment manufacturer's instructions.

3 In certain territories, the use of a CO meter is essential and if this is used then the throttle adjusting screw and the mixture screw must be turned to provide a reading on the meter of 1.5% $\pm$

0.5% at the specified engine idling speed.

4 As a temporary measure, the adjustment screws may be rotated progressively, first one and then the other until the engine idles at the correct speed without any 'hunting' or stalling. Turning the mixture screw clockwise weakens the mixture and anti-clockwise richens it. Never screw the mixture screw in too far or the idle limiter cap will break. Should this happen, a new cap must be fitted in accordance with the installation diagram, first making sure that the mixture screw has been correctly set to give the specified CO exhaust gas analysis.

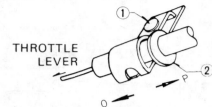

THROTTLE LEVER

Fig. 3.16. Accelerator cable adjustment diagram

1 Clamp bolt
2 Outer cable socket

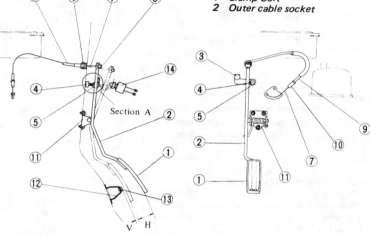

Section A

Fig. 3.17. Accelerator control components and adjustment diagram

1	Pedal	4	Stop bolt	8	Knurled nut	12	Stop bracket
2	Arm	5	Stop nut	9	Outer cable	13	Stop rubber buffer
3	Kickdown switch striker plate	6	Spring clamp	10	Socket	14	Kickdown switch
	(automatic transmission)	7	Inner cable	11	Bracket and spring		

H = 2.32 in (59.0 mm)

V = 0 to 0.079 in (0 to 2.0 mm)

Fig. 3.17A Hitachi type DCG 306 carburettor

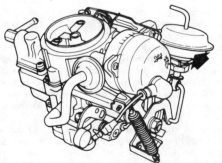

Fig. 3.18. Type DCH 306 carburettor (manual transmission) note throttle opener device (arrowed)

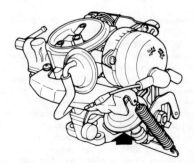

Fig. 3.19. Type DCH 306 carburettor (automatic transmis note dashpot (arrowed)

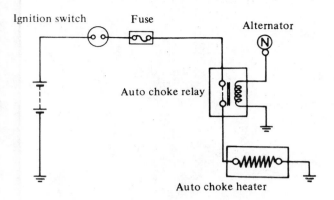

Fig. 3.20. Circuit diagram for automatic choke

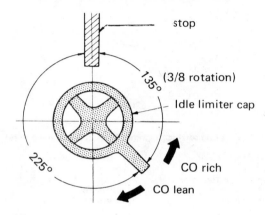

Fig. 3.22. Idle limiter cap installation diagram

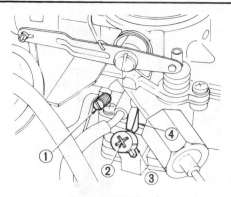

Fig. 3.21. Carburettor adjustment screws

1 *Throttle speed screw*
2 *Mixture control screw*
3 *Limiter cap*
4 *Limiter cap stop*

16.1 DCG 306 carburettor. Note crankcase breather valve screwed into inlet manifold

18 Float level - adjustment

1 Where the appropriate adjustments have been carried out and there is evidence of fuel starvation or conversely, flooding or excessively rich mixture, the float level should be checked.
2 Remove the carburettor as described in Section 25.
3 Disconnect choke connecting rod, accelerator pump lever and return spring.
4 Unscrew and remove the five securing screws which secure the upper choke chamber to the main body.
5 Turn the float chamber upside down and check the dimension 'H' with the float hanging down under its own weight, (Fig. 3.23).
6 Now gently push the float upwards to the full extent of its travel and check the clearance 'h' between the end face of the inlet needle valve and the float tongue. Adjustment to correct either of these dimensions is carried out by bending the float tongue or the stopper tag (3).

19 Fast idle adjustment

Type DCG 306 - manual choke

1 Ensure that the choke control is fully out and that the air cleaner having been removed, the choke butterfly valve can be seen to be in the fully closed position.
2 Check the position of the primary throttle valve plate. This should be open sufficiently to give a clearance of 0.050 in (1.27 mm) between the edge of the plate and the venturi wall.

3 Where adjustment is required, bend the choke connecting rod.

Type DCH 306 - automatic choke

4 Remove the automatic choke bi-metal cover.
5 Within the bi-metal housing, set the fast idle arm on the second step of the fast idle cam.
6 Turn the fast idle adjusting screw so that the clearance between the edge of the primary throttle valve plate and the carburettor is within the following tolerances:

Manual transmission 0.032 to 0.035 in (0.80 to 0.8 mm)
Automatic transmission 0.043 to 0.046 in (1.07 to 1.17 mm)

These settings will give a fast idle speed for a cold engine of (manual transmission) 1750 to 2050 rpm and (automatic transmission) 2650 to 2950 rpm.

20 Vacuum break (DCH 306 carburettor) - adjustment

1 Close the choke valve plate fully and retain it in this position by using a rubber band.
2 Grip the vacuum break stem with a pair of long-nosed pliers and extend it fully from the vacuum capsule. Now measure dimension 'B' (Fig. 3.25) which should be for manual transmission between 0.054 and 0.058 in (1.360 and 1.480 mm) and for automatic transmission 0.057 and 0.061 in (1.44 and 1.56 mm).
3 Where necessary, bend the vacuum break rod.

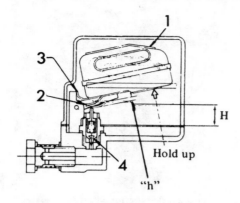

Fig. 3.23. Float level setting diagram

1 Float
2 Float tang
H = 0.748 in (19.0 mm)

3 Float stop
4 Inlet needle
h = 0.051 to 0.067 in (1.3 to 1.7 mm)

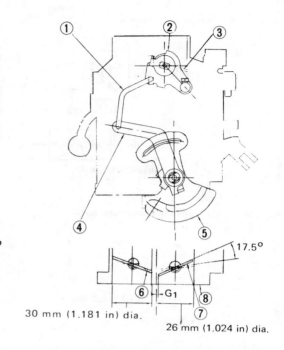

Fig. 3.23A. Fast idle setting diagram (DCG 306 manual choke)

1 Connecting rod
2 Choke lever
3 Choke butterfly valve
4 Choke connecting lever
5 Throttle lever

6 Secondary throttle butterfly valve
7 Primary throttle butterfly valve
8 Carburettor body

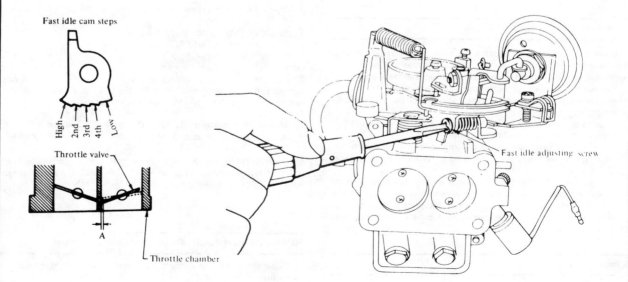

Fig. 3.24. Fast idle adjustment

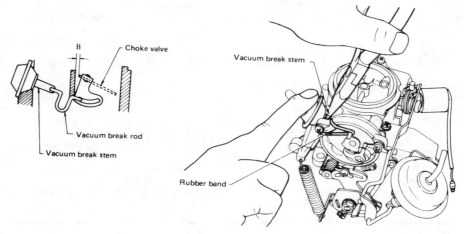

Fig. 3.25. Vacuum break adjustment

21 Choke valve release (DCH 306 carburettor) - adjustment

1 Close the choke valve plate fully and retain it in this position with a rubber band.
2 Open the throttle lever fully and then check the dimension 'C' (Fig. 3.26) between the edge of the choke valve and the carburettor body. This should be 0.079 in (2.01 mm) otherwise bend the unloader tongue.

22 Automatic choke bi-metal (DCH 306 carburettor) - adjustment and testing

1 If the choke cover and body index marks are observed before removal of the cover and then the cover is refitted in its original position, the setting of the automatic choke will not be disturbed. Where, however, new components have been fitted or due to changing characteristics of the engine because of wear or tuning, adjustment of the automatic choke is required, proceed in the following manner.
2 Release the choke cover screws enough to allow it to rotate. Set the cover so that the **centre** index and scale marks are in alignment. When the engine is started if there is any tendency to over-choke then rotate the cover in a clockwise direction. If there is any tendency to stall or hesitate, turn the cover in an anti-clockwise direction. Do not turn the cover more than half a division of the scale before retesting the starting performance. Re-tighten the cover screws.
3 Where there is evidence that the bi-metal resistance is unserviceable, this should be tested by connecting a sensitive ohmmeter between the choke heater wire terminal and the carburettor body. With the ignition off the resistance should be between 7.05 and 7.08 ohms measured at an ambient temperature of approximately 21°C (70°F).

23 Dashpot (automatic transmission) - adjustment (DCH 306 carburettor)

1 Run the engine to normal operating temperature.
2 Actuate the throttle linkage by hand until the dashpot just impinges upon the return spring lever. At this position the engine tachometer should register 2000 rpm. If this is not the case, adjust the dashpot stop nut.
3 Finally when the engine is running at 3,000 rpm release the throttle linkage and ensure that the engine speed falls smoothly from this level to 1000 rpm in about three seconds. If the speed does not fall smoothly and progressively then the dashpot is probably worn and must be renewed.

24 Primary and secondary throttle butterfly valves - adjustment of interlock mechanism

1 Actuate the primary throttle valve until the secondary throttle valve is just about to open. Measure the distance (G2) between the edge of the primary valve plate and the wall of the bore, this should be 0.23 in (5.8 mm).
2 If the clearance requires adjustment, bend the rod which connects the two throttle plates.

25 Carburettor - removal and installation

1 Remove the air cleaner.
2 Disconnect the fuel inlet pipe .
3 Disconnect the vacuum pipe from the distributor.
4 Disconnect the lead to the automatic choke, or the choke control cable according to type of carburettor. (photo)
5 Disconnect the lead from the anti-dieseling (anti-run on) solenoid on B210 vehicles, see Section 31.
6 Disconnect the throttle cable from the carburettor.
7 Remove the four nuts and washers which secure the carburettor to the inlet manifold and lift it away.
8 Installation is a reversal of removal but always use a new flange gasket between the carburettor and the manifold.

26 Carburettors - servicing general

1 In time, the components of a Hitachi carburettor will wear and fuel consumption will inevitably increase. The diameters of drillings and jets may increase due to the passage of air and fuel and leaks may develop round spindles and other moving parts. When a carburettor is well worn it is better to obtain a new or rebuilt unit rather than attempt to recondition the old one when so many parts need renewal.
2 Where it is decided to dismantle the carburettor for cleaning or to renew a jet or other small component, proceed by first obtaining the appropriate repair kit which will contain all the necessary gaskets and other components.
3 Never probe jets with wire to clear them but blow them out with air from a tyre pump.
4 Before starting to dismantle, clean the outside of the carburettor using a brush and some fuel.

27 Carburettor (DCG 306 - manual choke) - dismantling and reassembly

1 The main jets and needle valves are accessible from the ex-

terior of the carburettor.

2 These should be unscrewed, removed and cleaned by blowing them through with air from a tyre pump; never probe a jet or needle valve seat with wire.

3 Detach the choke chamber by removing the connecting rod, accelerator pump lever, return spring and the five securing screws.

4 The primary and secondary emulsion tubes are accessible after removing the main air bleeds.

5 Remove the accelerator pump cover, retaining the spring, piston and ball valve carefully.

6 Separate the float chamber from the throttle housing by unscrewing and removing three securing screws. Slide out the float pivot pin and remove the float.

7 Unless imperative, do not dismantle the throttle butterfly valves from their spindles.

8 Take great care when disconnecting the interlock rods that they are not bent or twisted or the settings and adjustments will be upset.

9 With the carburettor dismantled, clean all components in clean fuel and blow through the internal body passages with air from a tyre pump.

10 Inspect all components for wear and the body and chamber castings for cracks.

11 Clean the small gauze filter and if corroded or clogged, renew it.

12 If wear is evident in the throttle spindle, the carburettor should be renewed on an exchange basis.

13 Check all jet and air bleed sizes with those specified in Specifications in case a previous owner has changed them for ones of incorrect size.

14 Check the ejection of fuel when the accelerator pump is actuated.

15 Reassembly is a reversal of dismantling using all the items supplied in the repair kit.

16 Carry out the adjustments described in Sections 18, 19 and 24, of this Chapter.

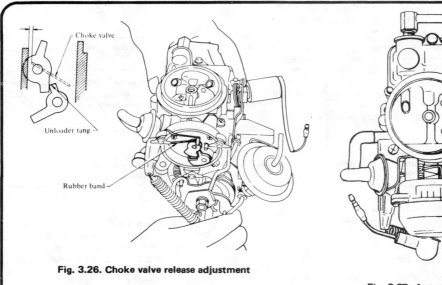

Fig. 3.26. Choke valve release adjustment

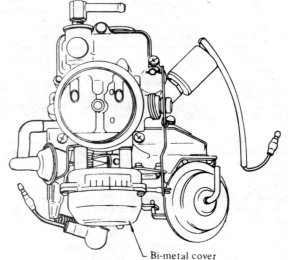

Fig. 3.27. Automatic choke bi-metal cover index

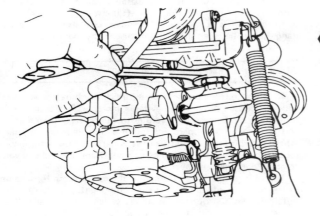

Fig. 3.29. Setting diagram for throttle valve interlock mechanism

1 *Connecting rod*
2 *Lever*
3 *Throttle lever*
4 *Secondary throttle butterfly valve*

5 *Primary throttle butterfly valve*
6 *Carburettor body*

Fig. 3.28. Dashpot adjustment (automatic transmission)

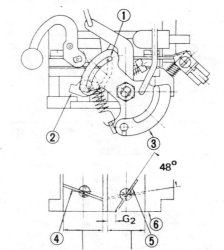

30 mm (1.181 in) dia.   26 mm (1.024 in) dia.

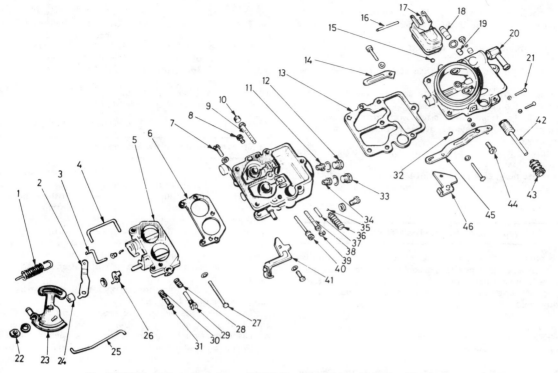

Fig. 3.29A Exploded view of type DCG-306 manually operated choke carburettor

1 Return spring	13 Float chamber gasket	25 Accelerator pump rod	36 Piston return spring
2 Choke lever	14 Spring support	26 Plate	37 Weight
3 Rod	15 Secondary slow air bleed	27 Screw	38 Primary emulsion tube
4 Choke connecting rod	16 Float pivot pin	28 Mixture screw spring	39 Primary main air bleed
5 Throttle chamber	17 Float	29 Mixture screw	40 Primary slow jet
6 Gasket	18 Inlet needle valve	30 Throttle screw spring	41 Accelerator cable connector
7 Screw	19 Filter	31 Throttle adjusting screw	42 Accelerator pump piston
8 Secondary slow jet	20 Choke chamber assembly	32 Primary slow air bleed	43 Accelerator pump cover
9 Secondary emulsion tube	21 Screw	33 Power valve	44 Accelerator pump lever shaft
10 Secondary main air bleed	22 Nut	34 Primary main jet	45 Accelerator pump lever
11 Secondary main jet	23 Throttle lever	35 Ball	46 Choke cable connector
12 Drain plug	24 Sleeve		

28 Carburettor (DCH 306 - auto choke) - dismantling and re-assembly

1 Remove the main jets and needle valves from the primary and secondary sides. They are accessible from outside the carburettor.

2 Detach the throttle return spring.

3 Unscrew the accelerator pump lever shaft, remove the pump operative lever and connecting rod.

4 Remove the rubber pipe from the choke piston.

5 Remove the servo-diaphragm (manual transmission models).

6 Remove the choke assembly bolts and withdraw the assembly, at the same time disconnecting the interconnecting rods.

7 Remove the air bleeds and extract the primary and secondary emulsion tubes.

8 Slide out the float pivot pin and remove the float.

9 Unscrew and remove the fuel inlet needle valve.

10 Invert the carburettor and eject the components of the accelerator pump. Take care not to lose the ball and weight.

11 Separate the throttle chamber from the main body by removing the three securing screws.

12 Do not dismantle the throttle valves unless absolutely essential.

13 Take great care when disconnecting the interlock rods that they are not bent or twisted or the settings and adjustments will be upset.

25.4 Choke and accelerator controls on DCG 306 carburettor

14 With the carbuettor dismantled, clean all components in clean fuel and blow through the body passages with air from a tyre pump.

15 Inspect all components for wear and the body and chamber castings for cracks.

16 Clean the small guaze filter and if corroded or clogged, renew it.

17 If wear is evident in the throttle spindle, the carburettor should be renewed on an exchange basis.

18 Check all jet and air bleed sizes with those specified in Specifications in case a previous owner has changed them for ones of incorrect size.

19 Reassembly is a reversal of dismantling, using all the items supplied in the repair kit.

20 During reassembly, always carry out all the checks and adjustments described in Sections 18 to 24, of this Chapter.

29 Exhaust emission control system - description

1 The maintenance of a 'clean exhaust' without loss of power or economy is dependent not only upon the correct adjustment of the specific components described in this Section but also upon the correct tune of other components of the engine.

2 Regularly check the adjustment of the following:

a) Valve clearances
b) Ignition timing
c) Contact breaker points
d) Spark plugs
e) All the carburettor adjustments described in this Chapter.

3 The emission control system incorporates the following:

(i) Exhaust gas recirculation (EGR)
(ii) Throttle opener control (manual transmission)
(iii) Transmission controlled vacuum advance (manual transmission)
(iv) Anti-dieseling (anti-run on) solenoid valve
(v) Crankcase emission control valve (refer to Chapter 1)
(vi) Fuel evaporative control (refer to Section 14, of this Chapter)
(vii) Temperature controlled air cleaner (refer to Section 3, of this Chapter).

4 Maintenance and servicing of these components is described in the following Sections.

30 Exhaust gas recirculation (EGR) system

1 The system is designed to recirculate exhaust gases into the inlet manifold where they will re-enter the combustion chambers of the engine and so help to reduce the combustion temperatures and reduce the emission of noxious gases.

2 The system incorporates a control valve, a solenoid valve, water temperature transmitter, relay, gas tube and vacuum pipe.

3 When the EGR valve opens, exhaust gases from the exhaust manifold are directed through the valve into the inlet manifold. Metering of the gases is controlled by the valve which itself is operated by vacuum pressure according to the throttle opening.

4 A solenoid valve is actuated by the engine water temperature transmitter and during starting or cold running conditions, it seals the vacuum passage to prevent gas recirculation.

5 At intervals specified in the Routine Maintenance Section, check the security of the solenoid lead and the vacuum pipes.

6 Visually check that with the engine running, the control valve is open at part throttle and shut at full throttle.

7 Remove the control valve and clean deposits from its seat with a wire brush.

8 Check the relay and solenoid valve and renew if faulty.

9 The water temperature switch can be checked by first draining the cooling system and unscrewing the switch from the cylinder block. Connect the switch to an ohmmeter and immerse it in water not exceeding 25°C (77°F) and check that the reading is infinity (switch open). Using a thermometer, heat the water and when the temperature is between 31 to 41°C (88 to 106°F) the reading should drop to zero. Above this temperature level, this reading should be maintained.

31 Throttle opener control system

1 A throttle opening device is fitted which is designed to open the throttle slightly during engine deceleration and to reduce the concentration of unburned hydrocarbons in the exhaust system by admitting a mixture sufficient to maintain complete combustion within the cylinders. The device comprises a servo diaphragm attached to the carburettor and a control valve bolted to the inlet manifold. The system is actuated by vacuum within the inlet manifold. A solenoid actuated by the speedometer needle, prevents the throttle opener device operating at speeds below 10 mph (16 km/h).

2 Run the engine until normal operating temperature is reached (choke valve plate fully open).

3 Disconnect the vacuum hose which runs between the inlet manifold and the automatic temperature controlled air cleaner.

4 Disconnect the leads from the throttle opener solenoid.

5 Check and adjust the engine idling if necessary to comply with the specified figures - 800 rpm at 5° btdc with exhaust emission (CO) 1.5% ± 0.5%.

6 Connect the servo diaphragm (using a temporary hose) directly to the inlet manifold bypassing the vacuum control valve.

7 The engine speed under these conditions should be between 1650 and 1850 rpm. If this is not the case, release the locknut and rotate the adjusting screw as necessary.

8 Remake the original vacuum hose connections and then increase the engine speed to 3000 rpm, moving the throttle by hand.

Release the throttle lever abruptly and time the period taken for the engine speed to drop to 100 rpm this should be between 3.5 and 4.5 seconds. If the time taken for the engine speed to drop is ouside the specified limits, loosen the locknut on the valve and adjust the screw, clockwise to increase the period, anti-clockwise to reduce it.

9 In the event of failure to respond to adjustment with either component, renew as assemblies as they are not capable of repair.

32 Transmission controlled vacuum advance

1 This system installed on manual transmission vehicles provides operation of the distributor vacuum advance only when top (4th) gear is selected. The retarded ignition timing in other gear positions helps to maintain complete combustion.

2 A switch screwed into the gearbox housing actuates a solenoid valve which in turn allows air to enter the distributor vacuum capsule in all gear positions except 4th therefore destroying the vacuum advance in the low gear positions.

3 To check the operation of the system, have the engine running and depress the clutch and select each forward gear in turn. Arrange for an assistant to pull the vacuum hose from the distributor and feel for vacuum at the open end of the hose. This should be apparent when top gear is selected but not in the other gears.

4 Where this check does not prove satisfactory, inspect the electrical leads and hose connections and for a faulty solenoid or gearbox switch.

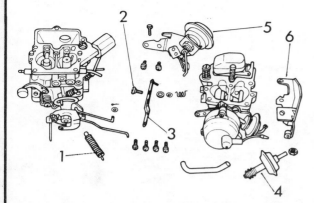

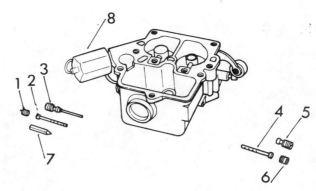

Fig. 3.30. Carburettor choke chamber and throttle opener components

1 Throttle return spring
2 Accelerator pump lever shaft
3 Accelerator pump lever
4 Dashpot (auto-trans)
5 Throttle opener device (manual trans.)
6 Throttle cable connector

Fig. 3.31. Location of emulsion tubes, bleeds and jets

1 Primary main air bleed
2 Primary emulsion tube
3 Primary slow jet
4 Secondary emulsion tube
5 Secondary slow jet
6 Secondary main air bleed
7 Weight
8 Anti-dieseling solenoid

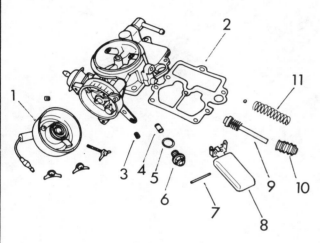

Fig. 3.32. Carburettor float, accelerator pump and bi-metal cover components

1 Bi-metal cover
2 Gasket
3 Inlet filter
4 Inlet valve
5 Washer
6 Inlet valve seat
7 Float pivot
8 Float
9 Accelerator pump piston
10 Accelerator pump cover
11 Accelerator pump spring

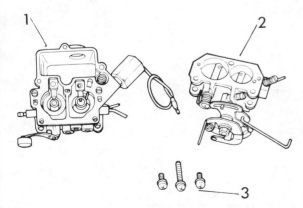

Fig. 3.33. Carburettor body (1) throttle chamber (2) and throttle chamber securing screws (3)

Fig. 3.34. Throttle valve operating components

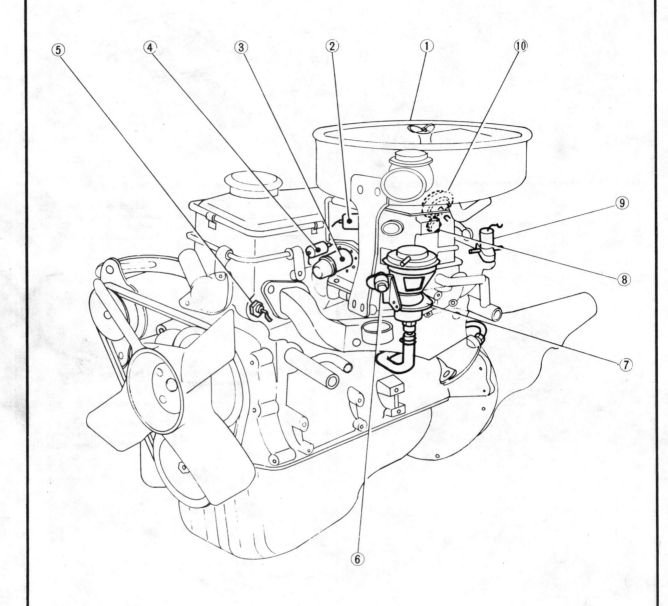

Fig. 3.35. Location of the emission control devices on the engine

1   Automatic temperature controlled type air-cleaner
2   Anti-dieseling (anti-run on) solenoid valve
3   Throttle opener vacuum control valve (manual transmission)
4   Throttle opener solenoid valve (manual transmission)
5   Water temperature switch
6   EGR solenoid valve
7   EGR control valve
8   Dashpot (automatic transmission)
9   Vacuum break solenoid valve (manual transmission)
10 Servo diaphragm (throttle opener control) - manual transmission

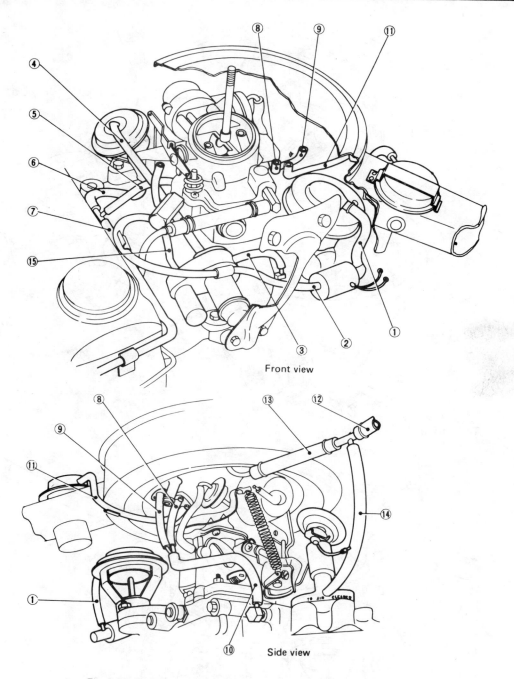

Front view

Side view

Fig. 3.36. Emission control system pipes (manual transmission)

1 EGR solenoid valve to EGR control valve
2 Throttle chamber to EGR solenoid valve
3 Inlet manifold to throttle opener control valve
4 Servo diaphragm to throttle opener control valve
5 Carburettor to 3-way connector
6 3-way connector to vacuum solenoid valve
7 3-way connector to distributor
8 Temperature sensor to 3-way connector
9 Idle compensator to 3-way connector
10 3-way connector to inlet manifold
11 Temperature sensor to air cleaner vacuum capsule
12 3-way connector to flow guide valve
13 3-way connector to air cleaner
14 3-way connector to vacuum break solenoid valve
15 Throttle opener solenoid valve to air cleaner

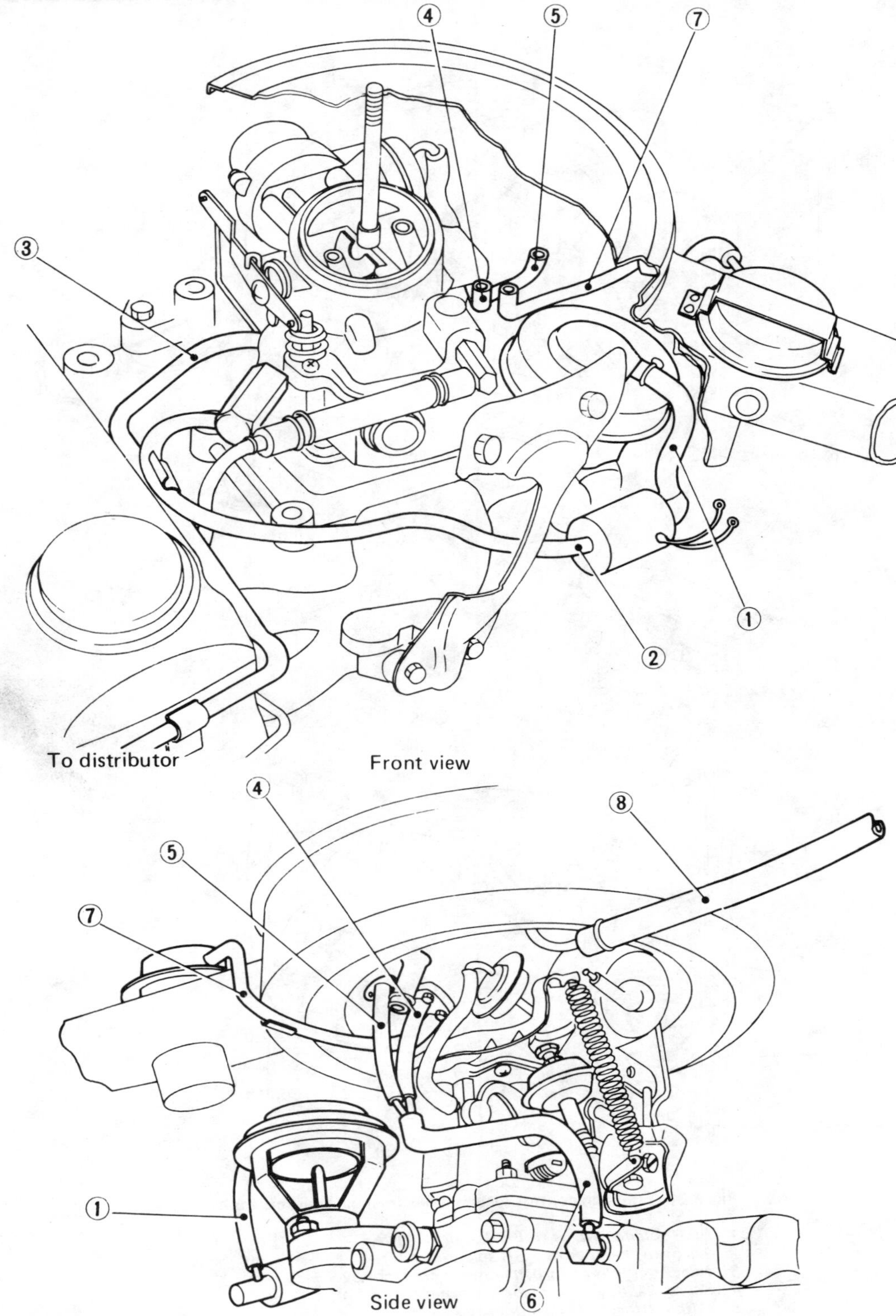

To distributor

Front view

Side view

Fig. 3.37. Emission control system pipes (automatic transmission)

1 *EGR solenoid valve to EGR control valve*
2 *Inlet manifold to EGR solenoid valve*
3 *Inlet manifold to distributor*
4 *Idle compensator to 3-way connector*
5 *Temperature sensor to 3-way connector*
6 *3-way connector to inlet manifold*
7 *Temperature sensor to vacuum capsule in air cleaner*
8 *Air cleaner to flow guide valve*

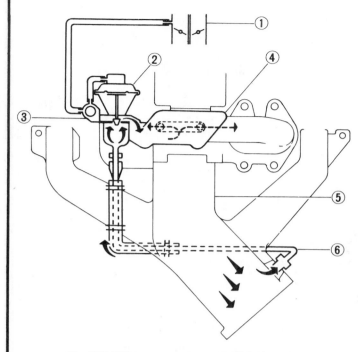

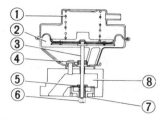

Fig. 3.39. Sectional view of the EGR control valve

1	Diaphragm spring	5	Valve (open)
2	Diaphragm	6	Valve (closed)
3	Valve	7	Valve seat
4	Seal	8	Valve chamber

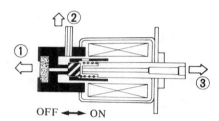

Fig. 3.38. Exhaust gas recirculation (EGR) system

1	Carburettor	4	Inlet manifold
2	EGR control valve	5	Exhaust manifold
3	EGR solenoid valve	6	EGR tube

Fig. 3.40. Sectional view of the EGR solenoid valve

| 1 | To atmosphere | 3 | To carburettor |
| 2 | To EGR control valve | | |

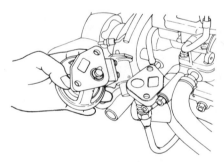

Fig. 3.41. Removing the EGR control valve

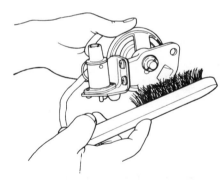

Fig. 3.42. Removing deposits from EGR control valve seat

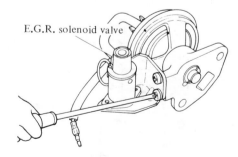

E.G.R. solenoid valve

Fig. 3.43. Removing the EGR solenoid valve

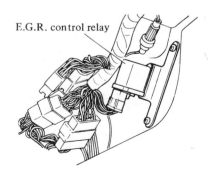

E.G.R. control relay

Fig. 3.44. Location of EGR control relay

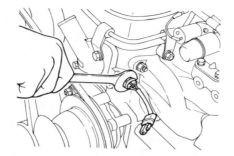

Fig. 3.45. Location of EGR water temperature switch

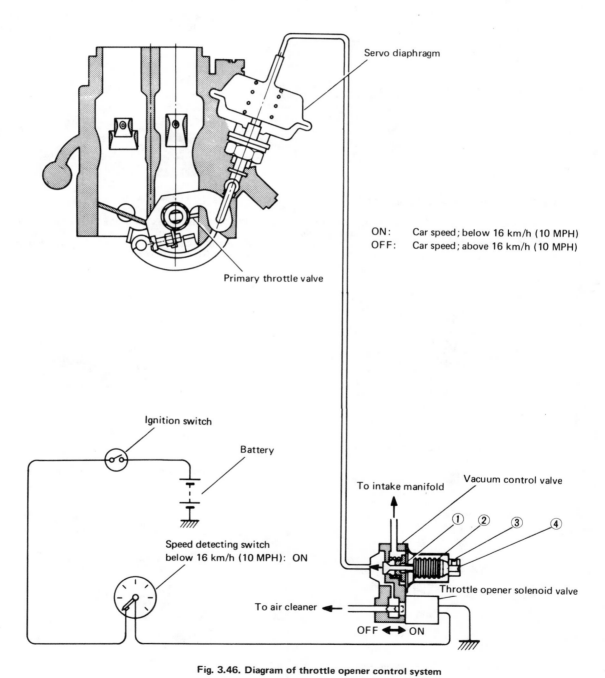

Servo diaphragm

ON: Car speed; below 16 km/h (10 MPH)
OFF: Car speed; above 16 km/h (10 MPH)

Primary throttle valve

Ignition switch

Battery

Speed detecting switch
below 16 km/h (10 MPH): ON

To intake manifold

Vacuum control valve

① ② ③ ④

Throttle opener solenoid valve

To air cleaner

OFF ↔ ON

Fig. 3.46. Diagram of throttle opener control system

| 1 Diaphragm | 2 Altitude corrector | 3 Locking screw | 4 Vacuum adjusting screw |

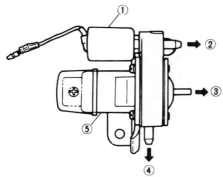

Fig. 3.47. Throttle opener solenoid valve

1 *Solenoid valve*	4 *To inlet manifold*
2 *To air cleaner*	5 *To control valve*
3 *To servo diaphragm*	

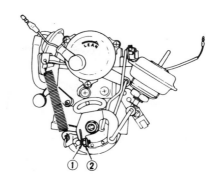

Fig. 3.48. Location of the throttle opener servo diaphragm adjusting screw (1) and locknut (2)

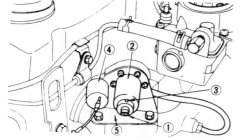

Fig. 3.49. Throttle opener system control valve location

1 *Adjusting screw*	4 *Solenoid*
2 *Control valve body*	5 *Mounting plate*
3 *Locking screw*	

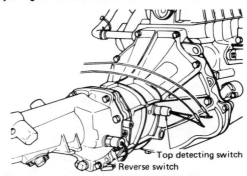

Fig. 3.50. Locations of reverse lamp switch and top gear detector switch

Top detecting switch
Reverse switch

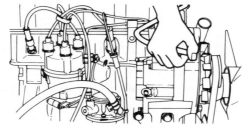

Fig. 3.51. Checking the operation of the vacuum advance

33 Anti-dieseling (anti-run on) valve

1   This is installed directly into the carburettor and operates by means of a solenoid which closes immediately the ignition is switched off to cut off fuel to the engine and prevent run-on. This can be caused by overheating or a heavy carbon built up within the combustion chambers causing ignition of the fuel mixture even though the ignition is switched off.

2   In the event of failure of the valve, check the electrical connection first. If renewal is required, carefully unscrew the solenoid valve and then screw in the new one after coating all threads with the thread locking compound.

3   Do not use the carbuettor for 12 hours to give the locking compound time to set.

34 Manifolds and exhaust system

1   The inlet manifold is of aluminium construction while the exhaust manifold is of cast iron. The latter incorporates a deflector valve with bi-metal coil spring to give quick warm up of the inlet manifold during initial starting of the engine when running during cold weather.

2   The exhaust system is of two section design and incorporates an expansion box and silencer. The system is supported on rubber rings and a flexible strap.

3   Examination of the exhaust pipe and silencers at regular intervals is worthwhile as small defects may be repairable when, if left they will almost certainly require renewal of one of the sections of the system. Also, any leaks, apart from the noise factor, may cause poisonous exhaust gases to get inside the car which can be unpleasant, to say the least, even in mild concentrations. Prolonged inhalation could cause sickness and giddiness.

4   As the sleeve connections and clamps are usually very difficult to separate it is quicker and easier in the long run to remove the complete system from the car when renewing a section. It can be expensive if another section is damaged when trying to separate a bad section from it.

5   To remove the system first remove the bolts holding the tail pipe bracket to the body. Support the rear silencer on something to prevent cracking or kinking the pipes elsewhere.

6   Unhook the rubber rings supporting the silencer.

7   Disconnect the manifold to downpipe connecting flange and then withdraw the conplete exhaust system from below and out to the rear of the vehicle. If necessary, jack up the rear of the vehicle to provide more clearance.

8   When separating the damaged section to be renewed cut away

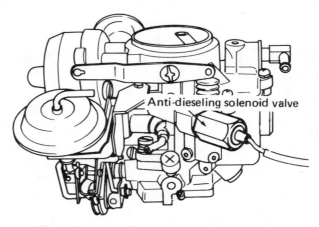

Fig. 3.52 Location of anti-dieseling (anti-run on) solenoid valve

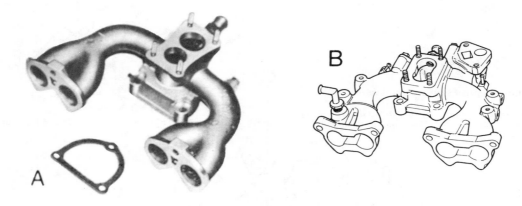

Fig. 3.53 The inlet manifold A = A12 engine B = A13 engine

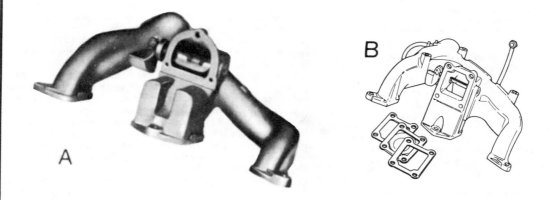

Fig. 3.54 The exhaust manifold A = A12 engine B = A13 engine

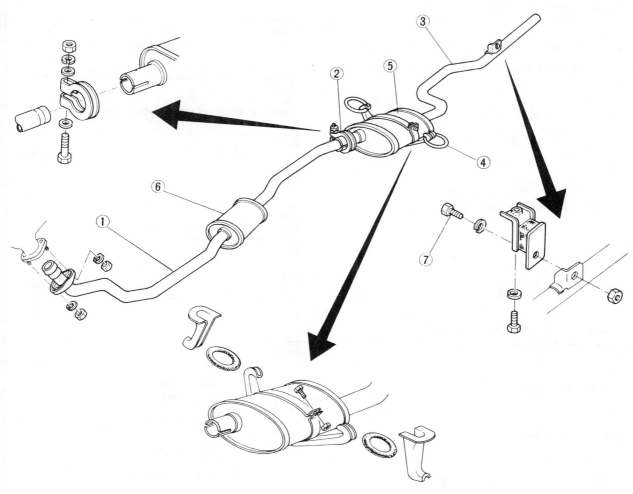

Fig. 3.55. The exhaust system

| 1 | Front pipe | 3 | Tailpipe | 5 | Main silencer | 7 | Rear support bolt |
| 2 | Clamp | 4 | Suspension ring | 6 | Expansion box | | |

the damaged part from the adjoining good section rather than risk damaging the latter.

9 If small repairs are being carried out it is best, if possible, not to try and pull the sections apart.

10 Refitting should be carried out after connecting the two sections together. De-burr and grease the connecting socket and make sure that the clamp is in good condition and slipped over the front pipe but do not tighten it at this stage.

11 Connect the system to the manifold and connect the rear support strap. Now adjust the attitude of the silencer so that the tension on the two rubber support rings will be equalized when fitted.

12 Tighten the pipe clamp, the manifold flange nuts and the rear suspension strap bolts. Check that the exhaust system will not knock against any part of the vehicle when deflected slightly in a sideways or upward direction.

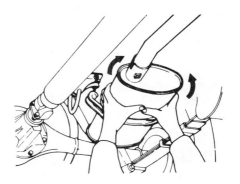

Fig. 3.56. Aligning the exhaust silencer

35 Fault diagnosis - carburation and fuel system

Symptom	Reason/s
Excessive fuel consumption	Air filter choked.
	Leakage from pump, carburettor or fuel lines or fuel tank.
	Float chamber flooding.
	Distributor capacitor faulty.
	Distributor weights or vacuum capsule faulty.
	Mixture too rich.
	Contact breaker gap too wide.
	Incorrect valve clearances.
	Incorrect spark plug gaps.
	Tyres under inflated.
	Dragging brakes.
Insufficient fuel delivery or weak mixture	Fuel tank air vent or pipe blocked or flattened.
	Clogged fuel filter.
	Float chamber needle valve clogged.
	Faulty fuel pump valves.
	Fuel pump diaphragm split.
	Fuel pipe unions loose.
	Fuel pump lid not seating correctly.
	Inlet manifold gasket or carburettor flange gasket leaking.
	Incorrect adjustment of carburettor.

36 Fault diagnosis - emission control system

Symptom	Reason/s
High engine idling speed	Sticking dash-pot (auto. trans.).
	Faulty throttle opener system (manual trans).
	Faulty automatic choke.
Rough or uneven idling	Faulty auto. temperature controlled air cleaner.
	Faulty EGR control valve.
	Faulty idle compensator in air cleaner.
Back fire	Faulty auto. temperature controlled air cleaner.
	Faulty EGR control valve.
Dieseling (running on)	Faulty anti-dieseling (anti-run on) solenoid.

Chapter 4 Ignition system

Contents

Specifications

System type	Battery, coil and distributor
Firing order	1 - 3 - 4 - 2
Ignition timing	
B210:	
Manual transmission	5° BTDC at 800 rpm
Automatic transmission ('D')	5° BTDC at 650 rpm
120Y:	
Manual transmission	7° BTDC at 600 rpm
Automatic transmission ('D')	7° BTDC at 650 rpm
Dwell angle	49 to 55°
Spark plugs	
Type:	
B210	Hitachi L46-PW or NGK BP−5ES
120Y	Hitachi L46−P or NGK BP−6E
Size	14 mm
Gap	0.031 to 0.035 in. (0.8 to 0.9 mm)
Coil	
Type:	
B210	Hitachi C6R−601
120Y	Hitachi C6R−200 or Hanshim HP5−13E
Condenser	
Capacity	0.20 to 0.24 uf
Distributor	
Type:	
B210	D4A2−02
120Y	D411−61
Rotational direction	Anti-clockwise
Contact breaker points gap	0.018 to 0.022 in. (0.45 to 0.55 mm)
Shaft to body wear limit	0.0031 in. (0.08 mm)
Counterweight pivot to hole clearance	0.0004 to 0.0018 in. (0.01 to 0.046 mm)

Torque wrench setting	lb f ft	kg f m
Spark plugs	14	2.0

1 General description

In order that the engine can run correctly it is necessary for an electrical spark to ignite the fuel/air mixture in the combustion chamber at exactly the right moment in relation to engine speed and load. The ignition system is based on feeding low tension (LT) voltage from the battery to the coil where it is converted to high tension (HT) voltage. The high tension voltage is powerful enough to jump the spark plug gap in the cylinders many times a second under high compression pressures, providing that the system is in good condition and that all adjustments are correct.

The ignition system is divided into two circuits. The low tension circuit and the high tension circuit.

The low tension (sometimes known as the primary) circuit consists of the battery lead to the control box, lead to the ignition switch, lead from the ignition switch to the low tension or primary coil windings (terminal +), and the lead from the low tension coil windings (coil terminal −) to the contact breaker points and condenser in the distributor.

The high tension circuit consists of the high tension or secondary coil windings, the heavy ignition lead from the centre of the coil to the centre of the distributor cap, the rotor arm, and the spark plug leads and spark plugs.

The system functions in the following manner. Low tension voltage is changed in the coil into high tension voltage by the opening and closing of the contact breaker points in the low tension circuit. High tension voltage is then fed via the carbon brush in the centre of the distributor cap to the rotor arm of the distributor cap, and each time it comes in line with one of the four metal segments in the cap, which are connected to the spark plug leads, the opening and closing of the contact breaker points causes the high tension voltage to build up, jump the gap from the rotor arm to the appropriate metal segment and so via the spark plug lead to the spark plug, where it finally jumps the spark plug gap before going to earth.

The ignition is advanced and retarded automatically, to ensure the spark occurs at just the right instant for the particular load at the prevailing engine speed.

The ignition advance is controlled both mechanically and by a vacuum operated system. The mechanical governor mechanism comprises two lead weights, which move out from the distributor shaft as the engine speed rises due to centrifugal force. As they move outwards they rotate the cam relative to the distributor shaft, and so advance the spark. The weights are held in position by two light springs and it is the tension of the springs which is largely responsible for correct spark advancement.

The vacuum control consists of a diaphragm, one side of which is connected via a small bore tube to the carburettor, and the other side to the contact breaker plate. Depression in the inlet manifold and carburettor, which varies with engine speed and throttle opening, causes the diaphragm to move, so moving the contact breaker plate, and advancing or retarding the spark. A fine degree of control is achieved by a spring in the vacuum assembly.

Vehicles equipped with a full emission control system have the distributor advance restricted by a gearbox mounted 4th gear switch and reference should be made to Chapter 3, Section 32.

2 Contact breaker - adjustment

1   To adjust the contact breaker points to the correct gap, first pull off the two clips securing the distributor cap to the distributor body, and lift away the cap. Clean the cap inside and out with a dry cloth. It is unlikely that the four segments will be badly burned or scored, but if they are the cap will have to be renewed.

2   Inspect the carbon brush in the top of the distributor cap and press it into its recess to test the spring.

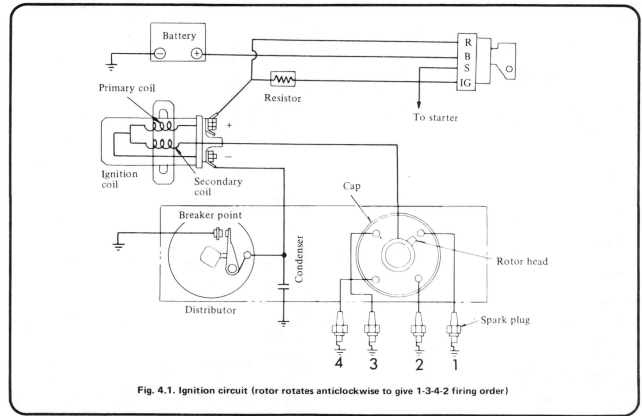

Fig. 4.1. Ignition circuit (rotor rotates anticlockwise to give 1-3-4-2 firing order)

3 Check the condition of the rotor arm and renew it if the metal contacts are burned or any cracks are evident.

4 Prise the contact breaker points apart and examine the condition of their faces. If they are rough, pitted, or dirty, it will be necessary to remove them for resurfacing, or for replacement points to be fitted.

5 Presuming the points are satisfactory, or that they have been cleaned and replaced, measure the gap between the points by turning the engine over until the heel of the breaker arm is on the highest point of the cam.

6 An 0.018 to 0.022 in (0.5 to 0.6 mm) feeler gauge should now just fit between the points.

7 If the cap varies from this amount slacken the contact plate securing screw.

8 Adjust the gap by turning the adjuster screw, which operates on an eccentric principle. When the gap is correct tighten the securing screw and re-check with the feeler gauge.

9 Make sure that the rotor arm is installed, refit the distributor cap and retaining spring clips.

3 Contact breaker points - removal and refitting

1 Slip back the spring clips which secure the distributor cap in position. Remove the distributor cap and lay it to one side, only removing one to two of the HT leads from the plugs if necessary to provide greater movement of the cap.

2 Pull the rotor from the distributor shaft.

3 Unscrew the contact breaker securing screws a turn or two and disconnect the LT lead from the contact breaker arm.

4 If necessary, unscrew the securing screws a turn or two more and slide the contact breaker arms sideways to remove them.

5 Inspect the faces of the contact points. If they are only lightly burned or pitted then they may be ground square on an oilstone or by rubbing a carborundum strip between them. Where the points are found to be severely burned or pitted, then they must be renewed and at the same time the cause of the erosion of the points established. This is most likely to be due to poor earth connections from the battery negative lead to body earth or the engine to earth strap. Remove the connecting bolts at these points, scrape the surfaces free from rust and corrosion and tighten the bolts using a star type lock washer. Other screws to check for security are: the baseplate to distributor body securing screws, the distributor body to lockplate bolt. Loose-

ness in any of these could contribute to a poor earth connection. Check the condenser (Section 4).

6 Refitting the contact breaker assembly is a reversal of removal and when fitted, adjust the points gap as described in the preceding Section.

4 Condenser (capacitor) - removal, testing and refitting

1 The condenser ensures that with the contact breaker points open, the sparking between them is not excessive to cause severe pitting. The condenser is fitted in parallel and its failure will automatically cause failure of the ignition system as the points will be prevented from interrupting the low tension circuit.

2 Testing for an unserviceable condenser may be effected by switching on the ignition and separating the contact points by hand. If this action is accompanied by a blue flash then condenser failure is indicated. Difficult starting, missing of the engine after several miles running or badly pitted points are other indications of a faulty condenser.

3 The surest test is by substitution of a new unit.

4 On some distributors, the condenser is secured to the distributor baseplate by the two contact breaker assembly screws and once these are loosened, the condenser can be removed by sliding it out from under the screw heads. On other types, the condenser is externally mounted.

5 Distributor - removal and refitting

1 To remove the distributor complete with cap from the engine, begin by pulling the plug lead terminals off the four spark plugs, Free the HT lead from the centre of the coil to the centre of the distributor by undoing the lead retaining cap from the coil.

2 Pull off the rubber pipe holding the vacuum tube to the distributor vacuum advance and retard take off pipe.

3 Disconnect the low tension wire from the coil.

4 Undo and remove the bolt which holds the distributor clamp plate to the crankcase and lift out the distributor.

5 Loosen the bolt which secures the clamp plate to the distributor body.

6 To install the distributor, refer to Chapter 1, Section 42.

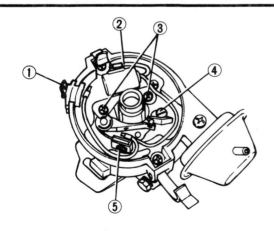

Fig. 4.3. Contact breaker components

1 LT terminal	4 Eccentric adjuster screw
2 Earth lead	5 Terminal screw
3 Securing screws	

2.6 Checking distributor points gap

6 Ignition - timing

1   This operation should be required only if the distributor has been removed and refitted or adjustment is necessary due to a change of fuel or engine condition.

2   Connect a timing light (stroboscope) between number one spark plug and number one HT lead terminal.

3   Mark the notch in the crankshaft pulley and the appropriate mark on the timing cover index with chalk or white paint (refer to Specifications Section for static ignition setting according to engine type). (photo)

4   Start the engine (which should be at normal operating temperature and let it run at the correct idle speed (see Specifications in Chapter 3 and 13).

5   By directing the timing light onto the chalked marks, the mark on the crankshaft pulley will appear to be stationary. Having previously loosened the distributor body clamp plate bolt, the distributor may be rotated slightly until the timing marks are in alignment. Where the limited adjustment provided by the clamp plate oval bolt hole is found to be insufficient to attain the correct alignment, then the distributor must be removed and re-meshed with the camshaft as described in Chapter 1, Section 42.

6   When the timing is correct, tighten the distributor body to clamp plate bolt. (photo)

7 Distributor - dismantling and inspection

1   Remove the distributor cap, rotor and contact breaker points as described in Section 3 of this Chapter, also the vacuum capsule (one screw).

2   Remove the two securing screws from the baseplate and remove the baseplate.

3   Unscrew and remove the screw from the centre of the cam. Should this be very tight, hold the cam using a close fitting spanner and take care not to damage the high-point surfaces. Always mark the relationship of the cam to the shaft so that it can be refitted in its original position.

4   Using a suitable drift, drive out the pin from the drive pinion end of the shaft.

5   Withdraw the distributor drive shaft complete with the mechanical advance assembly.

6   If it is necessary to dismantle this assembly, take care not to stretch the springs during removal and to mark their respective positions; also the counter weights in relation to their pivots so that they may be refitted in their original locations.

7   With the distributor dismantled, clean all the components in paraffin and inspect for wear. Renewal of components should be limited to the advance mechanism springs. Should wear in the shaft, bushes, the counter weight pivots or holes be outside the tolerances given in Specifications, then the distributor should be renewed on an exchange basis.

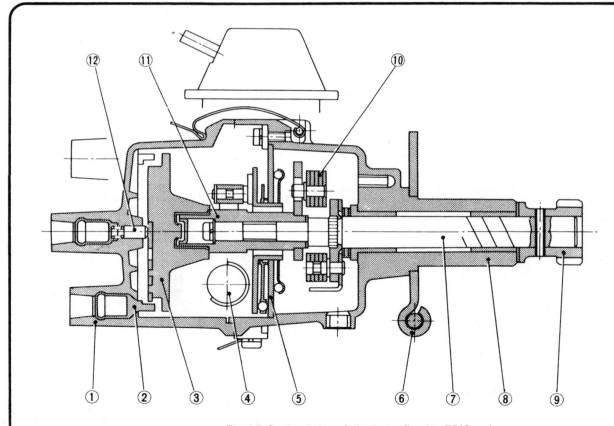

Fig. 4.5. Sectional view of distributor fitted to B210 engine

1 Cap	4 Condenser	7 Shaft	10 Counterweight
2 Contact segment	5 Baseplate	8 Body	11 Cam
3 Rotor arm	6 Clamp plate	9 Driven gear	12 Carbon brush

Measuring plug gap. A feeler gauge of the correct size (see ignition system specifications) should have a slight 'drag' when slid between the electrodes. Adjust gap if necessary

Adjusting plug gap. The plug gap is adjusted by bending the earth electrode inwards, or outwards, as necessary until the correct clearance is obtained. Note the use of the correct tool

Normal. Grey-brown deposits, lightly coated core nose. Gap increasing by around 0.001 in (0.025 mm) per 1000 miles (1600 km). Plugs ideally suited to engine, and engine in good condition

Carbon fouling. Dry, black, sooty deposits. Will cause weak spark and eventually misfire. Fault: over-rich fuel mixture. Check: carburettor mixture settings, float level and jet sizes; choke operation and cleanliness of air filter. Plugs can be re-used after cleaning

Oil fouling. Wet, oily deposits. Will cause weak spark and eventually misfire. Fault: worn bores/piston rings or valve guides; sometimes occurs (temporarily) during running-in period. Plugs can be re-used after thorough cleaning

Overheating. Electrodes have glazed appearance, core nose very white – few deposits. Fault: plug overheating. Check: plug value, ignition timing, fuel octane rating (too low) and fuel mixture (too weak). Discard plugs and cure fault immediately

Electrode damage. Electrodes burned away; core nose has burned, glazed appearance. Fault: pre-ignition. Check: as for 'Overheating' but may be more severe. Discard plugs and remedy fault before piston or valve damage occurs

Split core nose (may appear initially as a crack). Damage is self-evident, but cracks will only show after cleaning. Fault: pre-ignition or wrong gap-setting technique. Check: ignition timing, cooling system, fuel octane rating (too low) and fuel mixture (too weak). Discard plugs, rectify fault immediately

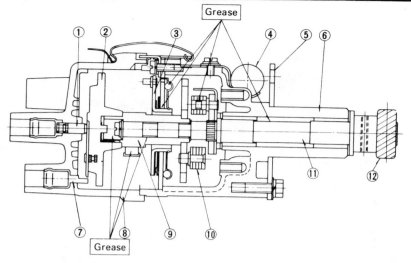

Fig. 4.5A. Sectional view of distributor fitted to 120Y engine

1 Carbon brush	4 Condenser	7 Contact segment	10 Counterweight
2 Rotor arm	5 Clamp plate	8 Cap	11 Shaft
3 Baseplate	6 Body	9 Cam	12 Driven gear

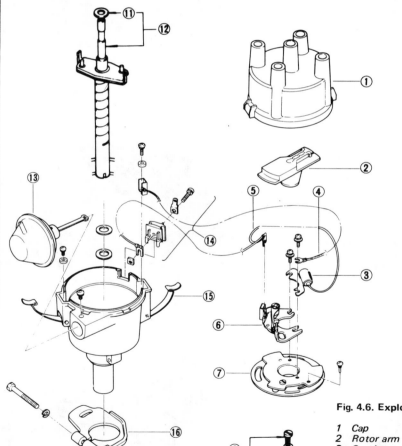

Fig. 4.6. Exploded view of distributor fitted to B210 engine

1 Cap	10 Counterweight
2 Rotor arm	11 Thrust washer
3 Condenser	12 Shaft
4 Earth lead	13 Vacuum capsule
5 LT lead	14 LT terminal
6 Contact set	15 Cap clip
7 Baseplate	16 Clamp plate
8 Cam	17 Gear
9 Spring	

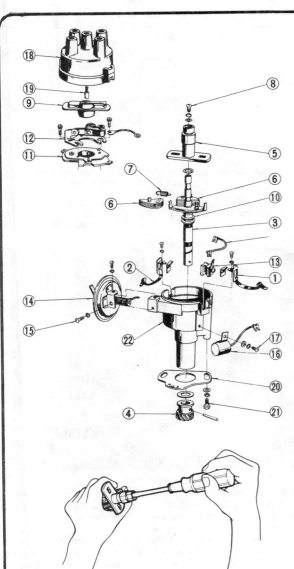

Fig. 4.6A. Exploded view of distributor fitted to 120Y engine

1	Cap clip	12	Contact breaker arm assembly
2	Cap clip	13	LT terminal and insulator
3	Drive shaft	14	Vacuum capsule
4	Pinion	15	Capsule securing screw
5	Cam assembly	16	Condenser (capacitor)
6	Counterweight	17	Condenser securing screw
7	Spring	18	Distributor cap
8	Cam to shaft securing screw	19	Carbon brush
9	Rotor	20	Distributor lock plate
10	Thrust washer	21	Lockplate bolt
11	Baseplate	22	Distributor body

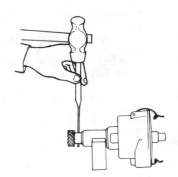

Fig. 4.7. Removing distributor cam

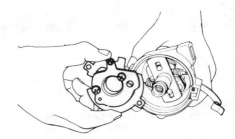

Fig. 4.8. Removing the distributor baseplate

Fig. 4.9. Removing the pinion pin

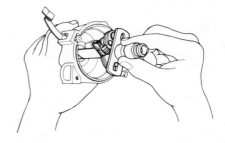

Fig. 4.10. Removing the distributor driveshaft assembly

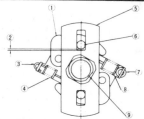

Fig. 4.11. Correct assembly of counterweights and springs (type
D4A2-02 distributor)

1 Counterweight	*6 Pin*
2 Clearance	*7 Circular hooked spring*
3 'U' shaped hooked spring	*8 Spring coils*
4 Spring coils	*9 Flat on cam for rotor arm*
5 Cam plate	

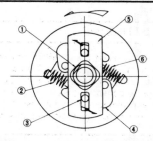

Fig. 4.11A. Correct assembly of counterweights and springs
(type D411-61 distributor)

1 Flat on cam for rotor arm	*4 Counterweights*
2 'U' shaped hooked spring	*5 Cam plate*
3 Pin	*6 Circular hooked spring*

6.3 Ignition timing marks

6.6 Distributor showing clamp plate bolt

8 Distributor - reassembly

1   Reassembly is largely a reversal of dismantling but apply high
melting point grease to all friction surfaces.
2   Always use a new pin to secure the pinion to the driveshaft.
3   If the mechanical advance mechanism has been dismantled,
then it should be reassembled in accordance with the appropriate diagram.

9 Coil - description and polarity

1   High tension current should be negative at the spark plug
terminals. To ensure this, check the LT connections to the coil
are correctly made.
2   The LT wire from the distributor must connect with the (—)
negative terminal on the coil.
3   The coil (+) positive terminal is connected to the ignition/
start switch.
4   An incorrect connection can cause as much as a 60% loss of
spark efficiency and can cause rough idling and misfiring at
speed.

10 Spark plugs and HT leads

1   The correct functioning of the spark plugs is vital for the
correct running and efficiency of the engine. The plugs fitted as
standard are listed on the Specification page.
2   At intervals of 2000 miles (19000 km) the plugs should be
removed, examined, cleaned and, if worn excessively, renewed.
The condition of the spark plug will also tell much about the
overall condition of the engine.

3   If the insulator nose of the spark plug is clean and white,
with no deposits, this is indicative of a weak mixture, or too hot
a plug. (A hot plug transfers heat away from the electrode slowly
- a cold plug transfers it away quickly).
4   If the top and insulator noise is covered with hard black
looking deposits, then this is indicative that the mixture is too
rich. Should the plug be black and oily, then it is likely that the
engine is fairly worn, as well as the mixture being too rich.
5   If the insulator nose is covered with light tan to greyish
brown deposits, then the mixture is correct and it is likely that
the engine is in good condition.
6   If there are any traces of long brown tapering stains on the
outside of the white portion of the plug, then the plug will have
to be renewed, as this shows that there is a faulty joint between
the plug body and the insulator, and compression is being
allowed to leak away.
7   Plugs should be cleaned by a sand blasting machine, which
will free them from carbon more thoroughly than cleaning by
hand. The machine will also test the condition of the plugs under
compression. Any plug that fails to spark at the recommended
pressure should be renewed.
8   The spark plug gap is of considerable importance, as, if it is
too large or too small the size of the spark and its efficiency will
be seriously impaired. The spark plug gap should be set to
between 0.031 and 0.035 in (0.8 to 0.9 mm) for the best results.
9   To set it, measure the gap with a feeler gauge, and then bend
open, or close, the outer plug electrode until the correct gap is
achieved. The centre electrode should never be bent as this may
crack the insulation and cause plug failure, if nothing worse.
10 When replacing the plugs, remember to use new plug washers
and replace the leads from the distributor in the correct firing
order 1,3,4,2, No 1 cylinder being the one nearest the radiator.
11 The plug leads require no routine attention other than being
kept clean and wiped over regularly.

11 Ignition system - fault diagnosis

Failures of the ignition system will either be due to faults in the HT or LT circuits. Initial checks should be made by observing the security of spark plug terminals, Lucar type terminals, coil and battery connection. More detailed investigation and the explanation and remedial action in respect of symptoms of ignition malfunction are described in the next Section.

12 Ignition system - fault symptoms

Engine fails to start

1 If the engine fails to start and the car was running normally when it was last used, first check there is fuel in the fuel tank. If the engine turns over normally on the starter motor and the battery is evidently well charged, then the fault may be in either the high or low tension circuits. First check the HT circuit. Note: If the battery is known to be fully charged; the ignition light comes on, and the starter motor fails to turn the engine **check the tightness of the leads on the battery terminals** and also the secureness of the earth lead to its **connection to the body**. It is quite common for the leads to have worked loose, even if they look and feel secure. If one of the battery terminal posts gets very hot when trying to work the starter motor this is a sure indication of a faulty connection to that terminal.

2 One of the commonest reasons for bad starting is wet or damp spark plug leads and distributor. Remove the distributor cap. If condensation is visible internally, dry the cap with a rag and also wipe over the leads. Replace the cap.

3 If the engine still fails to start, check that current is reaching the plugs, by disconnecting each plug lead in turn at the spark plug end, and hold the end of the cable about 3/16th inch (5.0 mm) away from the cylinder block. Spin the engine on the starter motor.

4 Sparking between the end of the cable and the block should be fairly strong with a regular blue spark. (Hold the lead with rubber to avoid electric shocks). If current is reaching the plugs, then remove them and clean and regap them. The engine should now start.

5 If there is no spark at the plug leads take off the HT lead from the centre of the distributor cap and hold it to the block as before. Spin the engine on the starter once more. A rapid succession of blue sparks between the end of the lead and the block indicate that the coil is in order and that the distributor cap is cracked, the rotor arm faulty, or the carbon brush in the top of the distributor cap is not making good contact with the spring on the rotor arm. Possibly the points are in bad condition. Clean and reset them as described in this Chapter.

6 If there are no sparks from the end of the lead from the coil, check the connections at the coil end of the lead. If it is in order start checking the low tension circuit.

7 Use a 12v voltmeter or a 12v bulb and two lengths of wire. With the ignition switch on and the points open test between the low tension wire to the coil (it is marked (+) and earth. No reading indicates a break in the supply from the ignition switch. Check the connections at the switch to see if any are loose. Refit them and the engine should run. A reading shows a faulty coil or condenser, or broken lead between the coil and the distributor.

8 Take the condenser wire off the points assembly and with the points open, test between the moving point and earth. If there now is a reading, then the fault is in the condenser. Fit a new one and the fault is cleared.

9 With no reading from the moving point to earth, take a reading between earth and the (—) terminal of the coil. A reading here shows a broken wire which will need to be replaced between the coil and distributor. No reading confirms that the coil has failed and must be replaced, after which the engine will run once more. Remember to refit the condenser wire to the points assembly. For these tests it is sufficient to separate the points with a piece of dry paper while testing with the points open.

Engine misfires

10 If the engine misfires regularly run it at a fast idling speed. Pull off each of the plug caps in turn and listen to the note of the engine. Hold the plug cap in a dry cloth or with a rubber glove as additional protection against a shock from the HT supply.

11 No difference in engine running will be noticed when the lead from the defective circuit is removed. Removing the lead from one of the good cylinders will accentuate the misfire.

12 Remove the plug lead from the end of the defective plug and hold it about 3/16 inch (5.0 mm) away from the block. Restart the engine. If the sparking is fairly strong and regular the fault must lie in the spark plug.

13 The plug may be loose, the insulation may be cracked, or the points may have burnt away giving too wide a gap for the spark to jump. Worse still, one of the points may have broken off. Either renew the plug, or clean it, reset the gap, and then test it.

14 If there is no spark at the end of the plug lead, or if it is weak and intermittent, check the ignition lead from the distributor to the plug. If the insulation is cracked or perished, renew the lead. Check the connections at the distributor cap.

15 If there is still no spark, examine the distributor cap carefully for tracking. This can be recognised by a very thin black line running between two or more electrodes, or between an electrode and some other part of the distributor. These lines are paths which now conduct electricity across the cap thus letting it run to earth. The only answer is a new distributor cap.

16 Apart from the ignition timing being incorrect, other causes of misfiring have already been dealt with under the section dealing with the failure of the engine to start. To recap - these are that:

a) *The coil may be faulty giving an intermittent misfire*
b) *There may be a damaged wire or loose connection in the low tension circuit*
c) *The condenser may be short circuiting*
d) *There may be a mechanical fault in the distributor (broken driving spindle or contact breaker spring).*

17 If the ignition timing is too far retarded, it should be noted that the engine will tend to overheat, and there will be a quite noticeable drop in power. If the engine is overheating and the power is down, and the ignition timing is correct, then the carburettor should be checked, as it is likely that this is where the fault lies.

Chapter 5 Clutch

Contents

Specifications

Type	Single dry plate with diaphragm spring pressure plate
Driven plate	
Friction disc diameter	7.09 in. (180 mm)
Thickness	0.140 in. (3.5 mm)
Number of cushion springs	6
Adjustment data (hydraulic operation)	
Pedal height from floor	6.020 to 6.260 in. (153.0 to 159.0 mm)
Pedal free-movement	0.630 to 1.300 in. (16.0 to 33.0 mm)
Pushrod to release lever free-movement	0.039 to 0.079 in. (1.0 to 2.0 mm)
Adjustment data (mechanical operation)	
Pedal height from floor	6.020 to 6.260 in. (153.0 to 159.0 mm)
Pedal free-movement	0.430 to 0.590 in. (10.9 to 15.0 mm)
Cable clevis to release lever free-movement	0.098 to 0.138 in. (2.5 to 3.5 mm)
Clutch master cylinder (diameter)	0.6248 in. (15.87 mm)
Clutch slave cylinder (diameter)	0.6874 in. (17.46 mm)

Torque wrench settings	lb f ft	kg f m
Cover to flywheel bolts	15	2.1
Pedal pivot bolt nut	17	2.4
Slave cylinder bolts	30	4.1
Flexible hose to slave cylinder	15	2.1
Clutch bellhousing to engine bolts	16	2.2

1 General description

1 All vehicles are fitted with a 7 inch (178.0 mm) diameter diaphragm spring, single plate clutch. The unit comprises a pressed steel cover which is dowelled to the rear face of the flywheel and bolted to it and contains the pressure plate, pressure plate diaphragm spring and the fulcrum rings.

2 The clutch disc is free to slide along the splined first motion shaft and is held in position between the flywheel and the pressure plate by the pressure of the pressure plate spring. Friction lining material is rivetted to the clutch disc and it has a spring cushioned hub to absorb transmission shocks and to help ensure a smooth take-off.

3 The circular diaphragm spring is mounted on shouldered pins held in place in the cover by two fulcrum rings. The spring is also held to the pressure plate by three spring steel clips which are rivetted in position. (photo)

4 The clutch is either actuated hydraulically (B210 models and LHD 120Y models) or mechanically by cable on RHD 120Y models. Where the clutch is actuated hydraulically, the pendant clutch pedal is connected to the clutch master cylinder and hydraulic fluid reservoir by a short pushrod. The master cylinder and hydraulic reservoir are mounted on the engine side of the bulkhead in front of the driver.

5 Depressing the clutch pedal moves the piston in the master cylinder forwards, so forcing hydraulic fluid through the clutch hydraulic pipe to the slave cylinder.

6 The piston in the slave cylinder moves forward on the entry of the fluid and actuates the clutch release arm by means of a short pushrod.

7 The release arm pushes the release bearing forwards to bear against the release plate, so moving the centre of the diaphragm spring inwards. The spring is sandwiched between two annular rings which act as fulcrum points. As the centre of the spring is pushed in, the outside of the spring is pushed out, so moving the pressure plate backwards and disengaging the pressure plate from the clutch disc.

8 When the clutch pedal is released the diaphragm spring forces the pressure plate into contact with the high friction linings on the clutch disc and at the same time pushes the clutch disc a fraction of an inch forwards on its splines so engaging the clutch disc with the flywheel. The clutch disc is now firmly sandwiched between the pressure plate and the flywheel so the drive is taken up.

9 As the friction linings on the clutch disc wear the pressure plate automatically moves closer to the disc to compensate. There is therefore no need to periodically adjust the clutch.

10 Where a cable type clutch actuating mechanism is fitted, the principle of operation is similar to that already described for the hydraulic type but correct adjustment must at all times be maintained as described in Section 3 of this Chapter.

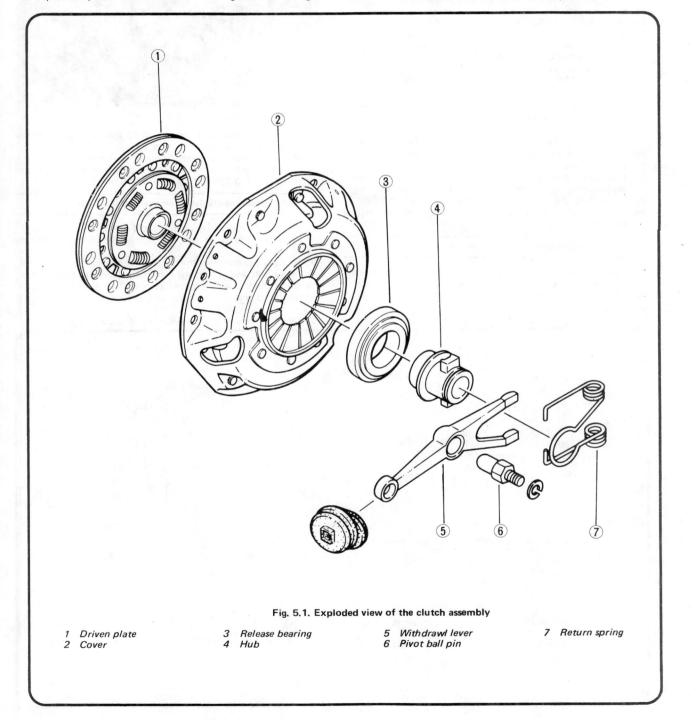

Fig. 5.1. Exploded view of the clutch assembly

1	Driven plate	3	Release bearing	5	Withdrawl lever	7	Return spring
2	Cover	4	Hub	6	Pivot ball pin		

2 Clutch (hydraulically operated) - adjustment

1   This adjustment or setting is normally carried out when the vehicle is built and will not be required unless new components have been fitted.
2   A clearance must be maintained between the slave cylinder pushrod nut and the withdrawal lever of between 0.039 and 0.079 in (1.0 and 2.0 mm).
3   Carry out any required adjustment by releasing the locknut on the pushrod and turning the adjuster nut.
4   When the clearance at the withdrawal lever is correct, there should be a free-movement at the centre of the pedal pad of between 0.630 and 1.300 in (16.0 to 33.0 mm).
5   Correct operation of the clutch will be affected if the pedal height is incorrectly set and the pedal height should be checked and adjusted as described in the next Section.

3 Clutch pedal height (hydraulic operation) - adjustment

1   The height of the centre of the upper pedal surface above the floor should be between 6.020 and 6.260 in (153.0 and 159.0 mm).
2   Adjustment is carried out by screwing the pedal stop in or out, after the master cylinder pushrod has been disconnected from the pedal arm.
3   Now adjust the length of the pushrod by releasing the locknut and turning the clevis fork so that when the pushrod is reconnected to the pedal arm, there is a free-movement at the pedal (before pressure on the master cylinder can be felt) of between 0.040 and 0.120 in. (1.0 to 3.0 mm).

4 Clutch (mechanically operated) - adjustment

1   With this type of clutch operation, adjust the clutch pedal arm stop to give a floor to upper surface of the pedal pad dimension of between 6.020 and 6.260 in (153.0 to 159.0 mm). Secure the stop locknut.
2   Loosen the clutch cable locknut and turn the adjuster nut to

1.3 Clutch assembly bolted to flywheel

give a free movement of between 0.43 and 0.59 in (10.9 and 15.0 mm) at the centre of the pedal pad.
3   If this adjustment is correctly made, then the total free movement at the connecting point of the cable clevis and release lever will be between 0.098 and 0.138 inin (2.5 and 3.5 mm).

5 Clutch pedal (hydraulic) - removal and installation

1   Extract the spring clip from the end of the clevis pin.
2   Withdraw the clevis pin and release the pushrod from the pedal arm.
3   Remove the nut from the pedal pivot bolt and then withdraw the pivot bolt and detach the pedal complete with return spring.
4   Installation is a reversal of removal but grease the moving surfaces and insert the pivot bolt and clevis pin from left to right.
5   Check the adjustment as described in Sections 2 and 3.

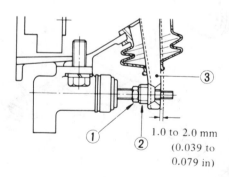

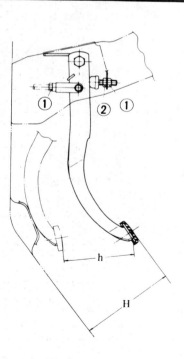

1.0 to 2.0 mm
(0.039 to 0.079 in)

Fig. 5.2. Clutch adjustment diagram (hydraulic operation)

1   *Locknut*   3   *Withdrawal lever*
2   *Adjusting nut*

Fig. 5.3. Pedal height adjustment diagram (hydraulic operation)

1   *Locknuts*   2   *Adjusting nut*

H = 6.02 to 6.26 in (153.0 to 159.0 mm)
h = 4.49 to 4.72 in (114.0 to 120.0 mm)

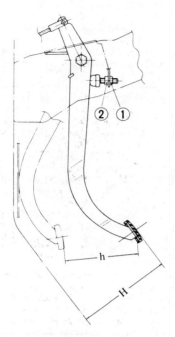

Fig. 5.4. Pedal height adjustment diagram (mechanical operation)

1 Locknut   2 Adjusting nut

H = 6.02 to 6.26 in (153.0 to 159.0 mm)
h = 4.49 to 4.72 in (114.0 to 120.0 mm)

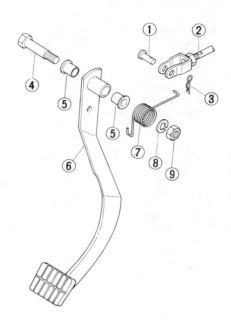

Fig. 5.5. Exploded view of the clutch pedal (hydraulic operation)

1 Clevis pin   5 Bush
2 Push-rod   6 Pedal
3 Spring clip   7 Return spring
4 Pivot bolt   8 Lockwasher
                               9 Nut

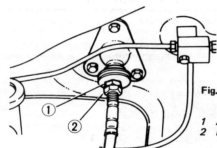

Fig. 5.6. Clutch cable adjustment nuts

1 Adjusting nut
2 Locknut

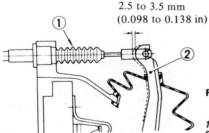

2.5 to 3.5 mm
(0.098 to 0.138 in)

Fig. 5.6A. Clutch cable free
movement diagram

1 Cable dust excluder
2 Withdrawal lever

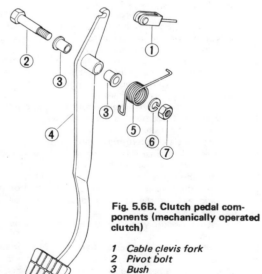

Fig. 5.6B. Clutch pedal components (mechanically operated
clutch)

1 Cable clevis fork
2 Pivot bolt
3 Bush
4 Pedal
5 Return spring
6 Lockwasher
7 Nut

6 Clutch pedal and cable - removal and installation

1 Loosen the locknut on the threaded section of the clutch outer cable at the engine bulkhead.
2 Release the adjustment nut sufficiently to enable the end of the cable to be detached from the end of the release lever.
3 Withdraw the spring clip and clevis pin from the upper end of

the clutch pedal and detach the cable. The cable can now be removed from the engine compartment.
4 Remove the clutch pedal pivot bolt and withdraw the pedal and return spring.
5 Installation is a reversal of removal but grease the moving surfaces and carry out the adjustment procedure described in Section 4. Ensure that the fuel hose clips do not rub against the clutch cable.

7 Hydraulic system - bleeding

1   The need for bleeding the cylinders and fluid line arises when air gets into it. Air gets in whenever a joint or seal leaks or part has to be dismantled. Bleeding is simply the process of venting the air out again.

2   Make sure the reservoir is filled and obtain a piece of 3/16 inch (4.8 mm) bore diameter rubber tube about 2ft (0.6 mm) long and a clean glass jar. A small quantity of fresh, clean hydraulic fluid is also necessary.

3   Detach the cap (if fitted) on the bleed nipple at the clutch slave cylinder and clean up the nipple and surrounding area. Unscrew the nipple ¾ turn and fit the tube over it. Put about 1 in (25.4 mm) of fluid in the jar and put the other end of the pipe in it. The jar can be placed on the ground under the car.

4   The clutch pedal should then be depressed quickly and released slowly until no more air bubbles come from the pipe. Quick pedal action carries the air along rather than leave it behind. Keep the reservoir topped up.

5   When the air bubbles stop tighten the nipple at the end of the down stroke.

6   Check that the operation of the clutch is satisfactory. Even though there may be no exterior leaks it is possible that the movement of the pushrod from the clutch cylinder is inadequate because fluid is leaking internally past the seals in the master cylinder. If this is the case, it is best to replace all seals in both cylinders.

7   Always use clean hydraulic fluid which has been stored in an airtight container and has remained unshaken for the preceding 24 hours.

8 Master cylinder - removal, dismantling, reassembly

1   The master cylinder and fluid reservoir are a single unit and indications of something wrong with it are if the pedal travels down without operating the clutch efficiently (assuming, of course, that the system has been bled and there are no leaks).

2   To remove the unit from the car first seal the cap with a piece of film to reduce fluid wastage whilst dismantling the pipes. Alternatively, the fluid may be pumped out from the clutch cylinder bleed nipple by opening the nipple and depressing the pedal several times.

3   From inside the car remove the split pin and clevis pin which attach the pushrod assembly to the clutch pedal.

4   Disconnect the fluid line which runs between the master cylinder and the slave (operating) cylinder.

5   Unscrew and remove the two bolts which secure the master cylinder to the engine rear bulkhead.

6   Withdraw the master cylinder from the bulkhead.

7   Peel back the rubber dust cover from the end of the master cylinder and extract the circlip and stop ring complete with pushrod.

8   The piston assembly will now be ejected by action of the return spring.

9   Clean all components in clean hydraulic fluid or methylated spirit. Examine the internal surface of the master cylinder for scoring or bright areas; also the surface of the piston. Where these are apparent, renew the complete master cylinder assembly.

10 Discard the cup seal and obtain a repair kit which will contain all necessary components.

11 Commence reassembly by dipping the new cup seal in clean hydraulic fluid and fitting it to the piston using only the fingers to manipulate it into position.

12 Insert the internal components and install the new circlip supplied.

13 Bolt the master cylinder to the bulkhead, connect the hydraulic pipe and reconnect the pushrod to the pedal. Bleed the system (Section 7).

14 Check the pedal height and clutch adjustment (Sections 2 and 3).

15 Finally top-up the fluid reservoir to the correct level.

9 Slave (operating) cylinder - removal, dismantling and re-assembly

1   Disconnect the rigid hydraulic pipe from the flexible hose at the support bracket on the body side frame.

2   Remove the locking clip from the bracket and release the flexible hose. Now unscrew the flexible hose from the slave cylinder.

3   Unscrew and remove the two bolts which secure the cylinder to the clutch bellhousing and remove it.

4   Peel off the rubber dust excluder and pull out the pushrod.

5   Extract the piston assembly either by tapping the cylinder on a piece of wood or applying air pressure to the fluid inlet hole.

6   Wash all components in clean hydraulic fluid or methylated spirit. Discard the seal and examine the piston and cylinder bore surfaces for scoring or bright areas. Where these are evident, renew the complete assembly.

7   Obtain a repair kit which will contain all necessary components.

8   Commence reassembly by dipping the new cup seal in clean hydraulic fluid and fitting it to the piston using only the fingers to manipulate it into position.

9   Dip the piston in clean fluid and insert it into the cylinder bore, fit the new dust cover supplied and install the pushrod.

10 Bolt the cylinder to the clutch bellhousing.

11 Reconnect the flexible hose taking care not to twist it or to route it near the exhaust pipe.

12 Bleed the system.

13 Check the clutch adjustment (Sec 2).

14 Finally top-up the fluid reservoir to the correct level.

10 Clutch assembly - removal

1   Remove the engine/gearbox as a unit as fully described in Chapter 1, or alternatively 'drop' the gearbox alone as described in Chapter 6.

2   Separate the gearbox from the engine by removing the clutch bellhousing to crankcase securing bolts.

3   Mark the position of the now exposed clutch pressure plate cover in relation to the flywheel on which it is mounted.

4   Unscrew the clutch assembly securing bolts a turn at a time in diametrically opposite sequence until the tension of the diaphragm spring is released. Remove the bolts and lift the pressure plate assembly away.

5   Lift the driven plate (friction disc) from the flywheel.

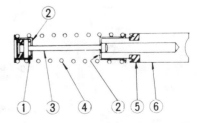

Fig. 5.7. Master cylinder piston assembly

1 *Valve spring*		4 *Return spring*
2 *Spring seat*		5 *Piston cup*
3 *Valve assembly*		6 *Piston*

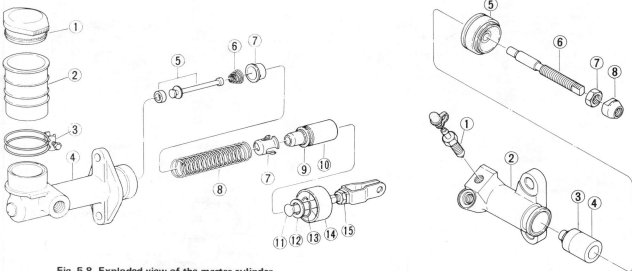

Fig. 5.8. Exploded view of the master cylinder

1	Cap	9	Cup seal
2	Reservoir	10	Piston
3	Clip	11	Push-rod
4	Body	12	Stop ring
5	Valve assembly	13	Circlip
6	Spring	14	Dust cover
7	Spring seat	15	Nut
8	Return spring		

Fig. 5.9. Exploded view of the slave cylinder

1	Bleed screw	5	Dust cover
2	Body	6	Push-rod
3	Cup seal	7	Locknut
4	Piston	8	Adjusting nut

11 Clutch - inspection and renovation

1   Due to the self adjusting nature of the clutch it is not always easy to decide when to go to the trouble of removing the gearbox in order to check the wear on the friction lining. The only positive indication that something needs doing is when it starts to slip or when squealing noises on engagement indicate that the friction lining has worn down to the rivets. In such instances it can only be hoped that the friction surfaces on the flywheel and pressure plate have not been badly worn or scored. A clutch will wear according to the way in which it is used. Much intentional slipping of the clutch while driving - rather than the correct selection of gears - will accelerate wear. It is best to assume, however, that the friction disc will need renewal at approximately 40,000 mile (64,000 km) intervals at least.
2   Examine the surfaces of the pressure plate and flywheel for signs of scoring. If this is only light it may be left, but if very deep the pressure plate unit will have to be renewed. If the flywheel is deeply scored it should be taken off and advice sought from an engineering firm. Providing it may be machined completely across the face the overall balance of engine and flywheel should not be too severely upset. If renewal of the flywheel is necessary the new one will have to be balanced to match the original.
3   The friction plate lining surfaces should be at least 1/32 in (0.8 mm) above the rivets, otherwise the disc is not worth putting back. If the lining material shows signs of breaking up or black areas where oil contamination has occurred it should also be renewed. If facilities are readily available for obtaining and fitting new friction pads to the existing disc this may be done but the saving is relatively small compared with obtaining a complete new disc assembly which ensures that the shock absorbing springs and the splined hub are renewed also. The same applies to the pressure plate assembly which cannot be readily dismantled and put back together without specialised riveting tools and balancing equipment. An allowance is usually given for exchange units.

12 Release bearing - removal and refitting

1   The release bearing is of ball bearing, grease sealed type and although designed for long life it is worth renewing at the same time as the other clutch components are being renewed or serviced.
2   Deterioration of the bearing should be suspected when there are signs of grease leakage or the unit is noisy when spun with the fingers.
3   Remove the rubber dust excluder which surrounds the release lever at the bellhousing aperture.
4   Disconnect and remove the return spring.
5   Detach the release lever from the release bearing retainer hub.
6   Withdraw the release bearing/hub assembly from the input shaft. (photo)
7   If necessary remove the release lever from its ball pivot.
8   Remove the bearing from its retainer hub using a suitable puller.
9   Fit the new bearing to the retainer hub using a press and ensuring that the pressure is exerted on the inner race of the bearing only.
10 Apply a dab of wheel bearing grease to the tip of the release lever pivot ball and pack the internal recess of the bearing retainer hub with the same type of lubricant.
11 Fit the hub/bearing assembly over the input shaft.
12 Refit the return spring and the rubber dust excluder.
13 Check that the release bearing turns freely and actuate the release lever only fractionally and check that the return spring is operating correctly.
Note: some release levers are of pressed steel construction but the principle of operation is the same as for the cast type. (photo)

13 Clutch - refitting

1   Before the driven plate and clutch pressure plate assembly

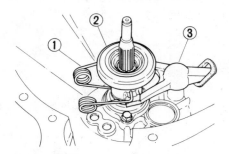

Fig. 5.10. Clutch release mechanism

1   *Return spring*   3   *Withdrawal lever*
2   *Release bearing*

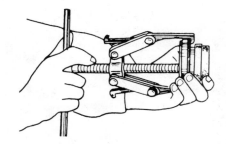

Fig. 5.11. Removing the release bearing from its hub

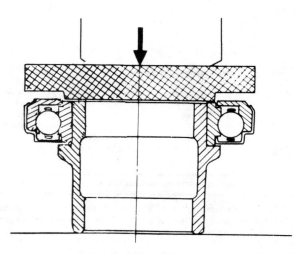

Fig 5.12 Pressing a release bearing onto its hub

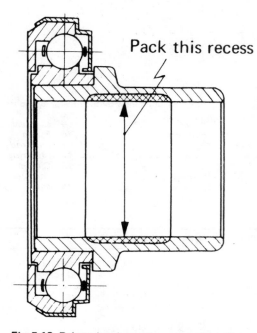

Pack this recess

Fig. 5.13. Release bearing hub grease packing diagram

can be refitted to the flywheel, a guide tool must be obtained. This may be either an old input shaft from a dismantled gearbox or a stepped mandrel similar to the one shown.

2   Examine the spigot bush located in the centre of the flywheel. If it is worn or damaged, the bush must be renewed as described in Chapter 1.

3   Locate the driven plate against the face of the flywheel, ensuring that the projecting side of the centre splined hub faces towards the gearbox.

4   Offer up the pressure plate assembly to the flywheel aligning the marks made prior to dismantling and insert the retaining bolts finger tight. Where a new pressure plate assembly is being fitted, locate it to the flywheel in a similar relative position to the original by reference to the index marking and dowel positions.

5   Insert the guide tool through the splined hub of the driven plate so that the end of the tool locates in the flywheel spigot bush. This action of the guide tool will centralise the driven plate by causing it to move in a sideways direction.

6   Insert and remove the guide tool two or three times to ensure that the driven plate is fully centralised and then tighten the pressure plate securing bolts a turn at a time and in a diametrically opposite sequence, to a torque of 15 lb/ft (2.1 kg/m) to prevent distortion of the pressure plate cover.

7   Reconnect the gearbox to the engine. Do this by supporting the gearbox and engaging the input shaft with the driven plate hub splines and the flywheel spigot bush. Keep the input shaft

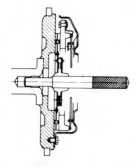

Fig. 5.14. Centralising the clutch driven plate

and gearbox perfectly square during the refitting operation and do not allow the weight of the gearbox to hang, even momentarily, upon the input shaft while it is only partially engaged with the driven plate otherwise damage to the clutch components may result.

8   Insert the clutch bellhousing to engine crankcase securing bolts and tighten them to a torque of 16 lb/ft (2.2 kg/m).

9   Adjust the clutch free-movement as described earlier in this Chapter.

12.6 Method of attachment of release bearing return spring to gearbox front cover

12.13 Pressed steel type release arm

14 Fault diagnosis - clutch

Symptom	Reason/s
Judder when taking up drive	Loose engine or gearbox mountings. Badly worn friction surfaces or contaminated with oil. Worn splines on gearbox input shaft or driven plate hub. Worn input shaft spigot bush in flywheel.
Clutch spin (failure to disengage) so that gears cannot be meshed	Incorrect release bearing to diaphragm spring finger clearance. Driven plate sticking on input shaft splines due to rust. May occur after vehicle standing idle for long period. Damage or misaligned pressure plate assembly.
Clutch slip (increase in engine speed does not result in increase in vehicle road speed - particularly on gradients)	Incorrect release bearing to diaphragm spring finger clearance. Friction surfaces worn out or oil contaminated.
Noise evident on depressing clutch pedal	Dry, worn or damaged release bearing. Insufficient pedal free travel. Weak or broken pedal return spring. Weak or broken clutch release lever return spring. Excessive play between driven plate hub splines and input shaft splines
Noise evident as clutch pedal released	Distorted driven plate. Broken or weak driven plate cushion coil springs. Insufficient pedal free travel. Weak or broken clutch pedal return spring. Weak or broken release lever return spring. Distorted or worn input shaft. Release bearing loose on retainer hub.

Chapter 6 Part 1: Manual gearbox

Contents

Specifications

Type

F4W56A	Four forward speeds and reverse, synchromesh on all forward gears
R3W56A	Three forward speeds and reverse

Ratios

	Four-speed	Three-speed
1st	3.757 : 1	3.380 : 1
2nd	2.169 : 1	1.734 : 1
3rd	1.404 : 1	1.000 : 1
4th	1.000 : 1	—
Reverse	3.640 : 1	3.640 : 1

Speedometer gear ratio 18/5

Gear tolerances (4 speed gearbox)

Backlash (all gears)	0.003 to 0.006 in. (0.08 to 0.15 mm)
End-play:	
1st and 2nd gears	0.006 to 0.010 in (0.15 to 0.25 mm)
3rd gear	0.004 to 0.012 in. (0.10 to 0.30 mm)
Counter gear	0 to 0.008 in. (0 to 0.2 mm)

Gear tolerances (3 speed gearbox)

Backlash (all gears)	0.003 to 0.006 in. (0.08 to 0.15 mm)
End-play:	
1st gear	0.006 to 0.010 in. (0.15 to 0.25 mm)
2nd gear	0.004 to 0.012 in. (0.1 to 0.3 mm)
Counter gear	0.000 to 0.008 in (0 to 0.2 mm)
Reverse idler gear	0.002 to 0.018 in. (0.05 to 0.45 mm)

Oil capacity ... ... 2 1/8 pt. (Imp), 2½ (US), 1.2 litre

Torque wrench settings

	lb f ft	kg f m
Clutch bellhousing to engine bolts	16	2.2
Rear mounting to gearbox bolts	20	2.8
Rear mounting to bodyframe	30	4.1
Starter motor bolts	30	4.1
Propeller shaft flange bolts	25	3.5
Rear extension housing bolts	16	2.2
Front cover bolts	10	1.4
Gearbox switches	22	3.0
Filler and drain plugs	22	3.0
Reinforcement plate to engine bolts	18	2.5
Reinforcement plate to gearbox bolts	36	5.0

1 General description

The gearbox is of four speed type with synchromesh on all forward speeds. The gearshift control is by means of a floor-mounted remote control lever.

The internal components of the gearbox are mounted on a cast-iron adaptor plate. The main transmission casing and the rear extension are secured to this plate by tie bolts, which when withdrawn and the casing and rear extension removed, will provide complete access to the gears and shafts.

Note: A RHD saloon or estate version is marketed in one or two isolated territories equipped with a three speed gearbox having steering column gearshift. Where this unit is encountered, refer to Specifications, and to Sections 9 and 10.

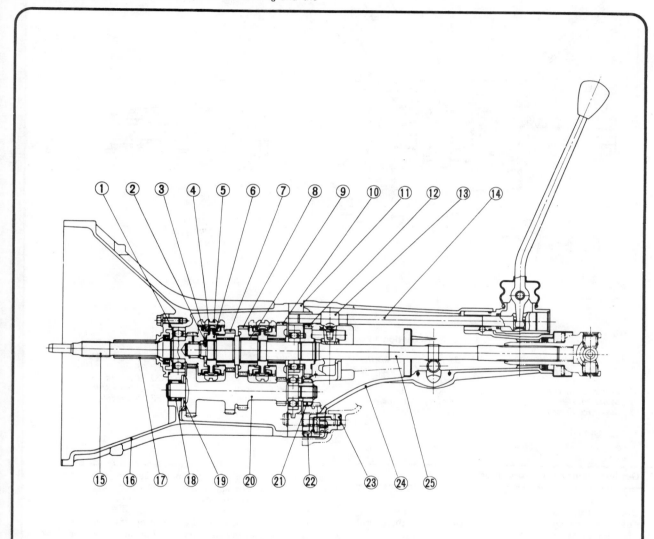

Fig. 6.1. Sectional view of the manual gearbox

1 Input shaft bearing shim	7 3rd gear	13 Selector cross lever	19 Countergear thrust washer
2 Synchro. thrust washer	8 2nd gear	14 Remote control rod	20 Countergear
3 Baulk ring	9 Needle bearing	15 Input shaft	21 Reverse gear
4 Shift key	10 1st gear	16 Casing	22 Reverse idler gear
5 Synchro. sleeve	11 Adaptor plate	17 Front cover	23 Reverse idler shaft
6 Synchro. hub	12 Reverse gear	18 Needle bearing	24 Rear extension housing
			25 Mainshaft

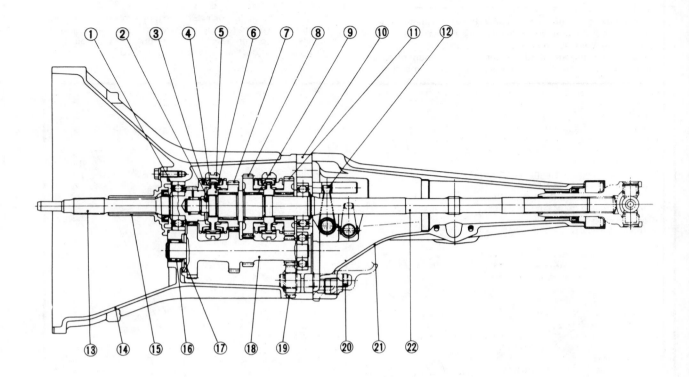

Fig. 6.1A. Sectional view of type R3W56A three speed gearbox

1 *Front cover shim*	7 *Second gear (mainshaft)*	13 *Input shaft*	18 *Counter gear*
2 *Thrust washer*	8 *First gear (mainshaft)*	14 *Casing*	19 *Reverse idle gear*
3 *Baulk ring*	9 *Needle bearing*	15 *Front cover*	20 *Reverse idler shaft*
4 *Synchro. shift key*	10 *Adaptor plate*	16 *Needle bearing*	21 *Rear extension*
5 *Synchro. sleeve*	11 *Reverse gear (mainshaft)*	17 *Thrust washer*	22 *Mainshaft*
6 *Synchro. hub*	12 *Selector lever*		

2 Gearbox - removal and installation

1 Disconnect the lead from the battery negative terminal.
2 *Four speed gearbox:* Inside the vehicle, remove the console from the transmission tunnel.
3 Unscrew and remove the rubber boot and retainer from the base of the gearshift lever. Make sure that the gearlever is in neutral and then remove the circlip and pivot pin from the remote control rod guide. Withdraw the gearlever.
4 *Three speed gearbox:* Remove the shift rods and cross-shaft assembly by unbolting the cross-shaft bracket from the sideframe.
5 If possible, obtain the use of a pit or hydraulic vehicle hoist. Failing this, jack the vehicle up sufficiently high so that the underbody clearance is slightly greater than the depth of the clutch bellhousing. Support the vehicle adequately on blocks or axle stands.
6 Disconnect the exhaust downpipe from the manifold.
7 Disconnect the leads from the reversing lamp switch.
8 Disconnect the leads from top gear and neutral switches (emission control and safety belt warning device).
9 Disconnect the speedometer cable from the rear extension housing. If the gearbox is to be dismantled, drain the oil.

10 Remove the propeller shaft as described in Chapter 7. It is a good idea to cover the opening in the rear extension housing with a plastic bag and retain it with a thick rubber band to prevent loss of oil from the gearbox, once the propeller shaft has been removed.
11 Unbolt the clutch slave cylinder from the bellhousing and tie it up out of the way (see Chapter 5) or disconnect the operating cable from the release lever according to type.
12 Place a jack under the sump, taking care that it does not foul the drain plug, using a piece of wood between the jack and the sump.
13 Unscrew the gearbox rear mounting bolts, place a supporting jack under the gearbox and remove the securing bolts from the mounting/body attachments.
14 Unscrew the starter motor cable connection and the two starter motor securing bolts and remove the starter.
15 Unscrew and remove the bellhousing to engine securing bolts, also the gusset plate bolts.
16 Lower both jacks progressively until the gearbox can be withdrawn rearwards from beneath the vehicle. Do not allow the weight of the gearbox to hang even momentarily upon the clutch driven plate while the input shaft is still engaged with it or the clutch assembly may be damaged. Do not lower the jacks more than is necessary for the gearbox to clear the underside of the body floor otherwise undue strain will be caused to the engine

mountings, the radiator hoses, the fuel inlet line and other components.

17 Refitting is a reversal of removal. If the clutch driven plate is inadvertently displaced during removal it will have to be centred, as described in Chapter 5. When the gearbox is installed, check the clutch adjustment (Chapter 5) and refill the gearbox with the correct grade and quantity of oil.

3 Gearbox (four speed) - dismantling into major components

1 Before dismantling, clean the external surfaces thoroughly with paraffin or water soluble solvent.
2 Detach the flexible dust cover from the release lever aperture in the clutch bellhousing and then remove the release lever and release bearing (see Chapter 5).
3 Remove the reversing lamp switch and the neutral and top gear switches (where fitted); see Section 9.
4 Unscrew and remove the two bolts which secure the speedometer pinion assembly to the extension housing and withdraw the pinion assembly. (photo)
5 Remove the circlip and the remote control rod guide stop pin.
6 Remove the threaded plug which is located above and slightly to the rear of the speedometer pinion aperture and then withdraw the plunger, return spring and bush.
7 From within the clutch bellhousing, unbolt and remove the front cover, 'O' ring and shim.
8 Unscrew and remove the rear extension housing to transmission casing tie-bolts.
9 Rotate the remote control rod guide as far as it will go in a clockwise direction and then drive off the rear extension housing using a soft-faced mallet.
10 Tap off the single piece clutch bellhousing/casing in a similar manner to that applied to the rear extension.
11 Make up a suitable support plate and secure it in the jaws of a

vice and then bolt the adaptor plate to it so that the countergear assembly is at the top.
12 Remove the countergear thrust washer.
13 Drive out the pins which secure the three shift forks to the selector rods. There is no need to remove the dogs from the ends of the selector rods unless they are to be renewed.
14 Remove reverse shift fork and reverse idle gear.
15 Invert the adaptor plate in the vice so that the shift forks and selector rods are uppermost.
16 Unscrew and remove the three detent ball plugs.
17 Tap out the selector rods from the adaptor plate (towards the rear) and take off the shift forks. Retain the detent balls, springs and interlock plungers as the selector rods are withdrawn. The selector rods need only be driven far enough to permit removal of the shift forks. The selector rods remaining attached to the adaptor plate will not impede removal of the shafts or gears later on.
18 At this stage, check for backlash in the gears, this should be within the tolerances given in Specifications Section. Also check the mainshaft gears for endfloat which again should be as specified for the particular gears. Where the tolerances are exceeded, the drive and driven gears must be renewed as matched sets.
19 Inspect the teeth of the gearwheels for wear or chipping which if evident will necessitate renewal of the gears concerned.
20 From the rear of the mainshaft, extract reverse gear circlip, the thrust washer and reverse gear.
21 Using a soft-faced mallet, tap the rear end of the mainshaft and eject both the mainshaft and countershaft assemblies from the adaptor plate. Hold the two gear trains in mesh during the removal operation and then detach the countergear also the input shaft from the front end of the mainshaft.
22 Unless the necessary press facilities are available, it is recommended that dismantling of the mainshaft, countergear and input shaft be left to your Datsun dealer. Where suitable equipment is available, proceed as described in the following Sections.

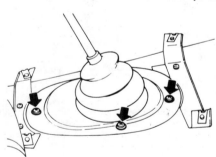

Fig. 6.2. Gearshift lever flexible boot

Fig. 6.3. Gearshift lever pivot pin and circlip

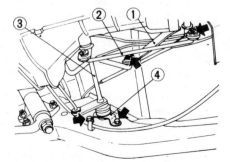

Fig. 6.3A. Gearchange rods, levers and shafts (3 speed gearbox)

| 1 | Shift lever | 3 | Cross-shaft |
| 2 | Shift rod | 4 | Cross-shaft bracket |

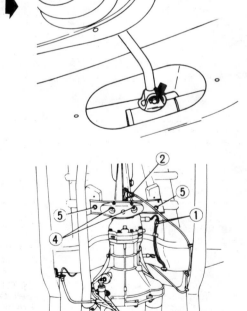

Fig. 6.4. Location of (1) reversing lamp leads (2) speedometer cable

3 Clutch operating cylinder (hydraulic actuation)
4 Rear mounting bolts
5 Mounting support bolts

3.4 Removing speedometer
drive pinion assembly

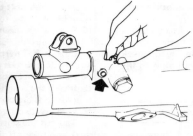

Fig. 6.5. Remote control rod
guide stop pin and circlip

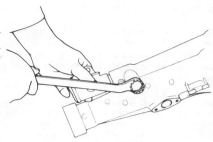

Fig. 6.6. Removing plunger
threaded plug

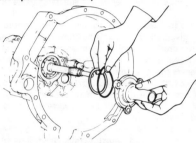

Fig. 6.7. Removing front
cover, 'O' ring and input
shaft bearing shim

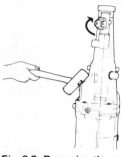

Fig. 6.8. Removing the rear
extension housing

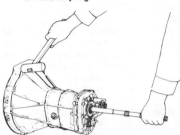

Fig. 6.9. Removing the gearbox
casing from the adaptor plate

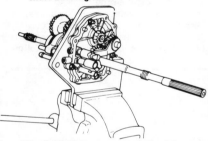

Fig. 6.10. Adaptor plate bolted
to support plate

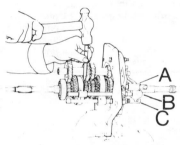

A
B
C

Fig. 6.11. Driving out a shift
fork retaining pin A - reverse,
B - 3rd/4th, C - 1st/2nd

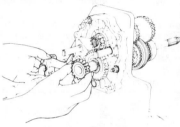

Fig. 6.12. Removing reverse
shift fork and reverse idler
gear

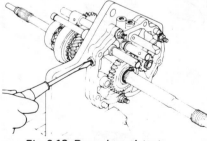

Fig. 6.13. Removing a detent
ball plug

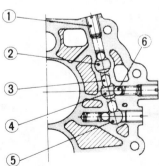

Fig. 6.14. Detent ball and
interlock plunger location
diagram

1 plug
2 1st/2nd selector rod
3 interlock plunger
4 3rd/4th selector rod
5 reverse gear selector rod
6 detent ball

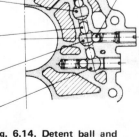

Fig. 6.15. Measuring the end-
play of gears

Thickness gauge

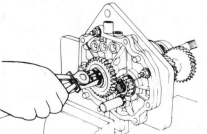

Fig. 6.16. Extracting reverse
gear circlip

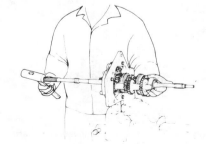

Fig. 6.17. Removing gear
assemblies from the adaptor
plate

4 Mainshaft (four speed) - dismantling, examination and re-assembly

1 From the front end of the mainshaft, remove the pilot needle roller bearing, the thrust washer and its steel locking ball, 3rd/4th synchro assembly, baulk rings, 3rd. gear and needle roller bearing. (photo)

2 Supporting the mainshaft bearing, press the mainshaft from it.

3 From the rear end of the mainshaft withdraw the thrust washer, 1st. gear, needle roller bearing, bush 1st./2nd. synchro assembly, baulk rings, 2nd. gear and another needle roller bearing.

4 With the mainshaft dismantled, check it for twist or spline wear and renew it if necessary.

5 Check the needle roller bearings and the main bearing for wear and renew if necessary.

6 Examine the synchronizer units for wear or damage. If there has been a history of noisy or slow gear selection, renew the synchronizer unit complete. If there is slight wear on any component (sleeve, hub, thrust washer etc), this should be renewed individually.

Examine each of the baulk rings for wear and damage. Place each baulk ring on its appropriage gear cone and measure the gap between them. This should be between 0.041 and 0.060 in (1.05 and 1.40 mm). Where the clearance is found to be smaller, renew the baulk ring.

7 To assemble a synchronizer, insert the hub into the sleeve and locate the three shift keys in grooves at equidistance points.

8 Install the springs which retain the shift keys but make quite sure that the ends of opposite springs are not engaged in the same key.

9 To the rear end of the mainshaft, assemble the 2nd gear needle bearing, 2nd gear, the baulk ring, 1st and 2nd speed synchro unit, 1st gear baulk ring, 1st gear bush and needle bearing, 1st gear and the thrust washer, in that sequence.

10 Now press on the mainshaft bearing making sure that pressure is applied only to the inner track.

11 To the front end of the mainshaft, fit the 3rd gear needle bearing, 3rd gear, the baulk ring, 3rd/4th synchro unit, the

thrust washer with its locking ball. Apply grease to the thrust washer before installing and make sure that the oil grooves are against the synchro hub.

5 Countergear (four speed) - dismantling, examination, re-assembly

1 Extract the circlip from the rear end of the countergear.

2 Support reverse gear and press the countergear assembly from it.

3 Remove the rear bearing in a similar manner.

4 Inspect the gearteeth for wear or chipping and renew if necessary the complete countergear assembly.

5 Examine the rear bearing for wear, roughness or noise when spinning it with the fingers and renew where necessary.

6 Press the rear bearing onto the countergear, applying pressure only to the bearing inner track.

7 Temporarily install a countershaft thrust washer into the recess at the front end of the gearbox casing. A height gauge (service tool ST 23050000) must now be borrowed from your Datsun dealer. With the tool held against the adaptor plate mating face of the gearbox casing and using feeler blades, measure the countershaft end-play which should be between 0.000 and 0.008 in (0 and 0.2 mm). In order to correct the end play, extract the thrust washer and substitute one of appropriate thickness from those available in the following range of sizes:

> 0.0906 to 0.0925 in (2.30 to 2.35 mm)
> 0.0925 to 0.0945 in (2.35 to 2.40 mm)
> 0.0945 to 0.0965 in (2.40 to 2.45 mm)
> 0.0965 to 0.0984 in (2.45 to 2.50 mm)
> 0.0984 to 0.1004 in (2.50 to 2.55 mm)
> 0.1004 to 0.1024 in (2.55 to 2.60 mm)

8 Remove the countergear assembly from the gearbox casing and press reverse gear onto the countergear.

9 Install the circlip to the rear end of the countergear.

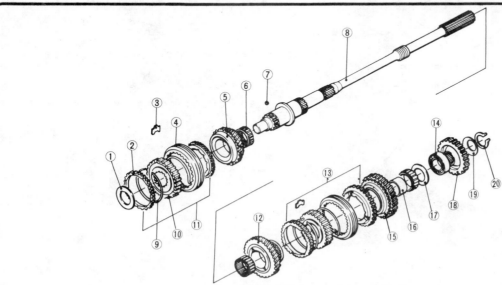

Fig. 6.18. Exploded view of the mainshaft assembly

1	Thrust washer	6	Needle bearing	11	3rd/4th synchro. assembly	16	Bush
2	Baulk ring	7	Ball	12	2nd gear	17	Thrust washer
3	Synchro. shift key	8	Mainshaft	13	1st/2nd synchro. assembly	18	Reverse gear
4	Synchro. sleeve	9	Synchro. spring	14	Mainshaft bearing	19	Thrust washer
5	3rd gear	10	Synchro. hub	15	1st gear	20	Circlip

4.1 Front end of mainshaft showing needle roller bearing, thrust washer and 3rd/4th synchro

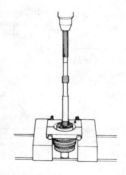

Fig. 6.19. Removing the mainshaft bearing

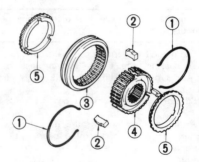

Fig. 6.20 Exploded view of a synchronizer unit

1 Spring
2 Shift key
3 Sleeve
4 Hub
5 Baulk ring

Fig. 6.21. Checking synchro. baulk ring to cone clearance

Fig. 6.22. Installing a synchro. unit spring

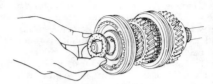

Fig. 6.23. Installing thrust washer to front of mainshaft

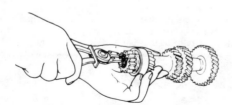

Fig. 6.24. Extracting circlip from end of counter gear

Fig. 6.25. Removing reverse gear from countershaft

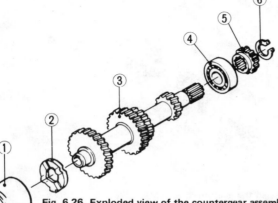

Fig. 6.26. Exploded view of the countergear assembly

1 Needle bearing
2 Thrust washer
3 Counter gear
4 Bearing
5 Countershaft reverse gear
6 Circlip

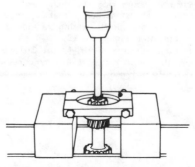

Fig. 6.27. Measuring counter gear end-play using height gauge

6 Input shaft (four speed) - examination, dismantling and re-assembly

1 Inspect the gearteeth and splines of the input shaft for wear or damage. If apparent, renew the shaft complete.
2 Check the bearing for wear or rough or noisy operation when it is turned with the fingers.
3 To remove the bearing, first extract the circlip and thrust washer and then using a suitable puller or press, draw the bearing from the shaft.
4 Press the new bearing onto the input shaft, applying pressure to the inner track only and making sure that the circlip groove on the shaft is fully exposed.
5 Locate the thrust washer on the bearing so that the chamfered face of the washer faces the front of the input shaft.
6 Fit a new circlip to the input shaft.
7 Finally, check the condition of the pilot needle bearing and renew it if it is worn.

7 Gearbox oil seals and casing

1 At time of major overhaul, always check the gearbox casing and rear extension housing for cracks.
2 Renew the front cover oil seal.
3 Renew the oil seal in the rear extension housing. If the bush in the rear extension is worn then the rear extension housing will have to be renewed complete.
4 If the countershaft needle bearing requires renewal, press it into the gearbox interior from the outside. Install the new one from the inside so that it will project by 0.079 in (2.0 mm) beyond the front face of the gearbox casing.
5 Finally, check the condition of the gearbox rear mounting and renew it if the rubber component has deteriorated.

8 Gearbox (four speed type) - reassembly

1 Fit the baulk ring to the input shaft and then joint the input shaft to the front of the mainshaft. (photo)
2 Mesh the mainshaft and countergear assemblies and then install them simultaneously into the adaptor plate by striking them alternately with a soft-faced mallet. (photo)
3 Fit the reverse gear and thrust washer to the rear end of the mainshaft and secure with circlip. Make sure that the chamfered face of the thrust washer is towards the front of the gearbox. Some washers are dished type, install with concave side to reverse gear. (photos)
4 Insert the spring and detent ball into the reverse hole in the adaptor plate. A useful tool can be made from a piece of rod having a sloping surface at one end to depress the detent ball and compress the spring pending installation of the reverse selector rod. (photo)
5 Install the reverse selector rod so that it displaces the tool without releasing the detent ball or spring.
6 Apply thread locking compound to the plug and screw it into the adaptor plate until it is flush with the surface of the plate. (photo)
7 Insert the interlock plunger which lies between reverse and 3rd/4th selector rods. Using the special tool maintain pressure on the plunger until by moving the reverse selector rod, the plunger can be felt to engage in the notch in the reverse selector rod.
8 Engage 3rd/4th shift fork with the groove in the 3rd/4th synchro sleeve (longer arm of fork **furthest** from countergear) and then slide 3rd/4th selector rod through the adaptor plate and shift fork. The 3rd/4th shift fork is identical with the 1st/2nd shift fork. (photo)
9 Install the detent ball, spring and plug into the 3rd/4th hole in the adaptor plate. Apply thread locking compound to the plug and screw it in until flush with the surface of the adaptor plate. Make sure that the detent notch in the selector rod is in the correct attitude to engage with the detent ball.
10 Engage the 1st/2nd shift fork with the groove in the 1st/2nd

synchro sleeve (longer arm of fork **nearest** countergear). (photo)
11 Insert the interlock plunger which lies between 1st/2nd and 3rd/4th selector rod holes in the adaptor plate. Make sure that the 3rd/4th selector rod notch is aligned to receive the plunger.
12 Slide the 1st/2nd selector rod through the adaptor plate and the shift fork.
13 Insert the detent ball, spring and plug into the 1st/2nd hole in the adaptor plate. Apply thread locking compound to the plug and screw it in until flush with the surface of the adaptor plate. Make sure that the detent notch in the selector rod is in the correct attitude to engage with the detent ball. (photos)
14 Install the reverse idler gear and shift fork.(photo)
15 Secure the three shift forks to their selector rods using new retaining pins. (photo)
16 Check the operation of the selector mechanism by moving the 3rd/4th selector rod to engage 3rd and then 4th gear. With either of these gears selected, movement of either of the other two selector rods should not cause any other gears to mesh. If they do, then the interlock plungers are not operating correctly which may be due to the selector rods having been installed with their notches 180° out of alignment.
17 Apply gear oil to all internal components and select each gear in turn to check for positive and smooth operation.
18 Clean the mating surfaces of the adaptor plate and the gearbox casing and apply jointing compound to both surfaces.
19 Stick the countergear thrust washer previously selected (see Section 5) into the recess at the front of the gearbox, holding it in positon with a dab of thick grease and making sure that the oil grooves on the washer are not visible when it is installed. (photo)
20 Connect the gearbox casing to the adaptor plate making sure that the locating dowel engages correctly and then tap the adaptor plate fully home with a soft-faced mallet. Take great care that the input shaft bearing enters the front face of the gearbox squarely and the nose of the countershaft enters the needle bearing in correct alignment during the later stages of the mating operation. (photo)
21 Clean the mating surfaces of the adaptor plate and the rear extension and apply jointing compound to them.
22 Set the selector rods in neutral and then gradually slide the rear extension onto the adaptor plate ensuring that the selector cross lever engages correctly with the dogs on the ends of the selector rods. During this operation, make sure that the remote control rod passes down the right-hand side of the mainshaft when viewed from the bottom of the gearbox. (photo)
23 Install the tie-bolts and washers and tighten them to the specified torque.
24 Apply jointing compound to the remote control rod guide stop in hole in the rear extension, insert the pin and secure with the circlip. (photo)
25 Grease the plunger, and springs and insert them into the hole in the rear extension housing. (photo)
26 Apply jointing compound to the threaded plug and install it. Install the speedometer pinion assembly (two bolts). (photo)
27 Using a vernier type depth gauge or feeler blades and a straight-edge, measure the distance by which the input shaft bearing outer race is recessed from the front cover mating face of the transmission casing. Select a shim from the range of thicknesses available - 0.020 in (0.5 mm) 0.008 in (0.2 mm) 0.004 in (0.1 mm) 0.012 in (0.03 mm) - which will reduce the dimension 'A' to between 0.1969 and 0.2029 in (5.00 and 5.15 mm). Stick the selected shim in position using a dab of thick grease. (photo)
28 Clean the mating surfaces of the front cover and the gearbox casing, install the front cover using a new 'O' ring seal and tightening the securing bolts to the specified torque. (photo)
29 Refit the reversing lamp switch, top gear and neutral indicator switches, apply jointing compound to their threads before screwing them in. Check that the breather on the rear extension housing has its directional arrow pointing to the front of the gearbox.
30 Install the release bearing and lever, coating the sliding and pivot surfaces with a little high melting point grease.
31 Temporarily connect the gear shift lever and check for smooth and positive gear selection.

8.1 Input shaft ready for coupling to mainshaft

8.2 Installing mainshaft and countergear assemblies to adaptor plate

8.3A Reverse gear installed on mainshaft rear end

8.3B Thrust washer installed on mainshaft rear end

8.3C Securing reverse gear and thrust washer to mainshaft with circlip

8.4 Detent ball and spring inserted into reverse hold in adaptor plate

8.6 Inserting plug into reverse detent hole in adaptor plate

8.8 Installing 3rd/4th selector rod and shift fork

8.10 Installing 1st/2nd selector rod and shift fork 1 = 1st/2nd, 2 = 3rd/4th, 3 = reverse

8.13A Inserting 1st/2nd detent ball and spring into adaptor plate

8.13B Inserting 1st/2nd detent plug

8.14 Reverse idler gear and shift fork correctly installed

8.15 Shift fork to selector rod tension pin

8.19 Countergear thrust washer at front of gear case interior

8.20 Connecting gearbox casing to adaptor plate

8.22 Installing gearbox extension housing to adaptor plate

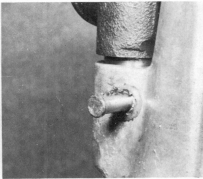

8.24A Gearshift remote control rod guide stop pin

8.24B Fitting circlip to remote control rod guide stop pin

8.25 Installing plunger assembly to rear extension housing

8.26 Installing speedometer drive pinion assembly

8.27 Input shaft bearing shim and recess

8.28 Front cover showing input shaft oil seal and 'O' ring

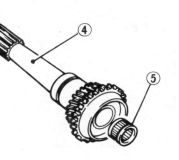

Fig. 6.28. Exploded view of the input shaft

1 Circlip
2 Thrust washer
3 Bearing
4 Input shaft
5 Pilot bearing

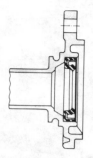

Fig. 6.29. Correct installation of front cover oil seal

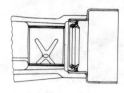

Fig. 6.30. Correct installation of rear extension housing oil seal

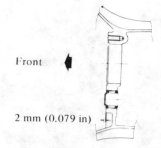

Front

2 mm (0.079 in)

Fig. 6.31. Countershaft needle bearing installation diagram

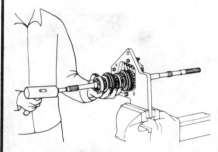

Fig. 6.32. Installing gear assemblies to adaptor plate

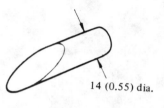

14 (0.55) dia.

Fig. 6.33. Detent ball and interlock plunger installation tool

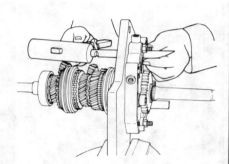

Fig. 6.34. Installing reverse selector rod

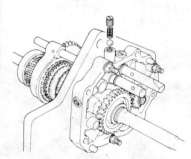

Fig. 6.35. Installing 3rd/4th selector rod detent ball and spring

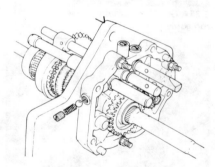

Fig. 6.36. Installing 1st/2nd selector rod detent ball and spring

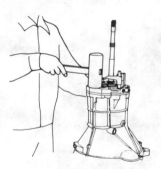

Fig. 6.37. Installing transmission casing

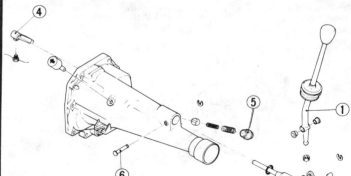

Fig. 6.38 Exploded view of the rear extension housing

1 Gearshift lever
2 Remote control rod guide
3 Remote control rod
4 Selector cross lever
5 Return spring plug
6 Guide stop pin
7 Gearshift lever pivot

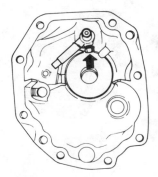

Fig. 6.39. Selector cross lever and securing bolt (arrowed)

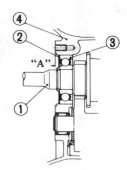

Fig. 6.41. Input shaft bearing shim selection diagram

1 Input shaft   3 Bearing
2 Shim   4 Casing

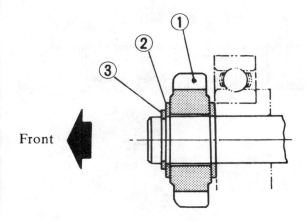

Front

Fig. 6.41A. Sectional view of reverse idler gear (3 speed gearbox)

1 Reverse idler gear   3 Circlip
2 Thrust washer

9 Gearbox (three speed type) - dismantling and reassembly

1 As this unit is very similar to the four speed gearbox, the operations described in the previous Sections will apply except for the following variations.
2 To dismantle the reverse idler gear, remove the circlip, thrust washer, the gear and the second thrust washer. Note the location of the mainshaft reverse gear which is to the front of the mainshaft rear bearing and the countershaft rear bearing. On the four speed types, reverse gear is to the rear of these bearings, otherwise the mainshaft and countershafts are similar.
3 To dismantle the selector mechanism, remove the rear extension housing and drive out the retaining pin from 1st/reverse cross-shaft. Pull out the cross-shaft and detach 1st and reverse operating lever.
4 Remove 2nd/3rd cross-shaft in a similar manner.
5 The detent plugs, balls and springs and the selector rods can then be extracted.
6 Check the gear backlash and endfloat in accordance with the tolerances given in Specifications Section.
7 If the rear extension bush is worn do not attempt to remove it but renew the housing complete.
8 Reassembly is similar to the procedure described in Section 8 for the four speed gearbox with the variations already described.

10 Steering column gearchange linkage (three speed gearbox)

1 After a high mileage the linkage will tend to wear and adjust-

ment will be required. To carry out this adjustment, release the locknuts on the shift rods so that they have adequate clearance in their trunnions.
2 Set both shift rods in the neutral position and then adjust the trunnion nuts until the groove in the lower support bracket is in alignment with those on the change levers. Fully tighten the nuts and check for smooth and positive operation in all gear positions.
3 If the linkage has to be removed in order to renew any components, first remove the steering wheel (see Chapter 11) followed by the steering column shrouds and the direction indicator switch.
4 Extract the two circlips and pivot pins from the hand control lever and withdraw the lever.
5 Disconnect the shift rods from the change levers by removing the split pins and washers.
6 Remove the items in the sequence shown in Fig. 6.41G.
7 Withdraw the control rod assembly from the vehicle interior and dismantle as necessary.
8 The cross-shaft assembly can be removed after unscrewing the two bolts from the cross-shaft bracket.

11 Transmission controlled vacuum advance (top gear switch)

1 This device is fitted to vehicles equipped with a full emission control system. Full details are given in Chapter 3, Section 30, to which reference should be made.

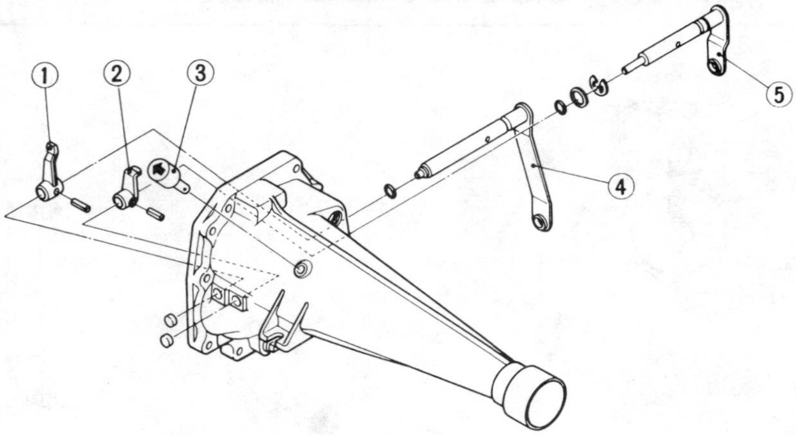

Fig. 6.41B. Gear selector mechanism (3 speed gearbox)

1 1st/reverse lever
2 2nd/3rd lever
3 Breather
4 1st/reverse cross-shaft
5 2nd/3rd cross-shaft

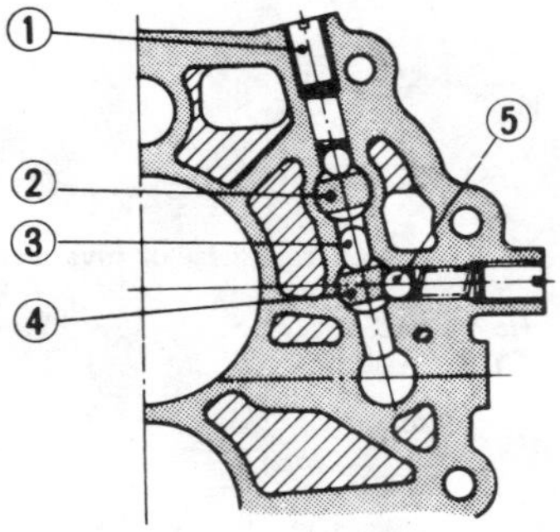

Fig. 6.41C. Sectional view of detent ball and interlock mechanism (3 speed gearbox)

1 Plug
2 1st/reverse selector rod
3 Interlock plunger
4 2nd/3rd selector rod
5 Detent ball

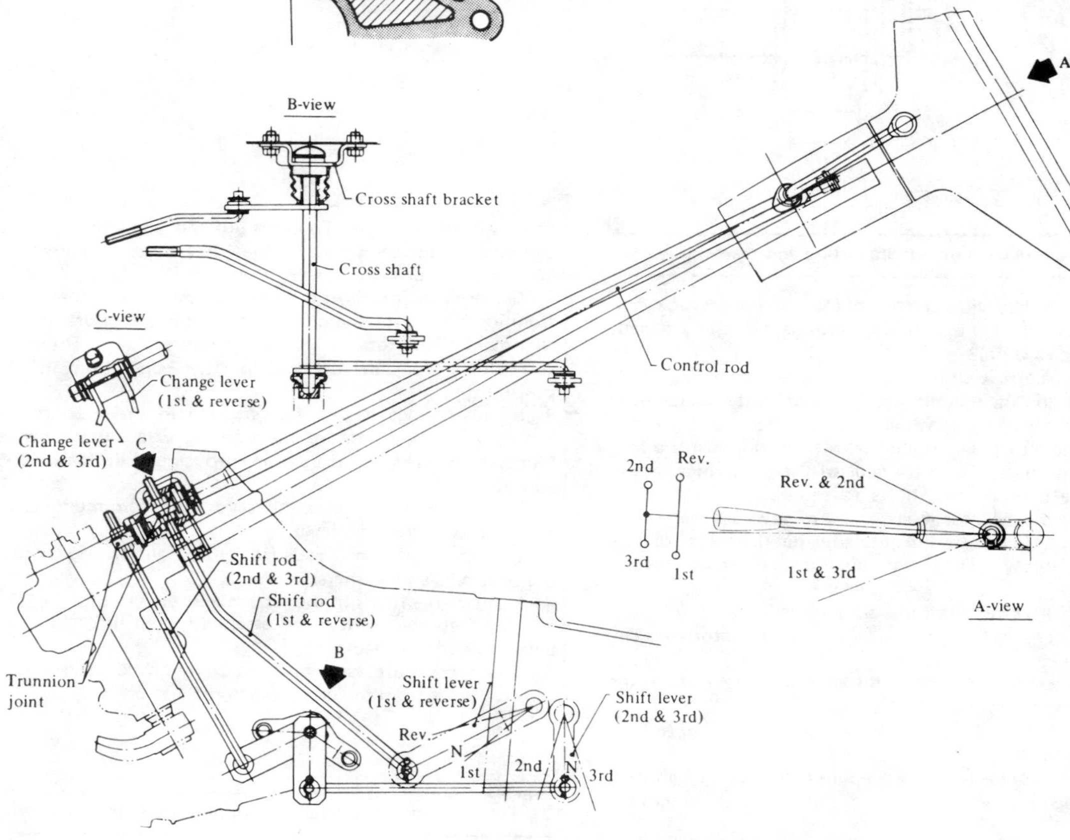

Fig. 6.41D. Steering column linkage (3 speed gearbox)

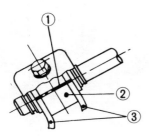

Fig. 6.41E. Steering column gearshift alignment marks

1   Neutral alignment groove   3   Change lever
2   Lower support bracket

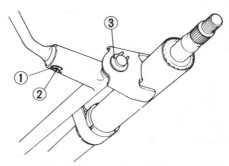

Fig. 6.41F. Steering column hand control lever attachment

1   Circlip   3   Circlip
2   Pivot pin

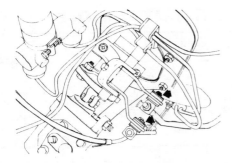

Fig. 6.41G. Disconnecting shift rods from change levers.
(Steering column change).

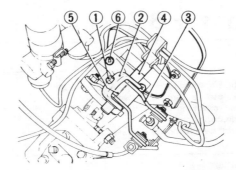

Fig. 6.41H. Steering column gearchange linkage disconnection
points

1   Retainer bolt   4   Control rod
2   Retainer   5   Lower bracket
3   Bush   6   Bracket bolts

12 Fault diagnosis - manual gearbox

Symptom	Reason/s
Ineffective synchromesh	Worn baulk rings or synchro hubs.
Jumps out of one or more gears (on drive or over-run)	Weak detent springs or worn selector forks or worn gears.
Noisy, rough, whining and vibration	Worn bearings and/or thrust washers (initially) resulting in extended wear generally due to play and backlash.
Noisy and difficult engagement of gears	Clutch fault (See Chapter 5).

Note: It is sometimes difficult to decide whether it is worthwhile removing and dismantling the gearbox for a fault which may be nothing more than a minor irritant. Gearboxes which howl, or where the synchromesh can be 'beaten' by a quick gearchange, may continue to perform for a long time in this state. A worn gearbox usually needs a complete rebuild to eliminate noise because the various gears, if re-aligned on new bearings will continue to howl when different wearing surfaces are presented to each other.

    The decision to overhaul therefore, must be considered with regard to time and money available, relative to the degree of noise or malfunction that the driver has to suffer.

Chapter 6 Part 2: Automatic transmission

Contents

Specifications

Type	3N71B (3 forward speeds and reverse)
Ratios:	
1st	2.458 : 1
2nd	1.458 : 1
3rd	1.000 : 1
Reverse	2.182 : 1
Lubrication system	by internal pump
Cooling	air flow
Fluid capacity:	
Excluding sealed torque converter	9¾ Imp. pints, (5 7/8 US qts, 5.5 litres)
Torque converter	4¾ Imp. pints, (2 7/8 US qts, 2.7 litres)
Engine idling speed (fume emission control fitted):	
Selector in 'N'	800 rev/min.
Selector in 'D'	650 rev/min.

Torque wrench settings	lb f ft	kg f m
Driveplate to crankshaft bolts	55	7.6
Driveplate to torque converter bolts	7	1.0
Torque converter housing to engine bolts	36	5.0
Transmission housing to converter housing	40	5.5
Rear extension to transmission casing bolts	20	2.8
Oil pan bolts	5	0.7
Inhibitor switch to transmission casing	5	0.7
Oil filler tube union nut	36	5.0
Selector range lever nut	30	4.1
Control rod locknuts	30	4.1

13 General description

The automatic transmission which may be optionally specified for Saloon and Coupe models is the type 3N71B.

The unit provides three forward ratios and one reverse. Changing of the forward gear ratios is completely automatic in relation to the vehicle speed and engine torque input and is dependent upon the vacuum pressure in the manifold and the vehicle road speed to actuate the gear change mechanism at the precise time.

The transmission has six selector positions:

P - parking position which locks the output shaft to the interior wall of the transmission housing. This is a safety device for use when the vehicle is parked on an incline. The engine may be started with 'P' selected and this position should always be selected when adjusting the engine while it is running. Never attempt to select 'P' when the vehicle is in motion.

R - reverse gear.

N - neutral. Select this position to start the engine or when idling in traffic for long periods.

2 - locks the transmission in second gear for wet road conditions or steep hill climbing or descents. The engine

can be over revved in this position.
*1 - the selection of this ratio above road speeds of approx-
imately 25 mph will engage second gear and as the speed
drops below 25 mph the transmission will lock into first
gear. Provides maximum retardation to steep descents.*

Due to the complexity of the automatic transmission unit,
any internal adjustment or servicing should be left to a main
Datsun agent. The information given in this Chapter is therefore
confined to those operations which are considered within the
scope of the home mechanic. An automatic transmission should
give many tens of thousands of miles service provided normal

maintenance and adjustment is carried out. When the unit finally
requires major overhaul, consideration should be given to
exchanging the old transmission for a factory reconditioned one,
the removal and installation being well within the capabilities of
the home mechanic as described later in this Chapter. The
hydraulic fluid does not require periodic draining or refilling but
the fluid level must be checked and topped-up if necessary, as
described in the following Section.

Periodically clean the outside of the transmission housing as
the accumulation of dirt and oil is liable to cause overheating of
the unit under extreme conditions.

Adjust the engine slow running as specified, 650 rpm in 'D'.

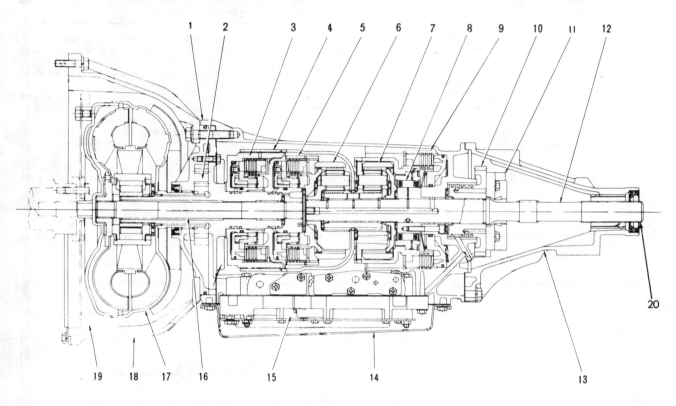

Fig. 6.42. Sectional view of the automatic transmission unit

1 Transmission housing	6 Front planetary gear	11 Governor	16 Input shaft
2 Oil pump	7 Rear planetary gear	12 Output shaft	17 Torque converter
3 Front clutch	8 One way clutch	13 Rear extension	18 Converter housing
4 Brake band	9 Low/reverse brake	14 Oil pan	19 Drive plate
5 Rear clutch	10 Oil distributor	15 Control valve	20 Rear extension oil seal

14 Fluid level - checking

1 At the intervals specified in Routine Maintenance Section,
run the car on the road until normal operating temperature is
reached.
2 Position the car on level ground and with the engine idling,
move the speed selector lever through all selector positions and
then place the lever in 'P'.
3 After a period of two minutes, withdraw the dipstick wipe it
clean on non-fluffy material and re-insert it, again withdrawing it
immediately it reaches the bottom of the guide tube. Immediate
withdrawal of the dipstick is very important as if it is allowed to
rest at the fully inserted position, the oil level reading will be incorrectly indicated or it may be impossible to obtain one at all
due to oil splash.

15 Automatic transmission - removal and installation

1 Removal of the engine and automatic transmission as a
combined unit is described and illustrated in Chapter 1 of this
manual. Where it is decided to remove the transmission leaving
the engine in position in the vehicle, proceed as described in the
following paragraphs. Note that there is no transmission drain
plug and care must be taken to prevent fluid spillage when
disconnecting the propeller shaft and fluid pipes to prevent
excessive loss.
2 Disconnect the battery negative lead.
3 Jack the car to an adequate working height and support on
stands or blocks.
4 Disconnect the exhaust down pipe bracket.
5 Disconnect the leads from the starter inhibitor switch.

6 Disconnect the leads from the downshift solenoid.

7 Withdraw the dipstick, unscrew the fluid filler tube union nut and then remove the tube from the transmission casing.

8 Where applicable, disconnect the oil cooler inlet and outlet tubes from the transmission case.

9 Disconnect the vacuum pipe from the vacuum capsule which is located just forward of the downshift solenoid.

10 Separate the selector lever from the selector linkage.

11 Disconnect the speedometer drive cable from the rear extension housing.

12 Mark the edges of the propeller shaft rear driving flange and the pinion flange (for exact refitting) remove the four retaining bolts and withdraw the propeller shaft from its connection with the transmission rear extension housing.

13 Support the engine sump with a jack and use a block of wood to prevent damage to the surface of the sump.

14 Remove the cover from the lower half of the torque converter housing. Mark the torque converter housing and drive plate in relation to each other for exact replacement.

15 Unscrew and remove the four bolts which secure the torque converter to the drive plate. Access to each of these bolts, in turn, is obtained by rotating the engine slowly, using a spanner on the crankshaft pulley bolt.

16 Unbolt and withdraw the starter motor.

17 Support the transmission with a jack (preferably a trolley type).

18 Detach the rear transmission mounting from the transmission housing and the vehicle body frame.

19 Unscrew and remove the transmission to engine securing bolts.

20 Lower the two jacks sufficiently to allow the transmission unit to be withdrawn from below and to the rear of the vehicle. The help of an assistant will probably be required due to the weight of the unit.

21 Installation is a reversal of removal but the following points must be observed:

- (i) *Ensure that the notch on the torque converter engages with the key on the oil pump. When the torque converter is correctly installed, the distance between the front faces of the torque converter securing bolts and the front face of the torque converter housing will be as shown in the diagram.*
- (ii) *Tighten all bolts to specified torque.*
- (iii)*Refill the unit with the correct grade and quantity of fluid.*

16 Speed selector linkage - adjustment

1 The importance of correct adjustment of the gear selector linkage cannot be over emphasised. Incorrect selection can cause damage, overheating and breakdown of the unit.

2 Check that the knob on the control lever is set as shown in dimension A (Fig. 6.46) in the diagram.

3 By adjustment of the length of the pushrod within the control lever, make sure that there is a clearance (dimension B) between the top surface of the gate pin and the gate.

4 Loosen the nuts (D) on the lower shift rod (2) and then set the hand control lever in the 'N' position, also the selector range lever on the side of the transmission casting to 'N'.

5 By adjustment of the shift rod nuts, provide a clearance (dimension C) at the hand control lever without disturbing the setting of the two levers in their detents.

6 Fully tighten the shift rod nuts and then check for correct operation of the linkage in all speed positions.

Faulty operation will probably indicate wear at the pivot pins, provided the adjustment procedure has been correctly carried out.

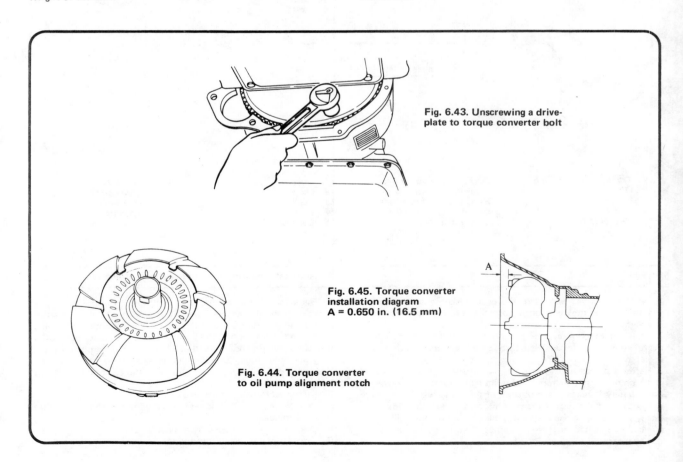

Fig. 6.43. Unscrewing a drive-plate to torque converter bolt

Fig. 6.45. Torque converter installation diagram
A = 0.650 in. (16.5 mm)

Fig. 6.44. Torque converter to oil pump alignment notch

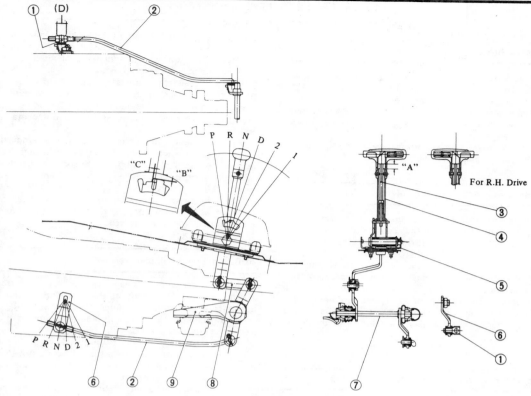

Fig. 6.46 Speed selector linkage

1	Trunnion	3	Push-rod	5	Control lever bracket	7	Cross-shift
2	Lower shift rod	4	Hand control lever	6	Selector range lever	8	Upper shift rod
						9	Cross-shaft bracket

A = 11-12 mm (0.43-0.47 in.)
B = 0.1-1.1 mm (0.0039-0.4331 in.)
C = 1 mm (0.039 in.)

Fig. 6.48. Components of the inhibitor switch assembly

1	Switch	6	Washer
2	Shaft	7	Securing nut
3	Spacer	8	Switch body (removed)
4	Nut	9	Range select lever
5	Plate		

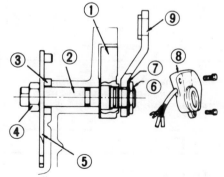

Fig. 6.47. Location of down-shift solenoid

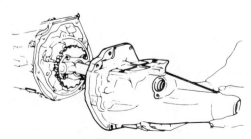

Fig. 6.49. Removing the rear extension housing

17 Speed selector linkage - removal and installation

1 Remove the knob from the hand control lever (two screws).
2 Remove the centre console.
3 Disconnect the shift rods from the cross-shaft.
4 Withdraw the hand control lever upwards and the remaining components downwards after unbolting the cross-shaft support and the selector range lever.
5 Installation is a reversal of removal but check the adjustment as described in the preceding Section.

18 'Kick-down' switch and downshift solenoid - checking

1 If the 'kick-down' facility fails to operate or operates at an incorrect change point, first check the security of the switch on the accelerator pedal arm and the wiring between the switch and the solenoid.
2 Turn the ignition key so that the ignition and oil pressure lamps illuminate but without operating the starter motor. Depress the accelerator pedal fully and as the switch actuates, a distinct click should be heard from the solenoid. Where this is absent, drain 2½ Imp. pints of fluid from the transmission unit unscrew the solenoid and fit a new one. Replenish the transmission fluid.

19 Starter inhibitor and reverse lamp switch - checking

1 Check that the starter motor operates only in 'N' and 'P' and the reversing lamps illuminate only with the selector lever in 'R'.
2 Any deviation from this arrangement should be rectified by adjustment, first having checked the correct setting of the selector linkage.
3 Refer to Fig. 6.48 and detach the range selector lever (9) from the selector rod which connects it to the hand control. Now move the range selector lever to the 'N' position.
4 Connect a ohmmeter to the black and yellow wires of the inhibitor switch. With the ignition switch on, the meter should indicate continuity of circuit when the range select lever is within 3 degrees (either side) of the 'N' and 'P' positions.
5 Repeat the test with the meter connected to the red and black wires and range lever in 'R'.
6 Where the switch requires adjusting to provide the correct moment of contact in the three selector positions, move the range lever to 'N' and then remove the retaining nut (6), the two inhibitor switch securing bolts and the screw located below the switch.
7 Align the hole, from which the screw was removed, with the pinhole in the manual shaft (2). A thin rod or piece of wire may be used to do this. Holding this alignment, fit the inhibitor switch securing bolts and tighten them. Remove the alignment rod and refit the screw.
8 Refit the remaining switch components and test for correct operation as previously described. If the test procedure does not prove positive, renew the switch.

20 Rear extension oil seal - renewal

1 After a considerable mileage, leakage may occur from the seal which surrounds the shaft at the rear end of the automatic transmission extension housing. This leakage will be evident from the state of the underbody and from the reduction in the level of the hydraulic fluid.
2 Remove the propeller shaft (Chapter 7).
3 Taking care not to damage the spined output shaft and the alloy housing, prise the old oil seal from its location. Drive in the new one using a tubular drift.
4 Should the seal be very tight in its recess, then support the transmission unit under the oil pan, remove the rear mounting, the speedometer drive cable and the rear extension to main transmission housing securing bolts.
5 Pull the extension housing straight off over the output shaft and governor assembly.
6 Using a suitable drift applied from the interior of the rear extension housing, remove the old oil seal.
7 Refitting is a reversal of removal, but always use a new gasket between the rear extension and main housing and tighten the securing bolts to the specified torque.

21 Fault diagnosis - automatic transmission

1 *In addition to the information given in this Chapter reference should be made to Chapter 3 for the servicing and maintenance of the emission control equipment fitted to automatic transmission vehicles.*
2 *The most likely causes of faulty operation are incorrect oil level and linkage adjustment.*

Symptom	Reason/s
Engine will not start in 'N' or 'P'	Faulty starter or ignition circuit. Incorrect linkage adjustment. Incorrectly installed inhibitor switch.
Engine starts in selector positions other than 'N' or 'P'	Incorrect linkage adjustment. Incorrectly installed inhibitor switch.
Severe bump when selecting 'D' or 'R' and excessive creep when hand brake released	Idling speed too high. Vacuum circuit leaking.
Poor acceleration and low maximum speed	Incorrect oil level. Incorrect linkage adjustment.

   Any other faults or mal-operation of the automatic transmission unit must be due to internal faults and should be rectified by your Datsun dealer. An indication of a major internal fault may be gained from the colour of the oil which under normal conditions should be transparent red. If it becomes discoloured or black then burned clutch or brake bands must be suspected.

Chapter 7 Propeller shaft

Contents

Specifications

Type	Single piece tubular steel with two universal joints and sliding sleeve at front end
Maximum out of balance (at 5800 rpm)	0.42 in oz (30 g/cm)
Maximum shaft out of round	0.024 in (0.6 mm)

Torque wrench setting	lb f ft	kg f m
Propeller shaft flange bolts	24	3.3

1 General description

1 The propeller shaft is of one piece tubular steel construction having a universal joint at each end to allow for vertical movement of the rear axle.
2 At the front end of the shaft is a sliding sleeve which mates with the splined output shaft of the transmission unit.
3 There is a difference in length and design of this sliding sleeve on the shafts used with manual gearbox and automatic transmission and the assemblies are not interchangeable.
4 The needle bearing cups of the universal joints are staked in position and in the event of wear occuring in the joints, the propeller shaft must be renewed complete.

2 Universal joints - testing for wear

1 Wear in the needle roller bearings is characterized by vibration in the transmission, 'clonks' on taking up the drive, and in extreme cases lack of lubrication, metallic squeaking and ultimately grating and shrieking sounds as the bearings break up.
2 It is easy to check if the needle roller bearings are worn with the propeller shaft in position, by trying to turn the shaft with one hand, the other hand holding the rear axle flange when the rear universal joint is being checked, and the front half coupling when the front universal joint is being checked. Any movement between the propeller shaft and the front half couplings, and round the rear half couplings, is indicative of considerable wear. A final test for wear is to attempt to lift the shaft and note any movement between the yokes of the joints.
3 If wear is evident, the complete propeller shaft assembly must be renewed.

3 Propeller shaft - removal and installation

1 Jack-up the rear of the vehicle and support it securely. Alternatively, place the vehicle over a pit.
2 Apply the handbrake fully and then mark the edges of the propeller shaft rear flange and the rear axle pinion driving flange so that they can be refitted in the same relative position.
3 Unscrew and remove the bolts which secure the flanges together and then push the propeller shaft slightly forward to separate the flanges, lower the shaft and withdraw it to the rear. Some loss of oil may occur from the rear of the transmission unit.
4 Installation is a reversal of removal but note that the heads of the flange bolts are nearer the front of the car. (photo)

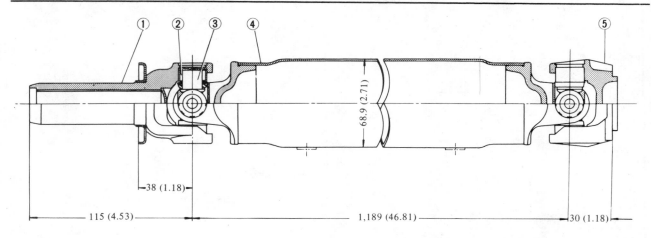

Unit: mm (in)

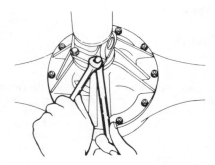

Fig 7.1 Propeller shaft dimensional diagram (inset) different front section on shaft fitted in conjunction with automatic transmission

1   Sliding (internally splined) sleeve/yoke assembly
2   Needle bearing assembly
3   Journal
4   Tubular shaft
5   Flange yoke

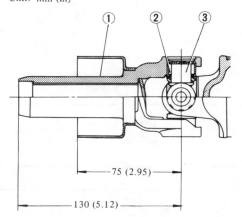

Fig 7.2 Releasing a propeller shaft flange bolt

3.4 Propeller shaft rear flange bolts

4 Fault diagnosis - propeller shaft

Symptom	Reason/s
Vibration when vehicle running on road	Out of balance or distorted propeller shaft
	Backlash in splined shaft
	Loose flange securing bolts
	Worn universal joint bearings

Chapter 8 Rear axle

Contents

Specifications

Type	Rigid, semi-floating with hypoid gear
Construction	Pressed steel casing, cast-iron differential carrier
Ratio	3.90 : 1
Oil capacity	1 5/8 pints (Imp.), 1 7/8 pints (US), 0.9 litre

Torque wrench settings	lb f ft	kg f m
Propeller shaft flange bolts	24	3.3
Oil drain and filler plugs	72	10.0
Brake backplate nut	14	2.0
Differential carrier to cassing nuts	18	2.5
Rear spring 'U' bolt nuts	36	5.0
Shock absorber lower mounting (Saloon & Estate Wagon)	33	4.5
Shock absorber lower mounting (Coupe)	9	1.2

1 General description

The rear axle is of semi-floating type and is held in place by two semi-elliptic road springs which provide the axle with the necessary lateral and longitudinal support.

The pressed steel banjo type axle casing carries the malleable cast iron differential assembly which is of hypoid type and comprises a crownwheel and pinion together with the side gears.

The differential assembly can be removed leaving the axle casing in the vehicle. It is not recommended that the differential unit is dismantled or repaired due to the need for special tools and equipment but in the event of wear occurring or a fault developing, the unit should be repaired by your Datsun dealer or an exchange unit obtained.

2 Routine maintenance

1 At least every 30,000 miles (48000 km), drain the oil (warm) from the rear axle and refill with the correct grade and quantity. It is preferable not to mix different brands of oil in the rear axle.
2 Regularly wipe accumulated oil and dirt from the breather outlet located on the top of the axle casing.

3 Rear axle - removal and refitting

1 Remove the hub caps from the roadwheels and loosen the wheel nuts.
2 Jack-up the bodyframe at the rear of the vehicle and support it on stands or blocks.
3 Place a jack under the centre of the rear axle casing and raise it sufficiently to take its weight but without raising the vehicle any higher.
4 Disconnect the rear shock absorber lower mountings.
5 Mark the edges of the propeller shaft rear flange and the pinion driving flange so that they may reconnected in the same relative position to maintain the balance of the shaft.
6 Unscrew and remove the four bolts which secure the flanges and then remove the propeller shaft.
7 Loosen the locknut on the handbrake turnbuckle located above the propeller shaft, unscrew the turnbuckle to disconnect the cable.
8 Disconnect the flexible brake hose at the support bracket on the body side frame. Plug the open ends of the rigid and flexible lines.
9 Unscrew the nuts from the rear road spring 'U' bolts. Remove the 'U' bolts, spring seat location plates and seat pads.

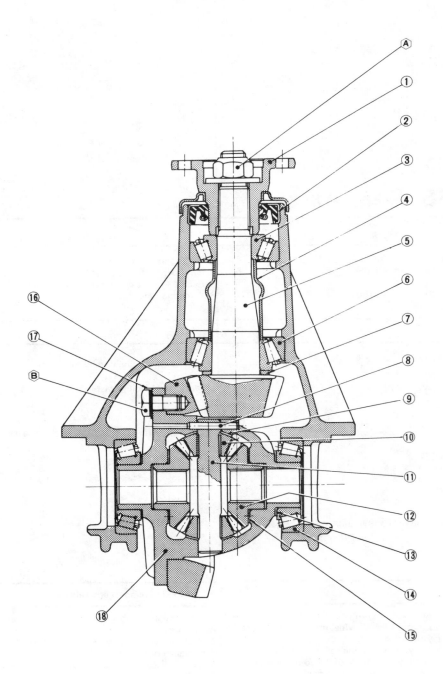

Fig 8.1 Sectional view of the differential carrier

1 Pinion driving flange	7 Pinion height adjusting washer	11 Pinion shaft	16 Crown wheel
2 Oil seal	8 Lock pin	12 Side gear	17 Lockplate
3 Pinion front bearing	9 Thrust washer	13 Thrust washer	18 Differential casing
4 Collapsible spacer	10 Pinion gear	14 Side bearing	A Pinion self-locking nut
5 Drive pinion		15 Shim	B Crownwheel bolt
6 Pinion rear bearing			

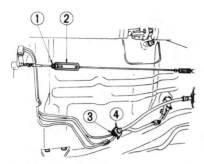

Fig 8.2 Location of brake components

1 *Locknut*
2 *Handbrake cable turnbuckle*
3 *Union nut*
4 *flexible hose retaining clip*

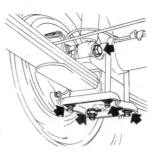

Fig. 8.3. Location of rear
shock absorber lower mounting
(Saloon and estate) and spring
'U' bolt nuts

Fig. 8.4. Location of rear
shock absorber lower mounting (Coupe) and spring 'U'
bolt nuts

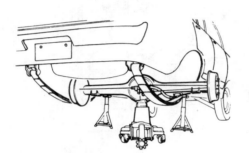

Fig 8.5 Removing rear axle complete

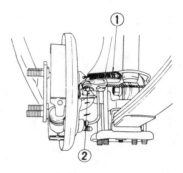

Fig 8.6 Handbrake cable (1) and
brake pipe (2) connections at
rear brake backplate

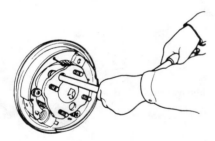

Fig 8.7 Removing a brake backplate securing nut

Fig 8.8 Extracting a halfshaft
using a slide hammer

The rear axle complete is now supported solely by the jack and may be withdrawn sideways through the space between the rear road spring and the bodyframe side member.

10 Refitting is a reversal of removal but the following points must be observed:

Tighten the nuts and bolts to specified torque.
Align the propeller shaft flange marks made before removal.
Bleed the brakes, as described in Chapter 9.
Adjust the handbrake cable, as described in Chapter 9.

4 Axle-halfshaft - removal and refitting

1 Jack-up the rear of the vehicle and support the axle casing securely on stnads.
2 Remove the roadwheel.
3 Disconnect the handbrake linkage and the hydraulic pipeline at the brake backplate. Plug the open end of the brake pipe and

the wheel cylinder to prevent loss of fluid and ingress of dirt.
4 Remove the brake drum.
5 Using a socket inserted through the hole in the axle-shaft flange, unscrew the four nuts from the bolts which retain the backplate to the axle casing.
6 A slide hammer should now be used to extract the axle-shaft complete with bearing and brake assembly. It is useless to attempt to pull the shaft from the axle casing, you will only succeed in pulling the vehicle from the stands. If a slide hammer is not available, an old wheel can be bolted to the hub and hammer blows given simultaneously at two opposite points on the rear (inner) edge of the wheel rim.
7 Refitting is a reversal of removal but before doing so it is recommended that a new oil seal is always installed as described in the next Section.

    Pass the halfshaft carefully through the oil seal, keeping the shaft quite parallel with the axle casing tube. When the splines on the end of the shaft engage with those in the differential unit carefully tap the shaft right home. Using a straight edge and

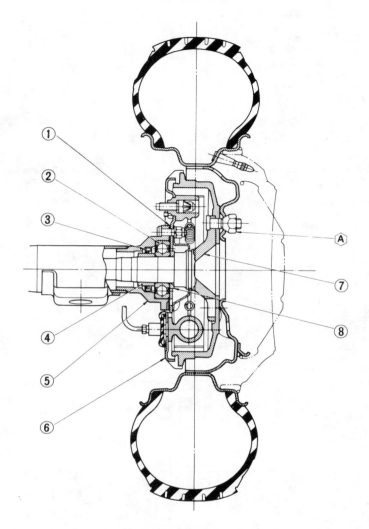

Fig 8.9 Sectional view of rear hub assembly

1 Shim	4 Bearing retaining collar	6 Brake backplate	8 Bearing spacer
2 Bearing	5 Casing	7 Halfshaft	A Wheel nut
3 Oil seal			

feeler gauge, check that the front face of the bearing does not project more than 0.0039 in. (0.1 mm) above the end face of the axle casing. If it does then a bearing adjusting shim must be obtained and fitted to the end face of the axle casing flange.

8 Tighten the backplate bolts to the specified torque, connect the handbrake linkage and brake pipe and then bleed the brakes, as described in Chapter 9.

9 Refit the roadwheel and lower the vehicle to the ground.

5 Axle-shaft oil seal - renewal

1 Oil seepage into the rear brake drums is an indication of failure of the axle housing oil seals. Where oil contamination is observed, always check that this is not, in fact, hydraulic brake fluid leaking from a faulty wheel operating cylinder.

2 Remove the axle halfshaft as described in the preceding Section.

3 Using a screwdriver as a lever prise the oil seal from the recess in the end of the axle casing.

4 Tap the new oil seal squarely into position using a piece of tube as a drift. Fill the space between the lips of the seal with grease.

5 Refit the axle-halfshaft, as described in Section 4.

6 Axle-shaft bearing - removal and refitting

1 The removal and fitting of halfshaft bearings and spacer/ collars is best left to a service station having suitable extracting and pressing equipment. Where the home mechanic has such facilities available, proceed as follows.

2 With the halfshaft removed as described in Section 4 secure it in a vice fitted with jaw protectors.

3 Using a sharp cold chisel, make several deep cuts in the collar at equidistant points. The collar can then be easily withdrawn from the axle shaft. Take great care not to damage or distort the axle shaft during this operation.

4 Using a suitable extractor, remove the bearing from the axle shaft and finally the bearing spacer.

5 Press wheel bearing grease into the bearing and then locate

the spacer, new bearing and new collar in position on the shaft. Press the components into position on the axle shaft using a suitable press to bear on the end of the collar.

6 Refit the axle-halfshaft (now reassembled) to the rear axle casing, as described in Section 4.

7 Differential carrier - removal and refitting

1 The overhaul of the rear axle differential unit is not within the scope of the home mechanic due to the specialized gauges and tools which are required. Where the unit requires servicing or repair due to wear or excessive noise it is most economical to exchange it for a factory reconditioned assembly and this Section is limited to a description of the removal and refitting procedure

2 Drain the oil from the rear axle.

3 Jack-up the axle and partially withdraw the axle-halfshafts, as described in Section 4 of this Chapter.

4 Disconnect and remove the propeller shaft as previously described.

5 Unscrew, evenly and in opposite sequence, the nuts from the ten differential unit securing studs. Pull the differential unit from the main axle casing.

6 Although only of academic interest, the new exposed crown wheel teeth should show a pinion tooth contact area as shown provided the differential unit was correctly set up originally.

7 Scrape all trace of old gasket from the mating surface of the axle casing. Locate a new gasket in position having first lightly coated it with jointing compound.

8 Clean the mating surface of the differential carrier and remove any burrs. Install the carrier so that the pinion is at the lowest point.

9 Tighten the securing nuts to the specified torque.

10 Refit the halfshafts and the propeller shaft.

11 Refit the roadwheels and lower the jack.

12 Fill the differential unit to the correct level with the specified grade of oil.

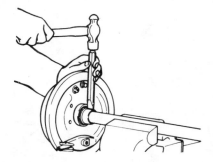

Fig 8.10 Cutting an axle-shaft bearing retaining collar

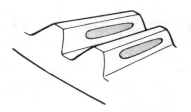

Fig 8.11 Crownwheel tooth marking when differential components correctly adjusted

8 Fault diagnosis - rear axle

Symptom	Reason/s
Noise on drive or overrun	Low oil level Loose crownwheel bolts Loose bearing cap bolts General wear in bearings or gearteeth.
Noise on turn	Seized, broken or damaged pinion or side gear or thrust washers.
Knock during gearshift or when taking up drive	Excessive crownwheel to pinion backlash Worn gears Worn halfshaft splines Drive pinion nut loose Loose crownwheel bolts or bearing cap bolts Worn side gear splines

Chapter 9 Braking system

Contents

Specifications

System type ...	Four wheel hydraulic with servo assistance. Front discs, rear drums, dual circuit. Mechanical handbrake on rear wheels only

Disc brakes

Disc outer diameter ...	9.65 in (245 mm))
Maximum run-out ...	0.0047 in. (0.12 mm)
Minimum disc thickness ...	0.331 in. (8.4 mm)
Pad dimensions:	
Long ...	2.496 in (63.4 mm)
Wide ...	1.622 in (41.2 mm)
Thick ...	0.394 in (10 mm)
Minimum thickness (friction material) ...	1/16 in. (1.6 mm)
Swept area (total front) ...	140 sq in. (903.3 sq cm)

Drum brakes

Drum inner diameter ...	8.000 in. (203.2 mm)
Out of round (maximum) ...	0.0008 in. (0.02 mm)
Internal diameter (regrind) limit ...	8.051 in. (204.5 mm)
Lining dimensions	
Long ...	7.680 in. (195.0 mm)
Wide ...	1.380 in. (35.0 mm)
Thick ...	0.190 in. (4.8 mm)
Swept area (total rear) ...	69.3 sq in. (445.2 sq cm)
Minimum thickness (friction material) ...	0.059 in. (1.5 mm)

Pedal height (top surface above metal floor)

Manual gearbox ...	6.140 in (156.0 mm)
Automatic transmission ...	6.220 in (158.0 mm)
Pedal free-play ...	0.039 to 0.197 in. (1.0 to 5.0 mm)
Master cylinder internal diameter ...	0.75 in (19.05 mm)
Wheel cylinder internal diameter ...	13/16 in. (20.64 mm)

Torque wrench settings	lb f ft	kg f m
Caliper securing bolt ...	53 to 72	7.3 to 9.9

Disc to hub bolts	...	...	...	...	...	...	...	...	40	5.5
Brake pedal pivot	...	...	...	...	...	...	...	...	20	2.8
Rear brake adjuster nuts	...	...	...	...	...	...	...	5	0.7
Rear brake backplate bolts	...	...	...	...	...	...	15	2.1
Master cylinder non-return valve plugs	...	...	...	...	40	5.5

1 General description

The braking system is four wheel, hydraulically operated with discs on the front and drums on the rear.

The hydraulic circuit is of dual type using a tandem master cylinder to ensure that in the event of a break or fault developing in one circuit, the remaining circuit remains fully operational.

A vacuum servo brake booster and fluid leakage indicator are fitted to all later model vehicles as in a pressure regulator valve to prevent the rear wheels locking under heavy braking applications.

A mechanically-operated handbrake is incorporated which operates on the rear wheels only.

2 Routine maintenance

1   Every 250 miles (400 km) or weekly, whichever occurs first, check the fluid level in both the master cylinder reservoirs. If necessary, top-up with fluid of the specified type which has been stored in an airtight container and has remained unshaken for the previous 24 hours.
2   Check that the reservoir cap breather holes are clear.
3   If topping-up is required frequently in one reservoir, inspect the hydraulic pipes of that particular circuit for leaks.
4   Every 3,000 miles (4,800 km) or more frequently if pedal travel becomes excessive, adjust the rear brakes, as described in Section 3.
5   At similar mileage intervals, remove the rear brake drums, inspect the linings and renew them if they are worn to 1/32in (0.8 mm) with bonded type, or with rivetted linings, down to the rivet heads. Where the linings are in good condition, brush out any dust from the rivet head recesses and the interior of the drums before refitting the drums.
6   Examine the thickness of the friction lining material of the front disc brake pads. If it is worn down to 1/16 in (1.6 mm) then all the disc pads should be renewed at one end the same time as a set. No adjustment is required to disc brakes.
7   Every 24,000 miles (38,000 km), bleed the hydraulic system of old fluid and refill with fresh.

8   Every 48,000 miles (77,000 km) renew all flexible hoses and rubber seals within the hydraulic components.

3 Rear drum brakes - adjustment

1   Release the handbrake fully and depress the footbrake pedal several times to position the shoes.
2   Chock the front wheels and then raise the rear roadwheels from the ground by placing a jack under the differential housing.
3   Turn the single adjuster on each brake backplate **in the same direction as the normal forward rotation of the roadwheel** until by turning the wheel, the brakes can be felt to bind. Now back off the adjuters until the shoes are no longer in contact with the drums.
4   Do not confuse transmission drag with rubbing shoe linings.
5   Apply the foot brake pedal hard and re-check the adjustment.

4 Rear brake shoes - renewal

1   Jack-up the rear axle differential carrier and support the axle casing on axle stands.
2   Remove the roadwheel and brake drum. (photo)
3   Release the backplate adjuster fully.
4   Using a pair of pliers, depress the shoe steady spring cup and turn it through 90°, then withdraw the cup and spring from the steady post. (photo)
5   Note and mark (or sketch if necessary), the relative positions of the shoes with regard to leading and trailing ends. (photo)
6   Using a pair of pliers, unhook the return springs from the holes in one of the shoe webbs and then remove the shoes and springs. (photos)
7   On no account depress the brake foot pedal while the shoes are removed or the wheel cylinder pistons will be ejected.
8   Install the new brake shoes by reversing the removal procedure but apply a trace of grease as shown to the backplate shoe engagement slots. Refit the drum and adjust the brakes as described in Section 3.
9   Check the reservoir fluid level for the rear hydraulic circuit.

4.2 Removing a rear brake drum

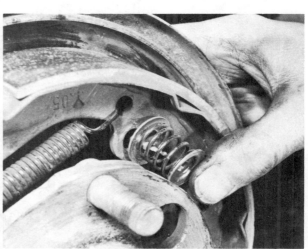

4.4 Removing a shoe steady spring and cup

4.5 Left rear brake assembly showing shoe positions

4.6A Removing shoe lower return spring

4.6B Prising away the lower end of the brake shoe

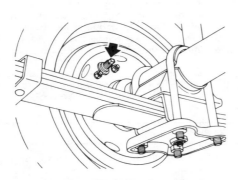

Fig 9.1 Rear brake adjuster

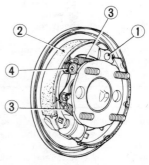

Fig 9.2 View of rear brake (drum removed)

1 Adjuster
2 Shoe
3 Shoe return springs
4 Shoe steady spring

Fig 9.3 Exploded view of a rear brake

1	Backplate	4	Brake shoe	7	Shoe steady spring and cup retainer
2	Bleed nipple	5	Shoe return spring	8	Shoe steady post
3	Wheel cylinder	6	Adjuster		

9 Handbrake lever
10 Lockplates and shims
11 Dust excluder

Fig 9.4 Grease application points on backplate

5 Front disc pads - renewal

1   Raise the front of the vehicle, support securely and remove the roadwheels.

2   Remove the spring clips from the retaining pins and then extract the retaining pins, coil springs and pad springs. (photos)

3   Using pliers, withdraw the pads from the caliper, together with anti-squeal shims (if fitted). (photos)

4   With the pads removed, on no account depress the brake foot pedal.

5   Brush out any dust from within the caliper body.

6   Unscrew the caliper bleed nipple so that by using the fingers, held square to the face of the outer piston, the piston can be depressed into the cylinder far enough to accommodate the new, thicker, inner pad. Only depress the piston the minimum amount needed to provide a wide enough gap for the pad, if it is pushed in too far, the piston seal will be damaged by the piston groove.

7   Now depress the inner piston into its cylinder by pulling the yoke of the caliper until sufficient gap is made to enable the new thicker outer pad to be installed. Install the anti-squeal shims (where fitted) with the arrow pointing upwards.

8   Tighten the bleed nipple, fit the pad pins and clips and then depress the brake pedal several times to settle the new pads.

9   Refit the roadwheel and lower the vehicle to the ground.

10 Check the reservoir fluid level for the front hydraulic circuit.

6 Flexible brake hoses - inspection, removal and installation

1   Periodically, inspect the condition of the flexible brake hoses. If they appear swollen, chafed or when bent double with the fingers tiny cracks are visible, then they must be renewed.

2   Always uncouple the rigid pipe from the flexible hose first, then release the end of the flexible hose from the support bracket. Now unscrew the flexible hose from the caliper or connector. If this method is followed, no kinking of the hose will occur. (photo)

3   When installing the hose, always use a new copper sealing washer.

4   When installation is complete, check that the flexible hose does not rub against the tyre or other adjacent components. Its attitude may be altered to overcome this by releasing its bracket support locknut and twisting the hose in the required direction by not more than one quarter turn.

5   Bleed the hydraulic system (Section 8).

5.2A Removing a clip from a disc pad retaining pin

5.2B Withdrawing a disc pad retaining pin

5.3A Withdrawing a disc pad

5.3B Disc pad anti-squeal shim

6.2 Flexible to rigid brake pipe union and support bracket

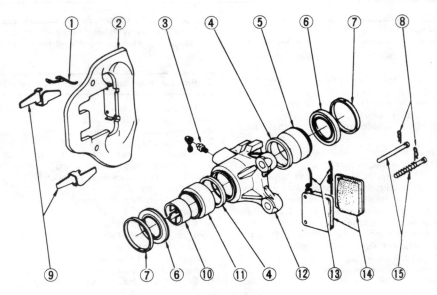

Fig 9.5 Exploded view of a disc caliper

1 Bias spring	5 Outer piston	9 Yoke spring	13 Pad spring
2 Yoke	6 Boot	10 Bias ring	14 Pad
3 Bleed nipple	7 Retaining ring	11 Inner piston	15 Retaining pin
4 Seal	8 Clip	12 Body	

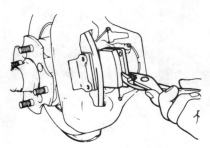

Fig 9.6 Withdrawing a disc pad

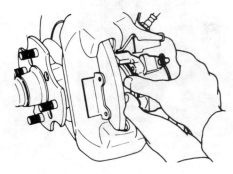

Fig 9.7 Depressing a caliper outer piston to accept new disc pad

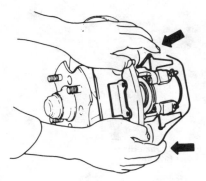

Fig 9.8 Depressing a caliper inner piston by pulling the yoke

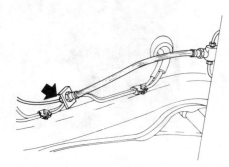

Fig 9.9 Typical installation of a flexible brake hose showing support bracket

7 Rigid brake lines - inspection, removal and installation

1 At regular intervals wipe the steel brake pipes clean and examine them for signs of rust or denting caused by flying stones.
2 Examine the fit of the pipes in their insulated securing clips and bend the tongues of the clips if necessary to ensure a positive fit.
3 Check that the pipes are not touching any adjacent components or rubbing against any part of the vehicle. Where this is observed, bend the pipe gently away to clear.
4 Any section of pipe which is rusty or chafed should be renewed. Brake pipes are available to the correct length and fitted with end unions from most Datsun dealers and can be made to pattern by many accessory suppliers. When installing the new pipes use the old pipes as a guide to bending and do not make any bends sharper than is necessary.
5 The system will of course have to be bled when the circuit has been reconnected.

8 Wheel cylinder seals - renewal

1 If hydraulic fluid is leaking from one of the brake cylinders it will be necessary to dismantle the cylinder and replace the dust cover and piston sealing rubber. If brake fluid is found running down the side of the wheel, or it is noticed that a pool of liquid forms alongside one wheel and the level in the master cylinder has dropped, and the hoses are in good order proceed as follows, there being no need to remove the wheel cylinder from the brake backplate.
2 Remove the brake drum and shoes as described in Section 4, remove the circlip and dust cover from the cylinder.
3 Take the piston complete with its seal out of the cylinder bore. Should the piston and seal prove difficult to remove, gentle pressure on the brake pedal will push it out of the bore. If this method is used place a quantity of rag under the brake backplate to catch the hydraulic fluid as it pours out of the cylinder.
4 Inspect the cylinder bore for score marks caused by impurities in the hydraulic fluid. If any are found the cylinder and piston will require renewal together as an exchange unit.
5 If the cylinder bore is sound, thoroughly clean it out with fresh hydraulic fluid.
6 The old rubber seal will probably be visibly worn or swollen. Detach it from the piston, smear a new rubber seal with hydraulic fluid and assemble it to the piston with the flat face of the seal next to the piston rear shoulder.
7 Reassembly is a direct reversal of the above procedure. If the rubber dust cap appears to be worn or damaged this should also be renewed.
8 Replenish the hydraulic fluid, replace the brake shoes and drum and bleed the braking system, as described in Section 16.

9 Wheel cylinder - removal and installation

1 Remove the brake drum and shoes.
2 Disconnect the handbrake cable from the lever on the wheel cylinder.
3 Unscrew the union and disconnect the brake pipe from the wheel cylinder. Plug the line to prevent loss of fluid and ingress of dirt.
4 Remove the dust cover from the wheel cylinder aperture and slide out the lockplate and adjustment shims. Note their sequence of fitting and number according to make of cylinder.
5 Installation is a reversal of removal but smear the lockplates and shims with grease before installing them in their correct sequence.
6 When installation is complete, bleed the hydraulic system and check the sliding resistance of the cylinder. This should be between 5 and 15 lb (2.3 and 6.8 kg) checked with a spring balance attached to the wheel cylinder.

10 Caliper unit - removal and installation

1 Remove the disc pads, as described in Section 5.
2 Disconnect the brake hose from the caliper. To do this, first disconnect the rigid line from the flexible hose at the support bracket union and then unscrew the flexible hose. Plug the open ends of the pipes.
3 Unbolt the caliper from the stub axle and lift it away from the disc.
4 Installation is a reversal of removal but tighten the securing bolts to specified torque and when installation is complete, bleed the hydraulic system.

11 Caliper unit - dismantling and reassembly

1 Drain the brake fluid from the caliper through the flexible hose connection.
2 Unscrew and remove the bleed nipple.
3 Depress each piston in turn as described in Section 5.
4 Secure the longer edge of the caliper yoke in a vice and tap the top of the yoke lightly with a hammer. This action will disconnect the caliper body from the yoke.
5 Remove the bias ring from the inner piston.
6 Remove the retaining rings and boots from the ends of both pistons.
7 Eject both pistons. This may be achieved by blocking the fluid inlet hole and applying air pressure at the bleed nipple hole.
8 Carefully extract the piston seals from their grooves in the cylinders.
9 Detach the spring from the yoke.
10 Clean all components in methylated spirit or clean hydraulic fluid. Inspect the cylinder walls for scoring, bright spots or corrosion. Where these are evident, renew the complete caliper assembly.
11 Obtain a repair kit which will contain all the necessary seals and replacement parts. Check that the rubber seals have not deteriorated or become deformed in storage.
12 Dip the new seals in hydraulic fluid and locate them in their grooves in the cylinder bores. Use only the fingers to manipulate them into position. Note the correct fitting of the seal chamfer.
13 Insert the bias ring into the inner piston so that the radiused corner of the ring is to the bottom. Make sure that the inner and outer pistons are correctly identified.
14 Dip each of the pistons in clean hydraulic fluid and insert them into their respective cylinders. Do not push the pistons too far into their cylinders or the seal will be damaged by the piston groove. Position the inner piston so that the yoke groove of the bias ring coincides with the yoke groove of the cylinder.
15 Install the boots and retaining rings.
16 Install the yoke springs.
17 Fit the bias spring to the yoke.
18 Apply a smear of brake grease to the yoke sliding surface of the cylinder body then reposition the bias ring so that the groove of the bias ring coincides with the yoke.
19 With the yoke spring located in the groove in the cylinder, connect the cylinder body and yoke by applying pressure with the thumbs.
20 Screw in the bleed nipple.

12 Master cylinder - removal and installation

1 Disconnect both fluid pipes from the master cylinder body and push a cap over the open ends of the pipes to prevent dirt entering the system.
2 Unscrew and remove the two master cylinder flange securing nuts and withdraw the unit from the front of the brake vacuum servo unit (later vehicles) or from the engine compartment rear bulkhead (early models).
3 Installation is a reversal of removal but the hydraulic system must be bled as described in Section 16.

120

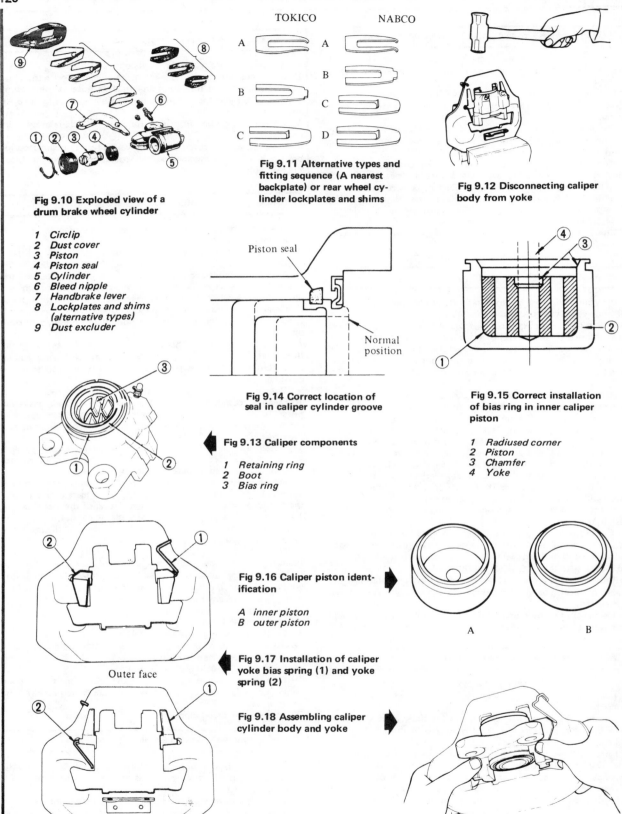

TOKICO **NABCO**

Fig 9.11 Alternative types and fitting sequence (A nearest backplate) or rear wheel cylinder lockplates and shims

Fig 9.12 Disconnecting caliper body from yoke

Fig 9.10 Exploded view of a drum brake wheel cylinder

1 Circlip
2 Dust cover
3 Piston
4 Piston seal
5 Cylinder
6 Bleed nipple
7 Handbrake lever
8 Lockplates and shims (alternative types)
9 Dust excluder

Piston seal

Normal position

Fig 9.14 Correct location of seal in caliper cylinder groove

Fig 9.15 Correct installation of bias ring in inner caliper piston

1 Radiused corner
2 Piston
3 Chamfer
4 Yoke

Fig 9.13 Caliper components

1 Retaining ring
2 Boot
3 Bias ring

Outer face

Inner face

Fig 9.16 Caliper piston identification

A inner piston
B outer piston

A   B

Fig 9.17 Installation of caliper yoke bias spring (1) and yoke spring (2)

Fig 9.18 Assembling caliper cylinder body and yoke

13 Master cylinder - dismantling and reassembly

1 Clean all dirt from the external surfaces of the master cylinder body, taking care that none enters the fluid outlet holes.
2 Remove the reservoir caps and filters and tip out the brake fluid.
3 Extract the circlip from the end of the cylinder body.
4 Unscrew and remove the stop bolt and then extract the stop ring, the primary piston assembly, the spring and the secondary piston assembly.
5 At this stage examine the surfaces of the pistons and cylinder bore. If there is evidence of scoring or 'bright' wear areas, the complete master cylinder must be renewed as an assembly.
6 Where the components are in good condition, discard all rubber seals and obtain a repair kit which will contain all the necessary items for renewal.
7 Do not detach the reservoirs from the master cylinder body. Should this be necessary for any reason, new reservoirs must be fitted.
8 If the non-return valves require attention, secure the master cylinder body in the jaws of a vice and unscrew the plugs.
9 Clean all components in methylated spirit or clean hydraulic fluid.
10 Manipulate the new seals into position using the fingers only.
11 Dip the internal components in clean hydraulic fluid and insert them into the master cylinder body in the reverse sequence to dismantling.
12 Tighten the non-return valve plugs to the specified torque.

14 Pressure regulating valve

1 This device is installed on the engine rear bulkhead and regulates the pressure applied in the front and rear hydraulic circuits to prevent the rear wheels locking before the front ones.
2 Periodically, test the functioning of the valve by driving the vehicle on a quiet or private road at about 31 mph (50 kmh) and apply the brakes suddenly. Observe the tyre tracks which should show that the front wheels lock ahead of the rear ones.
3 Where this is not the case, renew the valve and bleed the system.

15 Pressure differential indicator switch

1 With dual circuit hydraulic braking systems, a switch is fitted to the engine rear bulkhead to monitor any drop in pressure in either of the circuits.
2 The switch is essentially a piston which is kept in balance when the pressure in the front and rear hydraulic circuits is displaced by the greater pressure existing in the non-leaking circuit and makes an electrical contact to illuminate a warning lamp on the vehicle facia.
3 In the event of the warning lamp coming on, check immediately to establish the source of fluid leakage. This may be in the rigid or flexible pipes or more likely, at the wheel operating cylinders, master cylinder or caliper units.
4 When the faulty component has been repaired or renewed, bleed the brakes as described in Section 16, of this Chapter, when the pressure differential switch piston will automatically return to its 'in balance' position.
5 In the event of a fault developing in the switch itself, renew it as an assembly.

16 Hydraulic system - bleeding

1 Removal of air from the hydraulic system is essential to the correct operation of the brakes. Whenever either of the hydraulic circuits has been 'broken' or a component removed and replaced, the system must be bled.
2 If the master cylinder has been removed and replaced, initial bleeding should be carried out using the nipples on the master cylinder body.
3 An indication of air in the system is a 'spongy' pedal or when the pedal travel is reduced by repeated applications of the brakes. In the latter case, the trouble may be due to a worn or faulty master cylinder and this should be rectified immediately.
4 If there is any possibility of incorrect fluid having been put into the system, drain all the fluid out and flush through with methylated spirit. Renew all piston seals and cups since these will be affected and could possibly fail under pressure.
5 Gather together a clean jam jar, a length of tubing which fits tightly over the bleed nipples, and a tin of the correct brake fluid.
6 To bleed the system clean the areas around the bleed valves, and start on the front brakes first by removing the rubber cap over the bleed valve, and fitting a rubber tube in position. (photo)
7 Place the end of the tube in a clean glass jar containing sufficient fluid to keep the end of the tube submerged during the operation.

8 Open the bleed valve with a spanner and quickly press down the brake pedal. After slowly releasing the pedal, pause for a moment to allow the fluid to recoup in the master cylinder and then depress again. This will force air from the system. Continue until no more air bubbles can be seen coming from the tube. At intervals make certain that the reservoir is kept topped up, otherwise air will enter at this point again. Tighten the bleed valve when the pedal is fully depressed.
9 Continue the operations on the rear brakes.
10 Always discard fluid which has been bled from the system and top-up the system with fluid which has been stored in an airtight container and has remained unshaken for the preceding 24 hrs.

17 Handbrake - adjustment

1 The handbrake is adjusted automatically whenever the rear brake shoes are adjusted. However, due to cable stretch, additional adjustment may be required when the handbrake lever can be pulled more than six notches (clicks) to the full-on position.
2 Carry out the adjustment by slackening the locknut on the turnbuckle which is located above the propeller shaft and joints the handbrake cable sections together. Rotate the turnbuckle sufficiently to bring the handbrake lever movement within that specified and tighten the locknut. (photo)
3 Jack-up the rear roadwheels and check that the rear brake shoes do not bind when the handbrake is fully off.

18 Handbrake cables - renewal

1 Separate the primary and rear cables by unscrewing the turnbuckle which is located above the propeller shaft.
2 Remove the lockplate which is located just ahead of the turnbuckle.
3 From inside the vehicle, remove the cable clip.
4 Remove the handbrake lever shroud and then disconnect the lead from the handbrake warning switch (see next Section).
5 Unbolt the handbrake lever from the floor and withdraw the lever/cable assembly.
6 The primary cable may now be removed from the handbrake lever and a new one fitted.
7 To remove the rear cables, jack-up the rear of the vehicle and support securely on stands. Remove the roadwheels.
8 Detach the two return springs.
9 Disconnect the cables from the clevis forks on the wheel operating cylinder levers.
10 Remove the lockplate from the bracket on the rear axle casing and disconnect the cable.

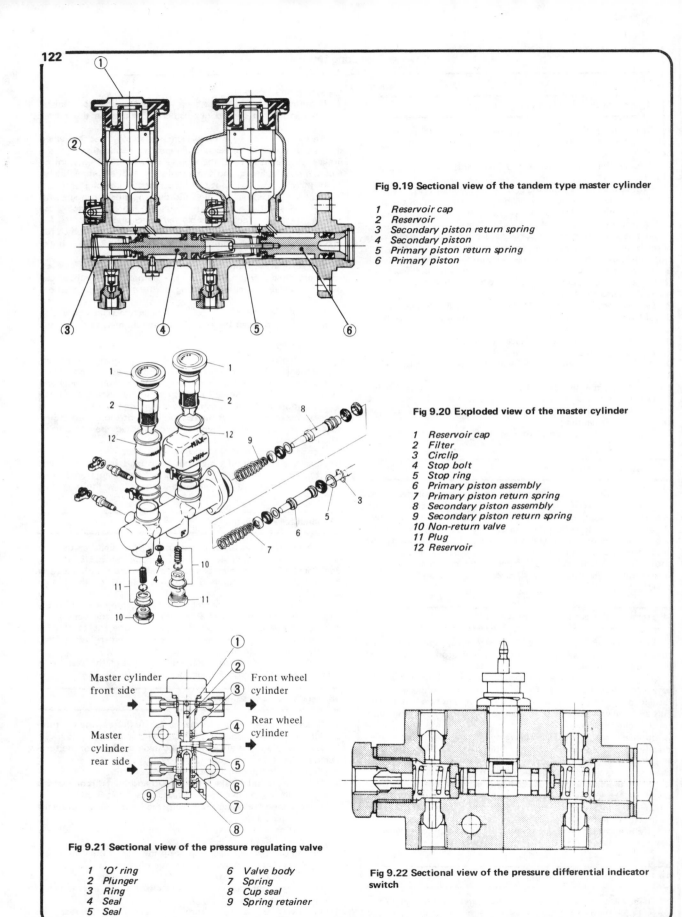

Fig 9.19 Sectional view of the tandem type master cylinder

1 Reservoir cap
2 Reservoir
3 Secondary piston return spring
4 Secondary piston
5 Primary piston return spring
6 Primary piston

Fig 9.20 Exploded view of the master cylinder

1 Reservoir cap
2 Filter
3 Circlip
4 Stop bolt
5 Stop ring
6 Primary piston assembly
7 Primary piston return spring
8 Secondary piston assembly
9 Secondary piston return spring
10 Non-return valve
11 Plug
12 Reservoir

Master cylinder front side

Front wheel cylinder

Master cylinder rear side

Rear wheel cylinder

Fig 9.21 Sectional view of the pressure regulating valve

1 'O' ring
2 Plunger
3 Ring
4 Seal
5 Seal
6 Valve body
7 Spring
8 Cup seal
9 Spring retainer

Fig 9.22 Sectional view of the pressure differential indicator switch

123

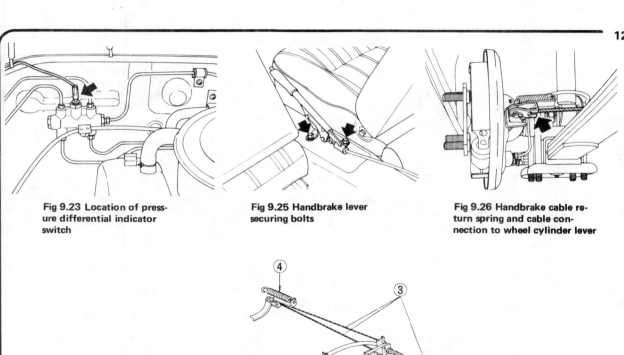

Fig 9.23 Location of pressure differential indicator switch

Fig 9.25 Handbrake lever securing bolts

Fig 9.26 Handbrake cable return spring and cable connection to wheel cylinder lever

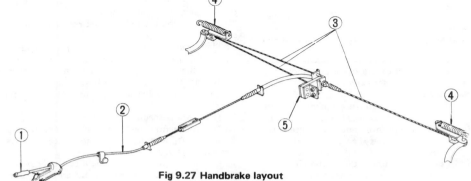

Fig 9.27 Handbrake layout

1 Lever
2 Primary cable

3 Rear cables

4 Return springs

5 Hanger

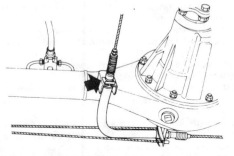

Fig 9.28 Handbrake lockplate and bracket on rear axle casing

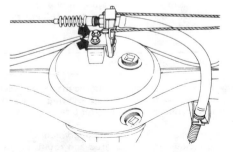

Fig 9.29 Handbrake cable hanger strap bolts

16.6 Caliper bleed nipple and cap with bleed hose attached

17.2 Handbrake cable turn-buckle adjuster

11 Unbolt the hanger strap from the rear of the axle casing and lift the complete rear cable assembly away.
12 The cables may now be renewed as necessary.
13 Installation of the primary cable or the rear cables is a reversal of removal. When installation is complete, adjust as described in the preceding Section.

19 Handbrake warning switch

1 The handbrake warning 'ON' switch is mounted to the rear of the handbrake lever and is actuated by a tab on the handbrake which depresses the switch plunger to break the warning lamp circuit in the 'lever released' position with the ignition switched on.
2 Apart from checking the security of the connecting lead, any fault will necessitate renewal of the switch which is a press fit in its support bracket.

20 Brake pedal and stop lamp switch - adjustment, removal and installation

1 The height of the upper surface of the pedal pad above the metal surface of the floor must be as shown in the diagram (Fig. 9.31) according to transmission type.
2 Adjustment is carried out by releasing the locknut on the stoplamp switch and moving the switch as necessary.
3 Now release the locknut on the pushrod and rotate the pushrod to give a pedal free-movement of between 0.039 and 0.197 in (1.0 to 5.0 mm).
4 To remove the brake pedal, withdrawn the spring clip from the clevis pin, withdraw the clevis pin and detach the pushrod from the pedal arm.
5 Unscrew and remove the pivot bolt and then withdraw the pedal and return spring.
6 Installation is a reversal of removal but lightly grease the pivot bolt, pedal arm bush and return spring before fitting. Ensure that the pivot bolt head is on the left-hand side when looking towards the front of the vehicle.

21 Brake servo unit - removal and installation

1 Disconnect the hydraulic pipes from the master cylinder.
2 Unscrew and remove the two flange securing nuts and withdraw the master cylinder from the front face of the vacuum servo unit.
3 Disconnect the vacuum hose from the servo unit.
4 Release the locknut on the pushrod and rotate the pushrod until it is unscrewed from the clevis fork.
5 Unscrew and remove the nuts from the four mounting studs and withdraw the servo unit from the engine compartment rear bulkhead.
6 Installation is a reversal of removal but adjust the pedal free movement as described in the preceding Section and bleed the hydraulic system (Section 16).
7 Whenever the fluid levels in the master cylinder reservoirs are being checked, inspect the condition and security of the vacuum hose which runs from the inlet manifold to the servo unit.
8 Incorporated in this hose is a non-return valve which is the most likely component to cause faulty operation of the brake booster facility.
9 Should the valve require renewal, make sure that it is installed in the vacuum hose the correct way round as shown in the illustration.

22 Brake servo unit - overhaul

1 A brake vacuum servo unit will normally give trouble-free service over a very high mileage and when a fault does eventually develop, it is recommended that the unit is renewed complete on an exchange basis.
2 For those wishing to undertake the servicing however, the following operations should be carried out.
3 Clean the external surfaces of dirt and grease.
4 Mark the relationship of the front and rear shells so that they can be refitted in their original positions.
5 Secure the unit vertically in a vice fitted with jaw protectors. Grip the edges of the front flange in the vice jaws.
6 Remove the pushrod locknut and the flexible bellows.
7 A tool will now have to be made up to unlock the rear shell from the front shell. The tool must locate securely on the four mounting studs of the rear shell and a diagram of a suitable device is shown. Do not improvise by placing a lever between two of the studs or irreparable damage will result.
8 Using the tool release the rear shell by turning it in an anti-clockwise direction.
9 Remove the diaphragm plate and valve body, followed by the diaphragm spring and pushrod.
10 Prise off the retainer and extract the bearing and valve body seal.
11 Place the diaphragm plate assembly on a clean surface and detach the diaphragm from the groove in the plate.
12 Prise the air silencer retainer from the diaphragm plate.
13 Extract the silencer and filter.
14 Extract the valve plunger stop key and remove the plunger assembly.
15 Remove the reaction disc.
16 Now dismantle the front shell by unscrewing the two flange securing nuts and removing the flange and the plate and seal assembly.
17 Obtain a repair kit which will contain new seals and specified grease. Commence reassembly by applying some of the grease supplied to the valve body seal lip and then install it in the rear shell using a tubular drift. The seal should be installed in accordance with the dimensions shown in the diagram. Install the bearing and retainer.
18 Apply specified grease to the new plunger assembly at the points indicated and install it, using a new stop key.
19 Fit a new silencer, silencer filter and silencer retainer.
20 Install a new diaphragm to the diaphragm plate/valve body assembly.
21 Lightly smear a new reaction disc with specified grease and install it in the diaphragm plate.
22 Install the plate and seal assembly to the front shell after smearing specified grease to the edge of the seal and the contact surface of the shell.
23 Apply a little specified grease to the shell contact surfaces of the diaphragm and then locate it correctly so that with the diaphragm spring in position, the rear shell can be assembled to the front shell by using the special tool and turning the shell in a clockwise direction to the limit of its travel in the retaining notches.
24 Adjust the projection of the pushrod in accordance with the diagram. To do this, grip the serrated portion of the pushrod and release the locknut.

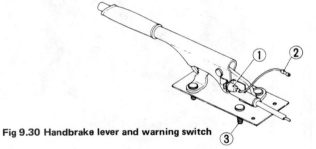

Fig 9.30 Handbrake lever and warning switch

1 *Switch*
2 *Terminal connector*
3 *Securing bolt*

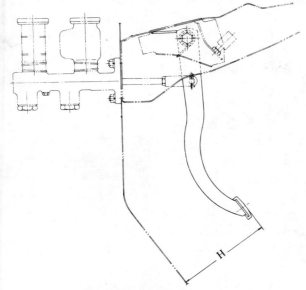

Fig 9.31 Pedal height setting diagram

H = Manual gearbox 6.14 in. (156.0 mm)
    Automatic transmission 6.22 in. (158.0 mm)

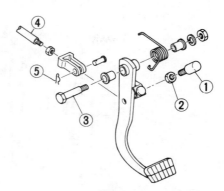

Fig 9.32 Exploded view of the brake pedal

1 Stoplamp switch
2 Locknut
3 Pivot bolt
4 Pushrod
5 Spring clip

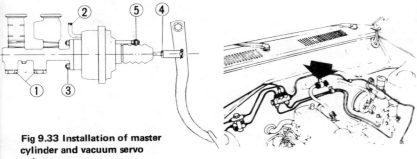

Fig 9.33 Installation of master
cylinder and vacuum servo
unit

1 Master cylinder
2 Vacuum connection
3 Mounting nut
4 Pushrod locknut
5 Filter silencer

Fig 9.34 Location of vacuum
servo non-return valve

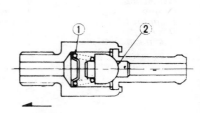

Manifold side

Fig 9.35 Correct orientation
of servo non-return valve

1 Spring
2 Valve

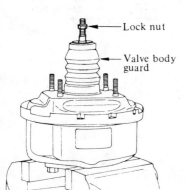

Lock nut

Valve body
guard

Fig 9.36 Servo unit ready for
dismantling

Fig 9.37 Suggested servo shell
removal tool

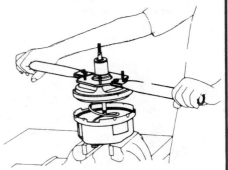

Fig 9.38 Releasing servo unit
rear shell

126

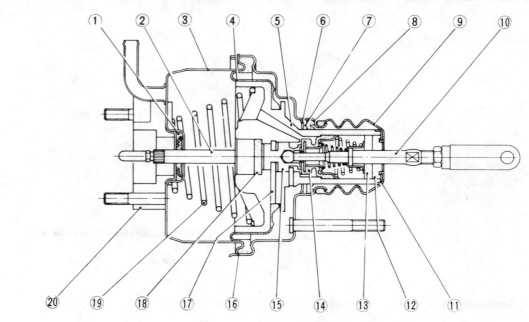

Fig 9.39 Sectional view of the vacuum servo unit

1 Front shell plate and
   seal assembly
2 Push-rod
3 Front shell
4 Diaphragm
5 Diaphragm plate and

   valve body
6 Retainer
7 Bearing
8 Valve body seal
9 Valve body boot
10 Operating rod

11 Silencer retainer
12 Filter
13 Silencer (rubber)
14 Poppet assembly
15 Plunger assembly
16 Rear shell

17 Valve plunger stop
   key
18 Reaction disc
19 Diaphragm return spring
20 Flange

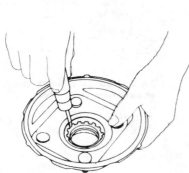

Fig 9.40 Prising off bearing retainer from rear shell of servo unit

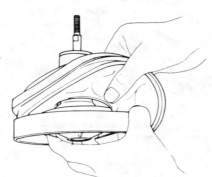

Fig 9.41 Separating flexible diaphragm from plate of servo unit

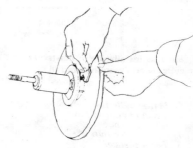

Fig 9.42 Removing servo unit valve plunger stop key

Fig 9.43 Removing servo unit valve plunger assembly

Fig 9.44 Removing the reaction disc from the servo unit

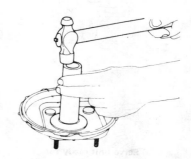

Fig 9.45 Installing valve body seal to servo rear shell

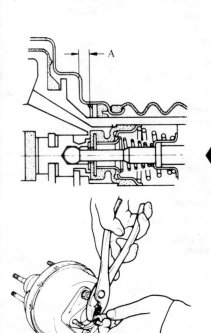

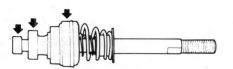

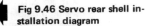

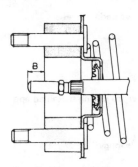

Fig 9.47 Servo plunger assembly grease application points

Fig 9.46 Servo rear shell installation diagram

A = 0.264 to 0.276 in. (6.7 to 7.0 mm)

Fig 9.48 Servo pushrod projection

B = 0.3839 to 0.3937 in. (9.75 to 10.0 mm)

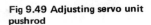

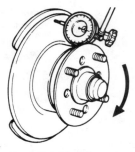

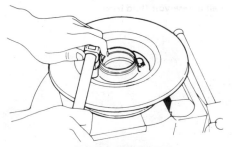

Fig 9.49 Adjusting servo unit pushrod

Fig 9.50 Checking disc run-out with a dial gauge

Fig 9.51 Removing disc from hub

23 Brake disc and drum - examination and renovation

1   After a considerable mileage the internal diameter of the rear drums may become out of round, worn beyond the permissible limit, or tapered.

2   Dependent upon whether the brake shoes have been renewed before the rivets have scored the internal surface of the drum, so the drums may require renewal or regrinding particularly if deep scoring is visible.

3   Where any of the foregoing conditions are evident, remove the drums and either renew them or have them professionally ground, always provided that the new dimensions do not exceed the tolerances given in Specifications Section.

4   The appearance of the front discs will show even light scoring which is normal. Any deep grooves will indicate the need for renewal or grinding as will excessive run-out, measured with a dial gauge.

5   Always check the tolerances specified in Specifications Section before having an original disc ground or refaced. A disc can be detached from the hub after unscrewing the securing bolts.

24 Fault diagnosis - braking system

Symptom	Reason/s
Brake grab	Out of round drums. Excessive run-out of discs. Rust on drum or disc. Oil stained linings or pads.
Brake drag	Faulty master cylinder. Foot pedal return impeded. Reservoir breather blocked. Seized caliper or wheel cylinder piston. Incorrect adjustment of handbrake. Weak or broken shoe return springs. Crushed, blocked or swollen pipe lines.
Excessive pedal effort required	Linings or pads not yet bedded-in. Drum, disc or linings contaminated with oil or grease. Scored drums or discs. Faulty vacuum servo unit.
Brake pedal feels hard	Glazed surfaces of friction material. Rust on disc surfaces. Seized caliper or wheel cylinder piston.

Excessive pedal travel

Low reservoir fluid level.
Disc run-out excessive.
Worn front wheel bearings.
Air in system.
Worn pads or linings.
Rear brakes requires adjustment.

Pedal creep during sustained application

Fluid leak.
Internal fault in master cylinder.
Faulty servo unit non-return valve.

Pedal "spongy"

Air in system.
Perished flexible hose.
Loose master cylinder mounting nuts.
Cracked brake drum.
Faulty master cylinder.
Reservoir breather blocked.
Linings not bedded-in.

Fall in reservoir fluid level

Normal due to pad or lining wear.
Leak in hydraulic system.

Chapter 10 Electrical system

Contents

Specifications

Battery

Capacity at 20 hour rate	40 amp/hr
Voltage	12
Earth (ground)	Negative (−)

Alternator

Types:

B210	Hitachi LT 135-13B or LT 150-05
120Y	Hitachi LT 125-06

	LT 125-06	LT 135-13B	LT 150-05
Rating	25 amp	35 amp	50 amp
Brush length (new)	0.57 in (14.5 mm)		
Minimum brush length	0.28 in (7.0 mm)		

Voltage regulator/cut-out

Type:

B210	Hitachi TL1Z-79
120Y	Hitachi TL1Z-37

Regulator

Regulating voltage	14.3 to 15.3 volts at 68°F (20°C)
Core gap	0.024 to 0.039 in (0.6 to 1.0 mm)
Points gap	0.012 to 0.016 in (0.3 to 0.4 mm)

Cut-out

Release voltage	4.2 to 5.2 volts at 'N' terminal
Core gap	0.031 to 0.039 in (0.8 to 1.0 mm)
Points gap	0.016 to 0.024 in (0.4 to 0.6 mm)

Starter motor

Make and type:

Manual transmission	Hitachi S114 - 87M
Automatic transmission	Hitachi S114 - 156
Drive	Pre-engaged
Output	1.0 kw

Brush length (new):

S114 - 87M	0.63 in (16.0 mm)
S114 - 156	0.55 in (14.0 mm)

Minimum brush length:
S114 - 87M	0.256 in (6.5 mm)		
S114 - 156	0.177 in (4.5 mm)		

Fuses

	B210		120Y
Number and rating	2 x 10 amp	RHD	4 x 15 amp
			3 x 10 amp
			1 x 8 amp
	6 x 15 amp	LHD	3 x 15 amp or 2 x 15 amp
			3 x 10 amp 6 x 10 amp

Bulbs (wattage)

	B210	120Y
Headlamp	50/40	
Front direction indicator/parking	23/8	21/5
Side marker	8	10
License plate	7.5	10
Rear direction indicator	23	21
Stop/tail	23/8	21/5
Reversing lamp	23	21
Interior	10	10
Automatic transmission speed indicator	3.4	3.4
Switch knob illumination	3.4	3.4
All indicator and instrumentation lamps	3.4	3.4

Torque wrench settings

	lb f ft	kg f m
Alternator pulley nut	30	4.1
Wiper arm to spindle nut	10	1.4

1 General description

The electrical system is of 12 volts, negative earth. The major components comprise a lead acid type battery; an alternator; belt driven from the crankshaft pulley; and a pre-engaged starter motor.

The battery supplies a steady current to the ignition system and for all the electrical accessories. The alternator maintains the charge in the battery and the voltage regulator adjusts the charging rate according to the battery's demands. The cut-out prevents the battery discharging to earth through the alternator when the engine is switched off and current generation stops.

2 Battery - removal and refitting

1   The battery is located at the front on the right-hand side of the engine compartment.
2   Disconnect the negative terminal first whenever servicing the battery.
3   Then remove the positive terminal, and remove the battery frame holding-down screws and lift the frame away.
4   Lift out the battery carefully to avoid spilling electrolyte on the paintwork.
5   Replacement is a reversal of removal procedure but when reconnecting the terminals, clean off any white deposits present and smear with petroleum jelly.

3 Battery - maintenance and inspection

1   Keep the top of the battery clean by wiping away dirt and moisture.
2   Remove the plugs or lid from the cells and check that the electrolyte level is just above the separator plates. If the level has fallen, add only distilled water until the electrolyte level is just above the separator plates.
3   As well as keeping the terminals clean and covered with petroleum jelly, the top of the battery, and especially the top of the cells, should be kept clean and dry. This helps prevent corrosion and ensures that the battery does not become partially discharged by leakage through dampness and dirt.
4   Once every three months, remove the battery and inspect the battery securing bolts, the battery clamp plate, tray and battery leads for corrosion (white fluffy deposits on the metal which are brittle to touch). If any corrosion is found, clean off the deposits with ammonia and paint over the clean metal with an anti-rust/anti-acid paint.
5   At the same time inspect the battery case for cracks. If a crack is found, clean and plug it with one of the proprietary compounds marketed, for this purpose. If leakage through the crack has been excessive then it will be necessary to refill the appropriate cell with fresh electrolyte as detailed later. Cracks are frequently caused to the top of the battery cases by pouring in distilled water in the middle of winter *after* instead of *before* a run.
This gives the water no chance to mix with the electrolyte and so the former freezes and splits the battery case.
6   If topping up the battery becomes excessive and the case has been inspected for cracks that could cause leakage, but none are found, the battery is being over-charged and the voltage regulator will have to be checked and reset (Section 12).
7   The specific gravity of a fully charged battery when tested with a hydrometer at an electrolyte temperature of 68°F (20°C) should be 1.260 with a variation between cells not exceeding 0.025.

Fig 10.1 Testing a battery for level of charge

1 *Thermometer*
2 *Hydrometer*

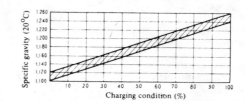

Fig 10.2 Relationship of specific gravity reading to battery charge

4 Electrolyte replenishment

1 If the battery is in a fully charged state and one of the cells maintains a specific gravity reading which is .025 or more lower than the others, and a check of each cell has been made with a voltage meter to check for short circuits (a four to seven second test should give a steady reading of between 1.2 to 1.8 volts), then it is likely that electrolyte has been lost from the cell with the low reading at some time.
2 Top-up the cell with a solution of 1 part sulphuric acid to 2.5 parts of water. If the cell is already fully topped up draw some electrolyte out of it with a pipette. The total capacity of each cell is ¾ pint.
3 When mixing the sulphuric acid and water **never add water to sulphuric acid** - always pour the acid slowly onto the water in a glass container. **If water is added to sulphuric acid it will explode.**
4 Continue to top-up the cell with the freshly made electrolyte and then recharge the battery and check the hydrometer readings.

5 Battery charging

1 In winter time when heavy demand is placed upon the battery, such as when starting from cold, and much electrical equipment is continually in use, it is a good idea to occasionally have the battery fully charged from an external source at the rate of 3.5 or 4 amps.
2 Continue to charge the battery at this rate until no further rise in specific gravity is noted over a four hour period.
3 Alternatively, a trickle charger charging at the rate of 1.5 amps can be safely used overnight.
4 Specially rapid 'boost' charges which are claimed to restore the power of the battery in 1 to 2 hours are most dangerous as they can cause serious damage to the battery plates.
5 Take extreme care when making circuit connections to a vehicle fitted with an alternator and observe the following. When making connections to the alternator from a battery always match correct polarity. Before using electric-arc welding equipment to repair any part of the vehicle, disconnect the connector from the alternator and disconnect the positive battery terminal. Never start the car with a battery charger connected. Always disconnect both battery leads before using a mains charger. If boosting from another battery, always connect in parallel using heavy cable.

6 Alternator - maintenance

1 Maintenance consists of occasionally wiping away any dirt or oil which may have collected on the unit.
2 Check the tension of the driving belt every 6,000 miles (9,600 km) and adjust if necessary as described in Chapter 1, Section 42 to give a ½ in (12.7 mm) total free-movement at the centre of the top run of the belt.
3 No lubrication is required as the bearings of the alternator are sealed for life.

7 Alternator - removal and refitting

1 Loosen the alternator mounting bracket bolts and strap, push the unit towards the engine block sufficiently far to enable the fan belt to be slipped off the alternator pulley.
2 Remove the cable connectors from the alternator and withdraw the mounting bracket bolts. Lift away the alternator.
3 Replacement is a reversal of removal procedure but ensure that the connections are correctly made and that the drivebelt is correctly tensioned.

8 Alternator - testing and servicing

1 It is not recommended that testing of an alternator should be undertaken at home due to the testing equipment required and the possibility of damage occurring during testing. It is best left to automotive electrical specialists.
2 To dismantle the alternator in order to renew faulty components carry out the following operations.
3 Remove the pulley nut and withdraw the pulley using a suitable extractor. Lift off the fan and spacer.
4 Unscrew the brush holder cover screws and remove the cover.
5 Push the brush holder forward and remove it together with the brushes. Do not disconnect the 'N' terminal from the stator coil lead.
6 Unscrew and remove the tie bolts.
7 Separate the rotor/front cover assembly from the stator/rear cover by carefully tapping the front bracket with a soft-faced mallet.
8 Unscrew the three set screws from the bearing retainer and separate the rotor from the front cover.
9 Remove the rear bearing from the rotor shaft using a two-legged extractor.
10 Remove the securing screw and withdraw the diode cover.
11 Disconnect the three stator coil leads from the diode terminal by the careful use of soldering iron.
12 Unscrew the 'A' terminal nut and diode securing nut and withdraw the diode assembly.
13 If the brushes are worn beyond their specified limit (indicated by a line on some brushes), renew them, making sure that they move freely in the holder.
14 Reassembly is a reversal of dismantling but observe the following:

(i) *When soldering each stator coil lead to the diode assembly, work as quickly as possible in order to localise the heat.*
(ii) *When fitting the diode 'A' terminal, check that the components are installed in the correct sequence as illustrated.*

15 Tighten the pulley retaining nut to the specified torque. In order to avoid distorting the pulley, locate an old drivebelt in the pulley groove and then grip the belt as close to the pulley as possible in the jaws of a vice. When the nut is tightened, the pulley will be prevented from turning.

9 Starter motor - general description

1 This type of starter motor incorporates a solenoid mounted on top of the starter motor body. When the ignition switch is operated, the solenoid moves the starter drive pinion, through the medium of the shift lever, into engagement with the flywheel starter ring gear. As the solenoid reaches the end of its stroke and with the pinion by now fully engaged with the flywheel ring gear, the fixed and moving contacts close and energise the starter motor to rotate the engine.
2 This fractional pre-engagement of the starter drive does much to reduce the wear on the flywheel ring gear associated with inertia type starter motors.

10 Starter motor - removal and refitting

1 Disconnect the cable from the battery negative terminal.
2 Disconnect the black and yellow wire from the S terminal on the solenoid and the black cable from the B terminal also on the end cover of the solenoid.
3 Unscrew and remove the two starter motor securing bolts, pull the starter forward, tilt it slightly to clear the motor shaft

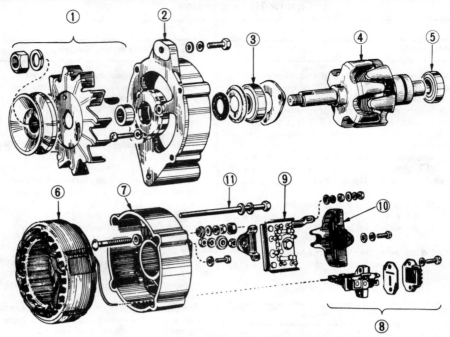

Fig 10.3 Exploded view of the alternator

1 Pulley assembly	4 Rotor	7 Rear cover	10 Diode cover
2 Front cover	5 Rear bearing	8 Brush assembly	11 Tie bolt
3 Front bearing	6 Stator	9 Diode plate	

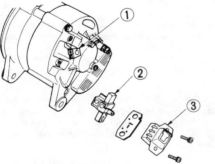

Fig 10.4 Alternator 'N' terminal (1) brush holder (2) and brush holder cover (3)

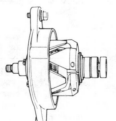

Fig 10.5 Alternator front cover/rotor separated from rear cover/stator

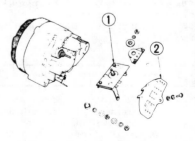

Fig 10.6 Alternator rotor separated from front cover showing spacer and washers

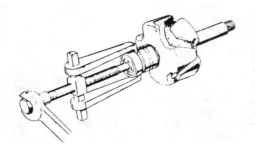

Fig 10.7 Removing alternator bearing

Fig 10.8 Alternator diode assembly (1) and diode cover (2)

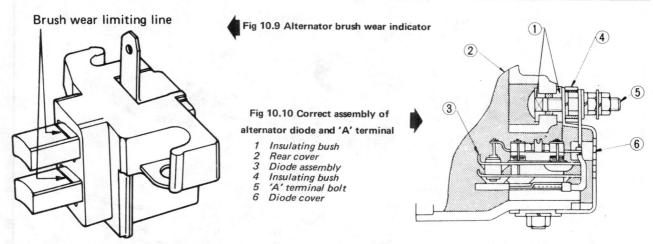

Brush wear limiting line

◀ Fig 10.9 Alternator brush wear indicator

Fig 10.10 Correct assembly of
alternator diode and 'A' terminal

1   Insulating bush
2   Rear cover
3   Diode assembly
4   Insulating bush
5   'A' terminal bolt
6   Diode cover

support from the flywheel ring gear and withdraw it.
4   Refitting is a reversal of removal.

11 Starter motor - dismantling, servicing, reassembly

1   Servicing operations should be limited to renewal of brushes, renewal of the solenoid, the overhaul of the starter drive gear and cleaning the commutator.
2   The major components of the starter should normally last the life of the unit and in the event of failure, a factory exchange replacement should be obtained.
3   The starter fitted to vehicles with automatic transmission is of heavy duty type but the descriptions given in this Section apply to both types.
4   Access to the brushes is obtained by slipping back the cover band. Unscrew and remove the screws which retain the brush lead tags. With an 'L' shaped roll pull aside the brush tension springs and pull the brushes from their holders.
5   Measure the overall length of each of the two brushes and where they are worn below the minimum recommended (see Specifications) renew them.
6   Ensure that each brush slides freely in its holder. If necessary, rub with a fine file and clean any accumulated carbon dust or grease from the holder with a fuel moistened rag.
7   Disconnect the cable which runs from the starter motor to the 'M' terminal on the solenoid cover. Withdraw the split pin and cotter pin from the shift fork and the two solenoid securing bolts. Remove the solenoid rearwards from the starter motor front housing.
8   Refitting a solenoid is a reversal of removal but the length of the plunger must be checked and adjusted if necessary. To do this, energise the solenoid by connecting to the battery and then measure the gap between the front face of the pinion and the face of the pinion stop button. This should be between 0.012 and 0.059 in (0.3 and 1.5 mm).
9   If the gap requires adjustment, release the solenoid plunger locknut and rotate the pillar nut. Retighten the locknut when adjustment is complete.
10 Normally, the commutator may be cleaned by holding a piece of non-fluffy rag moistened with fuel against it as it is rotated by hand. If on inspection, the mica separators are level with the copper segments then they must be undercut by between 0.020 and 0.032 in (0.5 and 0.8 mm).
11 Remove the brushes and solenoid as previously described. Unscrew and remove the two long bolts which secure the yoke to the front housing. Withdraw the yoke from the front housing, tapping it with a soft faced mallet if necessary to free it. Take great care not to damage the field coils of the yoke by catching them on the armature during removal.
12 Withdraw the armature with shift fork/pinion assembly attached.

13 Undercut the mica separators of the commutator using an old hacksaw blade ground to suit. The commutator may be polished with a piece of very fine glass paper - never use emery cloth as the carborundum particles will become embedded in the copper surfaces.
14 Refit the armature by reversing the removal procedure.
15 In the event of malfunction of pinion drive assembly, remove the armature as previously described in this Section. Prise the stop washer from the armature shaft using a screwdriver, detach the circlip from its groove and slide off the thrust washer, starter pinion and drive assembly.
16 Wash the components of the drive gear in paraffin and inspect for wear or damage, particularly to the pinion teeth and renew as appropriate. Refitting is a reversal of dismantling but stake a new stop washer in position and oil the sliding surfaces of the pinion assembly with a light oil, applied sparingly.

12 Voltage regulator and cut-out - description, testing and adjustment

1   The voltage regulator and cut-out unit is located forward of the right-hand front suspension strut mounting within the engine compartment. The resistance which is located next to the regulator prevents voltage drops in the ignition circuit when the starter motor is operated.
2   The voltage regulator controls the output from the alternator depending upon the state of the battery and the demands of the vehicle electrical equipment and it ensures that the battery is not overcharged. The cut-out is virtually an automatic switch which completes the charging circuit as soon as the alternator starts to rotate and isolates it when the engine stops so that the battery cannot be discharged to earth through the alternator. One visual indication of the correct functioning of the cut-out is the ignition warning lamp. When the lamp is out, the system is charging.
3   Before testing, check that the alternator drive belt is not broken or slack and that all electrical leads are secure.
4   Test the regulator voltage with the unit still installed in the vehicle. If it has been removed make sure it is positioned with the connector plug hanging downward. Carry out the testing with the engine compartment cold and complete the test within one minute to prevent the regulator heating up and affecting the specified voltage readings.
5   Establish the ambient temperature within the engine compartment, turn off all vehicle electrical equipment and ensure that the battery is in a fully charged state. Connect a DC (15 to 30V) voltmeter, a DC (0 to 10 amp) ammeter and a 0.25 ohm 100 watt resistor as shown.
6   Start the engine and immediately detach the short circuit wire. Increase the engine speed to 2,500 rpm and check the voltmeter reading according to the pre-determined ambient temperature as listed in the following table:

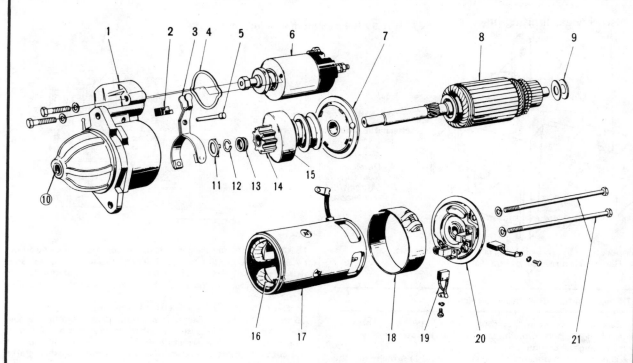

Fig 10.11 Exploded view of the starter motor

1	Front housing	6	Solenoid	11	Stop washer	16	Field coil
2	Dust cover	7	Bracket	12	Circlip	17	Yoke
3	shift fork	8	Armature	13	Thrust washer	18	Brush cover
4	Dust cover	9	Thrust washer	14	Pinion	19	Brush
5	Shift fork pin	10	Bush	15	Drive assembly	20	Rear cover
						21	Tie bolt

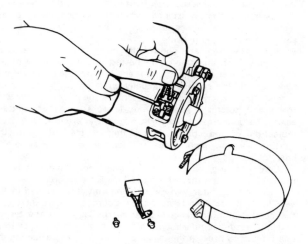

Fig 10.12 Removing a starter brush

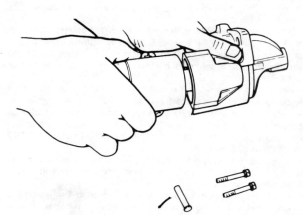

Fig 10.13 Removing the starter solenoid

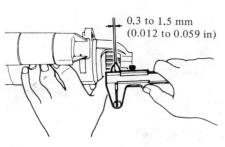

Fig 10.14 Measuring starter motor pinion face to stop clearance

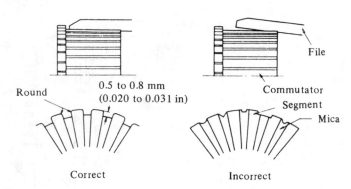

Fig 10.15 Starter motor commutator undercutting diagram

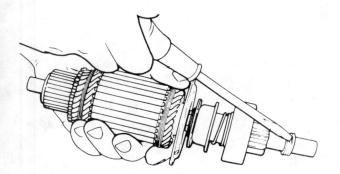

Fig 10.16 Prising off the starter pinion stop washer

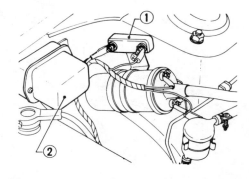

Fig 10.17 Location of voltage regulator (2) and resistance (1)

Ambient temperature °C (°F)	Rated regulating voltage (V)
-10 (14)	14.75 to 15.25
0 (32)	14.60 to 15.10
10 (50	14.45 to 14.95
20 (68)	14.30 to 14.80
30 (86)	14.15 to 14.65
40 (104)	14.00 to 14.50

7   If the voltage does not conform to that specified, continue to run the engine at 2,500 rpm for several minutes and then with the engine idling check that the ammeter reads below 5 amps. If the reading is above this, the battery is not fully charged and must be removed for charging as otherwise accurate testing cannot be carried out.

8   Switch off the engine, remove the cover from the voltage regulator and inspect the surfaces of the contacts. If these are rough or pitted, clean them by drawing a strip of fine emery cloth between them.

9   Using feeler gauges, check and adjust the core gap if necessary, to between 0.024 and 0.040 in (0.6 and 1.0 mm).

10 Check and adjust the contact point gap if necessary, to between 0.012 and 0.016 in (0.3 and 0.4 mm).

11 By now the voltage regulator will have cooled down so that the previous test may be repeated. If the voltage/temperature is still not compatible, switch off the engine and adjust the regulator screw. Do this by loosening the locknut and turning the screw clockwise to increase the voltage reading and anti-clockwise to reduce it.

12 Turn the adjuster screw only factionally before retesting the voltage charging rate again with the unit cold. Finally tighten the locknut.

13 If the cut-out is operating incorrectly, first check the fan belt and the ignition warning lamp bulb. Connect the positive terminal of a moving coil voltmeter to the yellow terminal of the regulator and the voltmeter terminal to earth as shown.

14 Start the engine and let it idle. Check the voltmeter reading. If the reading is O volts check for continuity between the N terminals of the regulator unit and the alternator. If the reading is below 5.2 volts and the ignition warning lamp remains on, check and adjust the core gap to between 0.032 and 0.040 in (0.8 to 1.0 mm) and the points gap to 0.016 and 0.024 in (0.4 to 0.6 mm). Remember that this time the adjustments are carried out to the cut-out not the voltage regulator although the procedure is similar.

15 If the reading is over 5.2 volts with the ignition warning lamp on and core and points gap are correctly set, the complete regulator unit must be renewed.

16 The cut-out is operating correctly if the voltmeter shows a reading of more than 5.2 volts (ignition lamp out).

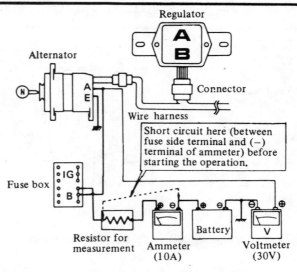

Regulator

Alternator

Connector

Wire harness

Short circuit here (between fuse side terminal and (−) terminal of ammeter) before starting the operation.

Fuse box

IG

B

Resistor for measurement

Ammeter (10A)

Battery

Voltmeter (30V)

Fig 10.18 Test diagram for voltage regulator A - cut-out, B - regulator

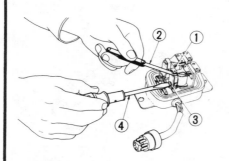

Fig 10.19 Adjusting core gap on voltage regulator

1　Contact
2　Feeler gauge
3　Adjusting screw
4　Screwdriver

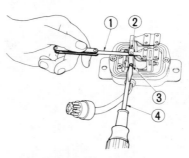

Fig 10.20 Adjusting points gap on voltage regulator

1　Feeler gauge
2　Upper contact
3　Adjusting screw
4　Screwdriver

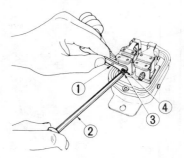

Fig 10.21 Adjusting regulating voltage

1　Spanner
2　Screwdriver
3　Adjusting screw
4　Locknut

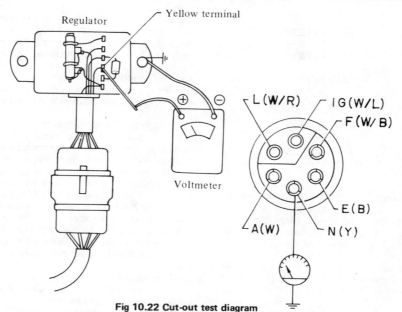

Regulator

Yellow terminal

Voltmeter

L(W/R)

IG(W/L)

F(W/B)

E(B)

A(W)

N(Y)

Fig 10.22 Cut-out test diagram

13 Fuses and fusible link

1 The fuse box is located under the fascia panel close the door pillar. The number and rating of the fuses varies according to model. The circuits and components protected by the individual fuses are indicated on the cover of the fuse box.

2 A fusible link is incorporated in the main power circuit and is situated just below the voltage regulator.

3 In the event of a fuse or fusible link blowing, always establish the cause before fitting a new one. This is most likely to be due to faulty insulation somewhere in the wiring circuit. Always carry a spare fuse for each rating and never be tempted to substitute a piece of wire or a nail for the correct fuse or a fire may be caused or, at least, the electrical component ruined.

14 Flasher unit (direction indicator) - faulty testing and renewal

1 If the direction indicators do not operate, carry out the following checks:
(i)   Inspect for blown fuse.
(ii)   Test security of all leads and connections.
(iii) Inspect switch mechanism.

2 If the indicator lamps flash too slowly or too quickly or the fascia indicator lamp does not go out, check the lamp units for a burnt out bulb and also for a loose connection. If the flashing cycle is irregular, check for a bulb of incorrect wattage.

3 Where the bulbs, switch and wiring are found to be in order, the flasher unit itself must be at fault.

4 To renew it, withdraw the ashtray and remove the ashtray cover (three screws). Unplug the leads from the flasher unit and then remove the single retaining screw.

15 Flasher unit (hazard warning) - fault testing and renewal

1 The hazard warning flasher unit is smaller in size than the one for the direction indicators.

2 Where a fault occurs, test in a similar way to that described in the preceding Section.

3 Access to the flasher unit is obtained by reaching up under the instrument panel. A single retaining screw is used and a plug-in type lead connector.

16 Headlamp - adjustment

1 The headlamp adjusting screws are accessible by inserting a screwdriver through the apertures in the radiator grille. (photo)

2 It is recommended that the headlamp beams are adjusted by a service station having modern optical beam setting equipment.

3 As a temporary measure, place the vehicle on a level surface with the tyres correctly inflated and check that the tops of the main beams do not rise above the level of the centres of the headlamps when projected onto a wall or screen.

4 In the dipped position, the beams should incline to the left or right (according to drive) to pick up the kerb for the maximum distance ahead compatible with there being no inclination to dazzle oncoming traffic.

17 Headlamp sealed beam unit or bulb - renewal

Sealed beam headlamp units.

1 Remove the six screws which secure the radiator grille and withdraw the grille.

2 Unscrew the headlamp retaining ring by rotating it in a clockwise direction after the three securing screws have been loosened (not removed). Do not confuse these screws with the adjusting screws which should not be disturbed.

3 Withdraw the headlamp sealed beam unit forward, peel back the rubber cover at the rear and disconnect the connecting plug. (photo)

4 Installation of the new lamp unit is a reversal of the removal operations but make sure that the word 'TOP' is correctly positioned.

Bulb type headlamps

5 Remove the radiator grille and loosen the three headlamp ring retaining screws, it is not necessary to remove them completely.

6 Remove the ring by rotating it clockwise and then withdraw the lamp unit.

7 Disconnect the electrical plug and peel back the dust excluding boot. Remove the bulb holder by rotating it in a clockwise direction. Renew the bulb and then reassemble by reversing the removal process.

18 Bulbs - renewal

1 This Section describes briefly the operations necessary to gain access to driving, warning and illumination lamp bulbs. Always renew a bulb with one of the specified type and wattage.

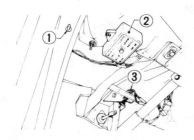

Fig 10.23 Location of fuse box

1 *Courtesy light/buzzer switch*
2 *Fuse box*
3 *Stop lamp switch*

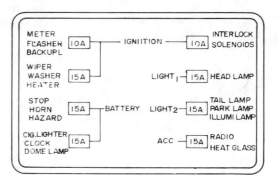

Fig 10.24 Fuse box cover (B210 models)

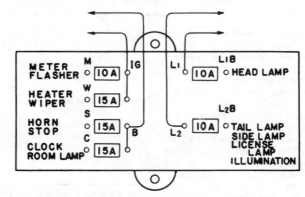

FOR L.H. DRIVE GENERAL AREA

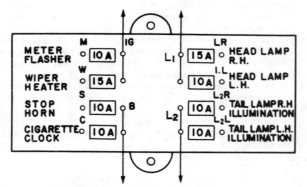

FOR L.H. DRIVE EUROPE

FOR R.H. DRIVE

Fig 10.24A Fuse box covers (120Y models)

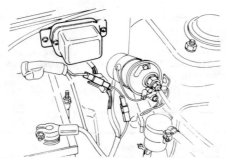

Fig 10.25 Location of the fusible link

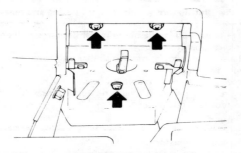

Fig 10.26 Ashtray cover screws

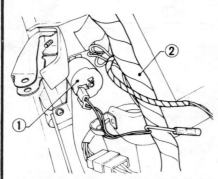

Fig 10.27 Location of direction indicator flasher unit

1 Flasher unit
2 Instrument harness

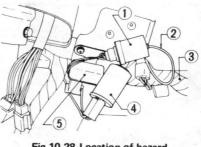

Fig 10.28 Location of hazard warning flasher unit

1 Wiper switch lamp
2 Tube
3 Instrument harness
4 Hazard flasher unit
5 Horn relay

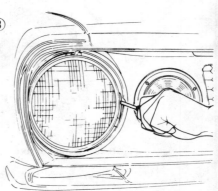

Fig 10.29 Adjusting a headlamp

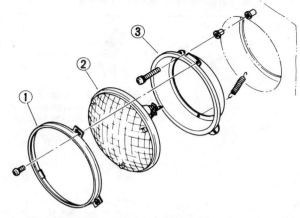

Fig 10.30 Exploded view of a sealed beam type headlamp

1   Retaining ring   2   Light unit   3   Mounting ring

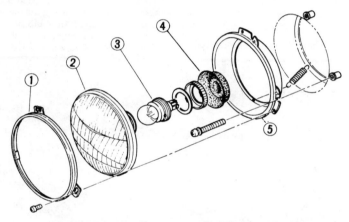

Fig 10.30A Exploded view of bulb type headlamp

1   Retaining ring   2   Reflector   3   Bulb   4   Boot
                                                                      5   Mounting

16.1 Headlamp vertical adjustment screw

17.3 Withdrawing a headlamp sealed beam unit

Front direction indicator/parking lamp

2 Remove the lamp bezel (three screws) and lens. The bulb is of conventional bayonet type fixing with offset pins to prevent incorrect installation.

Side marker lamps

3 Remove the two lens retaining screws and withdraw the lens. The bulb is of bayonet type fixing.

Rear lamp cluster

4 *On Saloon models*, work within the luggage compartment and remove the two screws which secure the bulb holder assembly to the back of the lamp. Withdraw the holder and remove the individual bulbs which are of bayonet type fixing.
On Coupe models, remove the cover from the back of the lamp body and remove the individual bulb holders by twisting them in an anti-clockwise direction and then withdrawing them.
On estate models, the bulbs are accessible after removing the external lens securing screws and withdrawing the lenses. (photo)

License plate lamp

5 The bulb is eccessible after removing the cover (two screws).

Interior lamp

6 Remove the lamp cover by twisting it in an anti-clockwise direction. The bulb is of festoon type and can be removed by prising the end contact supports apart.

Windscreen wiper switch illumination lamp

7 This is located under thyinstrument panel. Reach under the panel and twist the bulb holder from its socket.

Oil pressure and ignition warning and instrument illumination lamps

8 To renew these bulbs, twist the bulb holders from their sockets behind the combination instrument assembly.

Direction indicator (flasher) warning lamps

9 Remove the shrouds from the upper end of the steering column (4 screws). The bulb holders and their wedge base type bulbs can now be removed from the casing at the rear of the instrument panel.

Seat belt warning and rear window demister switch lamps

10 The seat belt warning lamp bulb may be renewed after unscrewing and removing the lamp body from the rear of the instrument panel. The bulb holder of the rear window demister switch can be reached after the switch retainers (one on each side) are depressed and the switch is withdrawn forward.

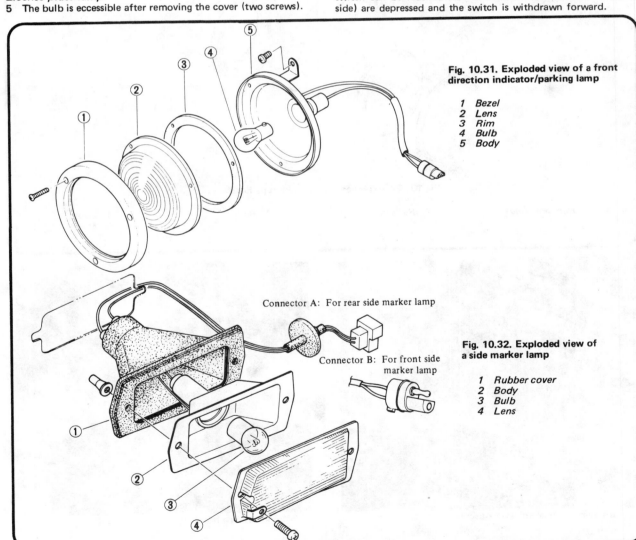

Connector A: For rear side marker lamp

Connector B: For front side marker lamp

Fig. 10.31. Exploded view of a front direction indicator/parking lamp

1 Bezel
2 Lens
3 Rim
4 Bulb
5 Body

Fig. 10.32. Exploded view of a side marker lamp

1 Rubber cover
2 Body
3 Bulb
4 Lens

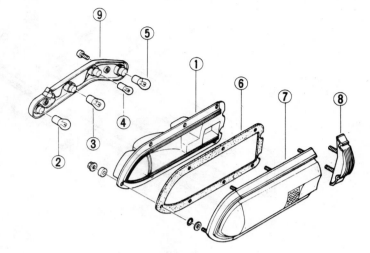

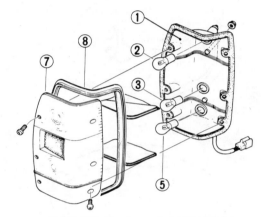

Fig 10.33 Rear lamp cluster (Saloon)

1 Body
2 Direction indicator bulb
3 Stop/tail bulb
4 Tail bulb
5 Reversing lamp bulb
6 Gasket
7 Lens
8 Retainer
9 Bulb holder

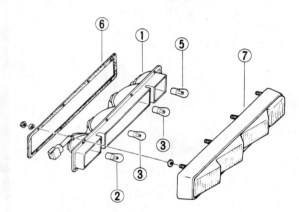

Fig 10.34 Rear lamp cluster (Coupe) Key as for Fig. 10.33

Fig 10.34A Rear lamp cluster (Estate)

1 Body
2 Direction indicator bulb
3 Stop/tail lamp
5 Reverse lamp bulb
7 Lens
8 Gasket

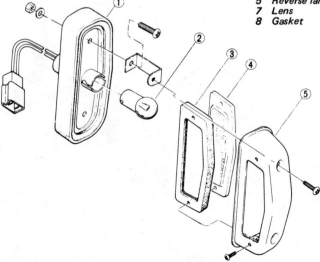

Fig 10.35 Exploded view of the licence plate lamp (B210 models)

1 Body   2 Bulb   3 Gasket   4 Lens
                                                5 Cover

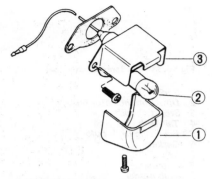

Fig 10.35A Exploded view of licence plate lamp (120Y Saloon and Coupe)
1 Lens
2 Bulb
3 Body

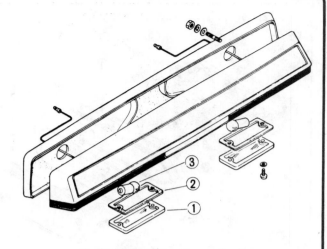

Fig 10.35B Exploded view of licence plate lamp (120Y Estate)
1 Lens
2 Rim
3 Bulb

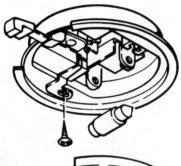

Fig 10.36 Interior lamp

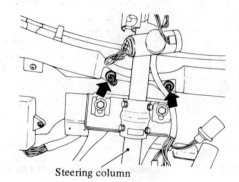

Steering column

Fig 10.37 Location of direction indicator warning lamps

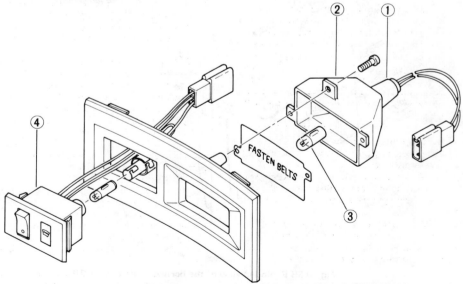

FASTEN BELTS

Fig 10.38 Seat belt warning lamp and demister switch

1 Bulb holder   2 Body   3 Bulb   4 Demister switch

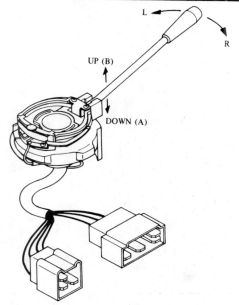

Fig 10.39 Steering column combination switch

18.4 Withdrawing Estate rear lamp cluster lens

19 Steering column combination switch

1 To remove this switch, which controls the headlamp beam positions and the direction indicator lamps, first withdraw the steering wheel as described in Chapter 11, Section 13.
2 Disconnect the lead from the battery negative terminal.
3 Remove the two halves of the steering column shroud.
4 Disconnect the two switch connector plugs.
5 Release the two screws which retain the switch to the steering column jacket and withdraw the switch.
6 Installation is a reversal of removal but ensure that the tongue on the switch locates in the hole in the steering column jacket.

20 Lighting switch - removal and installation

1 Disconnect the lead from the battery negative terminal.
2 Depress the switch knob fully and turn it in an anticlockwise direction. It can then be withdrawn from the switch spindle.
3 Unscrew the switch retaining ring nut, push the switch to the rear of the instrument panel and then disconnect the connector plug and remove the switch.
4 Installation is a reversal of removal.

21 Courtesy light/warning buzzer switch - removal and installation

1 The switch is a press fit in the door pillar.
2 To remove it, simply pull it from its location or carefully prise it out using a small screwdriver.
3 With the switch and leads withdrawn, disconnect the leads from the switch at the snap connectors, noting that of the three leads, two are for the warning buzzer and the third for the vehicle interior lamp.
4 The switch may cease to operate due to corrosion, causing a poor earth or bad switch electrical contact, in which case it should be renewed complete.
5 Installation is a reversal of removal. See also Section 33.

22 Hazard warning switch - removal and installation

1 Disconnect the lead from the battery netative terminal.

2 Remove the two halves of the steering column shroud.
3 Disconnect the connector plug.
4 Remove the switch from the upper section of the shroud to which it is attached by three screws.

23 Instrument panel and instruments - removal and installation

1 Disconnect the lead from the battery negative terminal.
2 Remove the steering column shroud.
3 Remove the steering wheel (Chapter 11) and the steering column switch (Section 19, of this Chapter).
4 Remove the ashtray and the ashtray cover.
5 Remove the knobs from the wiper, lighting and rheostat (wiper and heater switch illumination) switches. To remove the first two knobs, depress them fully and turn to the left (anticlockwise) and release them. The rheostat knob simply pulls off.
6 Pull off the radio control knobs.
7 Unscrew and remove the switch retaining ring nuts.
8 Unscrew and remove the nine screws which retain the cluster front cover to the instrument panel. Four of these screws are located on the upper edge, three on the bottom edge, one in the ashtray casing (centre one of three) and one in the glove compartment.
9 Withdraw the cluster front cover forward from the instrument panel enough to disconnect the leads for the cigar lighter, rear window demister switch, clock, seat belt warning lamp and the direction indicator warning lamps.
10 Remove the complete cluster front cover.
11 The individual instruments may now be removed. Unscrew and remove the four screws which retain the combination instrument in position. Pull the instrument assembly forward sufficiently to disconnect the speedometer cable and electrical connector also the leads from the clock and tachometer. Withdraw the instrument assembly.
12 The speedometer can be removed from the main assembly after having removed the glass (four screws), separated the upper and lower housings (six screws) and then extracted the two screws which retain the instrument to the lower housing.
13 The fuel, water temperature and oil pressure gauges can.all be removed from the lower housing after unscrewing the securing screws.
14 The tachometer can be removed after extracting the upper and lower retaining screws and disconnecting the four electrical leads. Removal of the clock is similar but only three electrical leads are used.
15 In all cases, installation is a reversal of removal.

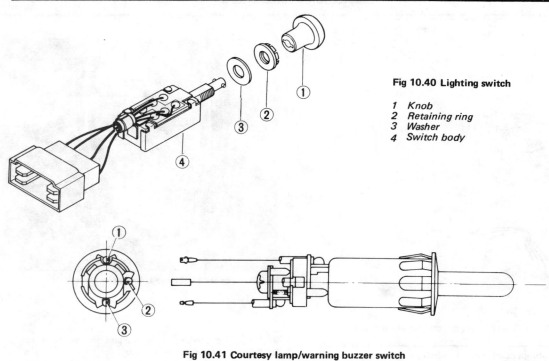

Fig 10.40 Lighting switch

1 Knob
2 Retaining ring
3 Washer
4 Switch body

Fig 10.41 Courtesy lamp/warning buzzer switch

Fig 10.42 Hazard warning switch

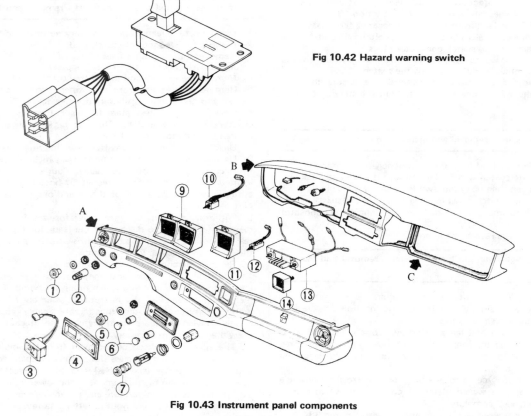

Fig 10.43 Instrument panel components

A Cluster front cover
B Crash pad
C Instrument panel
1 Lighting switch knob
2 Illumination brightness control
3 Demister switch
4 Escutcheon plate
5 Wiper switch knob
6 Radio control knob
7 Cigar lighter
9 Combination instrument
10 Lighting switch
11 Tachometer
12 Wiper switch
13 Radio
14 Clock

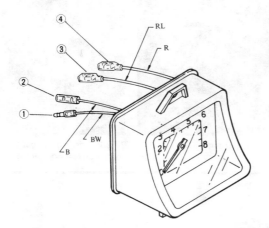

Fig 10.44 Tachometer and connections

1   To ignition coil
2   To 'A' combination instrument
3   To 'B' on combination instrument
4   To 'C' combination instrument
R   Red
RL Red with blue stripe
B   Black
BW Black with white stripe

24 Horns - description

1   Twin duo-tone horns are fitted together with the necessary relay.
2   The horn relay is located under the instrument panel adjacent to the hazard flasher unit.
3   No maintenance is normally required except to occasionally check the security of leads and terminal connectors.

25 Windscreen wiper and washer - description and maintenance

1   The wiper motor is of two speed type. It is mounted on the engine compartment rear bulkhead and drives the wiper arms through linkage located below the air intake grille just ahead of the windscreen.
2   The electrically operated windscreen washer unit (motor, tank and pump) is located to the left front of the engine compartment.
3   A combined wiper/washer switch is fitted. The switch operates the wipers by a two position push-pull action and the washer by twisting the switch knob clockwise. The washer knob is spring loaded and it should not be held in the 'ON' position for more than 30 seconds at a time.
4   At two yearly intervals or earlier if the screen is not being wiped effectively, renew the wiper blades.
5   Never operate the washer without liquid being in the tank.

26 Wiper arm and blade - removal and installation

1   Pull the wiper arm/blade assembly forward to raise it from the windscreen glass.
2   Unscrew and remove the arm to spindle securing nut and remove the arm/blade assembly from the spindle. (photo)
3   To remove the wiper blade, depress the tab to release the dimple from its recess and pull the blade from the arm. (photo)
4   Installation is a reversal of removal but with the wiper motor in the parked position, install the wiper arm/blade assemblies so that they are parallel with the bottom of the windscreen and tighten the arm to spindle nuts to the specified torque. Any fine adjustment can be made by releasing the nut and slightly moving the position of the arm on the spindle. Incorrect parking of the wiper arms may be caused by incorrect setting of the auto-stop device. Remove the cover and bend the relay plate as required.

27 Wiper motor and linkage - removal and installation

1   Remove the wiper arm/blade assemblies as previously des-

cribed.
2   Working within the engine compartment, disconnect the electrical connector plug adjacent to the wiper motor. (photo)
3   Remove the air intake grille from its location just in front of the windscreen.
4   Unscrew and remove the three wiper motor retaining bolts, pull the wiper motor forward enough to be able to disconnect the motor crank arm from the linkage, then remove the motor complete.
5   Unscrew and remove the two flange nuts which retain each of the drive spindles to the top cowl panel and withdraw the complete linkage assembly.
6   Installation is a reversal of removal.

28 Washer tank and motor - removal and installation

1   Disconnect the two electrical leads at their snap connectors.
2   Disconnect the hoses from the pump and allow the fluid to drain.
3   Unbolt the washer tank and pump assembly from their support bracket and remove from the engine compartment.
4   The pump may now be removed from the washer tank.
5   Installation is a reversal of removal.

29 Cigar lighter - removal and installation

1   Disconnect the lead from the battery negative terminal.
2   Withdraw the lighter element.
3   Remove the cluster front cover as described in Section 23 of this Chapter.
4   Disconnect the leads at their snap connectors.
5   Unscrew the cigar lighter housing cover and remove all the components.
6   Installation is a reversal of removal.

30 Rear window demister

1   The filament is of surface-applied, conductive silver type and in the event of failure due to a break in the filament circuit it can be repaired but this is definitely a job for your Datsun dealer.
2   On Coupe models, an interrupter switch is fitted to the rear tailgate stay to cut off the current to the demister when the tailgate is in the open position.

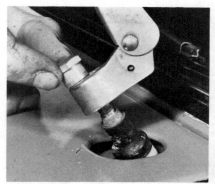

26.2 Removing a windscreen wiper arm

26.3 Removing a windscreen wiper blade

27.2 Windscreen wiper motor and electrical connector plug

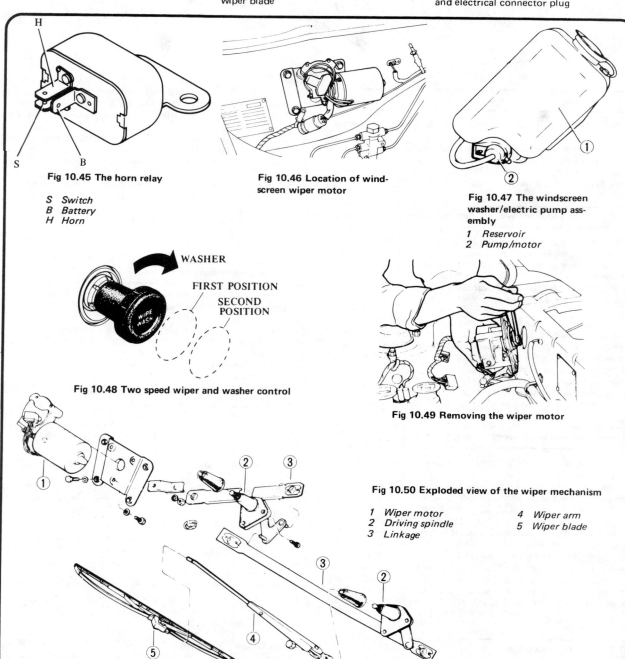

Fig 10.45 The horn relay

S Switch
B Battery
H Horn

Fig 10.46 Location of wind-screen wiper motor

Fig 10.47 The windscreen washer/electric pump ass-embly

1 Reservoir
2 Pump/motor

WASHER

FIRST POSITION

SECOND POSITION

Fig 10.48 Two speed wiper and washer control

Fig 10.49 Removing the wiper motor

Fig 10.50 Exploded view of the wiper mechanism

1 Wiper motor
2 Driving spindle
3 Linkage

4 Wiper arm
5 Wiper blade

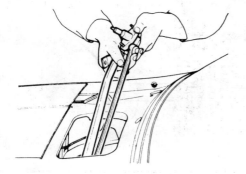

Fig 10.51 Removing the wiper linkage

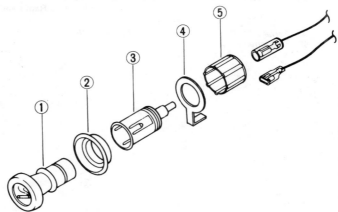

Fig. 10.52 Exploded view of the cigar lighter
1 Element
2 Escutcheon plate
3 Housing
4 Washer
5 Cover

31 Radio - removal and refitting

1 Pull off the radio control knobs and remove the ring retaining nuts if these are fitted.
2 Remove the cluster front cover from the instrument panel as described in Section 23, of this Chapter.
3 Disconnect all the leads and connector plugs and extract the radio securing screws. Lift the radio from the instrument panel.
4 Installation is a reversal of removal.

32 Radio aerial trimmer - adjustment

1 This operation will only be required if a new radio receiver or aerial has been fitted.
2 Extend the aerial fully and tune to the weakest station between 1200 and 1600 Hz.
3 Using a small screwdriver, turn the antenna trimmer first to the left and then to the right until sensitivity is at its best.
4 The trimmer screw varies in its location according to make of radio.

33 Theft protection system (where fitted)

1 The system comprises the ignition switch, the door pillar switch and a buzzer and is designed to prevent the driver leaving the vehicle while the ignition key is still in the lock.
2 Where a fault occurs in the system, first check the connecting wiring. The door pillar switch which also operates the interior courtesy lamp can be removed as described in Section 21.
3 The warning buzzer is located behind the instrument panel adjacent to the interlock relay (see Section 35).

4 Refer also to Chapter 11, for details of the steering column and ignition locks.

34 Starter interlock system - description and operation

1 This system is installed to meet regulations in North America (not Canada) and certain other territories. The engine can only be started when the following conditions have been complied with otherwise a warning buzzer and lamp will be actuated.

(i) The seat belts are fastened after each of the front seats is occupied.
(ii) The gearshift lever is in neutral (manual transmission) or the speed selector lever is in 'N' or 'P' (automatic transmission).

2 If the engine stalls, it can be restarted provided the driver remains seated and the ignition key remains in the 'ON' position or has been turned to the 'OFF' or 'ACC' position for a period not exceeding three minutes.
3 In an emergency, if a fault in the system is obviously preventing the engine from starting, turn the ignition key to 'ON', press the emergency over-ride button within the engine compartment and then turn the ignition key to 'START'.
4 For tuning and maintenance purposes, the engine can be started by reaching into the car to turn the ignition key so that no weight is placed upon the front seats.
5 Do not leave objects on either of the front seats or they will actuate the seat switch and discharge the battery.

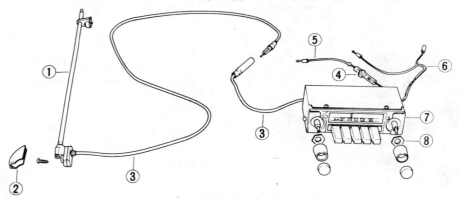

Fig 10.53 Radio and aerial

1 Aerial	3 Feeder cable	5 Power lead	7 Receiver
2 Escutcheon	4 Fuse	6 Speaker leads	8 Retaining nut

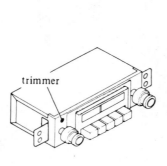

HITACHI

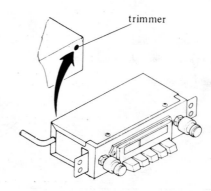

CLARION

Fig 10.54 Location of aerial trimmer

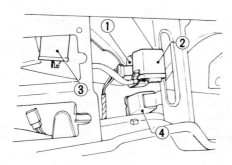

Fig 10.55 Location of theft protection warning buzzer

1 Warning buzzer
2 Interlock relay
3 Flasher unit
4 Neutral relay

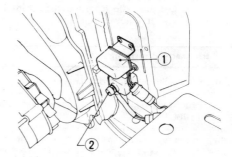

Fig 10.56 Location of starter interlock system override switch

1 Automatic choke relay
2 Override switch

35 Starter interlock system - components

1 Components of the system include the following items. Any malfunction in the system can be diagnosed by first checking the connecting wiring and then for continuity in the individual switches using a test lamp:

(i) The seat switch
(ii) The interlock unit, located under the passenger seat.
(iii) The belt switch.
(iv) The neutral switches (see Chapter 6).
(v) The interlock relay which is located behind the cluster front cover of the instrument panel.
(vi) The neutral relay (automatic transmission) which is also located behind the cluster front cover of the instrument panel.
(vii) The warning buzzer which is positioned adjacent to the interlock and neutral relays.
(viii) The engine compartment emergency switch which is fitted to the radiator support.

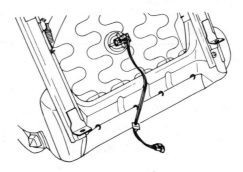

Fig 10.57 Seat switch (starter interlock system)

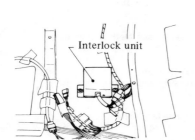

Fig 10.58 Interlock unit (starter interlock system)

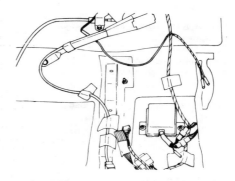

Fig 10.59 Belt switch (starter interlock system)

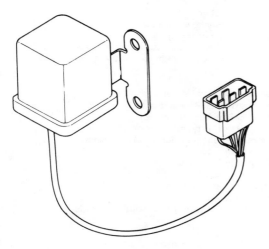

Fig 10.60 Interlock relay (starter interlock system)

Fig 10.61 Emergency override switch (starter interlock system)

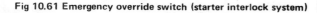
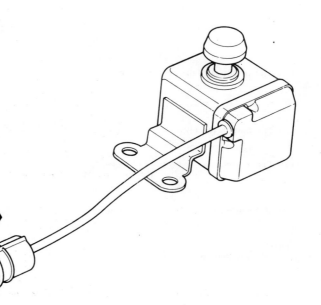

36 Fault diagnosis - electrical system

Symptom	Reason/s
Starter motor fails to turn engine	
No electricity at starter motor	Battery discharged
	Battery defective internally
	Battery terminal leads loose or earth lead not securely attached attached to body
	Loose or broken connections in starter motor circuit
	Starter motor switch or solenoid faulty
Electricity at starter motor: faulty motor	Starter motor pinion jammed in mesh with flywheel gear ring
	Starter brushes badly worn, sticking, or brush wires loose
	Commutator dirty, worn or burnt
	Starter motor armature faulty
	Field coils earthed
Starter motor turns engine very slowly	
Electrical defects	Battery in discharged condition
	Starter brushes badly worn, sticking, or brush wires loose
	Loose wires in starter motor circuit
Starter motor operates without turning engine	
Mechanical damage	Pinion or flywheel gear teeth broken or worn
Starter motor noisy or excessively rough engagement	
Lack of attention or mechanical damage	Pinion or flywheel gear teeth broken or worn
	Starter motor retaining bolts loose
Battery will not hold charge for more than a few days	
Wear or damage	Battery defective internally
	Electrolyte level too low or electrolyte too weak due to leakage
	Plate separators no longer fully effective
	Battery plates severely sulphated
Insufficient current flow to keep battery charged	Battery plates severely sulphated
	Fan belt slipping
	Battery terminal connections loose or corroded
	Alternator not charging
	Short in lighting circuit causing continual battery drain
	Regulator unit not working correctly
Ignition light fails to go out, battery runs flat in a few days	
Alternator not charging	Fan belt loose and slipping or broken
	Brushes worn, sticking, broken or dirty
	Brush springs weak or broken
	Commutator dirty, greasy, worn or burnt
	Alternator field coils burnt, open, or shorted
	Commutator worn
	Pole pieces very loose
Regulator or cut-out fails to work correctly	Regulator incorrectly set
	Cut-out incorrectly set
	Open circuit in wiring of cut-out and regulator unit
Horn	
Horn operates all the time	Horn push either earthed or stuck down
	Horn cable to horn push earthed
Horn fails to operate	Blown fuse
	Cable or cable connection loose, broken or disconnected
	Horn has an internal fault
Horn emits intermittent or unsatisfactory noise	Cable connections loose
	Horn incorrectly adjusted
Lights	
Lights do not come on	If engine not running, battery discharged
	Sealed beam filament burnt out or bulbs broken
	Wire connections loose, disconnected or broken
	Light switch shorting or otherwise faulty

Lights come on but fade out	If engine not running battery discharged
	Light bulb filament burnt out or bulbs or sealed beam units broken
	Wire connections loose, disconnected or broken
	Light switch shorting or otherwise faulty
Lights give very poor illumination	Lamp glasses dirty
	Lamp badly out of adjustment
Lights work erratically - flashing on and off, especially over bumps	Battery terminals or earth connection loose
	Light not earthing properly
	Contacts in light switch faulty

Wipers

Wiper motor fails to work	Blown fuse
	Wire connections loose, disconnected, or broken
	Brushes badly worn
	Armature worn or faulty
	Field coils faulty
Wiper motor works very slowly and takes excessive current	Commutator dirty, greasy or burnt
	Armature bearings dirty or unaligned
	Armature badly worn or faulty
Wiper motor works slowly and takes little current	Brushes badly worn
	Commutator dirty, greasy or burnt
	Armature badly worn or faulty
Wiper motor works but wiper blades remain static	Wiper motor gearbox parts badly worn
Wipers do not stop when switched off or stop in wrong place	Auto-stop device faulty

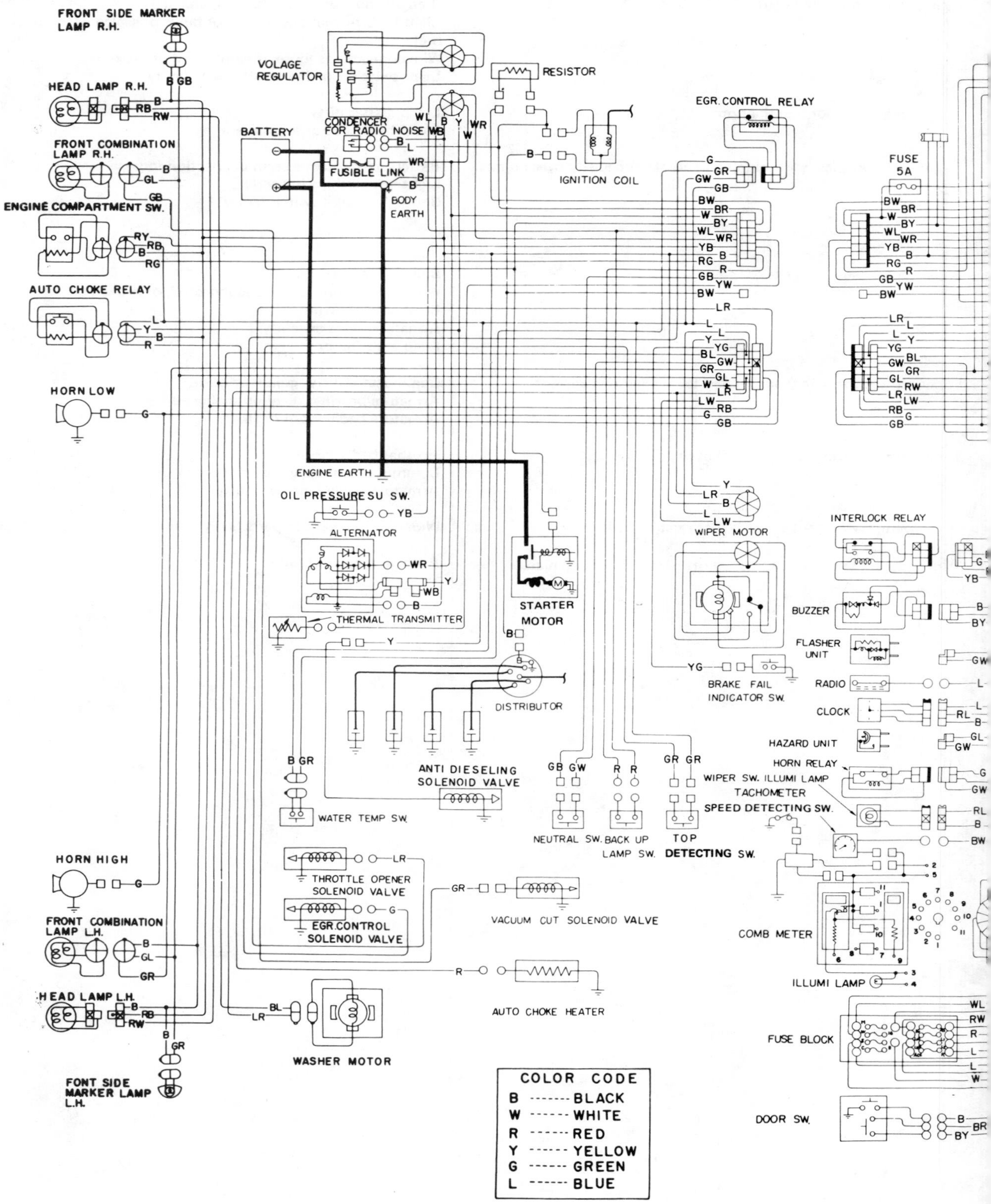

FRONT SIDE MARKER LAMP R.H.

HEAD LAMP R.H.

VOLAGE REGULATOR

RESISTOR

EGR.CONTROL RELAY

B GB

B RB

B RW

FRONT COMBINATION LAMP R.H.

BATTERY

CONDENCER FOR RADIO NOISE

WL B Y
WB

WR
W

IGNITION COIL

FUSE 5A

B
GL
GB

FUSIBLE LINK

WR
B

BODY EARTH

G
GW
GB
BW
W BR
WL BY
YB WR
RG
GB YW
BW

GR
GB

BW BR
W BY
WL WR
RG
GB YW
BW

ENGINE COMPARTMENT SW.

RY
RB
YB
RG

AUTO CHOKE RELAY

L
Y
B
R

LR
L
Y YG
BL GW
GR GL
W LR
LW RB
GB

LR
L
Y
YG
BL GW
GL GR
LR RW
RB LW
GB

HORN LOW

G

INTERLOCK RELAY

G
YB

ENGINE EARTH

OIL PRESSURE SU SW.

YB

ALTERNATOR

WR

WB
Y

B

STARTER MOTOR

Y
LR
B
L
LW

WIPER MOTOR

BUZZER

B
BY

FLASHER UNIT

GW

THERMAL TRANSMITTER

DISTRIBUTOR

YG

BRAKE FAIL INDICATOR SW.

RADIO

L

CLOCK

L
RL
L
GL
GW

HAZARD UNIT

B GR

ANTI DIESELING SOLENOID VALVE

GB GW

NEUTRAL SW.

R R

BACK UP LAMP SW.

GR GR

TOP DETECTING SW.

WIPER SW. ILLUMI LAMP

HORN RELAY

G

TACHOMETER

SPEED DETECTING SW.

RL
B

WATER TEMP SW.

BW

COMB METER

HORN HIGH

G

THROTTLE OPENER SOLENOID VALVE

LR

GR G

VACUUM CUT SOLENOID VALVE

FRONT COMBINATION LAMP L.H.

B
GL
GR

EGR.CONTROL SOLENOID VALVE

G

ILLUMI LAMP

HEAD LAMP L.H.

B
RB
RW

R

BL
LR

AUTO CHOKE HEATER

WL
RW
R
L
L
W

FUSE BLOCK

B GR

FONT SIDE MARKER LAMP L.H.

WASHER MOTOR

DOOR SW.

B
BR
B
BY

COLOR CODE	
B	BLACK
W	WHITE
R	RED
Y	YELLOW
G	GREEN
L	BLUE

USA models (automatic transmission)

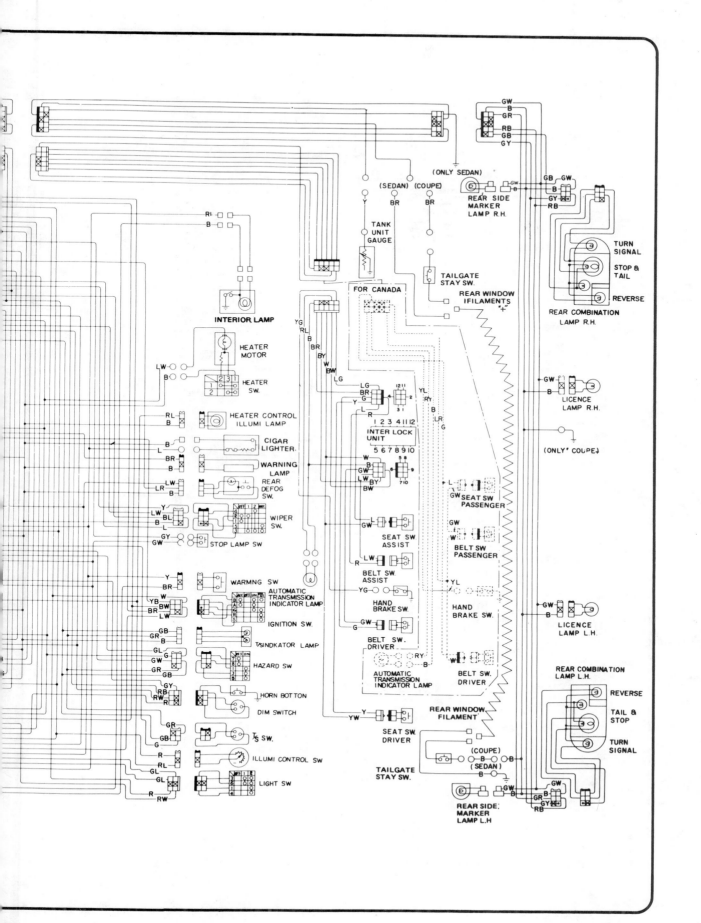

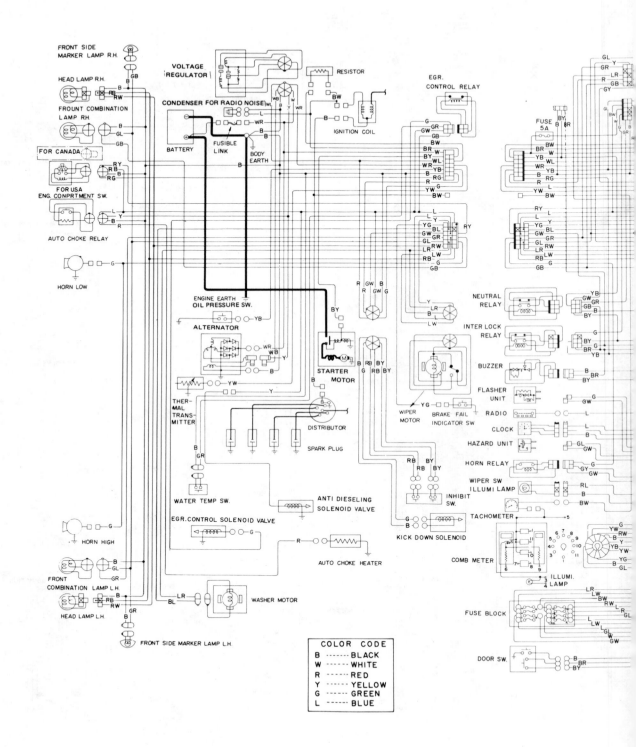

USA models (manual transmission)

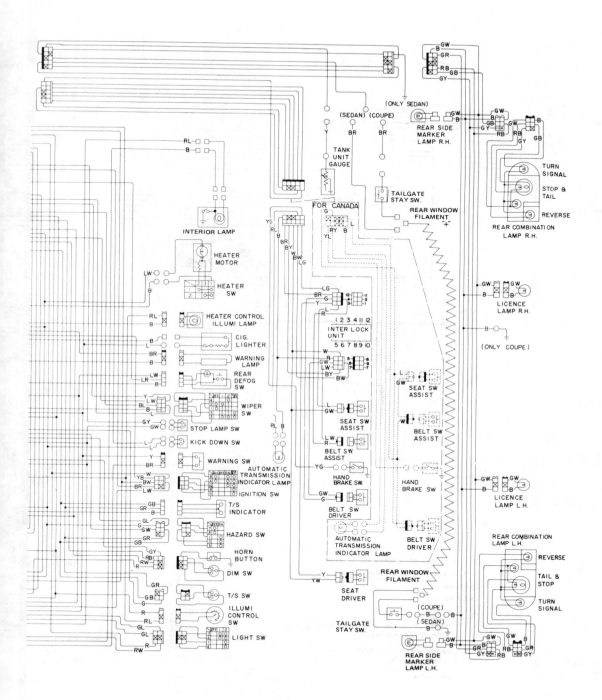

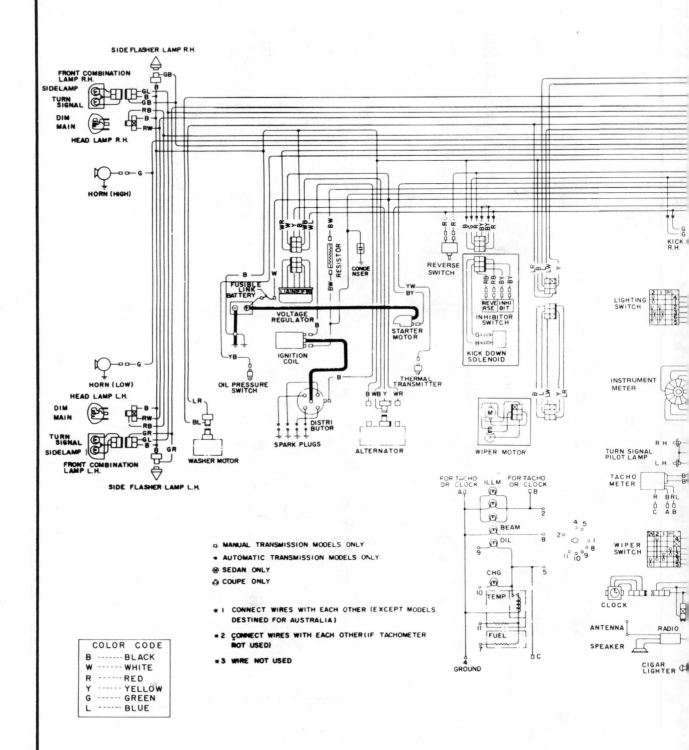

SIDE FLASHER LAMP R.H.

FRONT COMBINATION LAMP R.H.
SIDELAMP
TURN SIGNAL
DIM MAIN
HEAD LAMP R.H.

HORN (HIGH)

HORN (LOW)

HEAD LAMP L.H.
DIM MAIN
TURN SIGNAL
SIDELAMP
FRONT COMBINATION LAMP L.H.

SIDE FLASHER LAMP L.H.

WASHER MOTOR

FUSIBLE LINK
BATTERY
VOLTAGE REGULATOR
IGNITION COIL
OIL PRESSURE SWITCH

RESISTOR
CONDENSER

DISTRIBUTOR
SPARK PLUGS

STARTER MOTOR
THERMAL TRANSMITTER

ALTERNATOR

REVERSE SWITCH

INHIBITOR SWITCH
KICK DOWN SOLENOID

WIPER MOTOR

KICK R.H.

LIGHTING SWITCH

INSTRUMENT METER

TURN SIGNAL PILOT LAMP

TACHO METER

WIPER SWITCH

CLOCK

ANTENNA   RADIO

SPEAKER

CIGAR LIGHTER

FOR TACHO OR CLOCK
ILLM.
FOR TACHO OR CLOCK
BEAM
OIL
CHG.
TEMP.
FUEL
GROUND

☆ MANUAL TRANSMISSION MODELS ONLY

✱ AUTOMATIC TRANSMISSION MODELS ONLY

⊗ SEDAN ONLY

⊘ COUPE ONLY

✱ 1 CONNECT WIRES WITH EACH OTHER (EXCEPT MODELS DESTINED FOR AUSTRALIA)

✱ 2 CONNECT WIRES WITH EACH OTHER (IF TACHOMETER NOT USED)

✱ 3 WIRE NOT USED

COLOR CODE	
B	BLACK
W	WHITE
R	RED
Y	YELLOW
G	GREEN
L	BLUE

UK models

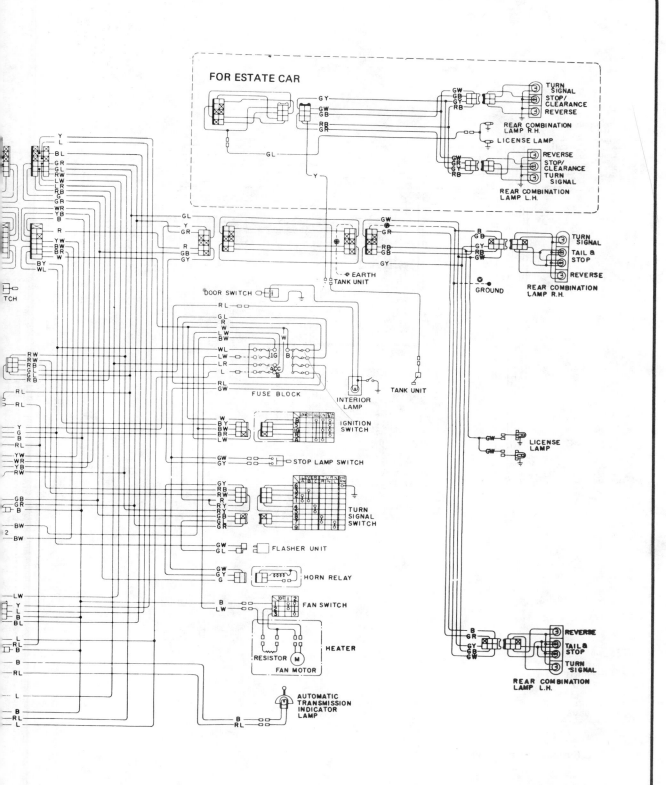

FOR ESTATE CAR

TURN SIGNAL
STOP/CLEARANCE
REVERSE

REAR COMBINATION LAMP R.H.

LICENSE LAMP

REVERSE
STOP/CLEARANCE
TURN SIGNAL

REAR COMBINATION LAMP L.H.

TURN SIGNAL
TAIL & STOP
REVERSE

REAR COMBINATION LAMP R.H.

EARTH
TANK UNIT

GROUND

DOOR SWITCH

FUSE BLOCK

INTERIOR LAMP

TANK UNIT

IGNITION SWITCH

STOP LAMP SWITCH

TURN SIGNAL SWITCH

FLASHER UNIT

HORN RELAY

FAN SWITCH

HEATER

RESISTOR   FAN MOTOR

AUTOMATIC TRANSMISSION INDICATOR LAMP

LICENSE LAMP

REVERSE
TAIL & STOP
TURN SIGNAL

REAR COMBINATION LAMP L.H.

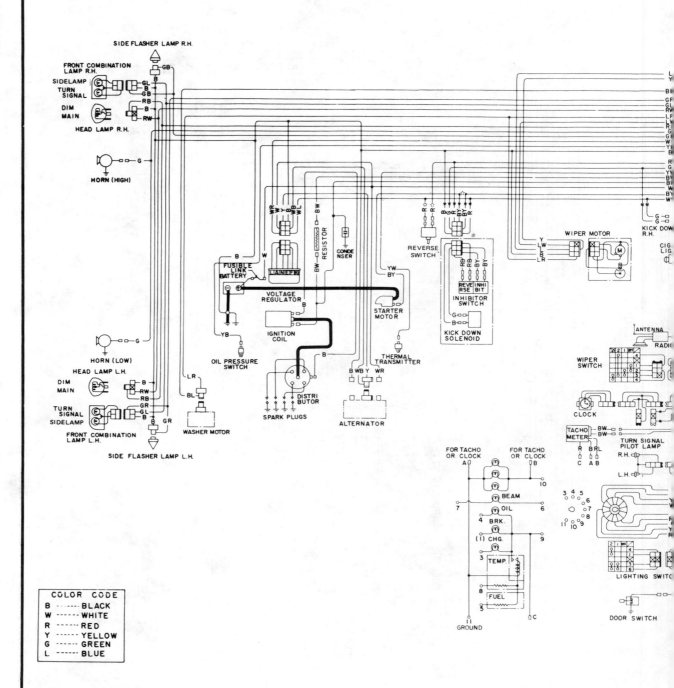

Left-hand drive models (other than US)

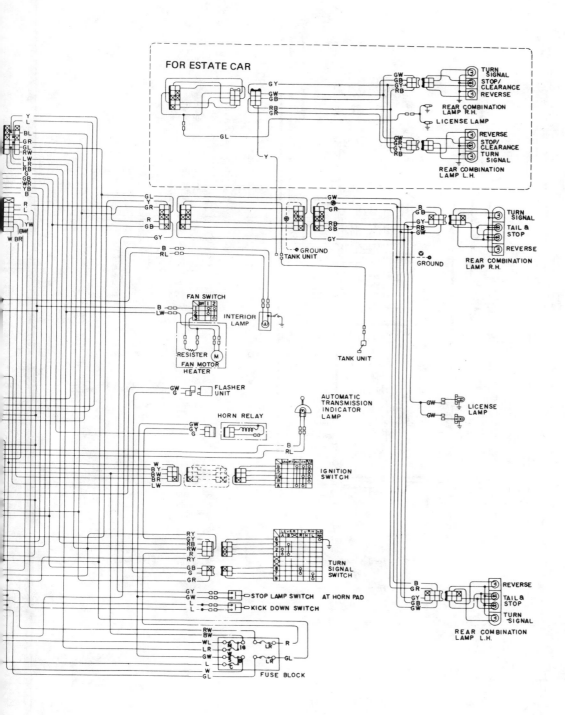

FOR ESTATE CAR

TURN SIGNAL
STOP/ CLEARANCE
REVERSE

REAR COMBINATION LAMP R.H.

LICENSE LAMP

REVERSE
STOP/ CLEARANCE
TURN SIGNAL

REAR COMBINATION LAMP L.H.

GROUND
TANK UNIT

GROUND

TURN SIGNAL
TAIL & STOP
REVERSE

REAR COMBINATION LAMP R.H.

FAN SWITCH

INTERIOR LAMP

RESISTER
FAN MOTOR HEATER

TANK UNIT

FLASHER UNIT

AUTOMATIC TRANSMISSION INDICATOR LAMP

HORN RELAY

LICENSE LAMP

IGNITION SWITCH

TURN SIGNAL SWITCH

STOP LAMP SWITCH   AT HORN PAD
KICK DOWN SWITCH

REVERSE
TAIL & STOP
TURN SIGNAL

REAR COMBINATION LAMP L.H.

FUSE BLOCK

FRONT SIDE MARKER LAMP R.H.

VOLTAGE REGULATOR

RESISTOR IGNITION COIL

EGR COMPARTMENT SW

NEUTRAL RELAY

WASHER MOTOR

AUTO CHOKE RELAY

DETECTOR DRIVE COUNTER (EXCEPT CANADA)

HEAD LAMP R.H.
DIM MAIN

FRONT COMBINATION LAMP R.H.
PARK TURN

HORN HIGH

BATTERY

CONDENCER FOR RADIO NOISE

FUSIBLE LINK

BODY EARTH

FOR CANADA

(USELESS)
FUSE IA
FUSE 5A

ENGINE EARTH

OIL PRESSURE SW

ALTERNATOR

THERMAL TRANSMITTER

YW WB WR
YB B Y

STARTER MOTOR

WIPER MOTOR

INTERLOCK RELAY

BRAKE FAIL INDICATOR SW

BUZZER

FLASHER UNIT

RADIO

CLOCK

HAZARD UNIT

HORN RELAY

DISTRIBUTOR

SPARK PLUGS

FUEL CUT SOLENOID

THROTTLE OPENER CUT SOLENOID

VACUUM CUT SOLENOID

AUTO CHOKE HEATER

GEAR SW

BACK UP LAMP SW

NEUTRAL SW

ODOMETER SW (EXCEPT CANADA)

WIPER SW ILLUMI LAMP SPEED SW

TACHOMETER

COMBINATION METER ILLUMI LAMP

FUSE BLOCK

HORN LOW

FRONT COMBINATION LAMP L.H.
PARK TURN

HEAD LAMP L.H.
DIM MAIN

CHECK CONNECTOR

DOOR SW

CHECK CONNECTOR

FRONT SIDE MARKER LAMP L.H.

USA models (non-Californian) 1975 (manual transmission)

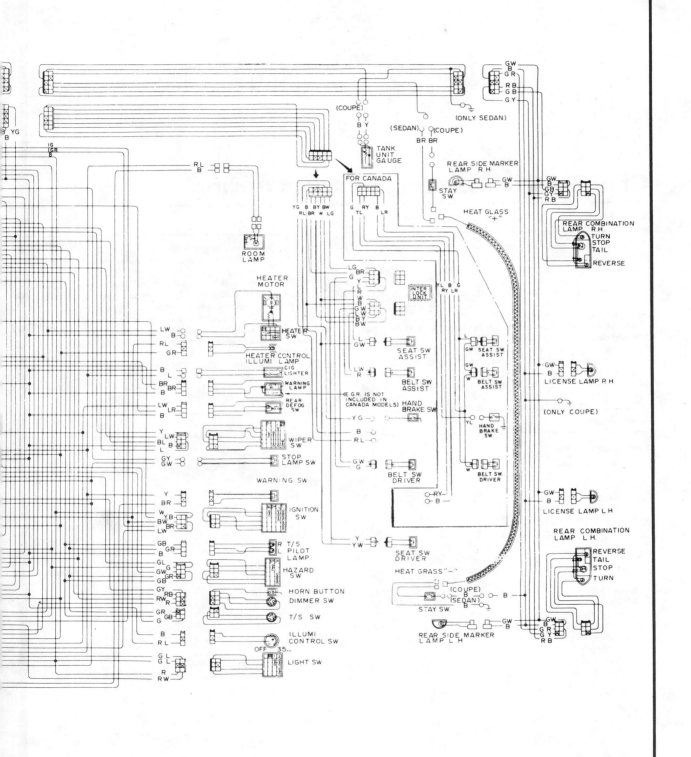

Chapter 11 Suspension and steering

Contents

Specifications

Front suspension

									B210	120Y
Type									Independent, MacPherson Strut with stabiliser bar	
Coil springs:										
No. of turns									9	9
Free-length									13.90 in. (352.5 mm)	14.07 in (357.5 mm)
Coil diameter									3.94 in. (100.0 mm)	3.94 in. (100.0 mm)
Wire diameter									0.413 in. (10.5 mm)	0.406 in. (10.3 mm)

Rear suspension

Type ... ...   Semi-elliptic leaf springs with double acting telescopic shock absorbers.

Spring length ... ...   45.90 in. (1165.0 mm)

Width ... ...   1.97 in. (50.0 mm)

Thickness of leaf:
  Saloon and Coupe ... ...   0.236 in. (6.0 mm) and 0.276 in. (7.0 mm)
  Estate ... ...   0.197 in. (5.0 mm) 0.236 in. (6.0 mm) 0.512 in. (13.0 mm)

No. of leaves:
  Saloon and Coupe ... ...   4 (two each of alternative thickness)
  Estate ... ...   6 (two x 5.0 mm - three x 6.0 mm - one x 13.0 mm)

Shock absorbers

Stroke:
  Saloon ... ...   8.07 in. (205.0 mm)
  Coupe ... ...   7.68 in. (195.0 mm)
  Estate ... ...   7.09 in. (180.0 mm)

Extended length:
  Saloon ... ...   20.75 in. (527.0 mm)
  Coupe ... ...   18.50 in. (470.0 mm)
  Estate ... ...   18.78 in. (477.0 mm)

Steering

Type ... ...   Worm and nut recirculating ball

	B210	120Y
Ratio ...	15.0 : 1	16.4 : 1
No. of turns (lock-to-lock) ...	3.54	
Turning circle ...	28 ft. (8.5 m)	
Oil capacity ...	½ pt (Imp.), 5/8 pt (US), 0.27 litre	

	B210	120Y
Camber angle:		
Saloon and Coupe ...	40' to 1° 40' (positive)	15' to 1° 15' positive
Estate ...		20' to 1° 20' positive
Castor angle:		
Saloon and Coupe ...	1° 15' to 2° 15' (positive)	1° 15' to 2° 15' positive
Estate ...		1° 10' to 2° 10' positive
Steering axis inclination:		
Saloon and Coupe ...	7° 47' to 8° 47'	7° 47' to 8° 47'
Estate ...		7° 42' to 8° 42'
Toe-in:		
B210 ...	0.08 to 0.16 in (2 to 4 mm)	
210Y*		
Early models ...	0.16 to 0.24 in (4 to 6 mm)	
Later models ...	0.08 to 0.16 in (2 to 4 mm)	
Wheels**		
B210 ...	4½J-13	
120Y ...	4½J-12	
Tyres**		
B210 ...	155 x 13 (6.00 x 13)	
120Y ...	155 x 12 (6.00 x 12)	

*For the correct setting for your car, consult your Datsun dealer.
**In some territories there may be variations in sizes, consult the handbook supplied with the car.

Torque wrench settings

	lb f ft	kg f m
Front suspension		
Suspension strut upper mounting nut ...	25	3.5
Suspension strut piston rod nut ...	54	7.5
Steering arm to suspension strut bolts ...	44	6.1
Brake caliper to stub axle bolts ...	53 to 72	7.3 to 9.9
Stabiliser bar bracket bolts ...	15	2.1
Stabiliser bar end link nuts ...	10	1.4
Drag strut bracket bolts:		
Front ...	31	4.3
Rear ...	15	2.1
Drag strut to track control arm ...	22	3.0
Drag strut to bracket nut ...	46	6.3
Track control arm pivot nuts ...	36	5.0
Front crossmember to bodyframe bolts ...	31	4.3
Balljoint to track control arm ...	22	3.0
Balljoint to lower swivel housing ...	55	7.6
Rear suspension		
Spring 'U' bolts:		
Saloon and Coupe ...	36	5.0
Estate ...	40	5.5
Shock absorber upper mounting:		
Saloon ...	17	2.4
Coupe ...	9	1.2
Estate ...	33	4.5
Shock absorber lower mounting:		
Saloon ...	33	4.5
Coupe ...	9	1.2
Estate ...	33	4.5
Spring front shackle pivot nut ...	14	2.0
Spring front pivot plate bolts (Estate only) ...	25	3.5
Spring rear shackle pivot nut ...	14	2.0
Steering		
Steering wheel nut ...	25	3.5
Column upper clamp bolts ...	13	1.8
Flexible coupling pinch bolt ...	16	2.2
Flexible coupling securing bolts ...	36	5.0
Steering box mounting bolts ...	58	8.0
Drop arm nut ...	100	13.8
Trackrod balljoint nuts ...	36	5.0
Trackrod-end locknuts ...	70	9.7

Idler shaft nut	...	...	...	...	...	...	50	6.9
Idler mounting bolts	...	...	...	...	...	...	50	6.9
Steering box rear cover bolts	...	...	...	...	...	20	2.8
Sector shaft cover bolts	...	...	...	...	...	20	2.8
Sector shaft adjuster screw locknut	...	...	...	...	22	3.0
Roadwheel nuts ...	...	...	...	...	...	...	60	8.3

1 General description

The front suspension is of MacPherson strut type incorporating a double acting hydraulic ram and outer coil spring. A drag strut and stablisier bar positively absorb any lateral or longitudinal thrust force. There are detail differences in the front systems of the B210 and 120Y models as shown in the illustrations.

The front hubs run on inner and outer tapered roller bearings.

Rear suspension is by conventional semi-elliptic leaf springs, the springs being mounted on rubber-bushed shackle pins. The springs are damped by telescopic double-acting shock absorbers. The steering gear is of recirculating ball, worm and nut type. The drop arm on the steering gear shaft transmits motion to the roadwheels through a relay rod and two outer trackrods which incorporate lubricant sealed balljoints. A collapsible type steering column is used on most models but a one piece steering column and box may be encountered on some vehicles.

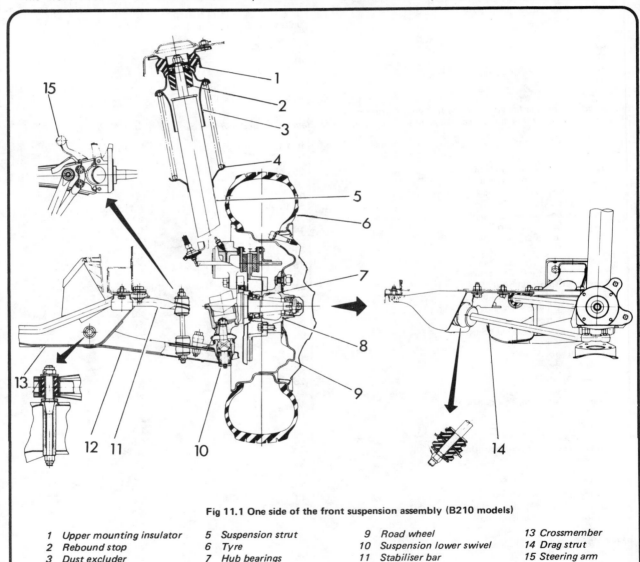

Fig 11.1 One side of the front suspension assembly (B210 models)

1 Upper mounting insulator	5 Suspension strut	9 Road wheel	13 Crossmember
2 Rebound stop	6 Tyre	10 Suspension lower swivel	14 Drag strut
3 Dust excluder	7 Hub bearings	11 Stabiliser bar	15 Steering arm
4 Coil spring	8 Hub	12 Track control arm	

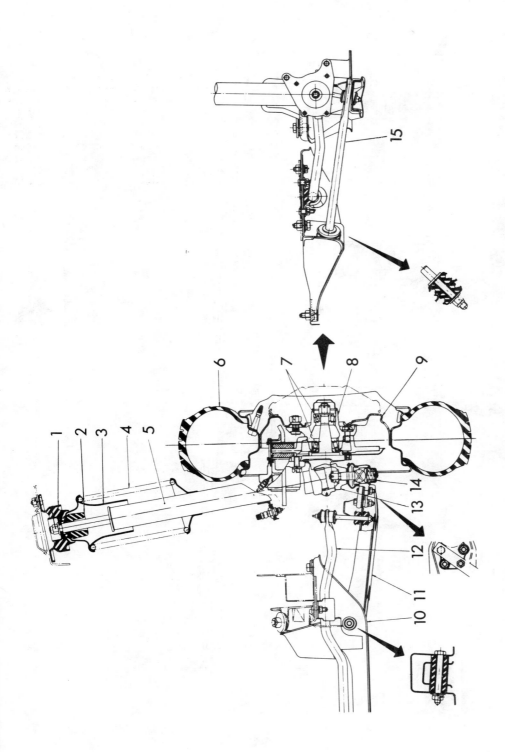

Fig 11.1A One side of the front suspension assembly (120Y models)

1 Upper mounting insulator
2 Rebound stop
3 Dust excluder
4 Coil spring

5 Suspension strut
6 Tyre
7 Hub bearings
8 Hub

9 Roadwheel
10 Crossmember
11 Track control
12 Stabiliser bar

13 Steering arm
14 Suspension lower swivel balljoint
15 Drag strut

166

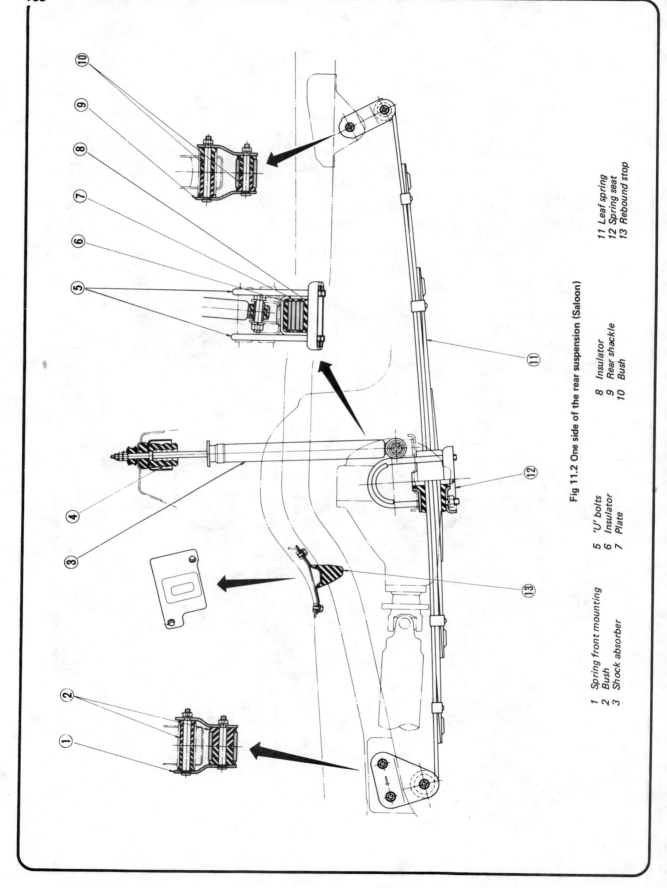

Fig 11.2 One side of the rear suspension (Saloon)

1 Spring front mounting
2 Bush
3 Shock absorber

5 'U' bolts
6 Insulator
7 Plate

8 Insulator
9 Rear shackle
10 Bush

11 Leaf spring
12 Spring seat
13 Rebound stop

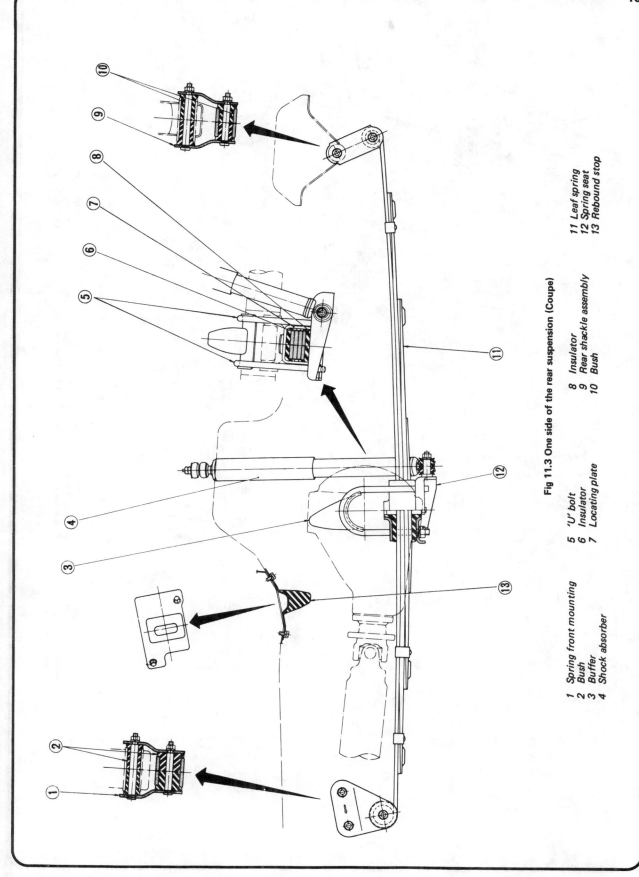

167

Fig 11.3 One side of the rear suspension (Coupe)

1 Spring front mounting
2 Bush
3 Buffer
4 Shock absorber

5 'U' bolt
6 Insulator
7 Locating plate

8 Insulator
9 Rear shackle assembly
10 Bush

11 Leaf spring
12 Spring seat
13 Rebound stop

168

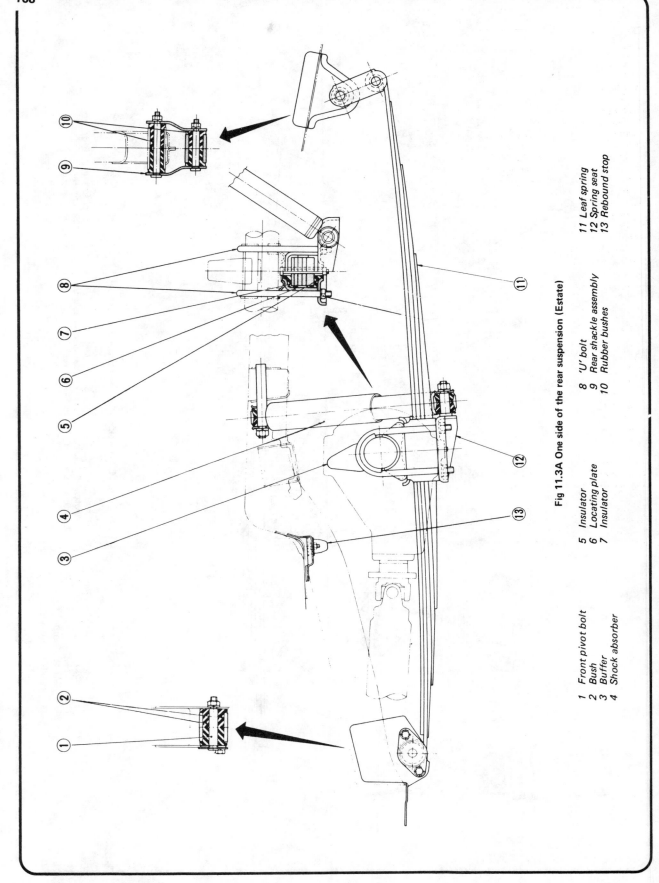

Fig 11.3A One side of the rear suspension (Estate)

1 Front pivot bolt
2 Bush
3 Buffer
4 Shock absorber

5 Insulator
6 Locating plate
7 Insulator

8 'U' bolt
9 Rear shackle assembly
10 Rubber bushes

11 Leaf spring
12 Spring seat
13 Rebound stop

2 Maintenance and inspection

1 Inspect the condition of all rubber gaiters, balljoint covers for splits or deterioration. Renew as necessary after reference to the appropriate section of this Chapter.
2 Check the security of the locknuts on the outer track rod ends, also the ball pin nuts.
3 Check the security of the front strut securing nuts and examine the condition of the radius rod and stabiliser bar rubber bushes and renew if necessary.
4 Every 24000 miles (38000 km), remove, clean, repack and adjust the front hub bearings and check the front wheel alignment (toe-in) as described in Sections 9 and 19, of this Chapter.
5 Every 30,000 miles (48000 km) remove the threaded plugs from the balljoints, screw in a grease nipple and inject wheel bearing grade grease.
6 Every 3000 miles (4800 km), remove the filler plug from the steering box and top up if required with EP grade oil.
7 No maintenance is required for the rear suspension other than periodically checking the security of 'U' bolt and shock absorber mounting bolts and nuts in accordance with the torque wrench settings given in the Specifications.

3 Suspension components - inspection for wear

1 The safety of the vehicle depends more on the steering and suspension than anything else and regular inspection of these components should be carried out.
2 Have an assistant lift the rear of the vehicle body up and down and check any movement in the top and bottom rear shock absorber mountings. Renew the bushes as necessary.
3 Also check for movement in the road spring shackles and eyes and for a broken or cracked spring leaf and renew as described later in this Chapter.
4 Any sign of oil on the outside of the rear shock absorber bodies will indicate that the seals have started to leak and the units must be renewed as assemblies. Where the shock absorber has failed internally, this is more difficult to detect although rear axle patter tramp, particularly on uneven road surfaces may provide a clue. When a shock absorber is suspected to have failed, remove it from the vehicle and holding it in a vertical position operate it for the full length of its stroke eight or ten times. Any

lack of resistance in either direction will indicate the need for renewal.
5 The front suspension should be checked by first jacking the car up so that the wheel is clear off the ground. Then place another jack under the track control arm near the outer end. When the arm is raised by the jack any movement in the suspension strut ball stud will be apparent. So also will any wear in the inner track control arm bush. The balljoint end float should not exceed 0.060 in. (1.5 mm). However, it is not possible to gauge this movement very accurately without removing the joint so if there is some doubt it is better to be on the safe side and dismantle it. There should be no play of any sort in the track control arm bush.
6 The top end of the suspension unit should have no discernible movement and to check it grip the strut at the lower spring seat and try pushing it from side to side. There should be no detachable movement either between the outer cylinder and the inner piston rod or at the top of the piston rod near the upper mounting.

4 Front suspension drag strut and stabiliser bar - removal and refitting

1 Jack-up the front of the vehicle and support it securely on axle stands. Remove the roadwheels.
2 Remove the splash shield from under the front of the engine compartment.
3 Release the nut which secures the end of the drag strut to the bracket.
4 Remove the bolts which secure the other end of the drag strut to the track control arm and remove the drag strut.
5 Remove the stabiliser bar drop link from the track control arm.
6 Loosen the drag strut bracket bolts and then unscrew and remove the stabiliser bracket bolts and remove the stabiliser bar from the vehicle
7 When refitting the stabiliser bar make sure that the white marks on the bar are visible from the outer edges of the support brackets.
8 Ensure that the drag strut to bracket bushes are correctly assembled and then tighten all nuts and bolts to the specified torque, making sure that the drag strut to bracket nut is tightened before the drag strut to track control arm bolt.

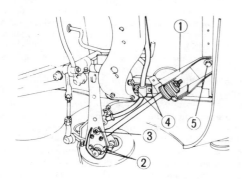

Fig 11.4 Stabiliser bar and drag strut attachment (B210 models)

1   Bracket
2   Drag strut to track control arm bolts
3   Stabiliser bar drop link nut
4   Stabiliser bar bracket bolts
5   Bracket bolts

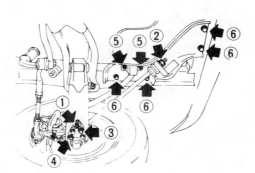

Fig 11.4A Front suspension component attachment points (120Y models)

1   Stabiliser bar drop link
2   Drag strut to bracket
3 and 4 drag strut to track control arm
5   Stabiliser bar bracket
6   Drag strut bracket

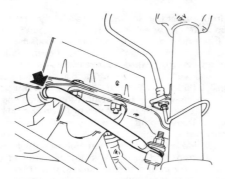

Fig 11.5 Stabiliser bar installation marks (B210 models)

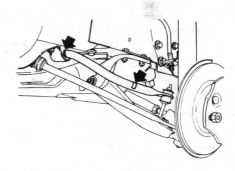

Fig 11.5A Stabiliser bar installation marks (120Y models)

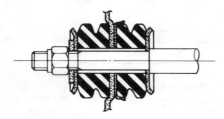

Fig 11.6 Correct assembly of drag strut to bracket bushes (B210 models)

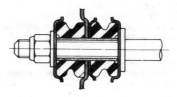

Fig 11.6A Correct assembly of drag strut to bracket bushes (120Y models)

5 Track control arm and balljoint - removal and refitting

1   Jack-up the front of the vehicle and support it on axle stands. Remove the roadwheel.
2   Unscrew and remove the nut from the outer balljoint on the outer track rod. Using a balljoint extractor or two wedges, separate the balljoint from the steering arm. Two club hammers of equal weight may be used to jar the balljoint taper pin from the steering arm eye. They should be used to strike the diametrically opposite edges of the eye simultaneously when the pin will be released.
3   Unscrew and remove the two bolts which secure the steering arm and balljoint housing to the bottom of the suspension strut. Disconnect the housing from the strut.
4   Disconnect the drag strut and the stabiliser bar from the track control arm.
5   Remove the pivot bolt which connects the track control arm to the front crossmember and then withdraw the track control arm complete with balljoint and steering arm.
6   Secure the track control arm in a vice and unbolt the balljoint from it.
7   Now grip the steering arm in the vice and unscrew the castellated nut from the taper pin of the balljoint. Tap the balljoint from the steering arm.
8   Clean all the dismantled components in paraffin and examine for cracks. Check the balljoints for up and down movement of the ball pin and if the taper pin moves too easily from side to side, it is worn and must be renewed. Ensure that the rubber dust excluder is not perished or torn. If the rubber bush at the inner end of the track control arm is worn or has deteriorated it must be renewed. A suitable press will be required and the new bush when correctly fitted must protrude equally either side of the arm.
9   Refitting is a reversal of removal and dismantling. Tighten all bolts and nuts to specified torque except the track control arm pivot bolt which should not be tightened until the weight of the vehicle is on the roadwheels.

10 If a new balljoint is being fitted, remove the plug, temporarily install a nipple and inject grease. Remove the nipple and refit the plug.

6 Front suspension struts - removal and installation

1   The strut assembly may be removed complete with hub, coil road spring and top thrust bearing unit. Removal for left and right hand assemblies is identical.
2   Apply the handbrake and jack-up the front of the car, supporting adequately under the body side members.
3   Remove the roadwheel from the side to be dismantled.
4   Loosen the union nut which connects the rigid brake pipe to the flexible hose. Extract the lockplate which retains the flexible hose and separate the two pipes. Plug the hydraulic line to prevent loss of fluid.
5   Unscrew and remove the two caliper securing bolts and withdraw the caliper unit complete.
6   Disconnect the steering arm from the bottom of the suspension strut as described in the preceding Section. A lever can be used to carefully prise the track control arm downwards against the tension of the stabiliser bar.
7   Raise the bonnet and unscrew the three upper mounting nuts. (photo)
8   Using a jack to support the strut/hub assembly, lower it carefully and then withdraw from under the front wing.
9   Using suitable coil spring compressing clamps, compress the coil springs. An alternative method of compressing the coil road springs is to make three clips from ½ inch diameter mild steel bar, of suitable length and with bent-over ends forming hooks, to span three coils of the spring. With the weight of a person on the wing before any dismantling takes place, the clips are slipped over the coils at equidistant points around the spring circumference. Whichever method is used for spring compression, a tough encircling safety strap should be used round the clips or compression after fixing them to the spring.
10 Remove the nut which secures the thrust bearing unit to the strut.

11 Remove the locating washer and bearing unit, push the damper rod into the strut and either gently release the spring compressors (evenly) or remove the coil spring complete with clips for subsequent detachment. The clips can easily be removed if a centrally placed screwed rod with nuts and end plates is used to further compress the coil spring.

12 When suspension struts become damaged, soft or faulty in action then it is recommended that they are renewed as units. The procedure described in this Chapter should be followed for dismantling the hub, brake and other components as the exchange or replacement unit will not include anything over the above the bare telescopic suspension leg.

13 Refitting of the suspension strut is a reversal of removal but the following points must be noted.

14 Where a new suspension strut is being installed it should be held vertically before fitting and the piston rod fully extended several times. Repeat the operation holding the strut upside down. This action will bleed the hydraulic fluid of any air which may have collected in the unit during storage.

15 Check that the coil spring is correctly located in its lower pan as indicated.

16 Make sure that the upper mounting components are installed in their correct sequence and grease is applied to the bearing and the piston rod self-locking nut is tightened to the specified torque.

17 When refitting the steering arm/lower balljoint housing to the bottom of the suspension strut, apply sealing compound to the mating surfaces to prevent entry of water and subsequent corrosion of the balljoint.

18 When installation is complete, bleed the brakes and check the front wheel alignment as described later in this Chapter.

7 Front crossmember - removal and installation

1 Jack-up the front of the vehicle and support it securely under the body side frame members.

2 Remove the roadwheels and the splash shield from under the engine.

3 Unscrew and remove the two track control arm pivot bolts, one from each side of the crossmember. Detach the track control arms from the crossmember and support them at their inner ends.

4 Using a suitable hoist take the strain of the weight of the engine and then unscrew and remove the nuts from the engine mountings.

5 Unscrew and remove the four crossmember securing bolts and lower the crossmember from the vehicle.

6 Check the condition of the engine mounting rubber insulators and renew them if necessary.

7 Installation is a reversal of removal. Tighten all nuts and bolts to specified torque except the track control arm pivot bolts which should not be tightened until the weight of the vehicle is on the roadwheels.

B210 models

8 With the steering in the straight-ahead position, there should be a clearance between the end of the track control arm pivot bolt and the leading edge of the steering idler arm of 0.276 in. (7.0 mm).

120Y models

9 The clearance should be as shown.

6.7 Front suspension strut upper mounting nuts

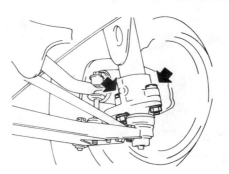

Fig 11.7 Location of the steering arm to suspension strut bolts

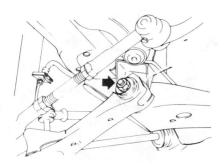

Fig 11.8 Track control arm pivot bolt (B210 models)

Fig 11.8A Track control arm pivot bolt (120Y models)

Fig 11.9 Disconnecting lower suspension balljoint from steering arm

Fig 11.10 Correct installation of track control arm bush (B210 models)

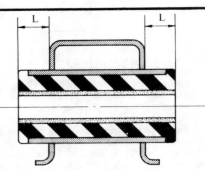

Fig 11.10A Correct install-ation of track control arm bush (120Y models)

L = equal dimensions

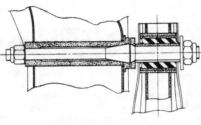

Fig 11.11 Sectional view of track control arm attach-ment to crossmember (B210 models)

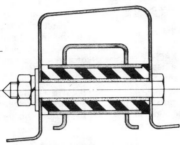

Fig 11.11A Sectional view of track control arm attachment to crossmember (120Y models)

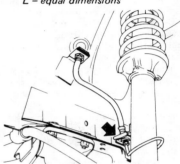

Fig 11.12 Location of a front flexible brake hose (body frame support bracket arrow-ed)

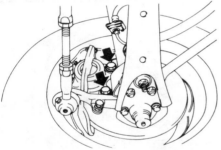

Fig 11.13 Location of caliper mounting bolts

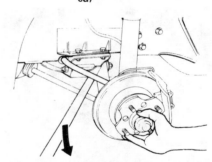

Fig 11.14 Using a lever to separate the steering arm from the suspension strut

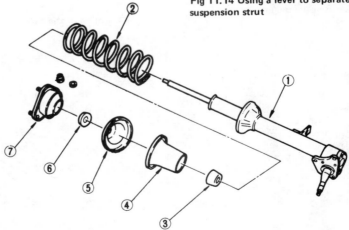

Fig 11.16 Exploded view of a front suspension strut upper mounting

1 Strut	2 Coil spring	3 Rubber damper	4 Dust excluder
5 Spring upper seat	6 Bearing	7 Insulator/mounting	

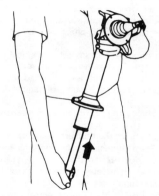

Fig 11.17 Expelling air from a front suspension strut

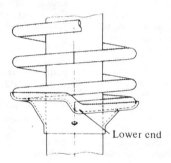

Fig 11.18 Correct mounting of a front suspension coil spring

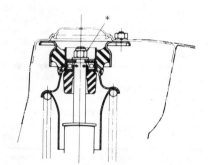

Fig 11.19 Sectional view of front suspension strut upper mounting

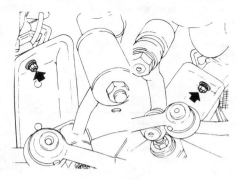

Fig 11.20 Engine mounting nuts

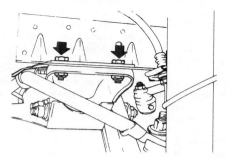

Fig 11.21 Crossmember securing bolts (one side)

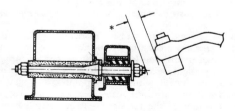

Fig 11.22 Drop arm to track control arm pivot bolt clearance diagram

*= 0.276 in. (7.0 mm) - B210 models

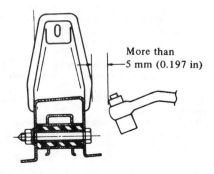

Fig 11.22A Drop arm to suspension crossmember clearance (120Y models)

8 Front wheel bearings - adjustment

1   Jack-up the front of the vehicle and support securely under the body sidemember.

2   Remove the roadwheel, the cap from the end of the hub and withdraw the split pin. Extract the nut retainer.

3   Using a socket and torque wrench, tighten the stub axle nut to 25 lb/ft (3.5 kg/m), at the same time rotating the hub in both directions to settle the bearings.

4   Unscrew the nut one quarter turn and then by attaching a spring balance to one of the roadwheels studs check the force needed to rotate the hub. With original components this should be 1.5 lb (0.7 kg) but if new bearings have been installed it should be 2.6 lb (1.2 kg).

5   When the adjustment is correct this will indicate that the bearings are correctly preloaded and the nut retainer, a new split pin and the cap can be refitted.

9 Front wheel hub and bearings - removal and installation

1   Jack-up the front of the vehicle, remove the roadwheel and remove the friction pads. Disconnect the hydraulic brake pipe at the suspension strut bracket and plug the pipe to prevent loss of fluid. Remove the caliper unit.

2   Knock off the cap from the end of the hub, remove the split pin and unscrew and remove the retainer, nut and thrust washer. (photo)

3   Pull the hub assembly forward and extract the outer roller bearing then pull the unit from the stub axle. (photo)

4   Wash all internal grease from the hub using paraffin. If the bearings and seal are in good order, repack the interior of the hub and end cap with wheel bearing grease so that it occupies the area shown.

5   If the bearings are worn or damaged, prise out the oil seal from the inner end of the hub and extract the inner roller race.

Drift out the inner and outer bearing tracks using a thin rod.

6   Fit the new bearing tracks using a piece of tubing as a drift. If both hubs are being dismantled at the same time, ensure that the bearings are kept as matched sets and do not mix up the races and tracks.

7   Press the new grease seal squarely into the inner end of the hub, with its lip towards the roller bearing.

8   Pack the hub with grease as described in paragraph 4.

9   Refitting is a reversal of removal, adjust the bearing pre-load as described in the preceding Section and bleed the hydraulic system.

10 Rear road springs and shock absorbers - removal, servicing and installation

1   To renew the rear shock absorber, jack-up the car under the axle and remove the wheel for rease of access. Then remove the lower anchor bolt, nut and lockwasher and pull the bottom of the shock absorber from its location. (photo)

2   From inside the boot remove the locknut from the top mounting spindle and then grip the flats on the spindle with the suitable spanner so that the second nut can be undone and removed. On Estate cars, both shock absorber mountings are accessible from below.

3   The shock absorber may then be taken out from underneath. When refitting make sure first that all the rubber mountings and steel bushes are in good condition. Renew them if necessary. New bushes may come with the shock absorber.

4   To test a shock absorber, hold it vertically by gripping its lower mounting in a vice and push and pull its upper body to the full extent of its stroke ten or twelve times. If there is any lack of resistance in either direction then it must be renewed. It cannot be repaired.

5   The rear springs must be detached either to renew a broken leaf or to renew the mounting bushes at the front or rear. Jack-up the car and support it on stands at the rear and then support the axle on a jack at a point away from the spring mountings. Remove the roadwheel.

6   Detach the lower end of the shock absorber from the mounting.

7   Thoroughly clean off all the dirt from the 'U' bolts and shackle pins and soak the nuts and threads with a suitable easing fluid.

8   Remove the 'U' bolt nuts and jack-up the axle a little way to separate it from the springs.

9   Unscrew the nuts and disconnect the spring rear shackle.

10 Unscrew the nuts and disconnect the front mounting plate assembly from the bodyframe.

11 A broken spring can be replaced as a complete unit or the individual leaf can be renewed. If the leaf only is being replaced

new spring clips, rivets and inserts will be required to reassemble the leaves. A replacement unit can usually be found at a breaker's and this is the simplest and cheapest way to go about it.

12 Examine the condition of the shackle bushes and bolts and renew them if they are worn. Bush renewal is best left to a service station, but they can be removed and refitted by using a threaded rod, nuts, washers and a tubular distance piece as an extractor.

13 When refitting a road spring, note that the centre bolt is offset toward the front.

14 When refitting the spring to the hangars it is usually easier to fit the front end first. Then replace the shackle pins and bushes. Replace the nuts but do not tighten them yet. Then lower the axle and position it so that it locates correctly onto the spring and put the 'U' bolts and clamp plate in position. Tighten up the 'U' bolt nuts only moderately. Make quite certain that the 'U' bolts are positioned absolutely vertically and not inclined at their tops along the axle casing.

15 The shock absorber should next be fitted to the lower mountings.

16 The car should then be lowered to the ground, bounced a few times to settle the bushes and then all the nuts tightened to the specified torque.

11 Steering gear linkage - inspection

1   Wear in the steering gear and linkage is indicated when there is considerable movement in the steering wheel without corresponding movement at the roadwheels. Wear is also indicated when the car tends to 'wander' off the line one is trying to steer. There are three main steering 'groups' to examine in such circumstances. These are the wheel bearings, the linkage joints and bushes and the steering box itself.

2   First jack-up the front of the car and support it on stands under the side frame members so that both front wheels are clear off the ground.

3   Grip the top and bottom of the roadwheel and try to rock it. It will not take any great effort to be able to feel any play in the wheel bearing. If this play is very noticeable it would be as well to adjust it straight away as it could confuse further examinations. It is also possible that during this check play may be discovered also in the lower suspension track control arm balljoint (at the foot of the suspension strut). If this happens the balljoint will need renewal as described in Section 5.

4   Next grip each side of the roadwheel and try rocking it laterally. Steady pressure will, of course, turn the steering but an

9.2 Removing a front hub dust cap

9.3 Withdrawing front hub outer bearing, thrust washer and nut

alternated back and forth pressure will reveal any loose joint. If some play is felt it would be easier to get assistance from someone so that while one person rocks the roadwheel from side to side, the other can look at the joints and bushes on the track rods and connections. Excluding the steering box itself there are eight places where the play may occur. The two outer balljoints on the two outer track rods are the most likely, followed by the two inner joints on the same rods where they join the centre relay rod. Any play in these means renewal of the balljoint. Next are the two swivel bushes, one at each end of the centre relay rod. Finally check the steering box drop arm balljoint and the one on the idler arm which supports the centre relay rod on the side opposite the steering box. This unit is bolted to the side frame member and any play calls for renewal of the unit.

5   Finally, the steering box itself is checked. First make sure that the bolts holding the steering box to the side frame member are tight. Then get another person to help examine the mechanism. One should look at, or get hold of, the drop arm at the bottom of the steering box while the other turns the steering wheel a little way from side to side. The amount of lost motion between the steering wheel and the drop arm indicates the degree of wear somewhere in the steering box mechanism. This check should be carried out with the wheels first of all in the straight ahead position and then at nearly full lock on each side. If the play only occurs noticeably in the straight ahead position then the wear is most probably in the worm and/or nut. If it occurs at all positions of the steering then the wear is probably in the rocker shaft bush. An oil leak at this point is another indication of such wear. In either case the steering box will need removal for closer examination and repair.

12 Steering linkage and balljoints - removal and refitting

1   The balljoints on the two outer track rods and the swivel

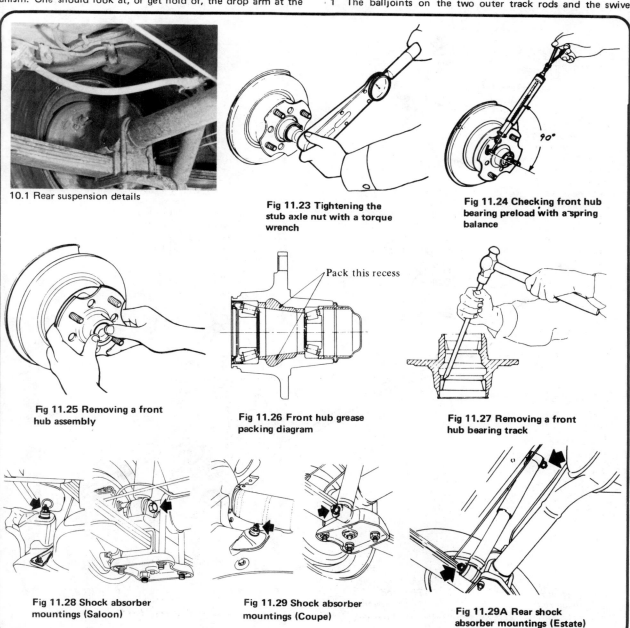

10.1 Rear suspension details

Fig 11.23 Tightening the stub axle nut with a torque wrench

Fig 11.24 Checking front hub bearing preload with a spring balance

Fig 11.25 Removing a front hub assembly

Pack this recess

Fig 11.26 Front hub grease packing diagram

Fig 11.27 Removing a front hub bearing track

Fig 11.28 Shock absorber mountings (Saloon)

Fig 11.29 Shock absorber mountings (Coupe)

Fig 11.29A Rear shock absorber mountings (Estate)

Fig 11.30 Road spring rear shackle nuts

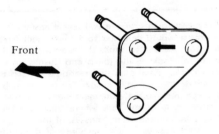

Front

Fig 11.31 Road spring front mounting plate (Saloon and Coupe)

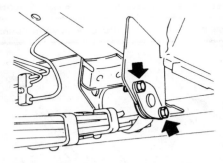

Fig 11.31A Front mounting plate (Estate)

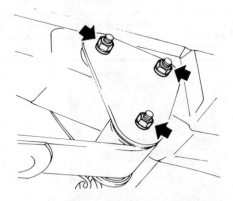

Fig 11.32 Road spring front mounting plate alignment

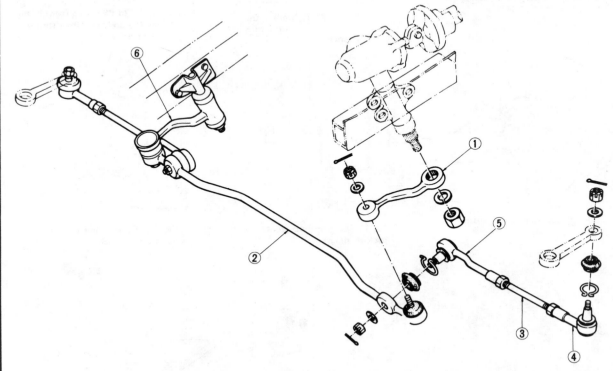

Fig 11.33 Steering linkage

| 1 | Drop arm | 3 | Trackrod | 5 | Trackrod-ends | 6 | Idler arm |
| 2 | Relay rod | 4 | Trackrod-ends | | | | |

bushes on the centre relay rod are all fitted into their respective locations by means of a taper pin into a tapered hole and secured by a self-locking or castellated nut. In the case of the four balljoints (two on each of the outer track rods) they are also screwed onto the rod and held by a locknut. The two outer balljoints have left-hand threads. (photo)

2 To disconnect a balljoint taper pin, first remove the castellated nut or self-locking nut then use an extractor or forked, tapered wedges to separate the balljoint from the eye of the attached component. Another method is to place the head of a hammer (or other solid metal article) on one side of the hole in the arm into which the pin is fitted. Then hit it smartly with a hammer on the opposite side. This has the effect of squeezing the taper out and usually works, provided one can get a good swing at it.

3 In the case of the trackrod-end balljoints, release the locknut and unscrew the trackrod-ends from the trackrods. If the locknut is only unscrewed by not more than one half turn then the new trackrod-end can be screwed on to take up (approximately) the original position but in any event the front wheel alignment will have to be checked and adjusted as described later in this Chapter.

4 If the balljoints of the centre relay rod require renewal then the complete rod assembly must be renewed after the trackrod balljoints have been disconnected from it and the steering box and idler drop arms also disconnected.

5 Any wear in the idler assembly will necessitate renewal of the split type rubber bushes. Smear a little brake fluid on them to facilitate installation.

6 Always check the front wheel alignment after any part of the steering linkage has been dismantled or renewed.

13 Steering wheel - removal and installation

1 Disconnect the lead from the battery negative terminal.

2 Remove the pad from the steering wheel spokes. The pad is retained by screws entered from the rear of the spokes.

3 Disconnect the horn wire.

4 Unscrew the steering wheel retaining nut and then using a suitable extractor, withdraw the steering wheel. On no account jar the end of the steering column in an attempt to free the wheel otherwise serious damage may be caused to the steering column which is of collapsible type.

5 Installation is a reversal of removal but apply grease to the wheel and shaft mating surfaces and with the roadwheels in the straight-ahead position, align the punch marks on the end of the shaft and the steering wheel boss.

6 Tighten the steering wheel nut to the specified torque.

14 Steering column (collapsible type) - removal and installation

1 Remove the steering wheel, as described in the preceding Section.

2 Open the bonnet and unscrew and remove the pinch bolt which secures the flexible coupling of the steering column to the worm shaft of the steering box.

3 Remove the two halves of the steering column shroud.

4 Remove the direction indicator switch from the top of the steering column (two screws), see also Chapter 11, Section 19.

5 Unscrew and remove the four screws which secure the column flange plate at its lower end.

6 Unscrew and remove the two bolts which secure the clamp at the upper end of the steering column.

7 Withdraw the steering column into the interior of the vehicle and then remove it.

8 The steering column bearings may be lubricated with multipurpose grease but apart from this operation no dismantling or overhaul can be carried out. If the bearings are worn, renew the column complete.

9 In the event of a front end collision having occurred, the

following demensional checks must be carried out and the column renewed if they are outside the specified tolerances.

10 Measure the distance (A) between the top edge of the jacket lower tube and the column clamp. This should be 7.035 in. (178.7 mm). If the dimension is smaller than the column has suffered partial collapse.

11 Now check that there is no gap between the end of the bolt insert and the end of the slot of the steering column clamp. If there is a measurable clearance then the jacket tube will have been crushed. In either case, renew the steering column complete.

12 Commence installation by setting the roadwheels in the straight-ahead position. Pass the steering column from the vehicle interior and connect the flexible coupling to the worm shaft making sure that the punch mark on the upper end of the steering shaft is at the top.

13 Insert the column clamp bolts finger-tight.

14 Loosen the column flange plate clamp bolt and slide the flange plate into engagement with the bulkhead. Insert the four securing bolts finger-tight.

15 Check for smooth operation of the steering wheel and column by temporarily installing the steering wheel and turning it from lock-to-lock.

16 If this proves satisfactory, tighten all bolts to the specified torque wrench settings.

17 Refit the direction indicator switch, the steering wheel and the column upper and lower shrouds.

15 Steering column lock - removal and installation

1 The steering column lock is combined with the ignition switch.

2 The ignition switch can be withdrawn after removing the small screw which retains it to the body of the lock.

3 Removal of the lock assembly can only be carried out after removing the steering column (Section 14) and drilling out the two shear bolts. If the lock is being renewed, it will probably be easier to remove the lock by sawing through the bolts by placing a hacksaw blade between the two halves of the body.

4 Position the new lock on the steering column and insert the securing bolts finger-tight. Now operate the ignition key several times to make sure that the tongue of the lock is in perfect alignment with the hole in the column tube and is operating smoothly.

5 Tighten the bolts evenly until their heads shear off.

16 Steering box - removal and installation

1 Remove the pinch bolt which secures the flexible coupling to the steering worm shaft. (photo)

2 Bend up the tab of the lockwasher and unscrew the nut which secures the drop arm to the sector shaft. Mark the relative position of the drop arm to the sector shaft to facilitate refitting.

3 Using a heavy duty puller, extract the drop arm from the sector shaft.

4 Unscrew the three bolts which secure the steering box to the body sideframe and remove the steering box from the engine compartment.

5 Installation is a reversal of removal but make sure that the drop arm and sector shaft marks made before dismantling, are in alignment. Do not drive the drop arm into position but draw it onto the sector shaft using the nut. Tighten all bolts to the specified torque.

17 Steering box - dismantling, adjustment, reassembly

1 With the steering box removed from the vehicle, first drain the oil from it by unscrewing the filler plug.

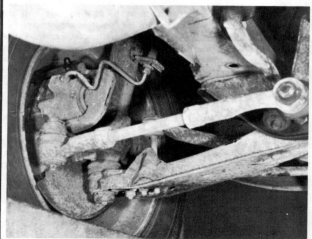

12.1 An outer trackrod

16.1 Steering box (engine removed)

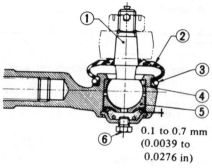

0.1 to 0.7 mm
(0.0039 to
0.0276 in)

Clearance
0.1 to 0.8 mm
(0.0039 to 0.0315 in)

Fig 11.33A Sectional views of steering linkage and front suspension balljoints

1 Ball stud	3 Clamp	5 Spring seat	6 Grease plug
2 Dust cover	4 Seat		

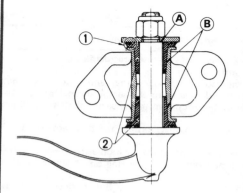

Fig 11.33B Sectional view of the steering idler

1 Seal
2 Rubber bushes
A Idler shaft
B Body

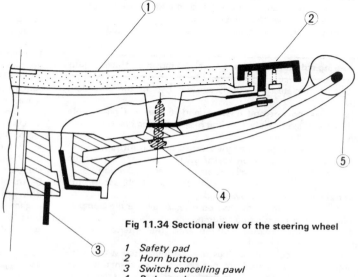

Fig 11.34 Sectional view of the steering wheel

1 Safety pad
2 Horn button
3 Switch cancelling pawl
4 Pad securing screw
5 Wheel rim

179

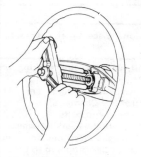

Fig 11.35 Removing the steering wheel with an extractor

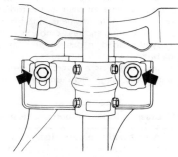

Fig 11.36 Flexible coupling pinch bolt (arrowed)

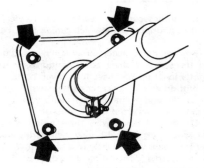

Fig 11.37 Steering column flange plate bolts

Fig 11.38 Steering column upper clamp bolts

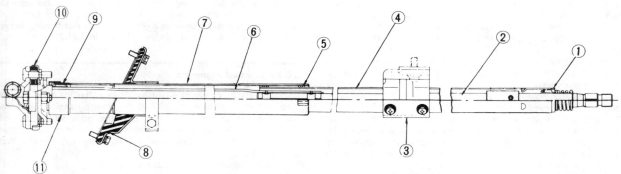

Fig 11.39 Sectional view of the steering column

1 Upper bearing
2 Shaft
3 Clamp
4 Column
5 Steel ball
6 Shaft
7 Lower column
8 Flange
9 Lower bearing
10 Flexible coupling
11 Dust cover

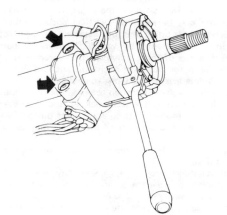

Fig 11.40 Steering column lock securing screws

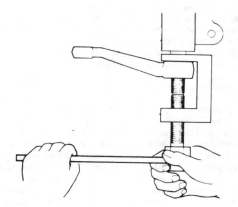

Fig 11.41 Removing drop arm from sector shaft

2 Carefully secure the steering box in a vice, preferably by bolting it to a support plate which can, in turn, be gripped in the vice jaws.

3 Release the adjuster screw locknut and unscrew and remove the three sector shaft cover bolts. Some steering boxes vary slightly in design and have four cover bolts.

4 Withdraw the cover complete with sector shaft. Using the slot in the end of the adjuster screw, turn the screw clockwise to release the cover from the sector shaft.

5 Unbolt the rear cover (three bolts), extract the bearing adjustment shims and withdraw the steering worm assembly. Some steering boxes vary slightly in design and have four cover bolts.

6 No further dismantling should be carried out except for renewal of the worm bearings and two oil seals if required.

7 Clean and check all components for wear or damage. Check the movement of the nut on the worm. Do not allow it to run from end-to-end or the ball guides will be damaged. Renewal of the worm/nut assembly is carried out by renewing the complete unit. Do not remove the sector shaft needle bearings from the steering box but if renewal is necessary, renew the complete steering box casing.

8 Commence reassembly by installing the oil seals so that their identification lettering is visible from the outside of the steering box.

9 Dip the worm assembly in clean lubricant and install it in the steering box.

10 Fig the rear cover, a new 'O' ring seal and the bearing shims (thicker shims to steering box side). Tighten the cover bolts to a torque of between 12 and 20 lb/ft (1.7 to 2.8 kg/m). Now use a spring balance and a cord wound round the splines of the worm shaft, to check the turning torque (bearing preload) which should be between 4 and 6 lbs. (9.0 to 13.0 kg). Always rotate the worm shaft a few turns in both directions to settle the bearings.

11 Where the preload is incorrect, remove the cover and add, remove or substitute shims as necessary. Shims are available in the following thickness:
0.030 in. (0.762 mm), 0.010 in. (0.254 mm)
0.005 in. (0.127 mm), 0.002 in. (0.050 mm)

12 Insert the adjuster screw into the recess in the top of the sector shaft and using feeler blades, measure the clearance at its lower face. The correct clearance is between 0.0004 and 0.0012 in. (0.01 and 0.03 mm) and if it is incorrect, insert a shim of suitable thickness from those available:
0.0620 to 0.0630 in. (1.575 to 1.600 mm)
0.0610 to 0.0620 in. (1.550 to 1.575 mm)
0.0600 to 0.0610 in. (1.525 to 1.550 mm)
0.0591 to 0.600 in. (1.500 to 1.525 mm)

13 Turn the worm shaft until the nut is in the centre of its travel on the worm then insert the sector shaft so that its centre tooth engages with the centre groove of the nut.

14 Smear both sides of a new gasket with jointing compound and locate it on the steering box. Fit the cover by turning the adjuster screw of the sector shaft in an anticlockwise direction. Tighten the cover bolts to the specified torque.

15 Using the slot in the end of the sector shaft adjuster screw, turn the screw until any up and down movement of the sector shaft just disappears (nut still centralised on worm shaft). Now give the adjuster screw a further 1/8 turn in a clockwise direction and tighten the locknut. Measure the turning torque of the wormshaft (as described in paragraph 10 using the cord and spring balance method) which should be between 4 and 11 lbs (9.0 to 24.0 kg). Readjust if necessary and check for smooth operation over the complete arc of travel of the worm shaft. Throughout the overhaul and adjustment operations, never be tempted to grip the splines of the worm shaft or sector shaft with pliers. Finger pressure will normally be sufficient to turn the wormshaft but if essential, slide on a piece of plastic or rubber tubing over the splines to provide protection and a gripping surface.

16 Fill the steering box with specified lubricant to the level of of the filler plug with the unit held in its operational attitude.

18 Steering column and box (one piece type) - removal, servicing and installation

1 To remove this type of unit, withdraw the steering wheel, shrouds and column switch.

2 If a three speed gearbox is fitted, disconnect and remove the steering column gearchange control (see Chapter 6).

3 Remove the two steering column clamp bolts.

4 Remove the four bolts which secure the blanking panel.

5 With the roadwheels in the straight-ahead position, remove the nut and lockwasher which secure the drop arm to the sector shaft of the steering box.

6 Mark the relationship of the drop arm to the end of the shaft and then using a suitable puller, remove the drop arm.

7 Unscrew the three bolts which secure the steering box to the body sideframe member and withdraw the steering box/column assembly into the engine compartment.

8 Dismantling and reassembly operations are similar to those already described in this Chapter for the independent type steering box.

9 Installation is a reversal of removal but install all bolts initially only finger-tight until the unit is checked for alignment.

19 Steering lock stop bolts - adjustment

1 A bolt and locknut is located on each of the steering arms to limit the travel of the steering gear when it is turned to full lock.

2 It is preferable to have the full-lock steering angles adjusted using alignment equipment but as a temporary expedient they should be adjusted to provide a clearance between the inside tyre wall and the drag strut of not less than 1¼ in. (31.75 mm).

20 Front wheel alignment

1 Accurate front wheel alignment is essential for good steering and tyre wear. Before considering the steering angle, check that the tyres are correctly inflated, that the front wheels are not buckled, the hub bearings are not worn or incorrectly adjusted and that the steering linkage is in good order, without slackness or wear at the joints.

2 Wheel alignment consists of four factors:
  Camber, which is the angle at which the front wheels are set from the vertical when viewed from the front of the car. Positive camber is the amount (in degrees) that the wheels are tilted outwards at the top from the vertical.
  Castor is the angle between the steering axis and a vertical line when viewed from each side of the car. Positive castor is when the steering axis is inclined rearward.
  Steering axis inclination is the angle, when viewed from the front of the car, between the vertical and an imaginary line drawn between the upper and lower suspension leg pivots.
  Toe-in is the amount by which the distance between the front inside edges of the roadwheels (measured at hub height) is less than the diametrically opposite distance measured between the rear inside edges of the front roadwheels.

3 All steering angles other than toe-in are set in production and are not adjustable. Front wheel tracking (toe-in) checks are best carried out with modern setting equipment but a reasonably accurate alternative and adjustment procedure may be carried out as follows:

4 Place the car on level ground with the wheels in the straight ahead position.

5 Obtain or make a toe-in gauge. One may be easily made from tubing, cranked to clear the sump and bellhousing, having an adjustable nut and setscrew at one end.

6 With the gauge, measure the distance between the two inner rims of the front roadwheels, at hub height and at the rear of the wheels.

7 Pull or push the vehicle so that the roadwheel turns through half a turn (180°) and measure the distance between the two

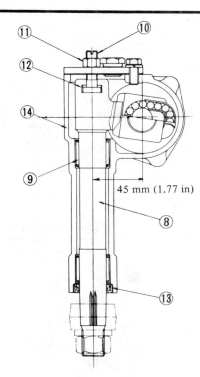

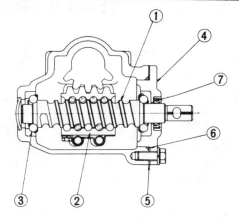

Fig. 11.42 Sectional views of the steering box

1	Worm shaft	8	Sector shaft
2	Ball nut	9	Needle bearings
3	Bearing	10	Adjusting screw
4	Rear cover	11	Locknut
5	Bearing adjuster shims	12	Shim
6	'O' ring	13	Oil seal
7	Oil seal	14	Casing

45 mm (1.77 in)

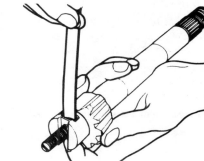

Fig 11.43 Withdrawing the steering worm assembly

Fig 11.44 Checking adjuster bolt clearance in sector shaft

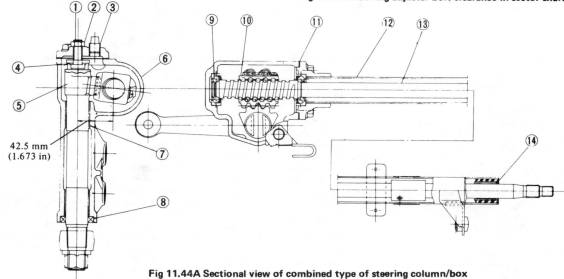

42.5 mm
(1.673 in)

Fig 11.44A Sectional view of combined type of steering column/box

1	Adjusting screw	5	Sector shaft	9	Bearing	12	Column tube
2	Locknut	6	Housing	10	Nut	13	Shaft
3	Filler plug	7	Bush	11	Shims	14	Top bush
4	Shim	8	Oil seal				

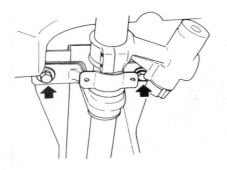

Fig 11.44B Steering column clamp bolts (one piece steering column/box)

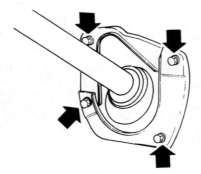

Fig 11.44C Blanking panel bolts (one piece steering column/box)

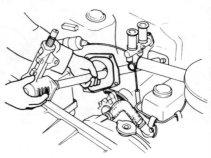

Fig 11.44D Withdrawing the one piece type steering column/box

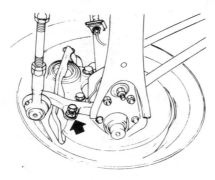

Fig 11.45 Location of a steering lock stop bolt

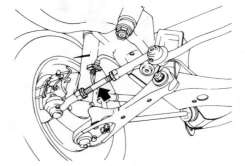

Fig 11.46 Outer trackrod (one side)

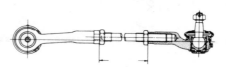

Fig 11.47 Trackrod basic setting diagram

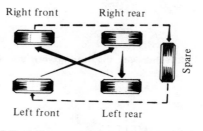

Fig 11.48 Typical tyre rotational pattern (not radial tyres)

inner rims at hub height at the front of the wheel. This last measurement should be less than the first by the specified toe-in (see Specifications Section).

8   Where the toe-in is found to be incorrect, slacken the lock-nuts on each outer track rod and rotate each track rod an equal amount but in opposite directions, until the correct toe-in is obtained. Tighten the locknuts ensuring that the balljoints are held in the centre of their arc of travel during tightening. If new trackrods or balljoints have been fitted, a starting point for adjusting the front wheel alignment is to set each outer trackrod so that the distance measured between the end faces of the track-rod end sockets is 4.0 in. (101.6 mm) for B210 models, and 4.35 in. (110.5 mm) for 120Y models.

21 Wheels and tyres

1   The roadwheels are of pressed steel type.
2   Periodically remove the wheels, clean dirt and mud from the inside and outside surfaces and examine for signs of rusting or rim damage and rectify as necessary
3   Apply a smear of light grease to the wheel studs before

screwing on the nuts and finally tighten them to specified torque.
4   The tyres fitted may be of crossply, bias belt or radial construction according to territory and specification. Never mix tyres of different construction and always check and maintain the pressures regularly.
5   If the wheels have been balanced on the vehicle then it is important that the wheels are not moved round the vehicle in an effort to equalise tread wear. If a wheel is removed, then the relationship of the wheel studs to the holes in the wheel should be marked to ensure exact replacement, otherwise the balance of wheel, hub and tyre will be upset.
6   Where the wheels have been balanced off the vehicle, then they may be moved round to equalise wear. Include the spare wheel in any rotational pattern. If radial tyres are fitted, do not move the wheels from side to side but only interchange the front and rear wheels on the same side.
7   Balancing of the wheels is an essential factor in good steering and road holding. When the tyres have been in use for about half their useful life the wheels should be rebalanced to compensate for the lost tread rubber due to wear.
8   Inspect the tyre walls and treads regularly for cuts and damage and where evident, have them professionally repaired.

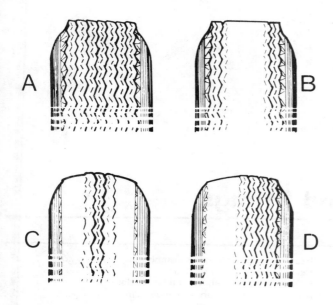

Fig 11.49 Tyre wear patterns and causes

A   'feathering' due to incorrect toe-in
B   over inflation
C   under inflation
D   wear due to incorrect camber, worn wheel bearings and
     fast cornering

22 Fault diagnosis - suspension and steering

Before diagnosing faults from the following chart, check that any irregularities are not caused by:
1   Binding brakes
2   Incorrect 'mix' of radial and crossply tyres
3   Incorrect tyre pressures
4   Misalignment of the bodyframe

Symptom	Reason/s
Steering wheel can be moved considerably before any sign of movement of the wheels is apparent	Wear in the steering linkage gear.
Vehicle difficult to steer in a consistent straight line - wandering	As above. Wheel alignment incorrect (indicated by excessive or uneven tyre wear). Front wheel hub bearings loose or worn. Worn suspension unit swivel joints.
Steering stiff and heavy	Incorrect wheel alignment (indicated by excessive or uneven tyre wear). Excessive wear or seizure in one or more of the joints in the steering linkage or suspension unit balljoints. Excessive wear in the steering gear unit.
Wheel wobble and vibration	Roadwheels out of balance. Roadwheels buckled. Wheel alignment incorrect. Wear in the steering linkage, suspension unit bearings or track control arm bushes. Broken fornt spring.
Excessive pitching and rolling on corners and during braking	Defective shock absorbers and/or broken spring.

Chapter 12 Bodywork and fittings

Contents

1 General description

The body and underframe is of unitary, all-welded steel construction. The range comprises two and four door Saloons and a Coupe. The Estate wagon version is only available in the 120Y model.

The front wings are of bolt-on type to ensure economical replacement in the event of damage.

There are minor differences in design of some components used on B210 and 120Y models and these include the radiator grille, the rear panel and the front and rear bumper assemblies.

2 Maintenance - bodywork and underframe

1 The general condition of a car's bodywork is the one thing that significantly affects its value. Maintenance is easy but needs to be regular. Neglect, particularly after minor damage, can lead quickly to further deterioration and costly repair bills. It is important also to keep watch on those parts of the car not immediately visible, for instance the underside, inside all the wheel arches and the lower part of the engine compartment.

2 The basic maintenance routine for the bodywork is washing - preferably with a lot of water, from a hose. This will remove all the loose solids which may have stuck to the car. It is important to flush these off in such a way as to prevent grit from scratching the finish.

3 The wheel arches and underbody need washing in the same way to remove any accumulated mud which will retain moisture and tend to encourage rust. Paradoxically enough, the best time to clean the underbody and wheel arches is in wet weather when the mud is thoroughly wet and soft. In very wet weather the underbody is usually cleaned of large accumulations auto-

matically and this is a good time for inspection.

4 Periodically it is a good idea to have the whole of the underside of the car steam cleaned, engine compartment included, so that a thorough inspection can be carried out to see what minor repairs and renovations are necessary. Steam cleaning is available at many garages and is necessary for removal of accumulation of oily grime which sometimes is allowed to cake thick in certain areas near the engine, gearbox and back axle. If steam facilities are not available, there are one or two excellent grease solvents available which can be brush applied. The dirt can then be simply hosed off.

5 After washing paintwork, wipe off with a chamois leather to give an unspotted clear finish. A coat of clear protective wax polish will give added protection against chemical pollutants in the air. If the paintwork sheen has dulled or oxidised, use a cleaner/polisher combination to restore the brilliance of the shine. This requires a little effort, but is usually caused because regular washing has been neglected. Always check that the door and ventilator opening drain holes and pipes are completely clear so that water can drain out. Bright work should be treated the same way as paintwork. Windscreens and windows can be kept clear of the smeary film which often appears if a little ammonia is added to the water. If they are scratched, a good rub with a proprietary metal polish will often clear them. Never use any form of wax or other body or chromium polish on glass.

3 Maintenance - upholstery and carpets

1 Mats and carpets should be brushed or vacuum cleaned regularly to keep them free of grit. If they are badly stained remove them from the car for scrubbing or sponging and make quite sure they are dry before replacement. Seats and interior trim panels can be kept clean by a wipe over with a damp cloth.

If they do become stained (which can be more apparent on light coloured upholstery) use a little liquid detergent and a soft nail brush to scour the grime out of the grain of the material. Do not forget to keep the head lining clean in the same way as the upholstery. When using liquid cleaners inside the car do not over-wet the surfaces being cleaned. Excessive damp could get into the seams and padded interior causing stains, offensive odours or even rot. If the inside of the car gets wet accidentally it is worthwhile taking some trouble to dry it out properly, particularly where carpets are involved. **Do not** leave oil or electric heaters inside the car for this purpose.

4 Minor body damage - repair

See photo sequences on pages 190 and 191.

Repair of minor scratches in the car's bodywork

If the scratch is very superficial, and does not penetrate to the metal of the bodywork - repair is very simple. Lightly rub the area of the scratch with a paintwork renovator (eg; T-Cut), or a very fine cutting paste, to remove loose paint from the scratch and to clear the surrounding bodywork of wax polish. Rinse the area with clean water.

Apply touch-up paint to the scratch using a thin paint brush; continue to apply thin layers of paint until the surface of the paint in the scratch is level with the surrounding paintwork. Allow the new paint at least two weeks to harden, then, blend it into the surrounding paintwork by rubbing the paintwork in the scratch area with a paintwork renovator (eg: T-Cut), or a very fine cutting paste. Finally apply wax polish.

An alternative to painting over the scratch is to use Holts Scratch-Patch. Use the same preparation for the affected area; then simply, pick a patch of a suitable size to cover the scratch completely. Hold the patch against the scratch and burnish its backing paper; the patch will adhere to the paintwork, freeing itself from the backing paper at the same time. Polish the affected area to blend the patch into the surrounding paintwork.

Where a scratch has penetrated right through to the metal of the bodywork, causing the metal to rust, a different repair technique is required. Remove any loose rust inhibiting paint (eg; Kurust) to prevent the formation of rust in the future. Using a rubber or nylon applicator fill the scratch with body-stopper paste. If required, this paste can be mixed with cellulose thinners to provide a very thin paste which is ideal for filling narrow scratches. Before the stopper paste in the scratch hardens, wrap a piece of smooth cotton rag around the tip of a finger. Dip the finger in cellulose thinners and then quickly sweep it across the surface of the stopper-paste this will ensure that it is slightly hollowed. The scratch can now be painted over as described earlier in this Section.

Repair of dents in the car's bodywork

When deep denting of the car's bodywork has taken place, the first task is to pull the dent out, until the affected bodywork almost attains its original shape. There is little point in trying to restore the original shape completely, as the metal in the damaged area will have stretched on impact and cannot be reshaped fully to its original contour. It is better to bring the level of the dent up to a point which is about 1/8 inch (3 mm) below the level of the surround bodywork. In cases where the dent is very shallow anyway, it is not worth trying to pull it out at all.

If the underside of the dent is accessible, it can be hammered out gently from behind, using a mallet with a wooden or plastic head. Whilst doing this, hold a suitable block of wood firmly against the outside of the dent. This block will absorb the impact from the hammer blows and thus prevent a large area of bodywork from being 'belled-out'.

Should the dent be in a section of the bodywork which has double skin or some other factor making it inaccessible from behind, a defferent technique is called for. Drill several small holes through the metal inside the dent area - particularly in the deeper sections. Then screw long self-tapping screws into the holes just sufficiently for them to gain a good purchase in the metal. Now the dent can be pulled out by pulling on the protruding heads of the screws with a pair of pliers.

The next stage of the repair is the removal of the paint from the damaged area, and from an inch or so of the surrounding 'sound' bodywork. This is accomplished most easily by using a wire brush or abrasive pad on a power drill, although it can be done just as effectively by hand using sheets of abrasive paper. To complete the preparations for filling, score the surface of the bare metal with a screwdriver or the tang of a file, or alternatively, drill small holes in the affected area. This will provide a really good 'key' for the filler paste.

To complete the repair see the Section on filling and respraying.

Repair of rust holes or gashes in the car's bodywork

Remove all paint from the affected area and from an inch or so of the surrounding 'sound' bodywork, using an abrasive pad or a wire brush on a power drill. If these are not available a few sheets of abrasive paper will do the job just as effectively. With the paint removed you will be able to gauge the severity of the corrosion and therefore decide whether to replace the whole panel (if this is possible) or to repair the affected area. Replacement body panels are not as expensive as most people think and it is often quicker and more satisfactory to fit a new panel than to attempt to repair large areas of corrosion.

Remove all fittings from the affected area except those which will act as a guide to the original shape of the damaged bodywork (eg; headlamp shells etc). Then, using tin snips or a hacksaw blade, remove all loose metal and any other metal badly affected by corrosion. Hammer the edges of the holes inwards in order to create a sligh depression for the filler paste.

Wire brush the affected area to remove the powdery rust from the surface of the remaining metal. Paint the affected area with rust inhibiting paint; if the back of the rusted area is accessible treat this also.

Before filling can take place it will be necessary to block the hole in some way. This can be achieved by the use of one of the following materials: Zinc gauze, Aluminium tape or Poly-urethane foam.

Zinc gauze is probably the best material to use for a large hole. Cut a piece to the approximate size and shape of the hole to be filled, then position it in the hole so that its edges are below the level of the surrounding bodywork. It can be retained in position by several blobs of filler plaste around its periphery.

Aluminium tape should be used for small or very narrow holes. Pull a piece off the roll and trim it to the approximate size and shape required, then pull off the backing paper (if used) and stick the tape over the hole; it can be overlapped if the thickness of one piece is insufficient. Burnish down the edges of the tape with the handle of a screwdriver or similar, to ensure that the tape is securely attached to the metal underneath.

Polyurethane foam is best used where the hole is situated in a section of bodywork of complex shape, backed by a small box section (eg; where the sill panel meets the rear wheel arch - most cars). The usual mixing procedure for this foam is as follows: Put equal amounts of fluid from each of the two cans provided in the kits, into one container. Stir until the mixture begins to thicken, then quickly pour this mixture into the hole, and hold a piece of cardboard over the larger apertures. Almost immediately the polyurethane will begin to expand, gushing frantically out of any small holes left unblocked. When the foam hardens it can be cut back to just below the level of the surrounding bodywork with a hacksaw blade.

Having blocked off the hole, the affected area must now be filled and sprayed - see Section on bodywork filling and respraying.

Bodywork repairs - filling and re-spraying

Before using this Section, see the Sections on dent, deep scratch, rust hole, and gash repairs.

Many types of bodyfiller are available, but generally speaking those proprietary kits which contain a tin of filler paste and a tube of resin hardener (eg; Holts Cataloy) are best for this type of repair. A wide, flexible plastic or nylon applicator will be found invaluable for imparting a smooth and well contoured finish to the surface of the filler.

Mix up a little filler on a clean piece of card or board - use the hardener sparingly (follow the maker's instructions on the pack), otherwise the filler will set very rapidly.

Using the applicator, apply the filler paste to the prepared area; draw the applicator across the surface of the filler to achieve the correct contour and to level the filler surface. As soon as a contour that approximates the correct one is achieved, stop working the paste - if you carry on too long the paste will become sticky and begin to 'pick-up' on the applicator.

Continue to add thin layers of filler paste at twenty-minute intervals until the level of the filler is just 'proud' of the surrounding bodywork.

Once the filler has hardened, excess can be removed using a Surform plane or Dreadnought file. From then on, progressively finer grades of abrasive paper should be used, starting with a 40 grade 'wet-and-dry' paper. Always wrap the abrasive paper around a flat rubber cork, or wooden block - otherwise the surface of the filler will not be completely flat. During the smoothing of the filler surface the 'wet-and-dry' paper should be periodically rinsed in water - this will ensure that a very smooth finish is imparted to the filler at the final stage.

At this stage the 'dent' should be surrounded by a ring of bare metal, which in turn should be encircled by the finely 'feathered' edge of the good paintwork. Rinse the repair area with clean water, until all of the dust produced by the rubbing-down operating is gone.

Spray the whole repair area with a light coat of grey primer - this will show up any imperfections in the surface of the filler. Repair these imperfections with fresh filler paste or body-stopper, and once more smooth the surface with abrasive paper. If bodystopper is used, it can be mixed with cellulose thinners to form a really thin paste which is ideal for filling small holes. Repeat this spray and repair procedure until you are satisfied that the surface of the filler, and the feathered edge of the paintwork are perfect. Clean the repair area with clean water and allow to dry fully.

The repair area is now ready for spraying. Paint spraying must be carried out in a warm, dry, windless and dust free atmosphere. This condition can be created artificially if you have access to a large indoor working area, but if you are forced to work in the open, you will have to pick your day carefully. If you are working indoors, dousing the floor in the work area with water will 'lay' the dust which would otherwise be in the atmosphere. If the repair area is confined to one body panel, mask off the surrounding panels; this will help to minimise the effects of a slight mis-match in paint colours. Bodywork fittings (eg; chrome strips, door handles etc) will also need to be masked off. Use genuine masking tape and several thicknesses of newspaper for the masking operation.

Before commencing to spray, agitate the aerosol can thoroughly, then spray a test area (an old tin, or similar) until the technique is mastered. Cover the repair area with a thick coat of primer; the thickness should be built up using several thin layers of paint rather than one thick one. Using 400 grade 'wet-and-dry' paper, rub down the surface of the primer until it is really smooth. While doing this, the work area should be thoroughly doused with water, and the wet-and-dry paper periodically rinsed in water. Allow to dry before spraying on more paint.

Spray on the top coat, again building up the thickness by using several thin layers of paint. Start spraying in the centre of the repair area and then using a circular motion, work outwards until the whole repair area and about 2 inches of the surrounding original paintwork is covered. Remove all masking material 10 to 15 minutes after spraying on the final coat of paint. Allow the new paint at least 2 weeks to harden fully, then using a paintwork renovation (eg; T-Cut) or a very fine cutting paste, blend the edges of the new paint into the existing paintwork.

Finally, apply wax polish.

5 Major body damage - repair

Where serious damage has occurred or large areas need renewal due to neglect, it means certainly that completely new sections or panels will need welding in and this is best left to professionals. If the damage is due to impact it will also be necessary to completely check the alignment of the body shell structure. Due to the principle of construction the strength and shape of the whole can be affected by damage to a part. In such instances the services of a Datsun agent with specialist checking jigs are essential. If a body is left misaligned it is first of all dangerous as the car will not handle properly and secondly uneven stresses will be imposed on the steering, engine and transmission, causing abnormal wear or complete failure. Tyre wear may also be excessive.

6 Maintenance - hinges and locks

1 Oil the hinges of the bonnet, boot and doors with a drop or two of light oil periodically. A good time is after the car has been washed.
2 Oil the bonnet release catch pivot pin and the safety catch pivot pin periodically.
3 Do not over lubricate door latches and strikers. Normally a little oil on the rotary cam spindle alone is sufficient.

7 Doors - tracing rattles and their rectification

1 Check first that the door is not loose at the hinges and that the latch is holding the door firmly in position. Check also that the door lines up with the aperture in the body.
2 If the hinges are loose or the door is out of alignment it will be necessary to reset the hinge positions, as described in Section 13.
3 If the latch is holding the door properly it should hold the door tightly when fully latched and the door should line up with the body. If it is out of alignment it needs adjustment as described in Section 20. If loose, some part of the lock mechanism must be worn out and requiring renewal.
4 Other rattle from the door would be caused by wear or looseness in the window winder, the glass channels and sill strips or the door buttons and interior latch release mechanism. All these are dealt with in Sections 17, 18 and 19.

8 Radiator grille - removal and installation

1 Open the bonnet and then remove the six screws which secure the radiator grille. Lift out the radiator grille. (photo)
2 Installation is a reversal of removal but make sure that the positioning spigots at the base of the grille are correctly located.

9 Front and rear bumpers (B210 models) - removal and installation

1 Unscrew the nuts which secure the bumper bar to the shock absorbers. Remove the bumper bar.
2 The shock absorbers may now be removed by unbolting them from the bodyframe.
3 Removal of front and rear bumper assemblies is similar except that with the shield fitted at the rear, the securing bolts are accessible from within the luggage boot.
4 The shock absorber units are gas-filled and must not be drilled or any attempt made to dismantle them. If they are faulty, renew them as complete units.
5 Installation is a reversal of removal but the bumpers must be adjusted for height as shown in the diagrams, before fully

tightening the securing nuts. In the case of the front bumper, this must be adjusted for horizontal location as well as for vertical position.

10 Front and rear bumpers (120Y models) - removal and installation

1   Bumpers on these models are simply attached by brackets and end bolts.
2   Before removing the front bumper, disconnect the leads to the side/flasher lamps.
3   Before removing the rear bumper on Saloon and Coupe models, disconnect the lead to the number plate lamp.
4   Installation is a reversal of removal.

11 Front wing - removal and installation

1   Open the bonnet fully.
2   Remove the radiator grille (Section 8).
3   Remove the front bumper (Section 9 or 10).
4   Unscrew and remove the two bolts which secure the front apron to the front wing.
5   Remove the windscreen wiper arms and the air intake grille.
6   With all models, disconnect the leads to the side marker lamps.
7   Remove the wing securing setscrews from the edge of the engine compartment, from the top cowl panel and from the body sill.

8   Installation is a reversal of removal but ensure that the mating flanges are clean and renew any beads of sealant to make a waterproof joint.
9   A new wing will require finishing to colour on its top surface and the application of body sealing compound to its under surface.

12 Bonnet - removal, installation and adjustment

1   Open the bonnet fully. Scribe round the hinge plates on the bonnet lid brackets so that they can be installed in their original positions.
2   Remove the hinge bolts and with the help of an assistant, lift the bonnet from its location.
3   Installation is a reversal of removal.
4   If necessary, the bonnet lid may be adjusted by loosening it on its hinges and moving it until there is an even gap between its rear edge and sides and the bodywork. Its rear surface must also be flush with the upper surfaces of the front wings.
5   The front surface of the bonnet lid can be adjusted to be flush with the upper surfaces of the front wings by screwing the rubber buffers in or out as required. If the buffers are adjusted, then almost certainly, the bonnet lock will require adjustment. To do this, release the locknut and screw the dovetail bolt in or out until the bonnet will close with gentle hand pressure and will not have a tendency to rattle when in the locked position.
6   Apply a little oil and grease to the moving parts of the bonnet lock mechanism at regular intervals.

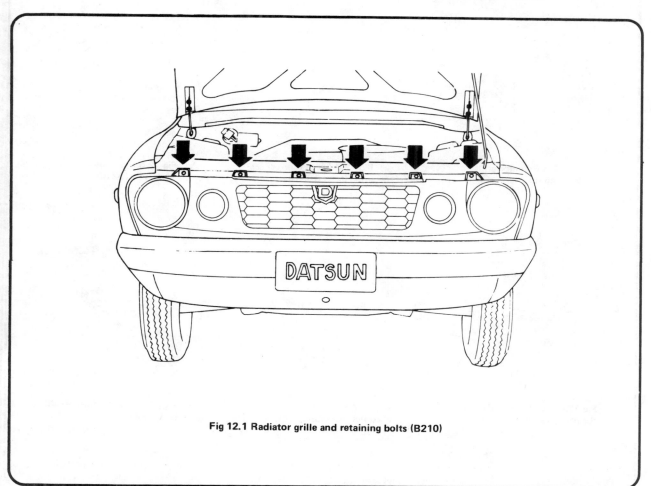

Fig 12.1 Radiator grille and retaining bolts (B210)

Fig 12.2 Radiator grille and retaining bolts (120Y)

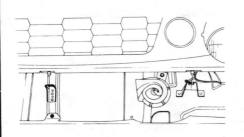

Fig 12.3 Radiator grille
locating spigots

Fig 12.4 Front bumper securing bolts (B210)

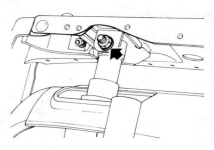

Fig 12.5 Rear bumper sec-
uring bolt (B210)

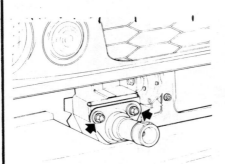

Fig 12.6 Front bumper shock
absorber mounting (B210)

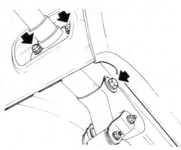

Fig 12.7 Rear bumper shock
absorber mounting (B210)

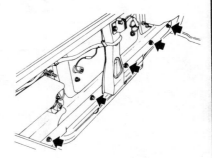

Fig 12.8 Rear bumper shield
bolts (B210)

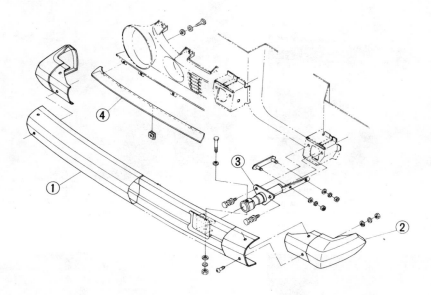

Fig 12.9 Exploded view of the front bumper (B210)

1 Bumper bar   2 Corner section   3 Shock absorber   4 Shield

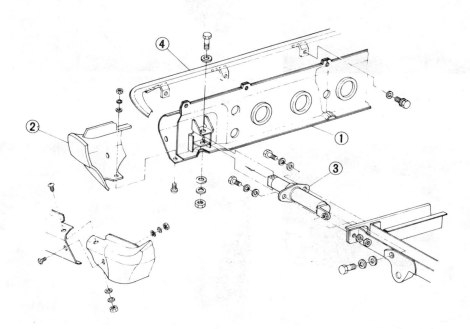

Fig 12.10 Exploded view of the rear bumper (B210)

1 Bumper bar   2 Corner section   3 Shock absorber   4 Shield

This sequence of photographs deals with the repair of the dent and paintwork damage shown in this photo. The procedure will be similar for the repair of a hole. It should be noted that the procedures given here are simplified — more explicit instructions will be found in the text

In the case of a dent the first job — after removing surrounding trim — is to hammer out the dent where access is possible. This will minimise filling. Here, the large dent having been hammered out, the damaged area is being made slightly concave

Now all paint must be removed from the damaged area, by rubbing with coarse abrasive paper. Alternatively, a wire brush or abrasive pad can be used in a power drill. Where the repair area meets good paintwork, the edge of the paintwork should be 'feathered', using a finer grade of abrasive paper

In the case of a hole caused by rusting, all damaged sheet-metal should be cut away before proceeding to this stage. Here, the damaged area is being treated with rust remover and inhibitor before being filled

Mix the body filler according to its manufacturer's instructions. In the case of corrosion damage, it will be necessary to block off any large holes before filling — this can be done with aluminium or plastic mesh, or aluminium tape. Make sure the area is absolutely clean before ...

... applying the filler. Filler should be applied with a flexible applicator, as shown, for best results; the wooden spatula being used for confined areas. Apply thin layers of filler at 20-minute intervals, until the surface of the filler is slightly proud of the surrounding bodywork

Initial shaping can be done with a Surform plane or Dreadnought file. Then, using progressively finer grades of wet-and-dry paper, wrapped around a sanding block, and copious amounts of clean water, rub down the filler until really smooth and flat. Again, feather the edges of adjoining paintwork

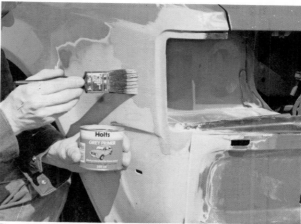

The whole repair area can now be sprayed or brush-painted with primer. If spraying, ensure adjoining areas are protected from over-spray. Note that at least one inch of the surrounding sound paintwork should be coated with primer. Primer has a 'thick' consistency, so will find small imperfections

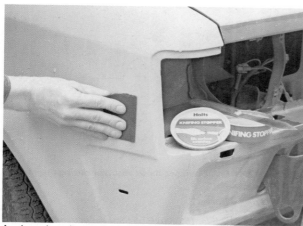

Again, using plenty of water, rub down the primer with a fine grade wet-and-dry paper (400 grade is probably best) until it is really smooth and well blended into the surrounding paintwork. Any remaining imperfections can now be filled by carefully applied knifing stopper paste

When the stopper has hardened, rub down the repair area again before applying the final coat of primer. Before rubbing down this last coat of primer, ensure the repair area is blemish-free — use more stopper if necessary. To ensure that the surface of the primer is really smooth use some finishing compound

The top coat can now be applied. When working out of doors, pick a dry, warm and wind-free day. Ensure surrounding areas are protected from over-spray. Agitate the aerosol thoroughly, then spray the centre of the repair area, working outwards with a circular motion. Apply the paint as several thin coats

After a period of about two weeks, which the paint needs to harden fully, the surface of the repaired area can be 'cut' with a mild cutting compound prior to wax polishing. When carrying out bodywork repairs, remember that the quality of the finished job is proportional to the time and effort expended

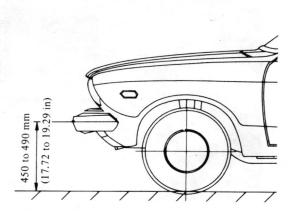

Fig 12.11 Front bumper setting diagram (all B210 models)

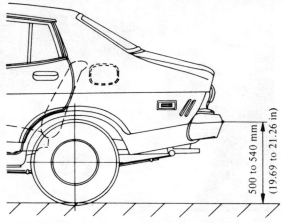

Fig 12.12 Rear bumper setting diagram (B210 Saloon)

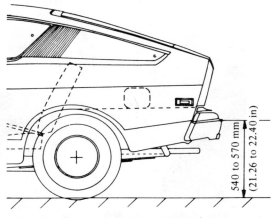

Fig 12.13 Rear bumper setting diagram (B210 Coupe)

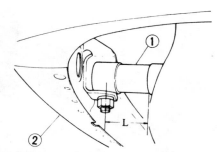

Fig. 12.14 Front bumper shock absorber setting diagram (B210 models)

1 Shock absorber
2 Bumper bar
L = 2.24 to 2.5 in. (56.8 to 63.5 mm) Ampco make
    2.30 to 2.60 in. (58.5 to 65.5 mm) Tokiko make

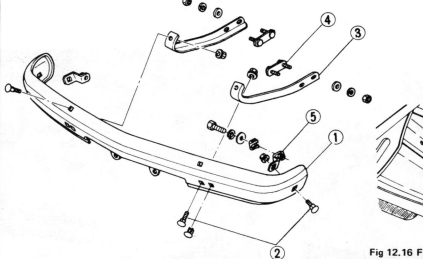

Fig 12.15 Exploded view of the front bumper (120Y)

1 Bumper bar
2 Bolt
3 Stay
4 Bolt
5 End bracket

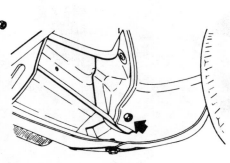

Fig 12.16 Front bumper end bracket bolt (120Y)

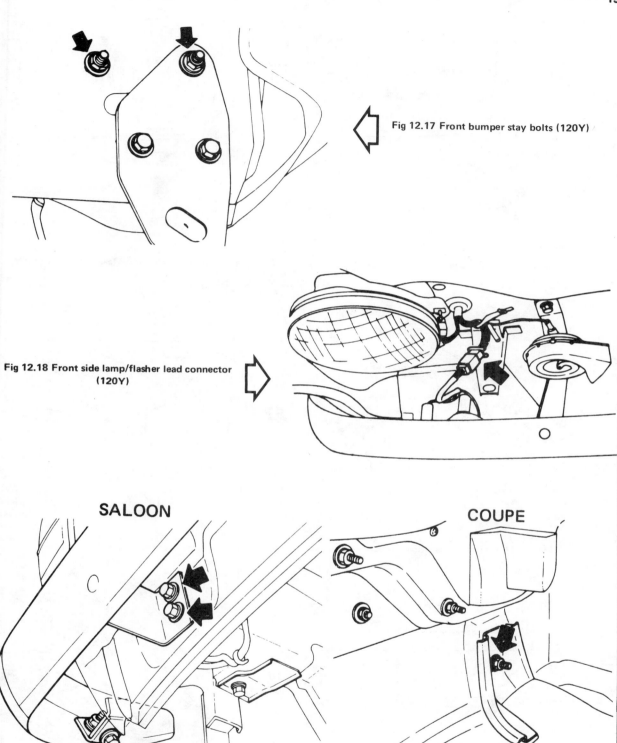

Fig 12.17 Front bumper stay bolts (120Y)

Fig 12.18 Front side lamp/flasher lead connector (120Y)

SALOON

COUPE

Fig 12.19 Rear bumper stay bolts (120Y saloon and coupe)

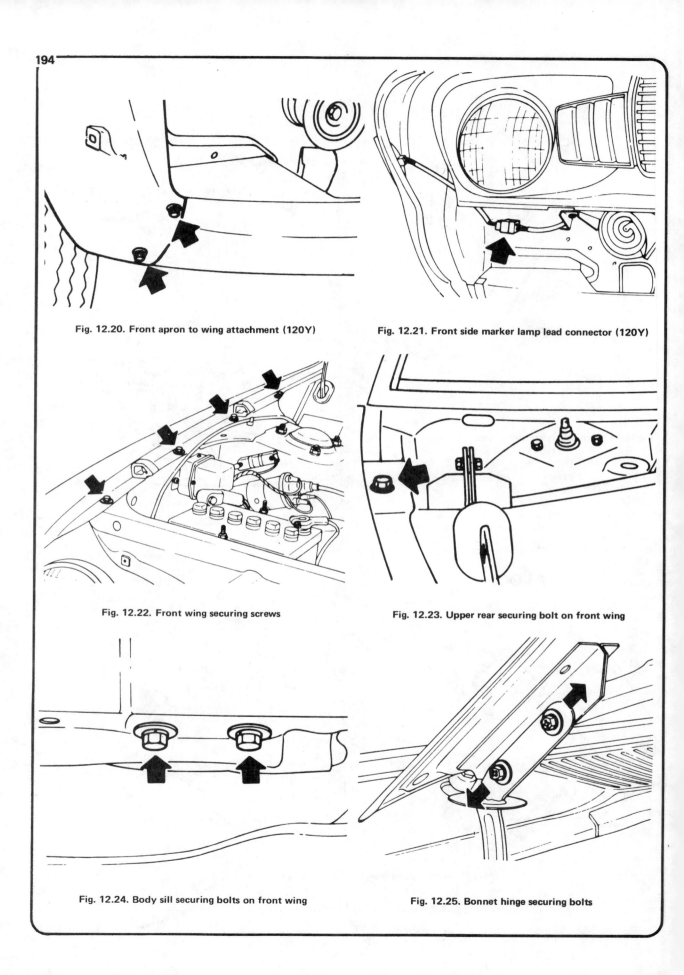

Fig. 12.20. Front apron to wing attachment (120Y)

Fig. 12.21. Front side marker lamp lead connector (120Y)

Fig. 12.22. Front wing securing screws

Fig. 12.23. Upper rear securing bolt on front wing

Fig. 12.24. Body sill securing bolts on front wing

Fig. 12.25. Bonnet hinge securing bolts

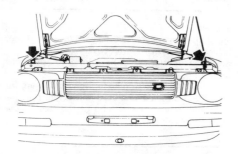

Fig 12.26 Location of bonnet lid buffers

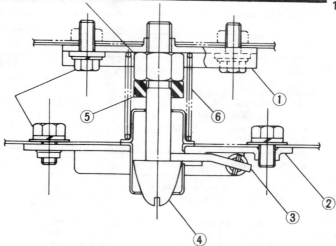

Fig 12.27 Sectional view of the bonnet lock

1   Male mounting plate
2   Female mounting plate
3   Latch
4   Dovetail bolt
5   Rubber buffer
6   Spring

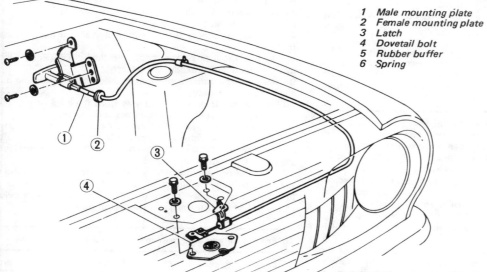

Fig 12.28 Components of the bonnet remote control lock

1   Cable
2   Grommet
3   Clamp
4   Latch assembly

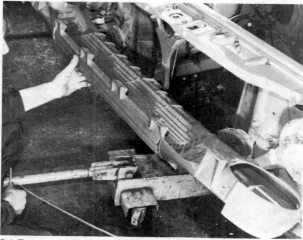

8.1 Removing the radiator grille (120Y)

13 Heater air intake grille - removal and installation

1   The grille can be removed without first having to remove the bonnet.
2   Remove the windscreen wiper arms.
3   Unscrew and remove the air intake grille securing screws. The grille can now be drawn forward and removed.
4   Installation is a reversal of removal.

14 Luggage boot lid - removal and installation

1   Open the lid fully and scribe round the hinge plates on the underside of the lid to ensure that the lid is refitted in its original position.
2   Remove the bolts which secure the hinges to the underside of the lid and with the help of an assistant, lift the lid from the car.
3   Installation is a reversal of removal. Any adjustment can be carried out by moving the position of the lid on the hinge plates with the securing bolts only finger-tight.
4   The lock and striker may then require re-positioning and they can both be moved after their securing screws have been released.
5   The luggage boot lid has a counterblance effect provided by two torsion bars. These may be removed if required by supporting the lid in the fully open position and levering each bar from its end bracket with a long screwdriver or similar tool.

15 Tailgate (Coupe) - removal and installation

1   Raise the tailgate to its fully open position and either prop it open with a length of wood or have an assistant hold it open. Disconnect the leads to the heated rear window.
2   Mark the positions of the hinge plates on the inner surface of the tailgate to facilitate replacement in its original position.
3   Unscrew and remove (from the tailgate) the hinge bolts and the counterblance strut bolts. Lift the tailgate from the car.
4   Never attempt to dismantle a counterbalance strut but if it becomes faulty, renew it as a unit.
5   Installation is a reversal of removal. Any adjustment of the position of the tailgate can be made by moving it with the hinge bolts only finger-tight. Always make sure that there is an even gap of between 0.160 and 0.280 in (4.0 and 7.0 mm) between the leading edge of the tailgate and the roof.
6   Any adjustment of the tailgate will necessitate adjustment of the lock or striker or both. Set the striker so that there is a clearance between the bottom edge of the tailgate and the rear panel of between 0.60 and 0.90 in (16.0 and 22.0 mm).

16 Tailgate (Estate) - removal and installation

1   Open the tailgate to its fullest extent and scribe round the hinge plates to ensure refitting in their original positions.
2   Disconnect the leads from the heated rear window.
3   With an assistant supporting the tailgate, unscrew and remove the bolts which secure the hinges to the tailgate and lift the tailgate away.
4   Installation is a reversal of removal. Any minor adjustment of the position of the tailgate within the body opening can be made by moving the tailgate on its hinges with the securing bolts only finger-tight. Further adjustment can be made if necessary, by removing the hinge covers and loosening (*not removing*) the hinge to body bolts.
5   After any adjustment of the hinges, the striker or lock (or both) may need re-positioning after slackening the securing screws. Access to the lock for removal can only be obtained after the tailgate interior trim panel has been removed.
6   The tailgate is counterbalanced by two torsion bars and where the tailgate no longer opens to its full height then they

must be renewed.
7   To remove the torsion bars, first withdraw the hinge covers and the luggage compartment lamp cover.
8   Peel back the rear edge of the headlining to gain access to the torsion bars.
9   Use a long bar as a lever to release the torsion bars from their end brackets. Keep the tailgate closed as much as possible during this operation and release the tension of the torsion bar slowly without letting the lever slip.

17 Door lock - removal and installation

1   Open the door fully and remove the arm rest. (photo)
2   Remove the screw which secures the door interior handle escutcheon and withdraw the escutcheon. (photo)
3   Remove the window regulator handle securing screw and detach the handle. (photo)
4   On rear doors, remove the ashtray (one screw).
5   Using a screwdriver, prise a corner of the door interior panel from the door frame and then insert the fingers and pull the panel complete with clips from the door frame. (photo)
6   Remove the waterproof sheet.
7   Remove the screws which secsure the door interior handle. (photo)
8   Remove the lock plunger knob and then disconnect the lock cylinder crank arm and control rod. (photo)
9   Unscrew and remove the two exterior handle securing nuts and remove the handle.
10 Remove the lock securing screws from the edge of the door frame and withdraw the lock from the door interior.
11 Installation is a reversal of removal but grease moving parts and adjust the exterior handle clearance by means of the nylon nut as shown in the diagram. When adjustment is complete, lock the nut with a dab of suitable adhesive.
12 The interior handle should be secured after it has been slid to the rear (within the limits of the elongated holes) as far as possible, using finger pressure only. Re-install the window regulator handle at the angle shown in the diagram.

18 Front door glass and regulator - removal and installation

1   Lower the glass fully and then remove the door interior handle, regulator handle and trim panel as described in the preceding Section.
2   Remove the weatherstrip and the moulding from the top edge of the door panel.
3   Remove the screws from the front lower glass guide and slide it from the edge of the glass.
4   Support the door glass and remove the screws which retain the bottom channel to the glass backplate. (photo)
5   The glass can now be drawn upwards and removed from the door interior.
6   Unscrew the screws which secure the guide channel and regulator assembly to the door interior panel and then withdraw the assembly through the door lower aperture. (photo)
7   Installation is a reversal of removal but adjust the glass for correct alignment and smooth operation by moving the position of the front and rear glass guides and the guide channel.

19 Rear door glass and regulator - removal and installation

1   Lower the glass fully and then remove the door interior handle, regulator handle and trim panel, as described in Section 17.
2   Remove the weatherstrip and moulding from the top edge of the door panel.
3   Peel back the top rubber weatherstrip for access to the divider channel upper securing screws and remove them. Remove the divider channel bottom screw and the screws which retain the bottom channel to the glass backplate.

4   Withdraw the quarterlight complete with divider channel and rubber weatherstrip.

5   Tilt the window glass and withdraw it upwards.

6   Unscrew and remove the regulator unit securing screws and withdraw it, through the door lower aperture.

7   Installation is a reversal of removal but adjust for alignment and smooth operation of the glass by moving the position of the divider channel (lower end) and the bottom glass channel.

20 Door - removal and installation

Rear door

1   First, open the front and rear doors fully.

2   Place some thick rag under the lower edge of the door and support it with a jack or blocks.

3   Unscrew and remove the bolts which secure the hinge plates to the centre body pillar and then carefully lift the door from the body.

Front door

4   Detach the windscreen wiper arms and unscrew and remove the heater air intake grille.

5   Remove the front wing, as described earlier in this Chapter.

6   Open the door fully and support it wiht a jack or blocks placed under its bottom edge.

7   Installation of both doors is a reversal of removal but adjust the position of the hinge plates to provide positive closure, an even gap all round and the door panel to be flush with the body panels.

21 Side window (Coupe) - removal and installation

1   Open the window and remove the hinge covers.

2   Remove the hinge to bodyframe screws also the handle securing screws and lift the window assembly from the car.

3   Installation is a reversal of removal.

17.1 Removing a door armrest

17.2 Removing a door interior handle escutcheon

17.3 Removing a window regulator handle

17.5 Withdrawing door interior panel

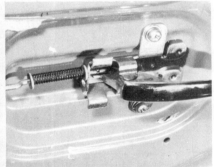
17.7 Door interior handle assembly

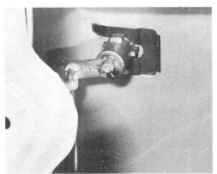
17.8 Lock cylinder crankarm and control rod

18.4 Door window glass backplate and bottom channel

18.6 Window regulator assembly securing bolts

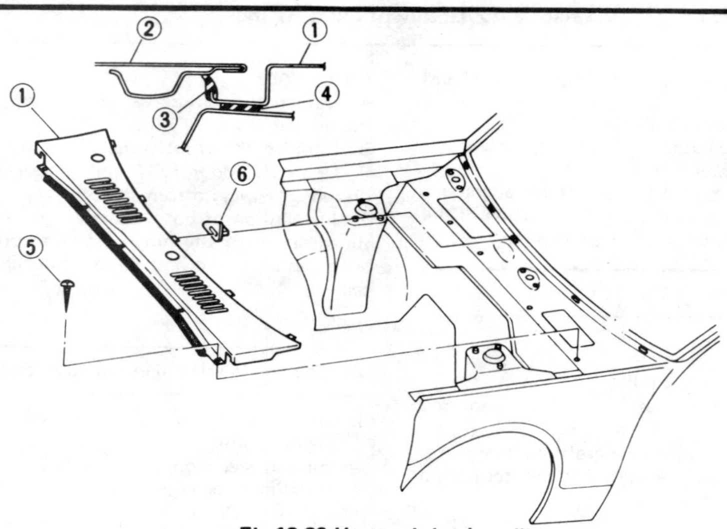

Fig 12.29 Heater air intake grille

1 Grille
2 Bonnet lid

3 and 4 seals

5 Screw

6 Locating plate

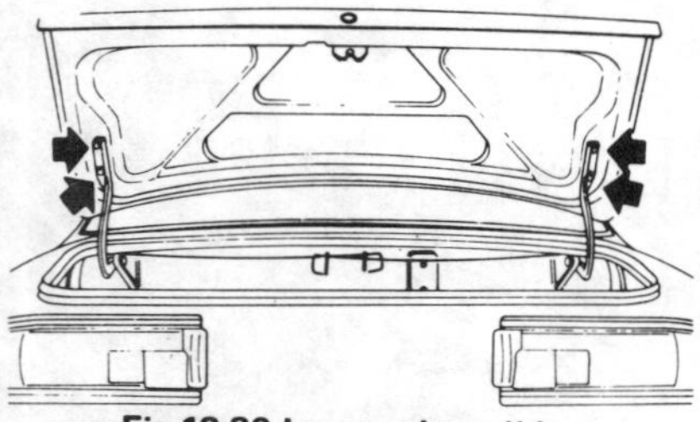

Fig 12.30 Luggage boot lid
hinges (Saloon models)

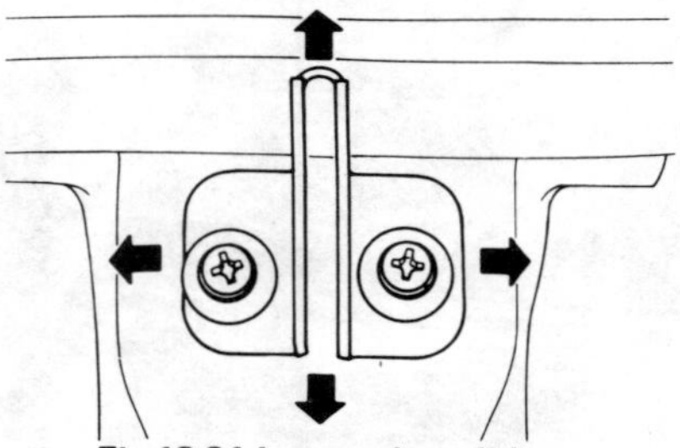

Fig 12.31 Luggage boot lid
lock striker plate

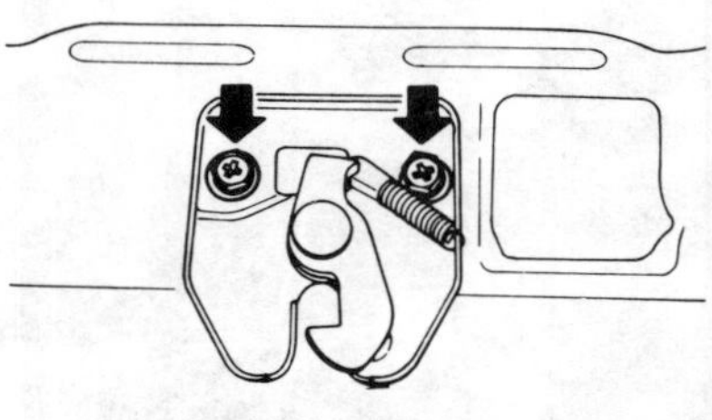

Fig 12.32 Luggage boot lid
lock

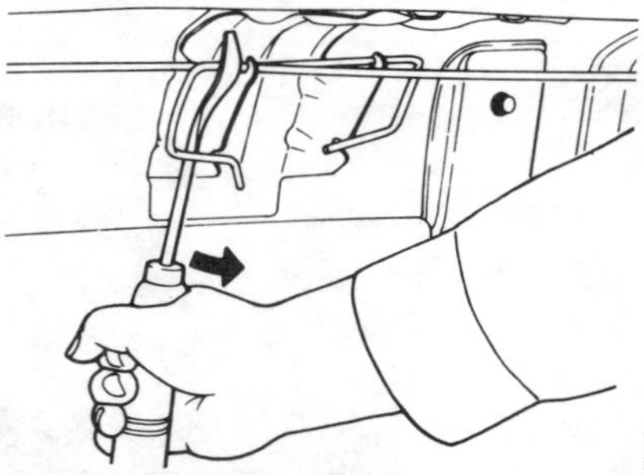

Fig 12.33 Removing a torsion
bar from the luggage boot lid

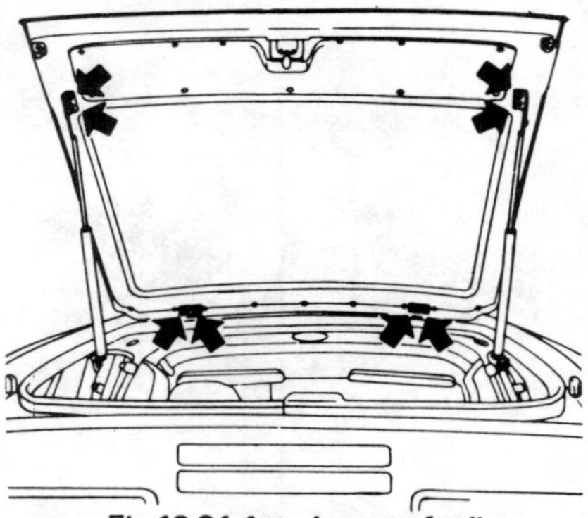

Fig 12.34 Attachment of tailgate (Coupe)

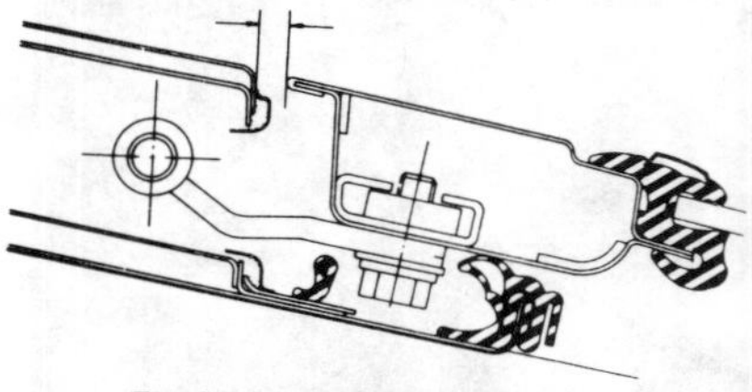

4 to 7 mm (0.157 to 0.276 in)

Fig 12.35 Tailgate to roof
clearance diagram (Coupe)

16 to 22 mm
(0.630 to
0.866 in)

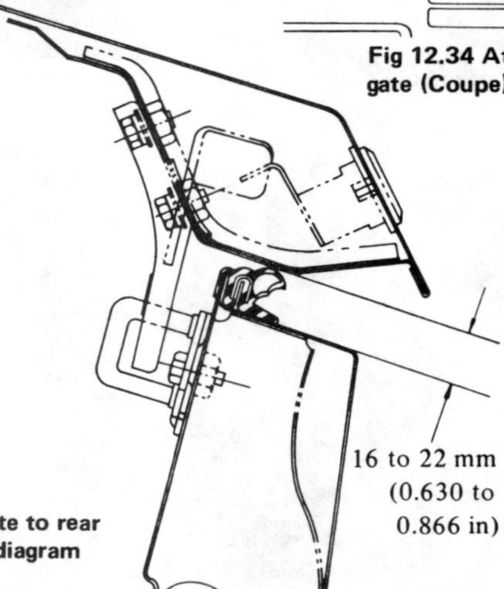

Fig 12.36 Tailgate to rear
panel clearance diagram
(Coupe)

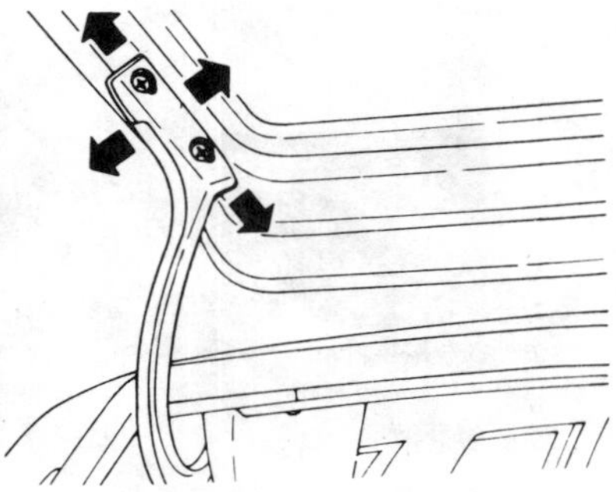

Fig 12.37 Tailgate hinge
(Estate wagon)

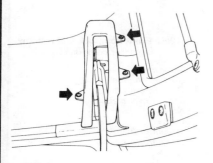

Fig 12.38 Tailgate hinge cover (Estate wagon)

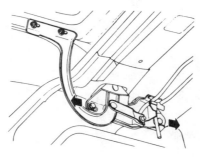

Fig 12.39 Hinge plate to body bolts (Estate tailgate)

Fig 12.40 Lock securing bolts (Estate tailgate)

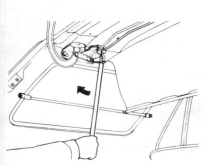

Fig 12.41 Removing Estate tailgate torsion bars

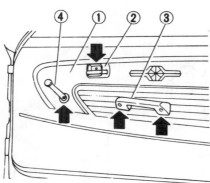

Fig 12.42 Door interior components

1 Trim panel
2 Interior handle
3 Arm rest
4 Window regulator

Fig 12.43 Removing door interior trim panel

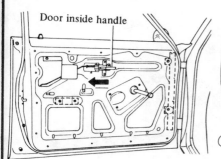

Fig 12.44 Door interior handle securing screws

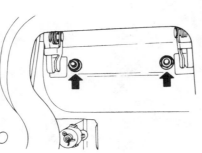

Fig 12.45 Door exterior handle securing nuts

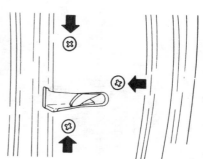

Fig 12.46 Door lock securing screws

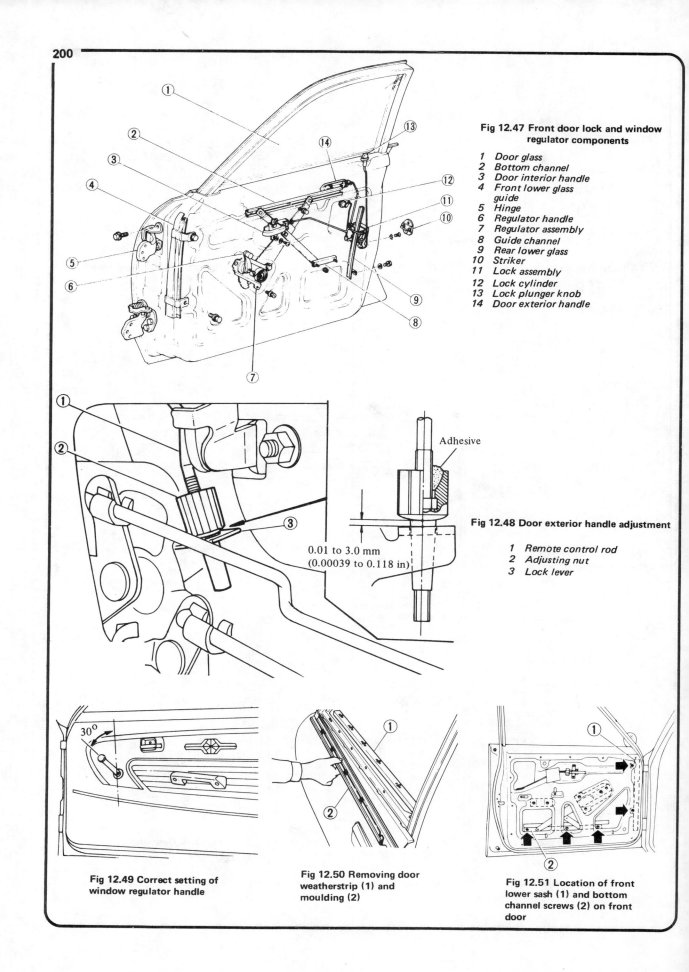

Fig 12.47 Front door lock and window regulator components

1 Door glass
2 Bottom channel
3 Door interior handle
4 Front lower glass guide
5 Hinge
6 Regulator handle
7 Regulator assembly
8 Guide channel
9 Rear lower glass
10 Striker
11 Lock assembly
12 Lock cylinder
13 Lock plunger knob
14 Door exterior handle

Fig 12.48 Door exterior handle adjustment

1 Remote control rod
2 Adjusting nut
3 Lock lever

0.01 to 3.0 mm
(0.00039 to 0.118 in)

Adhesive

Fig 12.49 Correct setting of window regulator handle

30°

Fig 12.50 Removing door weatherstrip (1) and moulding (2)

Fig 12.51 Location of front lower sash (1) and bottom channel screws (2) on front door

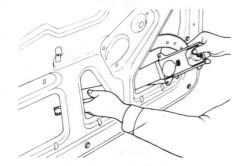

Fig 12.52 Removing window regulator mechanism

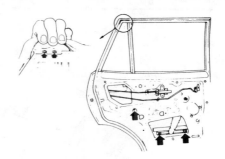

Fig 12.54 Exposing divider channel screws on a rear door

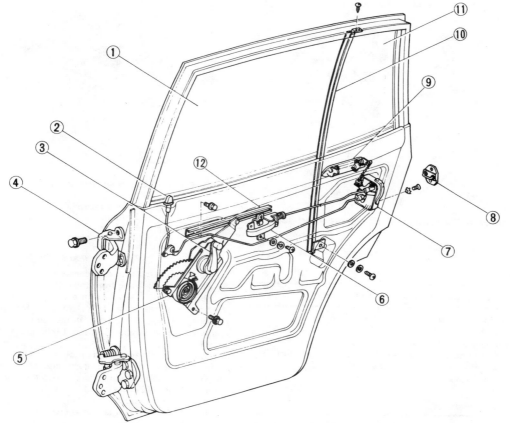

Fig 12.53 Rear door lock and regulator components

1 Door glass	4 Hinge	8 Lock striker plate	11 Quarter light
2 Door lock plunger knob	5 Regulator mechanism	9 Door exterior handle	12 Bottom channel
3 Window regulator handle	6 Door interior handle	10 Divider channel	
	7 Door lock assembly		

Fig 12.55 Removing quarter-light and divider channel (rear door)

Fig 12.56 Removing rear door glass

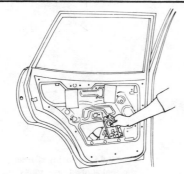

Fig 12.57 Removing rear door
window regulator assembly

Fig 12.58 Rear door hinge bolts

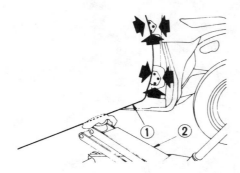

Fig 12.59 Front door (1) hinges and supporting jack (2)

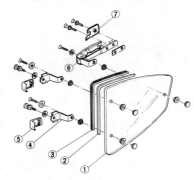

Fig 12.60 Exploded view of the Coupe side window

1   Glass
2   Weatherstrip
3   Frame
4   Hinge
5   Hinge cover
6   Handle
7   Handle escutcheon

22 Quarterlight (Coupe) - removal and installation

1   Open the side window and remove the handle assembly.
2   Remove the luggage compartment side trim panel.
3   Remove the rear quarter panel.
4   Unscrew and remove the nuts which secure the quarterlights in position and withdraw the glass and weatherstrip.
5   Installation is a reversal of removal.

23 Windscreen and rear window glass - removal and installation

1   Where a windscreen is to be replaced then if it is due to shattering, the facia air vents should be covered before attempting removal. Adhesive sheeting is useful to stick to the outside of the glass to enable large areas of crystallised glass to be removed.
2   Where the screen is to be removed intact then an assistant will be required. First release the rubber surround from the bodywork by running a blunt, small screwdriver around and under the rubber weatherstrip both inside and outside the car. This operation will break the adhesive of the sealer originally used. Take care not to damage the paintwork or cut the rubber surround with the screwdriver. Remove the windscreen wiper arms and interior mirror and place a protective cover on the bonnet.
3   Have your assistant push the inner lip of the rubber surround off the flange of the windscreen body aperture. Once the rubber surround starts to peel off the flange, the screen may be forced gently outwards by careful hand pressure. The second person should support and remove the screen complete with rubber

surround and metal trim as it comes out.
4   Remove the beading from the rubber surround.
5   Before fitting a windscreen, ensure that the rubber surround is completely free from old sealant, glass fragments and has not hardened or cracked. Fit the rubber surround to the glass and apply a bead of suitable sealant between the glass outer edge and the rubber.
6   Refit the bright trim to the rubber surround.
7   Cut a piece of strong cord greater in length than the periphery of the glass and insert it into the body flange locating channel of the rubber surround.
8   Apply a thin bead of sealant to the face of the rubber channel which will eventually mate with the body.
9   Offer the windscreen to the body aperture and pass the ends of the cord, previously fitted and located at bottom centre into the vehicle interior.
10 Press the windscreen into place, at the same time have an assistant pulling the cords to engage the lip of the rubber channel over the body flange.
11 Remove any excess sealant with a paraffin soaked rag.
12 Removal and installation of the rear window glass is carried out in an identical manner but (if fitted) disconnect the leads to the heating element in the glass.

24 Fascia panel - removal and installation

1   The cluster cover and the individual instruments may be removed, as described in Chapter 10, but where it is desired to withdraw the complete fascia panel as an assembly, proceed in the following manner.
2   Disconnect the lead from the battery negative terminal.
3   Remove the steering wheel and column shrouds.
4   Unscrew the fascia panel upper retaining screws.

5 Remove the screws which secure the fuse box.
6 Remove the bolts which secure the steering column upper bracket to the fascia panel.
7 Unscrew and remove the bolts which secure the ends of the fascia panel.
8 Withdraw the instrument panel/fascia assembly far enough forward to disconnect the leads from the instruments and the speedometer cable.
9 Installation is a reversal of removal.

25 Heater and ventilation system - general description

1 The heater system delivers fresh air to the windscreen for demisting purposes and to the car interior. The flow to each may be varied in respect of volume and temperature by the two facia mounted controls. A flow-through fresh air ventilation system is fitted which delivers unheated air through the two facia mounted controllable ducts and exhausts the stale air through outlets at the rear.
2 The heater assembly comprises a matrix heated by water from the engine cooling system and a booster fan controlled by a three-position switch. During normal forward motion of the car,

air is forced through the air intake just forward of the windscreen and passes through the heater matrix absorbing heat and carrying it to the car interior. When the car is stationary or travelling at low speed then the boost fan may be actuated.
    Two types of heater may be encountered, a standard unit and a heavy duty unit.

26 Heater - removal and installation

1 Disconnect the lead from the battery negative terminal.
2 Drain and retain the coolant if required for further use.
3 Disconnect the demister hoses from both sides of the heater unit.
4 Disconnect all leads from the heater.
5 Disconnect the water hoses from both sides of the heater. Take care that any coolant remaining in the heater matrix does not run out and stain the carpet.
6 Unscrew and remove the three heater securing bolts. One bolt is located on each side of the heater assembly and one on the top.
7 Pull the heater assembly forward and remove it from the vehicle interior.

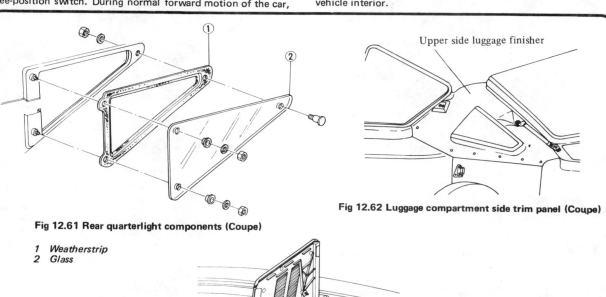

Fig 12.61 Rear quarterlight components (Coupe)

1 Weatherstrip
2 Glass

Fig 12.62 Luggage compartment side trim panel (Coupe)

Fig. 12.63 Removing rear quarter panel (Coupe)

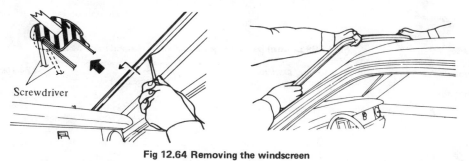

Screwdriver

Fig 12.64 Removing the windscreen

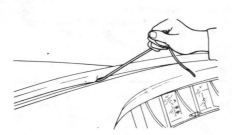

Fig 12.65 Using cord to install windscreen

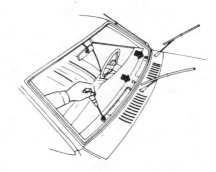

Fig 12.66 Facia panel upper retaining screws

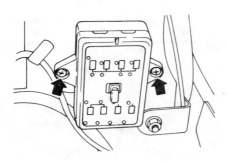

Fig 12.67 Fuse box securing screws

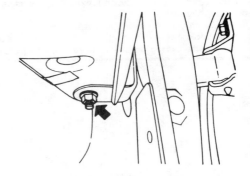

Fig 12.68 Fascia panel end securing bolts

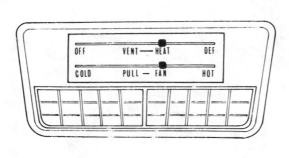

Fig 12.69 Control panel and sectional view of standard type heater

1 Air intake valve	4 Interior/demister outlet mixer valve	5 Matrix	7 Heater cock
2 Fan		6 Demister duct	8 demister nozzle
3 Air discharge valve			

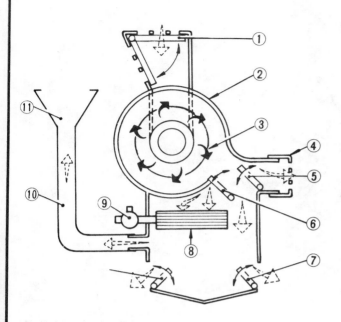

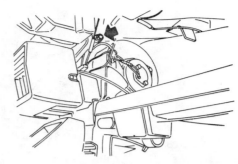

Fig 12.71 Location of heater upper securing bolt

Fig 12.70 Sectional view of heavy duty type heater

1 Air intake valve
2 Heater chamber
3 Fan
4 Air outlet
5 Air discharge Valve
6 Air mixer valve
7 Hot air discharge valve
8 Matrix
9 Heater cock
10 Demister duct
11 Demister nozzle

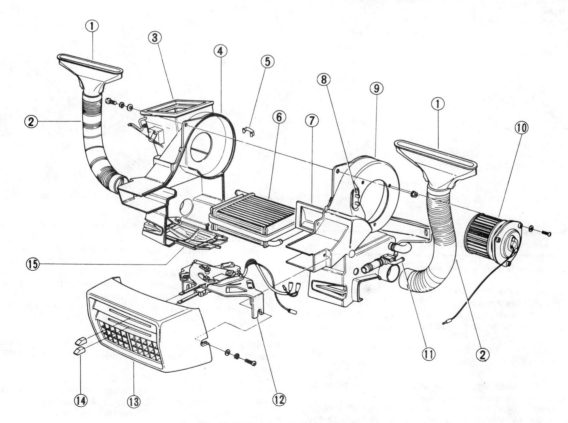

Fig 12.72 Exploded view of standard type heater

1 Demister nozzle	5 Heater box (right-hand side)	9 Heater box (right-hand side)
2 Demister duct	6 Matrix	10 Fan and motor
3 Air intake	7 Air mixer valve	11 Heater cock
4 Heater box (left-hand side)	8 .Resistor	12 Heater control

mechanism
13 Air outlet
14 Control knob
15 Interior/demister mixer valve

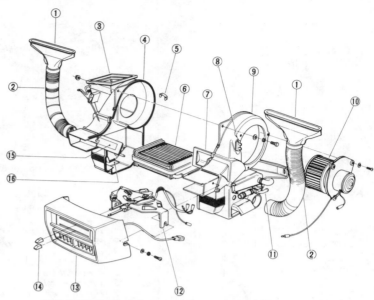

Fig 12.73 Exploded view of heavy duty type heater

1 Demister nozzle	5 Clip	side)	14 Control knob
2 Demister duct	6 Matrix	10 Fan and motor	15 Interior/demister mixer
3 Air intake	7 Air mixer valve	11 Heater cock	valve
4 Heater box (left-hand	8 Resistor	12 Heater control	16 Hot air discharge valve
side)	9 Heater box (right-hand	13 Air outlet	

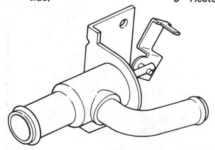

Fig 12.74 Heater cock and
lever arm

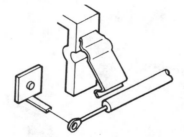

Fig 12.75 Heater cock control cable and clip

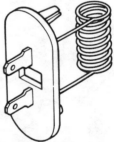

Fig 12.76 Heater resistor

27 Heater - dismantling and reassembly

1   Remove the small grub screws and pull the control knobs from the levers.

2   Remove the two screws from both sides of the centre ventilator. Remove the ventilator.

3   Disconnect the leads from the fan switch and the resistor. Disconnect control cables and rods by releasing the retaining clips.

4   Withdraw the control unit from the heater.

5   Disconnect the control cable from the heater cock by removing the clip.

6   Disconnect the hose from the cock and then remove the cock by unscrewing the two retaining screws.

7   Using a small screwdriver, lever the resistor from the right-hand side of the heater box and disconnect the leads at the connector plugs.

8   Remove the five clips which retain the left and right-hand heater boxes in the heater body.

9   Disconnect the heat valve control rod and separate the heater box into two sections. The heater matrix and the heat valve can now be removed.

10 Remove the ventilator valve return spring.

11 Unscrew the retaining nut and remove the fan from the motor shaft.

12 Remove the motor from the heater box (three screws).

13 Remove the air intake valve which is located at the top of the heater box, also the return spring.

14 With the heater completely dismantled, any faulty or damaged components should be renewed.

15 It is worth checking the condition of the motor brushes and renewing them if they are worn. This may save the expense of a new motor.

16 If the heater matrix is leaking, renew it. If it is blocked, try clearing it by reverse flushing. If this fails then it too will have to be renewed.

17 Reassembly is a reversal of dismantling but connect the controls in the follow manner. Move the upper control lever to 'OFF', attach the cable to the air intake valve and centre ventilator valve then secure the cables with the clamps.

18 Move the upper lever to the 'DEF' position. Connect the control cable to the lever of the heat valve and then secure the cable with a clamp.

19 Move the lower lever to the 'COLD' position. Connect the cable to the heater cock and then secure the cable with a clamp.

20 Check the movement of the controls for smooth and correct operation.

28 Fault diagnosis - heater

Symptom	Reason/s
Insufficient heat	Faulty or incorrect type cooling system thermostat. Coolant level too low. Faulty heater cock. Faulty ventilator valve.
Insufficient airflow	Ventilator or heat valve not operating correctly. Blower speed too low or non-existent due to blown fuse.
Faulty air deflection or temperature generally	Incorrectly adjusted cables. Disconnected demister hoses.

Chapter 13 Supplement

A Introduction

The purpose of this Supplement to the Owner's Workshop Manual is to bring the information up-to-date with current manufacturing specifications, to fill in a few gaps in information found in the first edition and lastly to cover alterations to the emission control equipment brought about by changes in Federal law.

B Routine maintenance

In addition to the tasks listed on pages 8, 9 and 10 of the manual, the following should be added, where applicable.

2 Check the condition and tension of the air conditioning compressor unit drive belt.

6000 miles (9600 km)

At intervals of 6000 miles (9600 km) or six months, whichever occurs first:
1 Check the condition and tension of the air pump drive belt.

12000 miles (19000 km)

At intervals of 12000 miles (19000 km) or 12 months, whichever occurs first:
1 Renew the air pump air cleaner element.

C General Data

Engine

Type	A14 (identical to A13 type unless indicated otherwise)
Displacement	85.24 cu in (1397 cc)
Bore	2.992 in (76 mm)
Maximum power (net)	80 BHP @ 6000 rev/min
Maximum torque...	83 lb/ft @ 3600 rev/min

Pistons

Diameter (standard)	2.9908 to 2.9927 in (75.967 to 76.017 mm)
Diameter (oversize 0.5 mm)	3.0105 to 3.0124 in (76.467 to 76.517 mm)
Diameter (oversize 1.0 mm)	3.0301 to 3.0321 in (76.967 to 77.017 mm)

Piston rings

Side clearance (2nd compression)	0.0012 to 0.0024 in (0.03 to 0.06 mm)
End gap (2nd compression)	0.0059 to 0.0118 in (0.15 to 0.30 mm)

Gudgeon pin

Diameter	0.7478 to 0.7480 in (18.995 to 19.00 mm)
Length	2.480 to 2.490 in (63.0 to 63.25 mm)
Clearance in piston	0.0003 to 0.0005 in (0.008 to 0.012 mm) @ 68°F (20°C)
Interference fit in small end bush	0.0007 to 0.014 in (0.017 to 0.035 mm)

Oil capacity (with filter)

1975 model	3 3/8 Imp qt (4 1/8 US qt, 3.9 litres)
Current model	3 1/8 Imp qt (3 7/8 US qt, 3.6 litres)

Cooling system (USA models)

Cooling capacity (with heater)

Manual transmission models	5 ¼ Imp qts (6¼ US qts, 5.9 litres)
Automatic transmission models	5 Imp qts (6 US qts, 5.7 litres)

Fuel system and Carburation

Carburettor make ... ... Hitachi

Application

Model 120Y ... ... DCG 306-5C, DCG 306-1E

Model B210 ... ... DCH 306-10B, DCH 306-14B

	Types DCG306/5C/1E		Types DCH306/10B/14B	
	Primary	Secondary	Primary	Secondary
Manifold port diameter	1.02 in (26 mm)	1.181 in (30 mm)	1.02 in (26 mm)	1.181 in (30 mm)
Venturi diameter	0.787 in (20 mm)	1.024 in (26 mm)	0.906 in (23 mm)	1.063 in (27 mm)
Main jet (variations dependent on altitude)	97	150	105	145
Main air bleed	80	80	95	80
Slow air bleed	220	100	—	—
Power jet	60		40	
Float height	0.75 in (19 mm)		0.75 in (19 mm)	

Ignition system

UK models

Manual transmission	7⁰ BTDC at 600 rpm
Automatic transmission ('D')	7⁰ BTDC at 650 rpm

USA models (non-Californian)

Manual transmission	10⁰ BTDC at 700 rpm
Automatic transmission ('D')	10⁰ BTDC at 650 rpm

Californian models

Manual and Automatic transmission	8⁰ BTDC at 650 rpm

Ignition coil

Type

B210 (non-Californian)	Hitachi C6R-608 or Hanshim H5-15-9
B210 (Californian)	Hitachi C1T-16 or STC-9
120Y	Hiatchi C6R-205 or Hanshim HP5-13E11

Distributor

Type

B210 (non-Californian)

Manual transmission	D4A5-13
Autaomatic transmission	D4A5-05

*B210(Californian)

Manual transmission	D4F5-03
Automatic transmission	D4F5-05
120Y	D411-89 or D411-97
*Air gap (Californian models)	0.008 to 0.016 in (0.2 to 0.4 mm)
*Contactor to cam clearance	0.12 in (0.3 mm)

*Fitted with transistorised ignition system

Manual gearbox

Type (B210)

F4W60 ... ... Four forward speeds and one reverse, synchromesh on all forward gears

FS5W63A   ...   .   Five forward speeds and one reverse, synchromesh on all forward gears

Ratios

									Four speed	Five speed
1st	...	...	...	...	...	...	...	...	3.513 : 1	3.382 : 1
2nd	...	...	...	...	...	...	...	...	2.170 : 1	2.013 : 1
3rd	...	...	...	...	...	...	...	...	1.378 : 1	1.312 : 1
4th	...	...	...	...	...	...	...	...	1.000 : 1	1.000 : 1
5th	...	...	...	...	...	...	...	...	—	0.854 : 1
Reverse	...	...	...	...	...	...	...	...	3.764 : 1	3.570 : 1

Oil capacity

4-speed	...	...	...	...	...	...	...	...	2 1/4 Imp pts (2 3/4 US pts, 1.3 litre)
5-speed	...	...	...	...	...	...	...	...	3 3/8 Imp pts (3 US pts, 1.7 litre)

Gearbox tolerances (5-speed gearbox)

Backlash (all gears)	...	...	...	...	...	...	...	...	0.003 to 0.006 in (0.08 to 0.25 mm)
End play									
1st gear	...	...	...	...	...	...	...	...	0.0126 to 0.0165 in (0.32 to 0.42 mm)
2nd gear	...	...	...	...	...	...	...	...	0.0087 to 0.0126 in (0.22 to 0.32 mm)
3rd and 5th gear	...	...	...	...	...	...	...	...	0.0020 to 0.0059 in (0.05 to 0.15 mm)
Baulk ring to gear clearance	...	...	...	...	...	...	...	...	0.0472 to 0.06360 in (1.20 to 1.60 mm)

Rear axle B210 (1977)

Ratio (manual transmission)   ...   .   3.70 : 1 (37/10)

Braking system (as given in Chapter 9 unless stated otherwise)

Disc brakes

Disc outer diameter   ...   .   9.65 in (245 mm)

Pad dimensions (European)

Length	...	...	...	...	...	...	...	...	2.417 in (61.4 mm)
Width	...	...	...	...	...	...	...	...	1.622 in (41.2 mm)
Thickness	...	...	...	...	...	...	...	...	0.394 in (10.0 mm)

Pad dimensions (USA)

Length	...	...	...	...	...	...	...	...	2.496 in (63.4 mm)
Width	...	...	...	...	...	...	...	...	1.622 in (41.2 mm)
Thickness	...	...	...	...	...	...	...	...	0.394 in (10.0 mm)

Electrical system (as given in Chapter 10 unless stated otherwise)

Alternator

Types:
B210 (A14 engine)	...	...	...	...	...	...	...		Hitachi LT 150-26
120Y (option)	...	...	...	...	...	...	...		Hitachi LY 150-12

									LT 150-26	LT 150-12
Rating	...	...	...	...	...	...	...	...	50 amp	50 amp
Minimum brush length	...	...	...	...	...	...	...		0.30 in (7.5 mm)	

Voltage regulator/cut out

Type:
B210	...	...	...	...	...	...	...	Hitachi TL1Z-82C
120Y	...	...	...	...	...	...	...	Hitachi TL1Z-57 or RQB2220B

Regulator
Core gap:
RQB2220B	...	...	...	...	...	...	...	0.0276 to 0.0512 in (0.7 to 1.3 mm)

Points gap:
TL1Z-82C	...	...	...	...	...	...	...	0.014 to 0.018 in (0.35 to 0.45 mm)

RQB2220B ...   .   0.011 to 0.017 in (0.35 to 0.45 mm)

Cut out
Core gap:
    RQB2220B ...   .   0.0354 to 0.0551 in (0.9 to 1.4 mm)
Points gap:
    RQB2220B ...   .   0.0275 to 0.0433 in (0.7 to 1.1 mm)

Starter motor
Type and application:
    Manual transmission   ...   .   Hitachi S114-160
    Automatic transmission   ...   .   Hitachi S114-163
Minimum brush length ...   .   0.47 in (12 mm)

Suspension and steering (as given in Chapter 11 unless stated otherwise)

Front suspension
Coil springs
No. of turns:
    USA (air conditioned models) 9¾
    Other USA and UK models   9
Free length:
    USA (air conditioned models)   ...   .   15.28 in (388 mm)
    Other USA models ...   .   14.76 in (375 mm)
    UK models ...   .   14.07 in (357.5 mm)
Wire diameter:
    USA (air conditioned models)   ...   .   0.425 in (10.8 mm)

Torque wrench settings

Gearbox (5 speed)

	lb f ft	kg f m
Mainshaft nut	17	123
Drain plug	25	3.5
Bellhousing to gearbox bolts	13	1.8
Front cover plate bolts	13	1.8
Check ball plugs	16	2.2
Main bearing retainer plate screws	9	1.3

Engine (A14) same as A13 engine unless stated otherwise

	lb f ft	kg f m
Main bearing cap bolts	43	6.0

D Engine

1 Engine - removal (A14 type)

1 In addition to the removal operation described in Chapter 1 it will be necessary to carry out the following on later B210 models.
2 Disconnect the two engine wiring harness connectors.
3 Disconnect the hoses from the air pump air cleaner and carbon canister.
4 Disconnect the hoses from the emergency air relief valve and altitude compensator (Californian models only).

5 Remove the catalytic convertor sensor protection plate and the two front exhaust pipe clamps (Californian models only).

2 Engine - dismantling general (A14 type)

1 The dismantling procedure is identical to that given in Chapter 1. However, when removing any of the additional emission control or air conditioning equipment not listed, refer to Section 6 of this Chapter for details.

E Cooling system

1 General description (USA models)

The general lay-out of the cooling system is conventional with only slight variations being found on air-conditioned and automatic transmission models.

On air-conditioned models a torque coupling is fitted to the cooling fan. The torque coupling is filled with a special silicone fluid which governs the maximum speed of the fan blades to 2,600 rpm. At speeds of more than 2,600 rpm the fluid coupling slips. The purpose of the coupling is to conserve power and reduce noise.

The radiators fitted to automatic transmission models have an integral oil cooler built into the radiator. The purpose of the

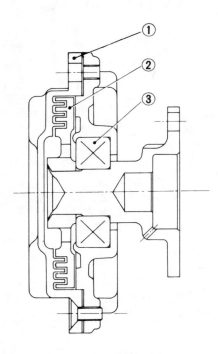

Fig. 13.1. Sectioned view through the torque coupling (air
conditioned models)

1 Wheel   2 Disc   3 Bearing

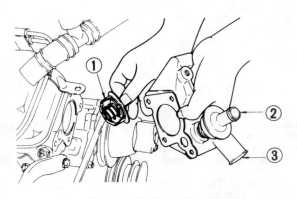

Fig. 13.2. Removing the thermostat on cars fitted with emission
control equipment

1   Thermostat   3   Water outlet tube
2   Air check valve

oil cooler is to prevent the automatic transmission fluid from
overheating. Part of the heat generated by the automatic
transmission is dissipated to the atmosphere while the remainder
is absorbed by the engine coolant via the radiator.

2 Radiator - removal and refitting (automatic transmission models)

1   Removal of the radiator is the same as detailed in Chapter 2
with one exception.
2   As stated in Section 5, Part 1, the automatic transmission oil
cooler is an integral part of the radiator and the connecting hoses
will have to be disconnected at the cooler when removing the
radiator.
3   On refitting the radiator it will be necessary to top up the
automatic transmission fluid level as described in Chapter 6, Part
2.

3 Thermostat - removal, inspection, testing and refitting

1   Removal, inspection, testing and refitting the thermostat is

4 Torque coupling - inspection, removal and refitting

1   If on inspection the bearings are found to be worn or the
special silicone oil is leaking from the coupling then it will be
necessary to fit a new coupling.
2   The coupling is made in such a way that it cannot be
dismantled and overhauled neither can the silicone oil level be
topped up.
3   To remove the coupling first slacken the fan belt.
4   Now remove the fan from the coupling.
5   Finally undo the securing nuts and remove the torque
coupling from the pulley and water pump hub.
6   Refitting the torque coupling is the reverse of the removal
operation.
identical to the procedure described in Chapter 2, except for the
following tasks.
2   USA models from 1975 onwards have a check valve screwed
into the thermostat housing and it will be necessary to
disconnect the air pipe from this valve.
3   It will also be necessary to slacken and remove the air pump
drive belt and to remove the idler pulley bracket.

F Carburation; fuel, emission control and exhaust systems

1 Carburettor - modifications and applications

Slight variations in the jetting and internal components have
brought about a modification in the type and model numbers of
the Hitachi carburettors fitted to the B210 and 120Y models.
For details of the jetting application; etc, refer to Section 3.

2 Idle compensator - modifications

Since 1975 some models have air cleaners fitted which house
two idle compensator valves. The valves fitted to this type open
at 140° to 158°F (60° to 70°C) and 158° to 176°F (70° to
80°C) respectively. The operation of the valves may be tested as

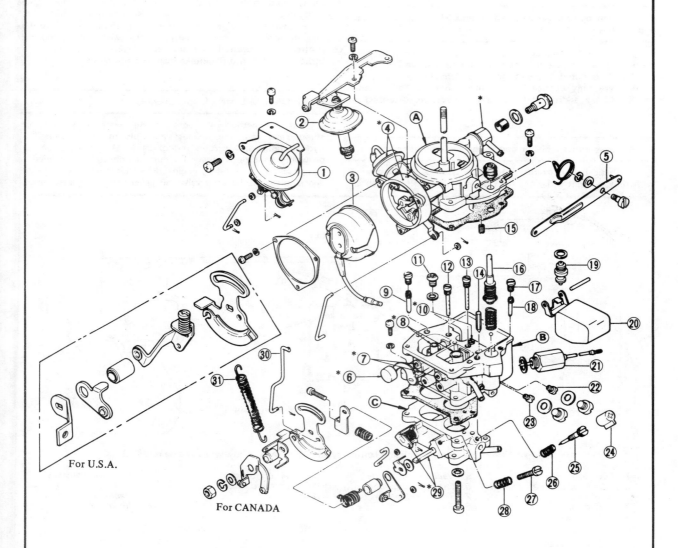

For U.S.A.

For CANADA

Fig. 13.3. An exploded view of the Hitachi carburettor fitted to USA models since 1975

A Choke chamber	7 *Venturi stopper screw	16 Accelerator pump	24 Idle limiter cap
B Centre body	8 *Primary and secondary	17 Plug	25 Idle adjust screw
C Throttle chamber	small venturi	18 Primary slow jet	26 Spring
1 Servo diaphragm of throttle	9 Secondary slow jet	19 Needle valve	27 Throttle adjust screw
opener	10 *Safe orifice	20 Float	28 Spring
2 Dash pot	11 Power jet	21 Anti-dieseling solenoid	29 *Primary and secondary
3 Automatic choke cover	12 Secondary main air bleed	valve	throttle valve
4 *Automatic choke body and	13 Primary main air bleed	22 Primary main jet	30 Accelerator pump rod
diaphragm chamber	14 Injector weight	23 Secondary main jet	31 Throttle return spring
5 Accelerator pump lever	15 Primary slow air bleed		
6 *Auxiliary valve	**Note:** do not remove the parts marked with an asterisk '*'.		

described in Chapter 3.

3 Emission control systems (USA models) - description and applications

Changes in the Federal laws concerning emission control have caused Datsun to redesign their systems to achieve the tighter restrictions imposed. Some of the components mentioned in this Section are only applicable to Californian cars. The systems mentioned are additional to the existing systems described in Chapter 3.

4 Fuel evaporative emission control system - modifications

The basic layout of the system is as described in Chapter 3 with only a slight variation. All USA models are fitted with an

activated carbon canister and purge control valve.

Fuel vapour from the sealed fuel tank is fed into the carbon canister and absorbed by the activated charcoal when the engine is idling or stopped. When the engine is running and the throttle valve opens the engine speed increases and the vacuum from the inlet manifold will open the purge control valve. When the purge control valve is opened the fuel vapour absorbed by the activated carbon is drawn into the intake manifold and burnt.

5 Air Injection System (AIS) - operation

This is a method of injecting air (generated in an external compressor) into the exhaust manifold in order to reduce hydrocarbons and carbon monoxide in the exhaust gas by providing conditions favourable for recombustion. The system comprises an air cleaner, engine driven air pump, relief valve, check valve, anti-backfire valve, air gallery and associated hoses.

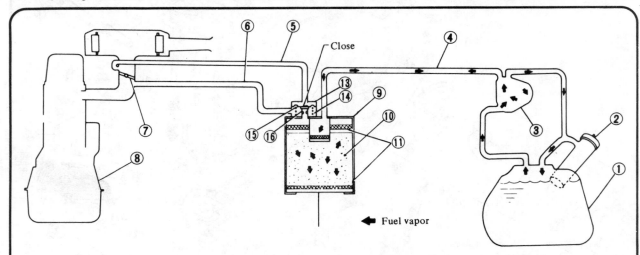

Fig. 13.4A. Evaporative emission control system (fuel vapour flow when engine is idling)

1 Fuel tank	5 Vacuum signal line	9 Carbon canister	13 Purge control valve
2 Fuel filler cap with vacuum relief valve	6 Canister purge line	10 Activated carbon	14 Diaphragm spring
3 Liquid vapour separator	7 Throttle flap valve	11 Screen	15 Diaphragm
4 Vapour vent line	8 Engine	12 Filter	16 Fixed orifice

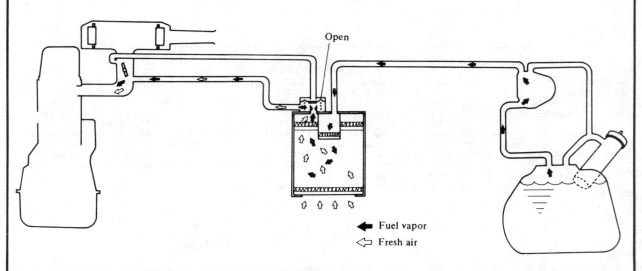

Fuel vapor

Fresh air

Fig. 13.4B. Evaporative emission control system (fuel vapour flow when engine is at rest or running faster than idling speed)

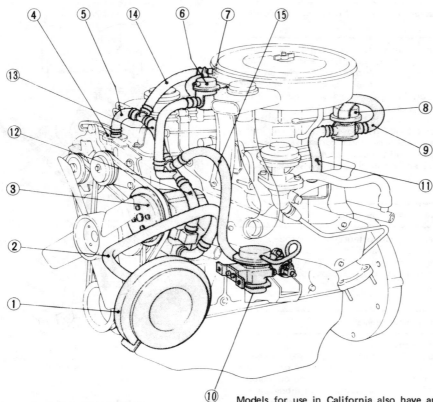

Fig. 13.5. Air injection system layout for Californian models from 1975 - 76

1 Air pump air cleaner
2 Air hose (air pump air cleaner to air pump)
3 Air pump
4 Check valve
5 Air hose (check valve to air hose connector)
6 Air control valve
7 Air relief valve
8 Anti-backfire valve (AB valve)
9 Air hose (AB valve to carburettor air cleaner)
10 Emergency air relief valve (EAR)
11 Air hose (AB valve to intake manifold)
12 Air hose (air pump to air hose connector)
13 Air hose (air hose connector to air hose connector)
14 Air hose (air hose connector to air relief valve)
15 Air hose (air hose connector to EAR valve)

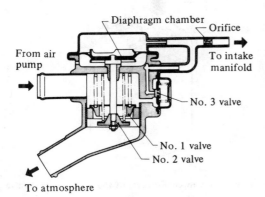

Fig. 13.6. Section through the combined air control (CAC) valve

Models for use in California also have an air control valve and emergency air relief valve to prevent excessive temperature rise in the catalytic converter.

Air is drawn through the air pump air cleaner, compressed, and directed through the check valve to the air gallery in the cylinder head. The air is then distributed to each exhaust port and injected near the exhaust valve. During high speed operation, excessive pump pressure is vented to the atmosphere through the relief valve in the carburettor air cleaner.

The check valve is fitted in the delivery line at the injection gallery. The function of this valve is to prevent any exhaust gases passing into the air pump should the manifold pressure be greater than the pump injection pressure. It is designed to close against the exhaust manifold pressure should the air pump fail as a result, for example, of a broken drive belt.

During deceleration the intake manifold vacuum opens the anti-backfire valve to allow fresh air to flow into the intake manifold. This ensures that the combustion cycle is more effective and reduces the amount of unburned gases exhausted.

On early Californian models the air control valve opens when the combined air pump pressure and intake manifold vacuum reach a predetermined level as happens during lightly loaded conditions. The air from the air pump is bled off to the air cleaner which means that the injection system is less effective, the exhaust gas temperature is lowered and the catalytic converter temperature can be maintained at the optimum operating temperature.

The Emergency Air Relief (EAR) valve bleeds air from the air pump when there is a prolonged condition of low manifold vacuum as happens during high continuous speed operation. This nullifies the air injection system, reduces the exhaust gas temperature and prevents the catalytic converter from over-heating.

On 1977 Californian models the air control valve and emergency air relief (EAR) valve are combined and form one assembly called the Combined Air Control (CAC) valve. The CAC valve consists of a diaphragm chamber, three valves and three pipe connections.

6 Altitude compensator (optional fitting on Californian models) - operation

This manually operated control device is fitted to Californian models so that they can meet Emission Standards when operating at both high and low altitudes. When the altitude compensator is set in the 'H' position air is guided through an air passage to the carburettor. The air passage is closed when the altitude compensator lever is set to the 'L' position.

The compensator should be set in the 'H' position at altitudes greater than 1,219 metres (4000 ft) above sea level. The idling speed and CO percentage will vary as the compensator lever is moved to a fresh position. It will therefore be necessary to adjust the carburettor idling speed and mixture screws when moving the compensator lever.

7 Early fuel evaporative system - operation

This system utilizes a thermostatically controlled heat control valve in the exhaust manifold to heat the intake manifold during the engine warm-up period. This improves the fuel atomization and results in lower hydrocarbon emissions from the exhaust.

8 Spark timing control systems - operation

These systems are used to control the ignition spark timing under specified conditions. The system functions as described in Section 32 of Chapter 3 with slight modifications on current models. A temperature control switch is now included on manual transmission models while automatic transmission models use a spark delay valve mounted in the distributor vacuum line. The purpose of the valve is to delay the spark advance during rapid acceleration and to cut off the spark advance immediately during deceleration.

9 Catalytic converter - operation

Fitted in the exhaust system of vehicles destined for California, this device speeds up the chemical reaction of the hydrocarbons and carbon monoxide present in the exhaust gases so that they change into harmless carbon dioxide and water. Air for the chemical process is supplied by the air injection pump.

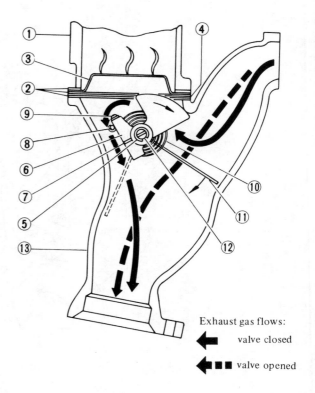

Exhaust gas flows:

⬅ valve closed

⬅■■ valve opened

Fig. 13.7. The early fuel evaporative system (EFE) sectioned view through the exhaust manifold and part of the inlet manifold

1 Inlet manifold	8 Stop pin
2 Stove gasket	9 Screw
3 Manifold stove	10 Thermostat spring
4 Heat shield plate	11 Heat control valve
5 Snap ring	12 Control valve shaft
6 Counterweight	13 Exhaust manifold
7 Key	

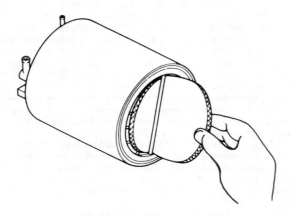

Fig. 13.8. Refitting the carbon canister filter

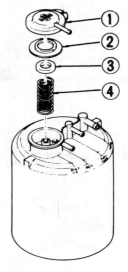

Fig. 13.9. The component parts of the purge control valve

1 Cover	3 Retainer
2 Diaphragm	4 Diaphragm spring

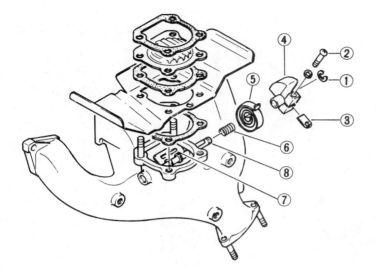

Fig. 13.10. The component parts of the early fuel evaporative system

1	Snap-ring	5	Thermostat spring
2	Lock bolt	6	Coil spring
3	Key	7	Heat control
4	Counterweight		valve
		8	Valve shaft

In the event of the system overheating, an increase in the floor temperature will result. This opens a temperature sensitive floor switch which illuminates a warning lamp through a relay becoming de-energized. During normal operating conditions, the warning lamp is illuminated during the engine start sequence as an indication of its serviceability. It is not unusual for the warning lamp to come on during periods of hard driving, or climbing gradients for long periods in low gears.

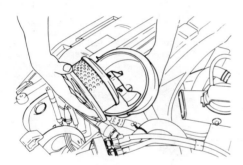

Fig. 13.11. Refitting the air pump air filter

10 Exhaust systems (USA models) - changes

The pattern of exhaust systems has been altered annually since 1974. The most noticeable change was the introduction of the catalytic converter on Californian models.

11 Fuel evaporative emission control system - maintenance and inspection

1 The purge control valve can be tested for fuel vapour leakage, by disconnecting the rubber hose, in the line between the T-connector and the carbon canister at the T-connector. Blow air, by mouth, down the rubber hose running to the vacuum hole in the carbon canister. If there is a leak, remove the top cover from the purge control valve and check for a dislodged or damaged diaphragm. A repair kit consisting of a new diaphragm, retainer and spring is available.

2 The filter fitted at the base of the activated carbon canister should be periodically renewed. The complete fuel evaporative system should be checked as described in Chapter 3.

12 Air Injection System (AIS) - maintenance and inspection

1 Check all the hoses, air gallery pipes and nozzles for security and condition.

2 Check and adjust the air pump drive belt tension to obtain a deflection of 0.3 to 0.47 in (8 to 12 mm). When a load of 22 lb (10 kg) is applied at the midpoint of the longest run of the belt.

3 With the engine at normal operating temperature, disconnect the hose leading to the check valve.

4 Run the engine at approximately 2000 rpm and then let it return to idling speed, all the time watching for exhaust gas leaks from the valve. Where these are evident, renew the valve.

5 Check the operation of the air pump relief valve by first disconnecting the hoses from the non-return valve and then

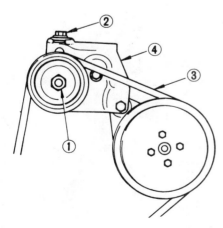

Fig. 13.12. Air pump drive belt and adjuster mechanism (1) Idler wheel pulley nut (2) Adjuster bolt (3) Drive belt (4) Idler pulley bracket

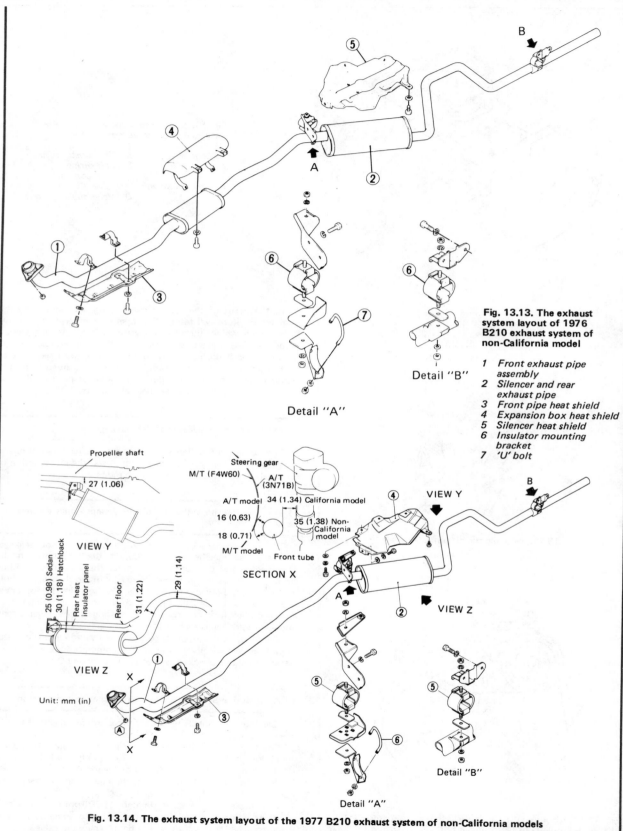

Fig. 13.13. The exhaust system layout of 1976 B210 exhaust system of non-California model

1 Front exhaust pipe assembly
2 Silencer and rear exhaust pipe
3 Front pipe heat shield
4 Expansion box heat shield
5 Silencer heat shield
6 Insulator mounting bracket
7 'U' bolt

Detail "B"

Detail "A"

Propeller shaft

27 (1.06)

VIEW Y

Steering gear

M/T (F4W60)   A/T (3N71B)

A/T model   34 (1.34) California model

16 (0.63)   35 (1.38) Non-California model

18 (0.71)   Front tube

M/T model

SECTION X

VIEW Y

VIEW Z

25 (0.98) Sedan
30 (1.18) Hatchback
Rear heat insulator panel
Rear floor
31 (1.22)
29 (1.14)

VIEW Z

Unit: mm (in)

Detail "A"

Detail "B"

Fig. 13.14. The exhaust system layout of the 1977 B210 exhaust system of non-California models

1 Front exhaust pipe
2 Silencer and rear exhaust pipe
3 Front pipe heat shield
4 Silencer heat shield
5 Exhaust mounting insulator
6 'U' bolt

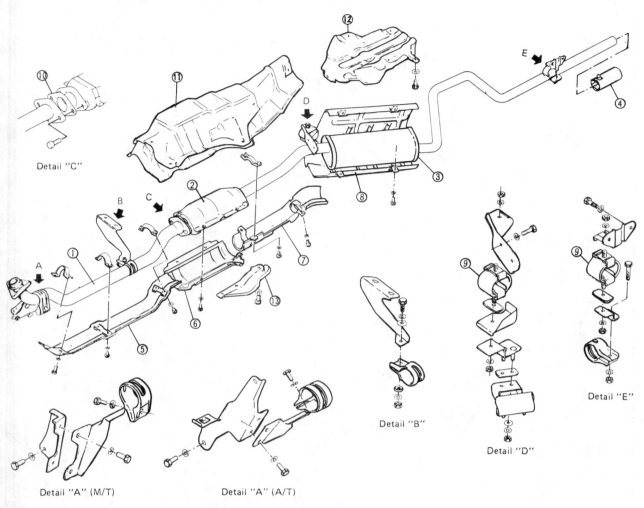

Fig. 13.15. The exhaust system of 1976 California models

1	Front exhaust pipe	5	Front exhaust pipe
2	Catalytic converter		heat shield
3	Silencer assembly	6	Lower heat shield
4	Diffuser	7	Centre pipe heat shield

8	Silencer heat shield	11	Front heat insulator panel
9	Exhaust mounting	12	Rear heat insulator panel
	insulator	13	Catalyst heat sensor wire
10	Gasket		protector

removing the air control valve from the hose connector. Plug the connector.

6 Run the engine at a steady 3000 rpm and place a hand on the air outlet of the emergency relief valve (Californian models). A good air pressure should be felt, but if not, renew the valve.

7 Now pull the vacuum hose from the air control valve. If air injection ceases from the outlet nozzle, the valve is in good condition but if it persists, renew the valve which must be faulty.

8 The anti-backfire valve (flame trap) can be checked, when the engine is at normal running temperature, by disconnecting the hose from the air cleaner and placing a finger over the end of the hose. Run the engine at about 3000 rpm and then let it return to the idling position. During this action, a strong sucking effect should be felt on the finger which indicates that the valve is in good order.

9 Every 12,000 miles (19000 km), renew the air pump air cleaner element. The assembly is located on the side of the engine compartment close to the air pump. The element and cleaner lower body are disposable, being an integral unit.

10 A faulty or worn air pump should be renewed as an exchange unit.

13 Early fuel evaporative system - maintenance and testing

1 Periodically inspect the operation of the heat control valve. On starting with the engine cold, the counterweight should be in its fully shut position.

2 During engine acceleration (engine still cold) the counterweight will rotate in a clockwise direction.

3 When the engine reaches its normal operating temperature, the counterweight will have moved fully clockwise.

4 External components of the device can be renewed but as the internal valve plate is welded to the operating shaft, any fault or wear in these items will necessitate renewal of the complete manifold assembly.

14 Altitude compensator - checking operation

1 To test the compensator unit try to blow air by mouth into the compensator air connections at the carburettor. This should not be possible below an altitude of 4000 ft (1,219 metres)

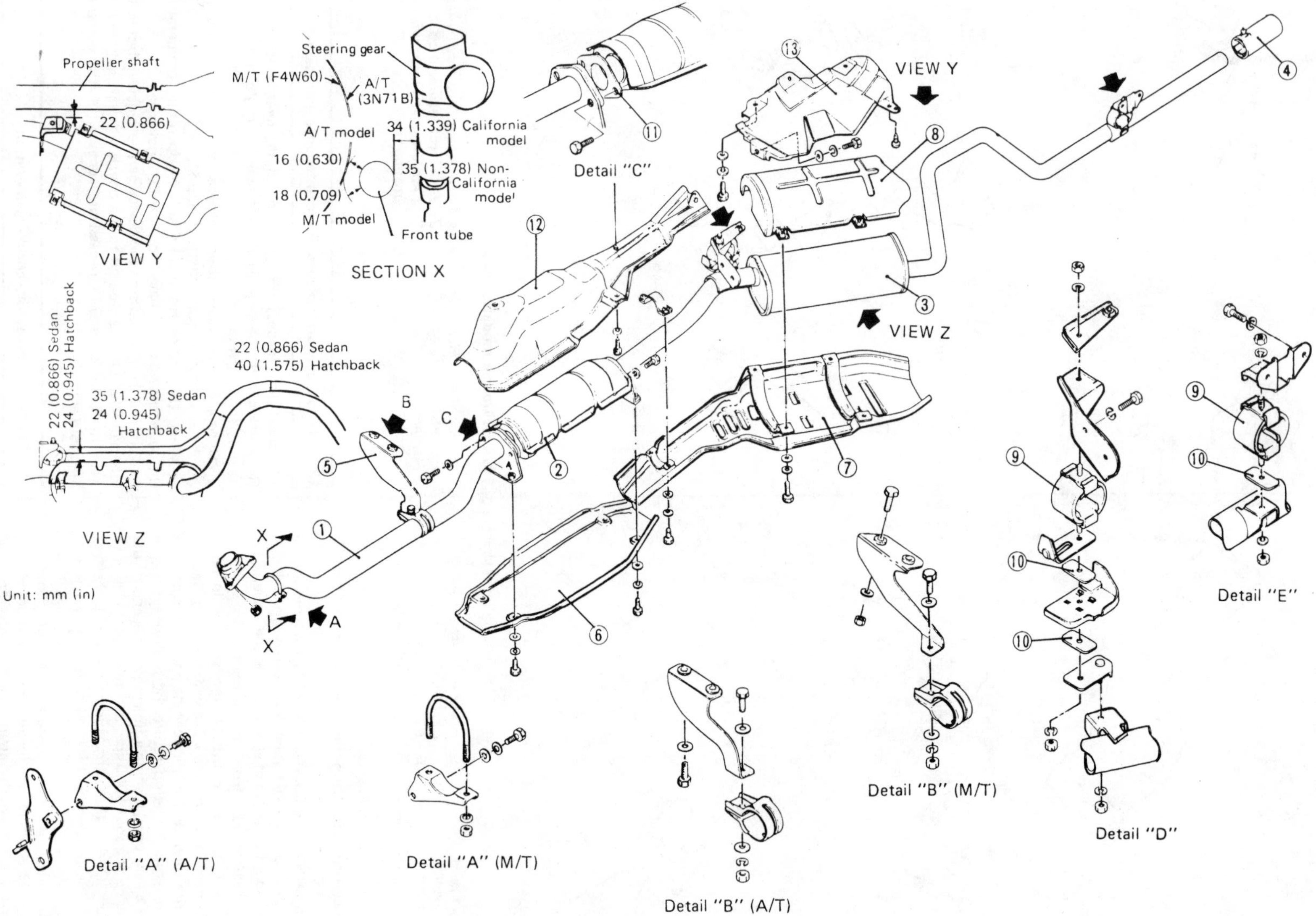

Detail "E"

Detail "D"

Detail "B" (M/T)

Detail "B" (A/T)

Detail "A" (M/T)

Detail "A" (A/T)

VIEW Y

VIEW Z

Detail "C"

SECTION X

Steering gear

M/T (F4W60)

A/T
(3N71B)

A/T model
16 (0.630)

34 (1.339) California model

35 (1.378) Non-California model

18 (0.709)
M/T model

Front tube

22 (0.866) Sedan
40 (1.575) Hatchback

35 (1.378) Sedan
24 (0.945) Hatchback

22 (0.866) Sedan
24 (0.945) Hatchback

Propeller shaft

22 (0.866)

VIEW Y

VIEW Z

Unit: mm (in)

Fig. 13.16. The exhaust system of 1977 California models

1	Front exhaust pipe	5	Front pipe mounting bracket	9	Exhaust mounting insulator	13	Rear heat shield
2	Catalytic converter	6	Catalytic converter shield	10	Heat shield plate	
3	Silencer box	7	Silencer box lower shield	11	Gasket	
4	Diffuser	8	Silencer box heat shield	12	Front heat shield	

above sea level and conversely should be possible above this altitude. Renew the compensator if it is found to be faulty.

2 A further test can be carried out by driving the car at altitudes greater and less than 4000 ft (1219 metres) above sea level. If the compensator operates below this altitude the engine will hesitate, falter or surge. If the compensator fails to operate above this altitude the engine will be hesitant and fail to accelerate cleanly.

15 Catalytic converter and exhaust system - removal and refitting

1 Faults associated with the catalytic converter or floor temperature warning system, which cannot be rectified by tightening the exhaust system clamps or reconnecting electrical leads, should be rectified by your nearest Datsun dealer.

16 Fault diagnosis - fuel system and carburation

Symptom	Reason/s
Excessive fuel consumption	Generally worn carburettor. Idling speed too high. Choke valve incorrectly set. Emission control system faulty (see later in this Section).
Insufficient fuel delivery or weak mixture	Too little fuel in fuel tank (prevalent when climbing steep hills). Split in fuel pipe on suction side of fuel pipe. Fault in altitude compensator (Californian models).

17 Fault diagnosis - emission control systems

Symptom	Reason/s
Erratic idling	Faulty anti-backfire valve. Carbon canister purge line disconnected.
Power reduced	Faulty spark timing control valve. Faulty altitude compensator (Californian models). Flap valve stuck (early fuel evaporative system).

2 Before disconnecting or removing the catalytic converter or exhaust system ensure that the system is cool enough to handle. Remember that the catalytic converter operates at a very high temperature.

3 The exhaust system is supported and clamped together in a conventional manner. Refer to the respective diagram for the layout of the system fitted to your car.

4 When assembling the exhaust system Datsun recommend that a special sealant is injected into the joining collars between the silencer boxes and connecting pipes.

5 During refitting of the system ensure that no strain is imposed on any of the mounting brackets or rubbers. Furthermore ensure that no part of the system contacts the vehicle floor or propeller shaft.

6 It is most important to fit the heat shields which will not only protect the catalytic converter and silencer but will also protect the body shell and surrounding units from the heat given off from the system.

G Ignition system

1 General description

The ignition systems have remained virtually unchanged except for Californian models which now have a transistorized ignition system fitted.

Basically the pulse controlled transistor ignition system functions as follows: A reluctor is fitted in place of the conventional distributor cam, and the regular contact breaker points are replaced by a pick-up coil. The reluctor is made with four protrusions, one for each cylinder. As the reluctor turns and a protrusion is aligned with the pick-up coil an electrical signal is sent by the coil to the transistor ignition pack. This signal causes the transistor unit to produce a high voltage in the coil. This high current is fed from the coil to the distributor cap and to the appropriate spark plug via the rotor head.

2 Checking and adjusting the distributor (transistor type)

1 The distributor cap and rotor head should be periodically inspected as specified in the Routine Maintenance Section.

2 The distributor cap and leads can be inspected as detailed in Chapter 4.

3 The air gap between the reluctor protrusion and the pick-up coil should be between 0.008 to 0.016 in (0.2 to 0.4 mm). If the gap is not within these limits the adjustment can be made by slackening the pick-up coil locating screws and moving the coil either in or out to obtain the necessary air gap.

4 A fault in the transistorized ignition system can only be checked and traced using an oscilloscope and this work should therefore be left to an auto-electrician.

3 Distributor (transistor type) - dismantling and reassembly

1 Remove the distributor cap and the rotor head.

2 Remove the two screws which secure the vacuum capsule, tilt it slightly to disengage the operating rod from the baseplate pivot.

3 Unscrew and remove the screws which hold the pick-up coil and remove it.

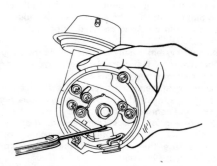

Fig. 13.17. Checking the air gap - transistor type distributor

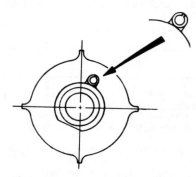

Fig. 13.18. Reluctor tension pin position

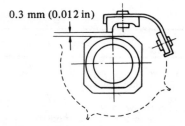

Fig. 13.19. Cam to contactor clearance dimension

4   Using two levers, pry the reluctor from the distributor shaft and then remove the tension pin.
5   Unscrew and remove the screws which secure the baseplate and lift off the baseplate.
6   Drive out the pin from the lower end of the shaft, remove the collar and then withdraw the upper counter weight assembly and shaft from the top of the distributor.
7   Unscrew and remove the screw from the recess at the end of the shaft then remove the camplate and weight assembly.
8   When the weights and springs are dismantled, take care not to stretch the springs. Mark one of the weights, springs and pivot posts to ensure that they are refitted correctly.
9   Renew any worn parts.
10 Reassembly is a reversal of the dismantling procedure but ensure that the following conditions are met:

   a) *The reluctor is correctly orientated on the distributor shaft with regard to the positions of the flat and tension pin. Note that the slot in the tension pin must face outwards (Fig. 13.18).*
   b) *If the contactor has been disturbed, adjust the cam to contactor clearance to 0.012 in (3 mm) on reassembly (Fig. 13.19).*
   c) *Grease the counterweight pivots and the top of the rotor shaft sparingly with a general purpose grease.*

4   Transistorized ignition unit - operation, removal and refitting

1   The unit is located on the right-hand dash side panel in the passenger compartment.
2   It performs the following functions:

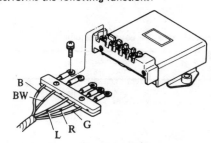

Fig. 13.20. Transistorized ignition unit connections

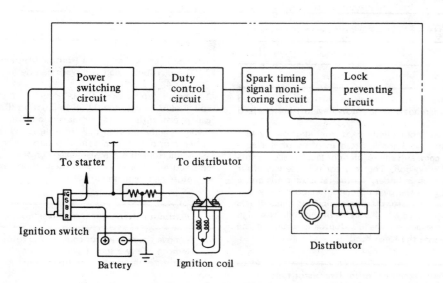

Fig. 13.21. Theoretical circuit diagram of transistorized ignition system

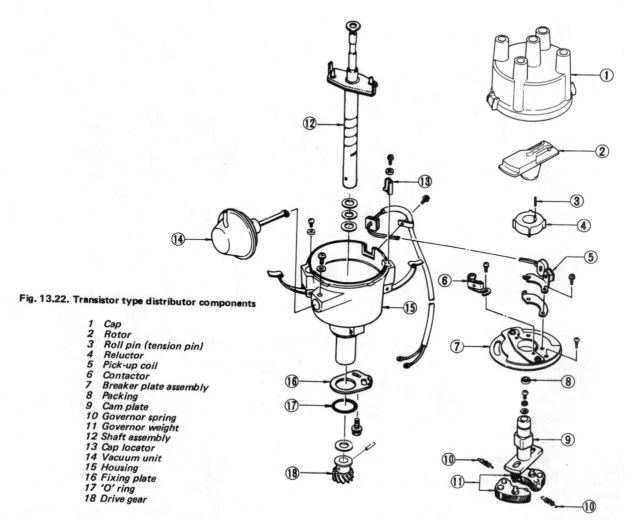

Fig. 13.22. Transistor type distributor components

1 Cap
2 Rotor
3 Roll pin (tension pin)
4 Reluctor
5 Pick-up coil
6 Contactor
7 Breaker plate assembly
8 Packing
9 Cam plate
10 Governor spring
11 Governor weight
12 Shaft assembly
13 Cap locator
14 Vacuum unit
15 Housing
16 Fixing plate
17 'O' ring
18 Drive gear

a) It 'makes' and 'breaks' the current in the primary circuit of the ignition coil.
b) Sets and maintains the make-and-break cycle according to engine speed.
c) Incorporates a delayed cut-out to disconnect the primary current within a period not exceeding ten seconds if the ignition is left switched on without the engine running.

3   As mentioned previously a fault in the transistorized ignition system can only be checked and traced using an oscilloscope.

4   Any fault occurring in the unit itself will require a new unit as the original cannot be repaired.
5   To renew a unit, disconnect the battery earth or ground (negative) lead.
6   Disconnect the wiring harness from the unit.
7   Unscrew and remove the securing set screws and lift the unit from its location.
8   Refitting is the reverse of the removal procedure but take care to connect the wiring harness correctly.
9   Where a transistorized ignition unit is fitted, do not disconnect the spark plug or coil wires when the engine is running.

H Manual transmission

1   Modifications

The hatchback version of the B210 is now available with an optional 5-speed manual gearbox. The fifth gear takes the form of an overdrive added to the fourth gear. The 5-speed gearbox is very similar in appearance and layout to the 4-speed gearbox. The introduction of this gearbox is to achieve fuel economy and to provide a closer spacing between the gear ratios.

2   Gearbox - removal and refitting

Identical to that described in Part 1, Chapter 6.

3   Gearbox dismantling

1   The dismantling of the 4-speed gearbox is identical to the

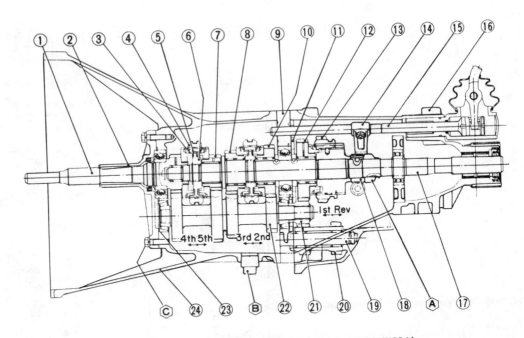

Fig. 13.23. Section through the 5-speed gearbox (type FS5W63A)

1 *Main drive (input) shaft*	7 *5th gear (mainshaft)*	13 *Reverse gear (mainshaft)*	19 *Reverse idler shaft*
2 *Front cover*	8 *3rd gear (mainshaft)*	14 *Striking lever*	20 *Reverse idler gear*
3 *Baulk ring*	9 *Adaptor plate*	15 *Striking rod*	21 *1st counter gear*
4 *Coupling sleeve*	10 *2nd gear (mainshaft)*	16 *Rear extension*	22 *Countergear*
5 *Shift key*	11 *Bearing retainer*	17 *Mainshaft*	23 *Countergear bearing shim*
6 *Synchronizer hub*	12 *1st gear (mainshaft)*	18 *Speedometer drive gear*	24 *Bellhousing*

procedure as described in Chapter 6, Part 1. As the 5-speed gearbox is slightly different the dismantling procedure is described in this section.

2 Before dismantling, clean the external surfaces thoroughly with paraffin or a water soluble solvent.

3 Remove the flexible dust cover from the release lever aperture in the clutch bellhousing and then remove the release lever and release bearing as described in Chapter 5.

4 Remove the reverse lamp switch and the neutral and top gear switches.

5 Unscrew and remove the two bolts which secure the speedometer pinion assembly.

6 Undo the front cover securing bolts and remove the front cover followed by the countershaft front bearing shim.

7 Now, using a pair of external circlip pliers, remove the circlip from the main drive bearing.

8 Remove the threaded plug which is located above and slightly to the rear of the speedometer pinion aperture and then withdraw the return spring and plunger from the housing.

9 Remove the rear extension housing bolts and using a suitably sized puller draw the rear extension housing off.

10 Using a soft mallet strike the back of the bellhousing to separate it from the adaptor plate.

11 Make up a suitable support plate and secure it in the jaws of a vice and then bolt the adaptor plate to it so that the countergear assembly is at the top.

12 Drive out the pins which secure the shift forks to the selector rods.

13 Now unscrew and remove the three detent ball plugs.

14 Tap out the selector rods from the adaptor plate (towards the rear) and take off the shift forks. Retain the three detent balls, the three springs and two interlock plungers as the selector rods are withdrawn. The selector rods need only be driven far enough to permit the removal of the shift forks. The selector rods that

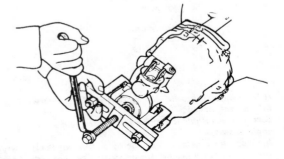

Fig. 13.24. Drawing off the rear extension using a conventional puller

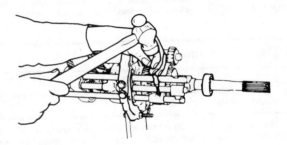

Fig. 13.25. Driving out the shift fork locking pins

remain attached to the adaptor plate will not impede removal of the shafts or gears later.

15 At this stage, check for backlash in the gears, which should be within the tolerances given in the General Data Section. Also check the mainshaft gears for endfloat which again should be as specified for the particular gears. Where the tolerances are exceeded, the drive and driven gears must be renewed as matched sets.

16 Inspect the teeth of the gearwheels for wear or chipping which if evident will necessitate the renewal of the gears concerned.

17 Remove the reverse idler gear and shaft.

18 Unless the necessary press facilities and bearing drawing tackle are available, it is recommended that further dismantling of the assemblies is left to your Datsun dealer. Where suitable equipment is available, proceed as follows.

19 Remove the circlip from the mainshaft end bearing and draw the bearing off.

20 Remove the circlip which is located behind the mainshaft end bearing.

21 Lock the gear assemblies by selecting 1st and 2nd gears and undo the mainshaft nut after having punched back the staked part of the nut.

22 With the mainshaft nut now removed slide the speedometer drive gear and its locking ball off the mainshaft followed by the reverse gear and synchro hub, the 1st gear with its needle bearings and bush, and finally the thrust washer and its locking ball. Take care not to lose the steel locking balls when removing these items. Their purpose is to retain the speedometer drivegear and thrust washer.

23 From the counter gearshaft end remove the circlip followed by the thrust washer.

24 Draw off the 1st counter gear.

25 The mainshaft and countershaft can now be pressed out of the adaptor plate. Take care when removing these shafts as they can be easily damaged if not supported correctly.

26 The mainshaft can now be further dismantled if it is so desired.

27 Remove the thrust washer and locating ball followed by the 2nd gear and needle bearings.

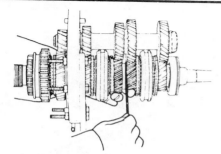

Fig. 13.26. Measuring the end-float of the gears using feeler gauges

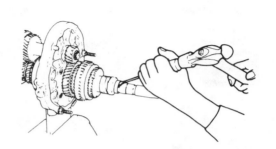

Fig. 13.27. Driving back the stacked part of the mainshaft nut

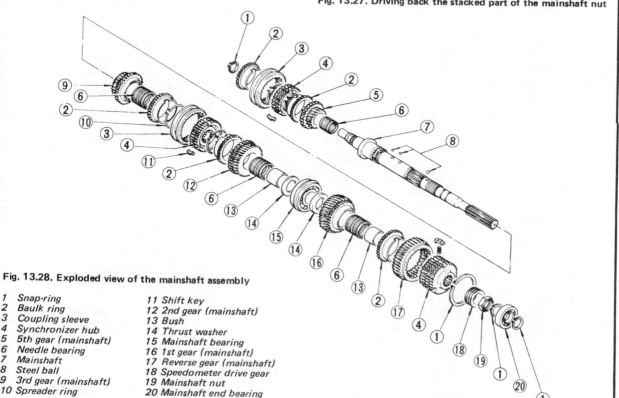

Fig. 13.28. Exploded view of the mainshaft assembly

1 Snap-ring	11 Shift key
2 Baulk ring	12 2nd gear (mainshaft)
3 Coupling sleeve	13 Bush
4 Synchronizer hub	14 Thrust washer
5 5th gear (mainshaft)	15 Mainshaft bearing
6 Needle bearing	16 1st gear (mainshaft)
7 Mainshaft	17 Reverse gear (mainshaft)
8 Steel ball	18 Speedometer drive gear
9 3rd gear (mainshaft)	19 Mainshaft nut
10 Spreader ring	20 Mainshaft end bearing

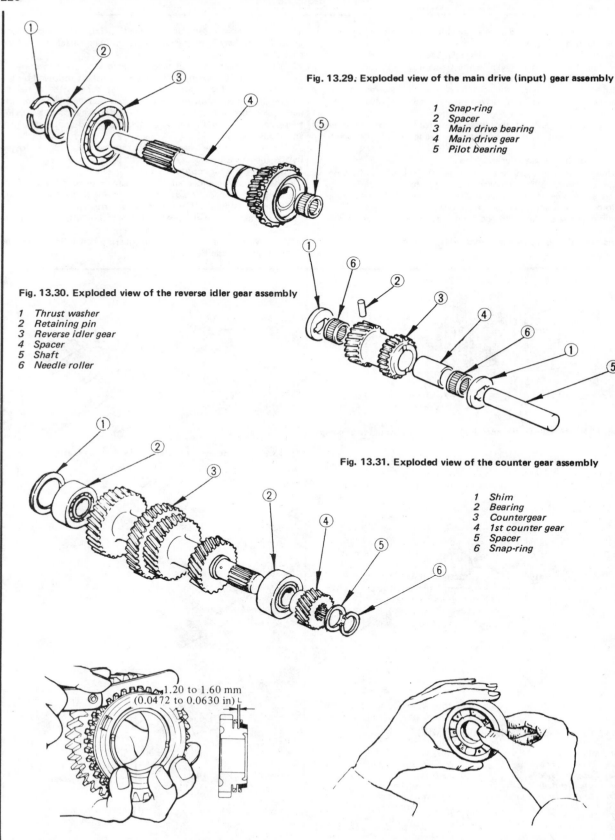

Fig. 13.29. Exploded view of the main drive (input) gear assembly

1 Snap-ring
2 Spacer
3 Main drive bearing
4 Main drive gear
5 Pilot bearing

Fig. 13.30. Exploded view of the reverse idler gear assembly

1 Thrust washer
2 Retaining pin
3 Reverse idler gear
4 Spacer
5 Shaft
6 Needle roller

Fig. 13.31. Exploded view of the counter gear assembly

1 Shim
2 Bearing
3 Countergear
4 1st counter gear
5 Spacer
6 Snap-ring

1.20 to 1.60 mm
(0.0472 to 0.0630 in)

Fig. 13.32. Measuring the gap between the baulk ring and gear cone

Fig. 13.33. Checking the condition of a roller bearing

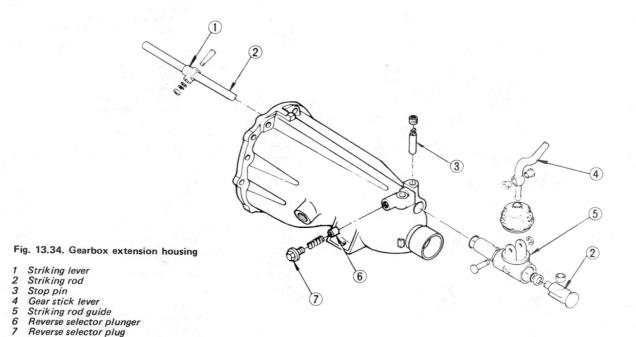

Fig. 13.34. Gearbox extension housing

1 *Striking lever*
2 *Striking rod*
3 *Stop pin*
4 *Gear stick lever*
5 *Striking rod guide*
6 *Reverse selector plunger*
7 *Reverse selector plug*

28 The following parts can be pressed out together from the 2nd and 3rd gears.

  a) *2nd gear mainshaft bush*
  b) *3rd gear and 2nd-3rd speed synchronizer.*

29 The main drive gear bearing can be pressed off its shaft after first removing the retaining circlip and spacing washer.

30 The counter shaft bearings can be pressed off the shaft if desired.

31 The reverse idler gear assembly can be dismantled if necessary. (Fig. 13.30 shows the layout of the assembly).

32 The mainshaft bearing fitted into the adaptor plate is held in position by a retainer plate. To remove the countersunk screws securing the retainer plate it will be necessary to use an impact driver as the screws are very tight.

33 With the retainer plate now removed it will be possible to extract the complete main bearing and the outer track of the counter gear bearing using a brass drift and a hammer.

34 Wash all parts in a suitable cleaning agent such as paraffin and carefully scrape the old gasket off. Remove any burrs from the mating faces using a fine file.

35 Examine the synchronizer units for wear or damage. If there has been a history of noisy or slow gear changes, renew the synchronizer unit complete. If there is slight wear on any component (sleeve, hub, thrust washer etc) they should be renewed individually.

36 Examine each of the baulk rings for wear and damage. Place each baulk ring on its appropriate gear cone and measure the gap between them. This should be between 0.047 to 0.063 in (1.20 to 1.60 mm). Where the clearance is found to be smaller renew the baulk ring.

37 Examine the bearings and races for wear and damage. Rotate the bearing outer race, by hand, while holding the inner track. If, when turning the bearing in this manner, you can feel roughness or tight spots the bearing is faulty and must be renewed.

38 After examining the whole of the gearbox assembly it will now necessary to obtain any new parts which are needed. It is always advisable to use new gaskets and oil seals when reassembling the gearbox. It is false economy to re-use the old ones.

4 Gearbox - reassembly

1 Reassembly of the gearbox is the reverse of the dismantling procedure; however, the following steps should be taken during this operation.

2 Press fit a new oil seal in the front cover after ensuring that the seat is clean. Check before fitting the seal that it is the correct way round. Finally, coat the oil seal with gear oil to provide the initial lubrication.

3 Now press fit a new oil seal in the rear extension housing ensuring that the seating is clean and the seal is facing in the correct direction. Coat the seal and bush with gear oil.

4 If the extension housing has been dismantled, the 'O' ring and plunger grooves should be lubricated with a multi-purpose grease before reassembly. Take care when tightening the striking rod lock pin nut as it can easily be overtightened.

5 Fit the outer race of the counter gear bearing and the mainshaft bearing in the adaptor plate using a hammer and a brass drift. Care must be taken when fitting the bearing and outer race to ensure that they are being inserted squarely or the bearing and adaptor plate will be damaged.

6 Refit the bearing retainer plate and tighten the four screws to the recommended torque wrench setting. Using a centre punchrod hammer, stake each screw at two points to prevent them from working loose.

7 The reassembly of 2nd, 3rd, 4th and 5th speed synchronizers is identical.

8 Insert the hub into the sleeve and locate the three shift keys in the grooves provided, at 120° intervals. Now locate the spreader springs which retain the shift keys. Make sure the ends of the opposite springs are not engaged in the same key.

9 The 1st and reverse synchronizer is slightly different to reassemble having additional springs fitted under the shift keys. Fit the three springs into their respective holes in the hub and place the shift keys in position. The problem arises when trying to hold all three keys and springs in a compressed position when sliding the hub into the sleeve. Refit the spreader rings as described in paragraph 8 of this Section.

10 Reassemble the mainshaft from the front end by fitting the 5th gear needle bearing followed by the 5th gear and baulk ring.

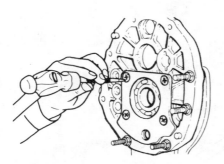

Fig. 13.35. Staking the countersunk screws

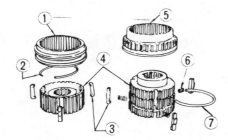

Fig. 13.36. Exploded view of the synchronizer assemblies

1 Coupling sleeve   5 Reverse gear
2 Spreader ring   6 Synchro spring
3 Shift key   7 Spreader ring
4 Synchro hub

Fig. 13.37. Fitting the spreader ring

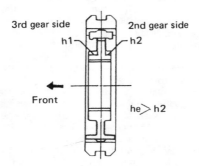

Fig. 13.38. Correct refitment of 2nd and 3rd speed synchronizer

Refit the 4th and 5th speed synchronizer assembly and locate these components using a snap-ring of the proper thickness so that it will fit the groove in the mainshaft.

11 Snap-rings for this purpose are available in the following thicknesses:

> 0.0551 to 0.0571 in (1.40 to 1.45 mm)
> 0.0571 to 0.0591 in (1.45 to 1.50 mm)
> 0.0591 to 0.0610 in (1.50 to 1.55 mm)
> 0.0610 to 0.0630 in (1.55 to 1.60 mm)
> 0.0630 to 0.0650 in (1.60 to 1.65 mm)

12 From the other end of the mainshaft fit the following parts in the order listed: 3rd gear needle roller bearing, 3rd gear, 3rd gear baulk ring, 2nd and 3rd speed synchronizer. Ensure that the 2nd and 3rd speed synchronizer is fitted the correct way round (Fig. 13.38 shows the correct fitting).

13 Gently tap onto the mainshaft the 2nd gear bush and main shaft bearing thrust washer using a soft faced hammer.

14 Now fit the 2nd gear baulk ring, needle bearing, 2nd gear, steel locking ball and thin thrust washer.

15 The main drive bearing can now be pressed onto the main drive (input) shaft. Now fit a snap-ring of a suitable thickness that will eliminate any endplay.

16 Snap-rings for this purpose are available in the following thicknesses:

> 0.0587 to 0.0610 in (1.49 to 1.55 mm)
> 0.0614 to 0.0638 in (1.56 to 1.62 mm)
> 0.0638 to 0.0661 in (1.62 to 1.68 mm)
> 0.0661 to 0.0685 in (1.68 to 1.74 mm)
> 0.0685 to 0.0709 in (1.74 to 1.80 mm)
> 0.0709 to 0.0732 in (1.80 to 1.86 mm)
> 0.0732 to 0.0756 in (1.86 to 1.92 mm)

17 The counter gear bearings can now be pressed onto the counter gear shaft.

18 The reverse gear idler components can be assembled as shown in Fig. 13.30. Ensure that the copper coated faces of the thrust washers are placed towards the gears.

19 Now secure the support plate to the adaptor plate and clamp the support plate in the vice.

20 Fit the mainshaft assembly into the adaptor plate and screw on the mainshaft nut temporarily.

21 Using service tools KV32101320 and KV32101330 draw the mainshaft through the adaptor plate until there is a clearance of 0.39 in (10 mm) between the thrust washer and bearing.

22 Alternatively this operation could be carried out using a mechanical press to push the mainshaft through the adaptor plate to achieve the desired clearance. However, extreme care must be taken when doing this to prevent damaging the adaptor plate and gear assemblies.

23 Position the 4th gear baulk ring on the conical face of the main drive gear and insert the pilot bearing into the rear of the main driveshaft having first lubricated it with gear oil.

24 Place the main drive gear and counter gear assemblies in position at the adaptor plate. The main drive gear assembly should be fitted to the main shaft first. The counter gear assembly will have to be tipped at an angle to facilitate refitment. Take care not to drop any of the gear assemblies on the floor, as they are damaged very easily.

25 Pull the mainshaft assembly, together with the main drive gear and counter gear, into the adaptor plate using the special service tools mentioned in paragraph 21 of this Section. Then remove the mainshaft nut.

26 The 1st counter gear can now be pressed onto the counter shaft and secured in place by a spacer and snap-ring.

27 Now fit the following parts to the rear of the mainshaft in the following order: steel ball, thick thrust washer, 1st gear bush, needle bearing, 1st gear, 1st gear baulk ring, 1st gear synchronizer, together with the reverse main gear, steel ball, speedometer drive gear and finally the mainshaft nut.

28 Tighten the mainshaft nut temporarily and lock the gearbox

by selecting 1st and 2nd gears at the same time.

29 Tighten the mainshaft nut to the recommended torque wrench setting and stake the nut using a hammer and punch. Release 1st and 2nd gears to set the gearbox in the neutral position.

30 Fit a 0.043 in (1.1 mm) thick snap-ring into the groove behind the mainshaft nut and then, using a suitable length of pipe as a drift, drive the mainshaft bearing into position against the snap-ring.

31 Fit a suitable snap-ring to the groove at the rear of the mainshaft bearing to eliminate any endplay.

32 Snap-rings for this purpose are available in the following thicknesses:

0.043 in (1.1 mm)
0.047 in (1.2 mm)
0.051 in (1.3 mm)
0.055 in (1.4 mm).

33 Now fit the reverse idler gear assembly.

34 Place the three selector forks in their respective grooves of the synchronizer sleeves.

35 Fit the 1st and reverse gear selector rod through the adaptor plate and shift fork. Now secure the shift fork to the selector rod using a new retaining pin.

36 Fit the check ball, spring and check ball plug. Note that the ball plug for the 1st and reverse fork rod is longer than those used for the other fork rods. A little jointing compound should be applied to the check ball plug before it is tightened.

37 Now align the centre notch in the 1st and reverse fork rod with the check ball by moving the rod back and forth until it aligns.

38 Fit the interlock plunger into the adaptor plate.

39 Fit the 2nd and 3rd fork rod through the adaptor plate and fork. Secure the fork to the rod using a new retainer pin.

40 Fit the check ball, spring and ball plug coated with a little jointing compound.

41 Align the centre notch in the 2nd and 3rd fork rod with the check ball.

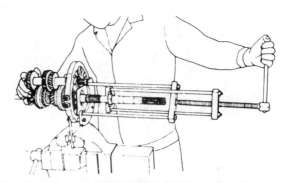

Fig. 13.39. Fitting the mainshaft assembly using service tools KV32101320 and KV32101330

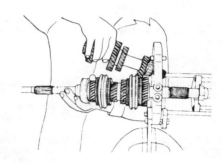

Fig. 13.40. Fitting the countergear assembly

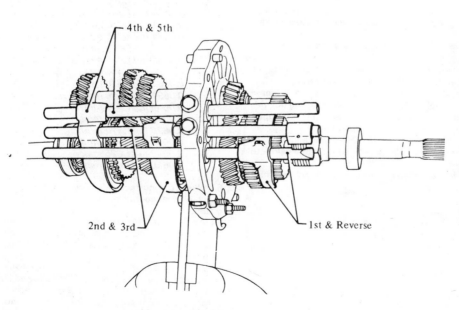

Fig. 13.41. Fitting the shift forks and rods

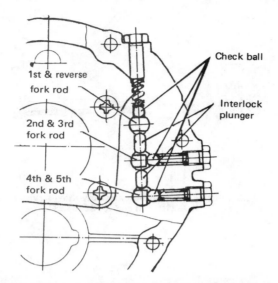

Fig. 13.42. Layout of the check balls and interlocking plungers

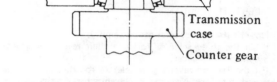

Fig. 13.43. Calculating the countershaft bearing shim thickness using service tool ST22500000

42 Repeat paragraphs 38 to 41 but applying the instructions to the 4th and 5th gear selector mechanisms.

43 Now apply gear oil to all the sliding surfaces and check to see that the selector rods slide correctly and that the gears engage smoothly.

44 Apply jointing compound to the mating surfaces of the adaptor plate and rear extension housing and gradually slide the rear extension onto the adaptor plate.

45 Apply jointing compound to the mating faces of the adaptor plate and bellhousing. It may be necessary to lightly tap the bellhousing into place against the adaptor plate.

46 Carefully fit the main drive bearing and counter shaft front bearing.

47 Check that the mainshaft rotates freely and refit the through bolts and washers. Tighten the bolts to the recommended torque wrench setting.

48 Using a pair of external snap-ring pliers fit the main drive bearing snap-ring.

49 Before refitting the front cover it is necessary to calculate the shim thickness required to load the countershaft bearing.

50 To calculate the shim thickness requirement use either a depth gauge or service tool ST22500000. When carrying out this calculation it is essential to ensure that the bearing is settled, by pressing on the bearing while turning the mainshaft.

51 When the height 'H' between the bearing casing and the face of the bellhousing has been calculated refer to the table below to select the correct shim.

52 The following shims are available to adjust the countershaft bearing.

Height 'H' ins (mm)

0.0467 to 0.0476 in (1.185 to 1.210 mm)
0.0476 to 0.0486 in (1.210 to 1.235 mm)
0.0486 to 0.0496 in (1.235 to 1.260 mm)
0.0496 to 0.0506 in (1.260 to 1.285 mm)
0.0506 to 0.0516 in (1.285 to 1.310 mm)
0.0516 to 0.0526 in (1.310 to 1.335 mm)
0.0526 to 0.0535 in (1.335 to 1.360 mm)
0.0535 to 0.0545 in (1.360 to 1.385 mm)
0.0545 to 0.0555 in (1.385 to 1.410 mm)
0.0555 to 0.0565 in (1.410 to 1.435 mm)
0.0565 to 0.0575 in (1.435 to 1.460 mm)
0.0575 to 0.0585 in (1.460 to 1.485 mm)
0.0585 to 0.0594 in (1.485 to 1.510 mm)

0.0594 to 0.0604 in (1.510 to 1.535 mm)
0.0604 to 0.0614 in (1.535 to 1.560 mm)
0.0614 to 0.0624 in (1.560 to 1.585 mm)
0.0624 to 0.0634 in (1.585 to 1.610 mm)
0.0634 to 0.0644 in (1.610 to 1.635 mm)
0.0644 to 0.0654 in (1.635 to 1.660 mm)

Thickness of countershaft shim ins (mm)

0.0472 in (1.200 mm)
0.0482 in (1.225 mm)
0.0492 in (1.250 mm)
0.0502 in (1.275 mm)
0.0512 in (1.300 mm)
0.0522 in (1.325 mm)
0.0531 in (1.350 mm)
0.0541 in (1.375 mm)
0.0551 in (1.400 mm)
0.0561 in (1.425 mm)
0.0571 in (1.450 mm)
0.0581 in (1.475 mm)
0.0591 in (1.500 mm)
0.0600 in (1.525 mm)
0.0610 in (1.550 mm)
0.0620 in (1.575 mm)
0.0630 in (1.600 mm)
0.0640 in (1.625 mm)
0.0650 in (1.650 mm)

53 When the correct shim has been obtained locate it to the front of the countershaft bearing using a little multi purpose grease.

54 Apply jointing compound to the mating faces of the bellhousing and cover plate. It is advisable to coat the threads of the cover plate securing bolts before tightening them to the recommended torque wrench setting.

55 Apply grease to the reverse gear selector return plunger and fit it in the rear extension housing followed by the return spring and return plug. Coat the threads of the return plug with jointing compound before screwing it into the extension housing.

56 Refit the various gearbox switches and speedo drive pinion.

57 Refit the clutch release lever and bearing assembly as described in Chapter 5.

58 The gearbox is now ready to be fitted as described in Chapter 6.

J Braking system

1 Braking system - modifications

Automatic rear brake adjusters are now offered as an option on all models. Automatic adjustment is made through application of the handbrake lever and when the clearance between the drum and brake shoes is large enough the adjusting bar will turn the adjuster wheel.

Rear brake adjustment on B210 models, not fitted with this optional equipment, is now achieved by rotating an adjuster wheel using a screwdriver. Access to the adjuster wheel is through a hole in the brake backplate which is covered by a rubber boot.

Other changes in the braking system are minor dimensional ones and details of these can be found in the General Data section of this Chapter. The system otherwise remains as detailed in Chapter 9 unless specifically mentioned in the following text.

2 Rear brakes - adjustment (B210 only)

1 Chock the front wheels and raise the car until the rear wheels are clear of the ground.
2 Ensure that the car is properly supported on axle stands or suitable wooden packing blocks.
3 Release the handbrake and check that the transmission is in the neutral position.
4 Now remove the rubber boot from the adjuster hole in the brake backplate.
5 Using a screwdriver turn the toothed adjusting wheel downwards to spread the brake shoes until it is no longer possible to turn the roadwheel by hand.
6 Now back the adjuster wheel off, until there is no longer contact between the drum and shoes. The roadwheel will now rotate easily when turned by hand.

7 Refit the rubber boot and repeat the operation for the other rear brake.

3 Rear brakes - removal, refitting and dismantling operations for cars fitted with automatic adjusters

Brake shoes - removal and refitting
1 Removal and refitting of the rear brake shoes is identical to the procedure detailed in Chapter 9, Section 4 except for one

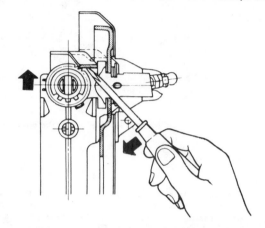

Fig. 13.44. Lifting the adjusting bar with a screwdriver inserted through the backplate

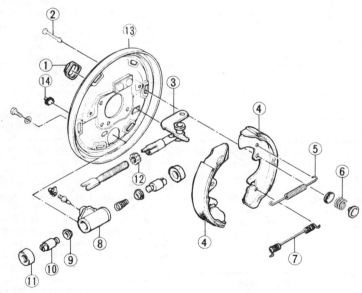

Fig. 13.45. The rear brake components fitted to current B210 models not equipped with automatic adjusters

1	Dust cover	4	Brake shoe	7	Shoe return spring (lower)	11	Dust cover
2	Steady post	5	Shoe return spring (upper)	8	Wheel cylinder	12	Adjuster wheel
3	Lever assembly	6	Shoe steady spring	9	Piston seal	13	Backplate
				10	Piston	14	Rubber boot

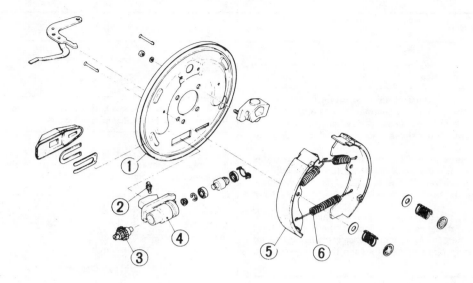

Fig. 13.46. The rear brake components fitted to models equipped with automatic adjusters

1 Backplate	3 Adjuster wheel	4 Wheel cylinder	5 Brake shoe
2 Bleed nipple			6 Shoe return spring

small detail.

2 Where reference to made to releasing the backplate adjuster this instruction should be ignored. Having said this it is necessary when refitting the brake shoes to screw the adjuster mechanism fully back to facilitate the refitment of the brake drum.

3 The adjuster mechanism can be backed off by inserting a screwdriver through the backplate and lifting the adjusting bar. With the adjusting bar now raised rotate the adjusting wheel in the appropriate direction.

4 Final adjustment of the rear brakes is made by applying the handbrake several times. The handbrake lever travel will diminish at every application as the automatic adjuster reduces the clearance between the rear brake shoes and the drum.

Wheel cylinder - removal, inspection, overhaul and refitting

5 The removal and refitting of the rear brake wheel cylinders is the same as detailed in Chapter 9 but note the instructions given in this Section for the removal and refitting of the brake shoes.

6 The wheel cylinder casting is different from that fitted to the rear braking system of early models. The difference being in the fitting of an adjuster wheel assembly on all models fitted with the optional automatic adjusters and current B210 models which are manually adjusted as described in the early part of this Section. (See Fig. 13.45 and 13.46 for details).

7 Chapter 9, Section 8 gives details of dismantling, inspection and overhauling the wheel cylinder assembly.

K Electrical system

1 Electrical system - changes

A different starter motor is now fitted to all models and details of the starter motor can be found in the General Data Section of this Chapter. The dismantling and overhaul of the unit is dealt with in the appropriate part of this Section.

Uprated alternators and voltage regulator/cut-outs have now been fitted to supply the needs of the extra equipment which together create an even heavier demand on the battery and charging system. Details of these changes and their applications can be found in the General Data Section of this Chapter.

2 Starter motor - dismantling, servicing and reassembly

1 The removal of the starter motor is identical to the instructions given in Chapter 10, Section 10.

2 With the starter motor now removed from the vehicle clean off the exterior using a suitable scraper followed by a rag soaked in paraffin. Never immerse the starter motor in a cleaning solvent as it will cause damage to the interior component parts and electrical units.

3 Servicing operations are normally limited to renewing the brushes, renewal of the solenoid, the overhaul of the starter drive gear and cleaning the commutator.

4 The major components of the starter should normally last the life of the unit and in the event of failure, a factory exchange unit should be obtained.

5 To dismantle the starter motor proceed as follows.

6 Remove the end dust cover which is retained by two screws, followed by the gasket.

7 Slide off the retaining clip followed by the thrust washers.

8 Undo the two through bolts and remove the end cover.

9 Remove the brushes from their holders. Use a piece of stiff wire fashioned to a hook at one end to draw the brush springs back to enable the brushes to be withdrawn.

10 Take the brush holder assembly off the starter.

11 Measure the length of the brushes. If they are worn to 0.472 in (12 mm) or less they should be renewed.

12 Ensure that each brush slides freely in its holder. If necessary, rub with a fine file and clean any accumulated carbon deposit or grease from the holder with a petrol moistened rag.

13 To dismantle the starter motor further remove the snap-ring from the front end of the armature assembly.

14 Slide off the pinion stopper followed by the pinion assembly

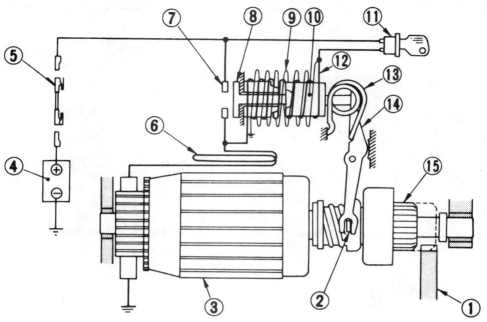

Fig. 13.47. Starting circuit

1	Flywheel ring gear	5	Fusible link	9	Shunt coil	13 Torsion spring
2	Shift lever guide	6	Field coil	10	Plunger	14 Shift lever
3	Armature	7	Stationary contact	11	Ignition switch	15 Pinion
4	Battery	8	Moving contact	12	Series coil	

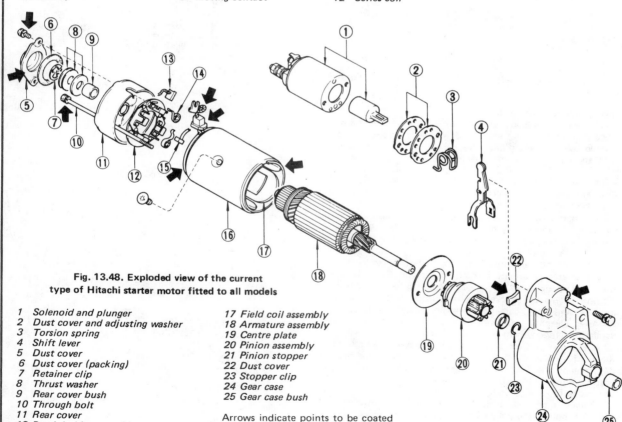

Fig. 13.48. Exploded view of the current
type of Hitachi starter motor fitted to all models

1 Solenoid and plunger
2 Dust cover and adjusting washer
3 Torsion spring
4 Shift lever
5 Dust cover
6 Dust cover (packing)
7 Retainer clip
8 Thrust washer
9 Rear cover bush
10 Through bolt
11 Rear cover
12 Brush holder assembly
13 Brush (−)
14 Brush spring
15 Brush (+)
16 Yoke

17 Field coil assembly
18 Armature assembly
19 Centre plate
20 Pinion assembly
21 Pinion stopper
22 Dust cover
23 Stopper clip
24 Gear case
25 Gear case bush

Arrows indicate points to be coated
with a non hardening sealant.

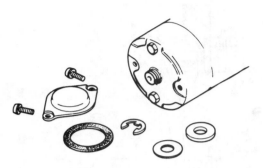

Fig. 13.49. Removing the dust cover, retainer clip and thrust washers

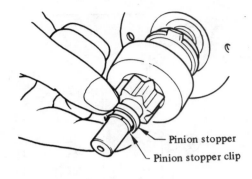

Pinion stopper
Pinion stopper clip

Fig. 13.50. Removing the pinion stopper

Fig. 13.51. Testing the field coil for ground (short circuiting)

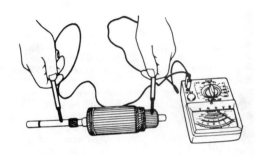

Fig. 13.52. Testing the armature for ground (short circuiting)

and finally the centre plate.

15 Normally, the commutator may be cleaned by holding a piece of non-fluffy rag moistened with petrol against it as it is rotated by hand. If on inspection, the mica separators are level with the copper segments they must be undercut by between 0.020 and 0.032 in (0.5 to 0.8 mm). An old hacksaw blade suitably ground is ideal for carrying out this task. (Fig. 10.15 of Chapter 10 shows examples of the correct and incorrect finishes that may occur).

16 The starter solenoid can be detached from the starter motor without dismantling any other components, after disconnecting the feed wires and removing the two locating bolts from the gear case.

17 Clean all the dismantled components but remember that the pinion assembly, armature assembly, solenoid and field coils should not be cleaned in a grease dissolving solvent as it would dissolve the grease packed in the clutch part of the pinion assembly and would damage the coils or other insulators.

18 After cleaning, examine all the components for wear or damage and renew them as necessary.

19 If you own or have access to an ohmmeter then you can test the fluid coil for continuity. To do this, connect one probe of the meter to the field coil positive terminal and the other to the positive brush holder. If no reading is indicated then the field coil circuit has a break in it.

20 Connect one probe of the meter to the field positive lead and the other one to the yoke. If there is a low resistance, then the field coil is earthed due to a breakdown in the insulation. If this fault is discovered, the field coils should be renewed by an automotive electrician, or a factory exchange unit obtained.

21 The armature may be tested for insulation breakdown, again by using the ohmmeter. Place one probe on the armature shaft

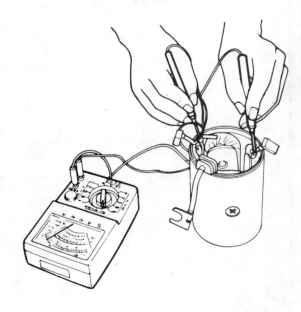

Fig. 13.53. Testing the field coil for continuity

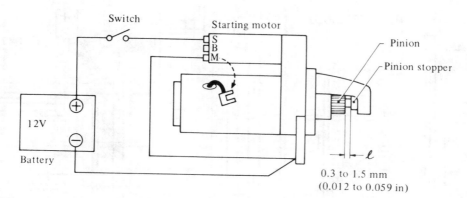

Fig. 13.54. Check the pinion to stopper clearance

and the other on each of the commutator segments in turn. If there is a reading indicated at any time during the test, the armature must be renewed.

22 Reassembly of the starter motor is the reverse of the dismantling procedure. When assembling, be sure to apply grease to the gear case and rear cover bushes. The pinion assembly can be lubricated using a light oil, applied sparingly. Points marked with an arrow in Fig. 13.48 should be assembled using a non-drying sealant.

23 When the starter motor has been fully reassembled, actuate the solenoid which will throw the pinion drive gear forward into its normal flywheel engagement position. Do this by connecting jumper leads between the battery negative terminal and the solenoid 'M' terminal and between the battery positive terminal and the solenoid 'S' terminal. Now check the gap between the end face of the drive pinion and the mating face of the pinion stopper. This should be between 0.012 to 0.059 in (0.3 to 1.5 mm) measured with either a vernier or feeler gauge. Adjusting washers are available in either 0.020 in (0.5 mm) or 0.030 in (0.8 mm) sizes.

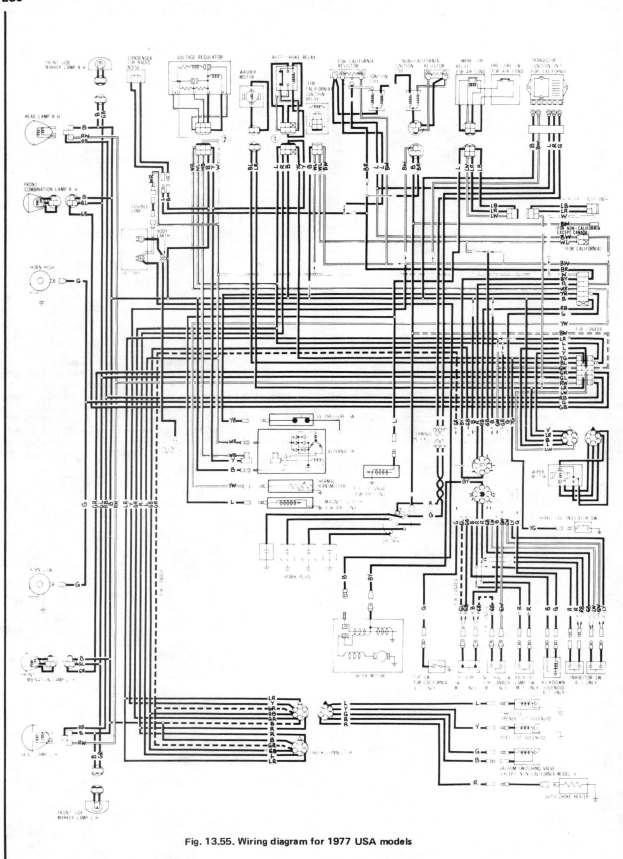

Fig. 13.55. Wiring diagram for 1977 USA models

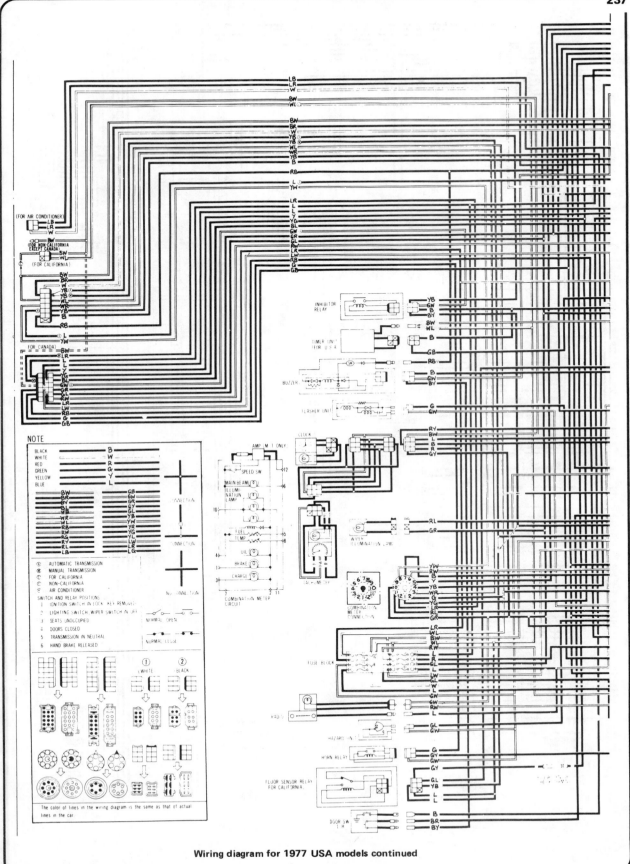

Wiring diagram for 1977 USA models continued

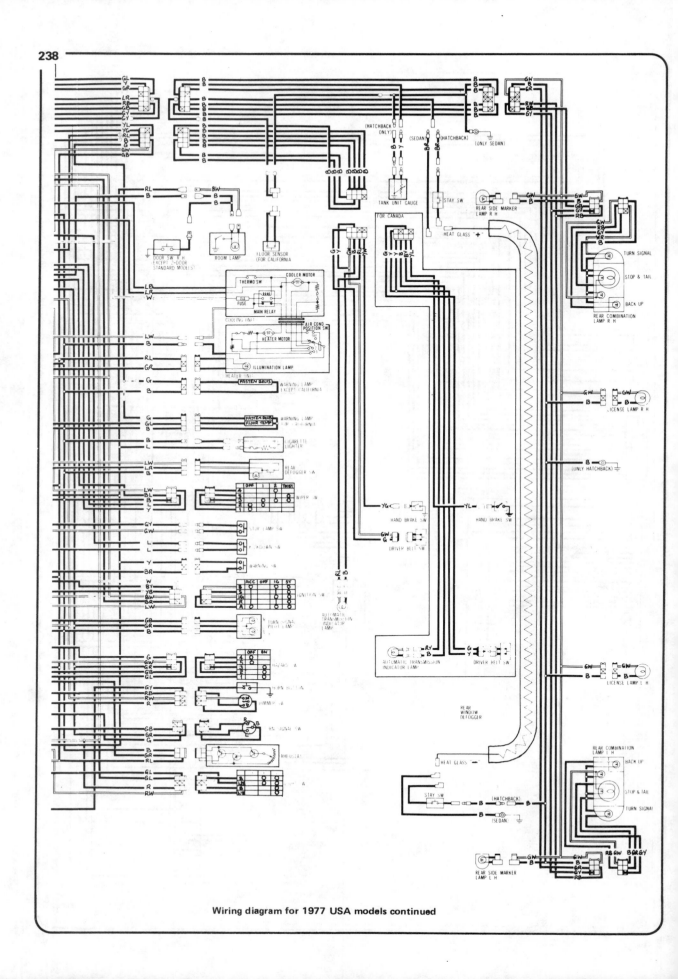

Wiring diagram for 1977 USA models continued

238

L Bodywork and fittings

1 Bodywork - alterations

The bodywork of the B240 has only undergone minor alterations. Body stripes have been added along with slight variations to the bumpers and radiator grille. The external overtaking mirror is now chromium plated and the carpets have been altered.

2 Air conditioning - general description

Since 1977 air conditioning has been offered as an optional factory extra on B210 models.

The air conditioning system comprises a cooling unit, an engine driven compressor, a condenser unit, a receiver/drier, and pipes connecting the units together. The cooling unit is mounted under the dash panel by three brackets in the position which is normally occupied by the package tray. The cooled air is directed into the passenger compartment via a duct to three outlets at the instrument panel.

The refrigerant flowing through the system is compressed by a compressor mounted on a bracket next to the engine block. The compressor is belt driven from the engine crankshaft pulley.

The condenser unit is located in front of the engine radiator and its function is to cool the refrigerant from the compressor.

The receiver/drier unit has two functions, in the first instance it is a storage container for refrigerant from the condenser and secondly it is a form of filter for the system, trapping particles and moisture which could block the fine operating clearances of the expansion valve.

Each component of the system is connected by either copper tubes or flexible hoses.

3 Air conditioning system - maintenance and inspection

1   Only two operations are possible for the home mechanic in connection with the cooling side of the air-conditioning system.

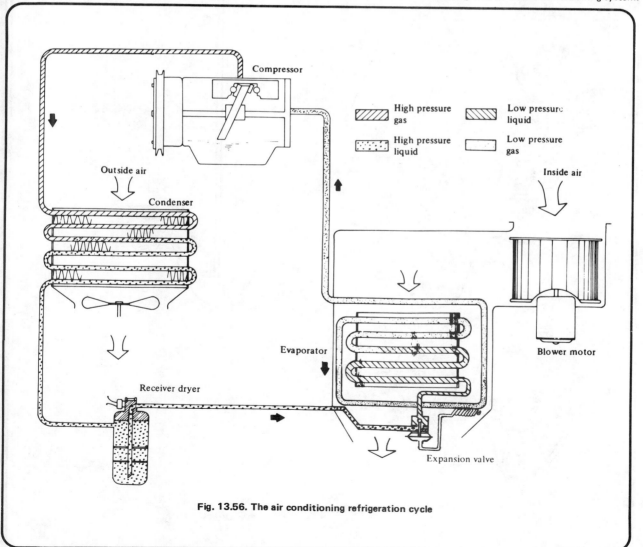

Fig. 13.56. The air conditioning refrigeration cycle

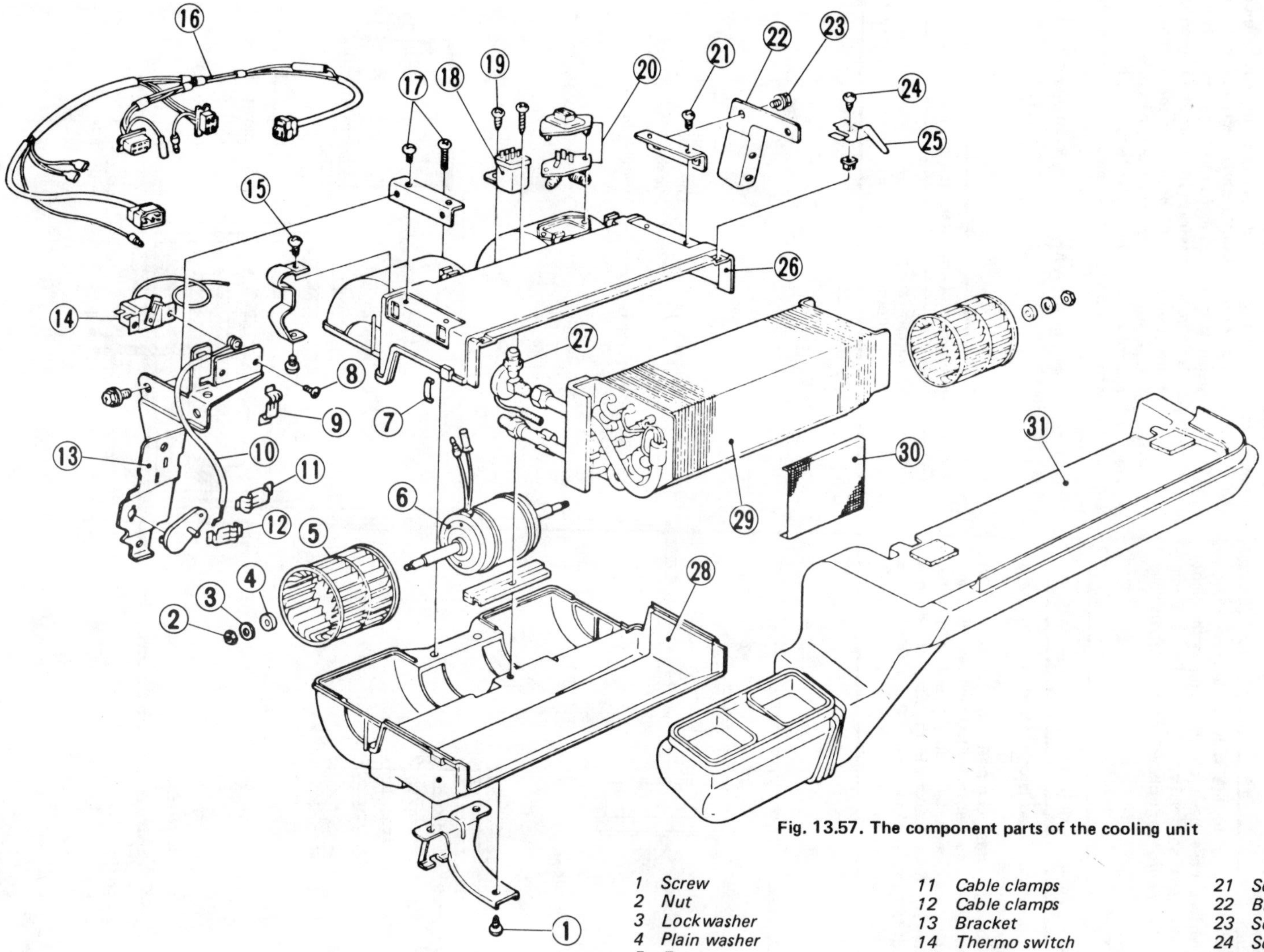

Fig. 13.57. The component parts of the cooling unit

1 Screw
2 Nut
3 Lockwasher
4 Plain washer
5 Fan
6 Motor assembly
7 Fixture
8 Screw
9 Cable clamps
10 Cable

11 Cable clamps
12 Cable clamps
13 Bracket
14 Thermo switch
15 Screw
16 Harness
17 Screw
18 Main relay
19 Screw
20 Resistance

21 Screw
22 Bracket
23 Screw
24 Screw
25 Spring stopper
26 Upper case
27 Expansion valve
28 Lower case
29 Evaporator assembly
30 Filter
31 Cooler duct

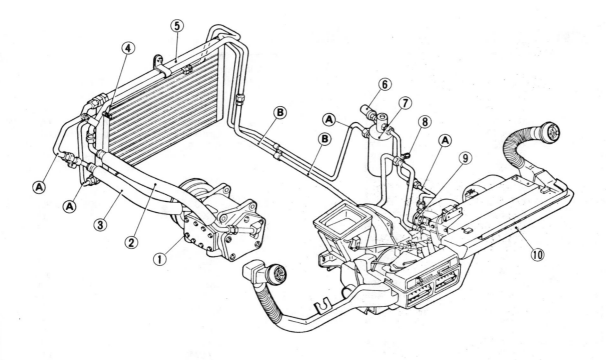

Fig. 13.58. The air conditioning cooling system

1	Compressor	4	Service valve (low pressure)	7	Receiver/drier unit	10	Cooling unit
2	Low pressure flexible hose	5	Condenser	8	Service valve (high pressure)	A	Copper tube (high pressure)
3	High pressure flexible hose	6	Pressure switch	9	Expansion valve	B	Copper tube (low pressure)

2 Periodically check the security and condition of the interconnecting hoses. If they are damaged or have deteriorated, they must be renewed. To do this the refrigeration circuit will have to be discharged. For safety reasons let your Datsun dealer discharge and recharge the unit.

3 At regular intervals, check the condition and tension of the compressor drive belt. There should be 0.31 to 0.47 in (8 to 12 mm) free play at the mid-point of the longest run of the belt.

4 Adjustment of the belt is carried out by slackening the idler pulley wheel nut and screwing the adjusting bolt inwards. After the correct belt tension has been obtained remember to retighten the idler pulley wheel securing nut.

5 The idler wheel is fitted with renewable bearings and is secured to a bracket bolted to the cylinder block.

Metric conversion tables

Inches	Decimals	Millimetres	Millimetres to Inches		Inches to Millimetres	
			mm	Inches	Inches	mm
1/64	0.015625	0.3969	0.01	0.00039	0.001	0.0254
1/32	0.03125	0.7937	0.02	0.00079	0.002	0.0508
3/64	0.046875	1.1906	0.03	0.00118	0.003	0.0762
1/16	0.0625	1.5875	0.04	0.00157	0.004	0.1016
5/64	0.078125	1.9844	0.05	0.00197	0.005	0.1270
3/32	0.09375	2.3812	0.06	0.00236	0.006	0.1524
7/64	0.109375	2.7781	0.07	0.00276	0.007	0.1778
1/8	0.125	3.1750	0.08	0.00315	0.008	0.2032
9/64	0.140625	3.5719	0.09	0.00354	0.009	0.2286
5/32	0.15625	3.9687	0.1	0.00394	0.01	0.254
11/64	0.171875	4.3656	0.2	0.00787	0.02	0.508
3/16	0.1875	4.7625	0.3	0.01181	0.03	0.762
13/64	0.203125	5.1594	0.4	0.01575	0.04	1.016
7/32	0.21875	5.5562	0.5	0.01969	0.05	1.270
15/64	0.234375	5.9531	0.6	0.02362	0.06	1.524
1/4	0.25	6.3500	0.7	0.02756	0.07	1.778
17/64	0.265625	6.7469	0.8	0.03150	0.08	2.032
9/32	0.28125	7.1437	0.9	0.03543	0.09	2.286
19/64	0.296875	7.5406	1	0.03947	0.1	2.54
5/16	0.3125	7.9375	2	0.07874	0.2	5.08
21/64	0.328125	8.3344	3	0.11811	0.3	7.62
11/32	0.34375	8.7312	4	0.15748	0.4	10.16
23/64	0.359375	9.1281	5	0.19685	0.5	12.70
3/8	0.375	9.5250	6	0.23622	0.6	15.24
25/64	0.390625	9.9219	7	0.27559	0.7	17.78
13/32	0.40625	10.3187	8	0.31496	0.8	20.32
27/64	0.421875	10.7156	9	0.35433	0.9	22.86
7/16	0.4375	11.1125	10	0.39370	1	25.4
29/64	0.453125	11.5094	11	0.43307	2	50.8
15/32	0.46875	11.9062	12	0.47244	3	76.2
31/64	0.484375	12.3031	13	0.51181	4	101.6
1/2	0.5	12.7000	14	0.55118	5	127.0
33/64	0.515625	13.0969	15	0.59055	6	152.4
17/32	0.53125	13.4937	16	0.62992	7	177.8
35/64	0.546875	13.8906	17	0.66929	8	203.2
9/16	0.5625	14.2875	18	0.70866	9	228.6
37/64	0.578125	14.6844	19	0.74803	10	254.0
19/32	0.59375	15.0812	20	0.78740	11	279.4
39/64	0.609375	15.4781	21	0.82677	12	304.8
5/8	0.625	15.8750	22	0.86614	13	330.2
41/64	0.640625	16.2719	23	0.90551	14	355.6
21/32	0.65625	16.6687	24	0.94488	15	381.0
43/64	0.671875	17.0656	25	0.98425	16	406.4
11/16	0.6875	17.4625	26	1.02362	17	431.8
45/64	0.703125	17.8594	27	1.06299	18	457.2
23/32	0.71875	18.2562	28	1.10236	19	482.6
47/64	0.734375	18.6531	29	1.14173	20	508.0
3/4	0.75	19.0500	30	1.18110	21	533.4
49/64	0.765625	19.4469	31	1.22047	22	558.8
25/32	0.78125	19.8437	32	1.25984	23	584.2
51/64	0.796875	20.2406	33	1.29921	24	609.6
13/16	0.8125	20.6375	34	1.33858	25	635.0
53/64	0.828125	21.0344	35	1.37795	26	660.4
27/32	0.84375	21.4312	36	1.41732	27	685.8
55/64	0.859375	21.8281	37	1.4567	28	711.2
7/8	0.875	22.2250	38	1.4961	29	736.6
57/64	0.890625	22.6219	39	1.5354	30	762.0
29/32	0.90625	23.0187	40	1.5748	31	787.4
59/64	0.921875	23.4156	41	1.6142	32	812.8
15/16	0.9375	23.8125	42	1.6535	33	838.2
61/64	0.953125	24.2094	43	1.6929	34	863.6
31/32	0.96875	24.6062	44	1.7323	35	889.0
63/64	0.984375	25.0031	45	1.7717	36	914.4

1 Imperial gallon = 8 Imp pints = 1.16 US gallons = 277.42 cu in = 4.5459 litres

1 US gallon = 4 US quarts = 0.862 Imp gallon = 231 cu in = 3.785 litres

1 Litre = 0.2199 Imp gallon = 0.2642 US gallon = 61.0253 cu in = 1000 cc

Miles to Kilometres		Kilometres to Miles	
1	1.61	1	0.62
2	3.22	2	1.24
3	4.83	3	1.86
4	6.44	4	2.49
5	8.05	5	3.11
6	9.66	6	3.73
7	11.27	7	4.35
8	12.88	8	4.97
9	14.48	9	5.59
10	16.09	10	6.21
20	32.19	20	12.43
30	48.28	30	18.64
40	64.37	40	24.85
50	80.47	50	31.07
60	96.56	60	37.28
70	112.65	70	43.50
80	128.75	80	49.71
90	144.84	90	55.92
100	160.93	100	62.14

lb f ft to Kg f m		Kg f m to lb f ft		lb f/in^2: Kg f/cm^2		Kg f/cm^2: lb f/in^2	
1	0.138	1	7.233	1	0.07	1	14.22
2	0.276	2	14.466	2	0.14	2	28.50
3	0.414	3	21.699	3	0.21	3	42.67
4	0.553	4	28.932	4	0.28	4	56.89
5	0.691	5	36.165	5	0.35	5	71.12
6	0.829	6	43.398	6	0.42	6	85.34
7	0.967	7	50.631	7	0.49	7	99.56
8	1.106	8	57.864	8	0.56	8	113.79
9	1.244	9	65.097	9	0.63	9	128.00
10	1.382	10	72.330	10	0.70	10	142.23
20	2.765	20	144.660	20	1.41	20	284.47
30	4.147	30	216.990	30	2.11	30	426.70

Index

Printed by
Haynes Publishing Group
Sparkford Yeovil Somerset
England